Malfeasance
In
Office

Frank E Cahill

American Ink Paperbacks

DEDICATION

To the next generation of free Americans.

May they accept the responsibility of independence and teach their children the legacy of self-government through refined public opinion and the common law of decent people. May they preserve the dreams of the last two hundred years for hundreds of years more. May they forever preserve the freedom of self-government.

ALSO BY FRANK E CAHILL

The Core Question

The Magic Of Flying

View AmericanInkPaperbacks.com for details

CONTENTS

FIGURES

ACKNOWLEDGMENTS

The background material for my narrative comes from years of squirreling away information, photocopying bits and pieces of newspaper and magazine articles, printing parts of Internet reports, and making personal notes from reading dozens, if not hundreds, of books on the various subjects. Unfortunately, this is the work of an amateur, and like any good amateur, I don't have a record of sources to cite in a bibliography. It's based purely upon the reading and interpretations of an everyday American.

There are several references to writing and quotations from the founding fathers and others. The words are mine, as I understood them, and are not directly accurate as word-for-word references. They are my take on forty years of undocumented scraps of paper.

I do have a few sources to acknowledge. For over twenty years I have carried a photocopy of an article that was given to me by a friend. I was so struck by its content that I have passed out more than a hundred copies of it to friends and acquaintances. The original is old, and I've seen it reprinted in various forms through the years. My ragged photocopy says it is an excerpt from *The Life of Colonel David Crockett*, compiled by Edward S. Ellis, published by Porter & Coates in 1884, and it's commonly called the "Not Yours to Give" speech. I've seen it reprinted in various forms through the years. It epitomizes the point of this book, and it is included in the text for your inspiration.

In some cases there are tables and statistics cited, and these are acknowledged where applicable. For example, items such as budget data from the U.S. Office of Management and Budget.

There is no greater gift from one individual to another than their time. My daughter read the manuscript and offered a variety of insights, suggestions, and encouragement. Thank you, Jenny, for your time, interest, and help.

CHAPTER ONE

AMERICAN DREAM

I AM AN ORDINARY MAN, a common American citizen who has lived the American Dream. I don't mean the American Dream of riches and wealth as most often described, but the American Dream of personal freedom. My life has been free. I have been free to enthusiastically work for a dollar, or to do nothing. I have been free to work for a corporate juggernaut, or to be left to the fruits of my own wits. My America has let me move freely and unfettered to live, work, or visit anywhere I choose. It has been my limitless pleasure to hunt, fish, drive, fly, and explore anywhere in this fabulous country, to raise a family in my own way, and to worship as I choose, where I choose, and how I choose. I can say what I want without fear of jail or restriction. I have been free to govern myself.

Our American Dream is the most wonderful dream of mankind and the greatest gift from the American men and women who lived before me. It was their dream to escape oppressive beliefs and to start anew with the freedom to choose their own way and to govern their own lives without hurting others. Millions left their homelands for a chance to worship without persecution. Others wanted to escape the class restrictions imposed by aristocratic nobility, or a crushing centralized government that left no opportunity to improve their lives or their children's lives.

Now, with recent events and worries of the country, I feel a need to help out somehow, to be a part of the solution in some way. By examining the American situation in more detail than I usually do, by returning to the ideas and advice of our founding fathers, and by writing some of my own ideas about freedom, I feel like it's a way to connect with the forefathers and fellow countrymen I admire.

1

Studious individuals will find little new here. Academic men and women spend their entire lives reading and studying the ideas of government and politics. Some have dozens of researchers to help them find sources and digest volumes of work that have preceded them. Numerous arguments have been iterated from one writer to another until they often are accepted as fact. I make no claim to join the scholastic study of government. Instead, my viewpoints are formed by a lifetime of government promises and interactions with its policies. Like most Americans, I have been promised many things by the federal government during my lifetime. But its promises are continually changing and reversing, which has left the country with a large portfolio of broken promises, unfair legislation, and unmanageable debt. Trillions of dollars have been spent on new programs and government agencies to give away the wealth of the country, but with poor result. Plans to help others and the economy have piled on more controls and restrictions on American freedom.

One hundred years of mismanagement by career politicians has sentenced America to be a nation of restricted freedom with debilitating debt. Their failure to honor their sworn oath to support and defend the Constitution of the United States has led them to restrict the power of a self-governing society in order to build the power and reach of federal regulators. By digging deeper into American lives in an unconstitutional attempt to guarantee the essentials of life, their lack of planning and controls have built a debt that has been passed from generation to generation until today the country faces a $16 trillion balance due on decades of fiscal malfeasance.

America has become a nation on the dole that is perpetually at war. It is shaken by the state of the Union that has left it with broken initiative. The generation today carries a tremendous financial debt it inherited from overspending measures implemented before its birth, and it is disillusioned with continued plans to bequeath more debt to its children. The combination of the new Health Care and Education Reconciliation Act and the Patient Protection and Affordable Care Act of 2010, more commonly called the health care act, has left freedom loving Americans in disbelief of the provisions and the legislative tactics used to pass them. It rivals the huge social insurance plans of the past, such as Social Security, Medicare, and Welfare, with its potential for spending and future debt. The health care act was created by a private organization and submitted to the Legislature. It was filled with social controls that were beyond the scope of health care, and then thrust upon the Congress for rapid approval. Legislators were left with little time to study its provisions; and smelly political tactics, with inequitable deals for the majority of American citizens, were used to muscle its approval.

Decades of job migration to foreign countries with accompanying unemployment have changed the face of America. There is fear that jobs may be gone forever. Instead of a country of producers, it has become a country of consumers, and nearly half of its citizens look for handouts from the other half. Phony mortgages and government manipulation of the financial system has added to the jobless malaise. Now, it seems America looks to the federal government for everything from an income allowance and food to health care and a home. It borders on completing the transition from a government by a free people to a centralized government by a bureaucratic elite.

Our country faces a moral dilemma today as it wrestles with the idea of maintaining a welfare society. The present generation, and at least four before it, has chosen to borrow from its children in order to provide extraordinary payouts to low-income and unemployed citizens. Isn't this immoral? If one generation of society decides that half its people should support the other half, then let there be extensive taxes to pay for it in full. But no generation should ever fail to fund its welfare programs by borrowing the money year after year, and then leaving its debt for the following generation to account for its excesses. Our forefathers knew this was wrong, and so do we.

It's past time to decide to stop borrowing. Shall we impose a colossal "care tax" on working America to fully fund its welfare handouts? Conversely, is it time to pare our give-away habit to an affordable size that fits the income of our national budget? Regardless of our choices or compromises, we must leave our children with a country that is free and clear of our obligations and vices. They must have an unencumbered opportunity to work, prosper, and manage the country's affairs during their lifetimes. It's our moral obligation.

This is the way things in the country seem to me today. But I wanted to verify my instincts, to see if my thoughts had merit, or if I was full of baloney. I returned to my history and civics books to refresh myself on the birth of our nation and its accomplishments and failures in the last two hundred years. I was inspired by the Constitution and the selfless genius of the country's founders. In studying the theoretical sources for developing the U.S. government, I began to understand the idea of self-government by public opinion. I don't think I ever truly understood the basis for our government until I dug deeper into the lessons from James Madison and others. It was an awakening to the idea of using public opinion to form the laws of the people and to put them into practice through the common law jury system.

I was swept up in reviewing the lives and writings of the forefathers. It was idealistic and stimulating, and I recognized the country had drifted considerably from the ideals of strong local governments and protection of individual choices. I wondered where and how the country changed course, so I began to examine major American programs and their history. The more I read, the deeper I was drawn in, and I was astounded by the long list of government programs and failures. They ranged into virtually every facet of American life, and slowly, in the name of good works, American freedoms have been dissolved and eliminated.

A lot of these changes took place during my lifetime. It has been a slow-moving process, and in my youth, I didn't recognize the harm to personal freedom that was fostered by many of these government programs. There were plenty of new programs that I disagreed with, or that offered me little confidence, but I accepted them in obedient silence as inevitable measures by a large government.

Finally, it's too much to quietly accept. I'm tired of professional politicians that serve only the self-interests of their own careers and not the business of the country. I don't want to hear more empty promises from a Congress that judges itself on the amount of legislative activity in each session, instead of how well it managed its financial responsibilities and its allegiance to the Constitution. I'm exhausted by insincere representatives that have made themselves federal employees, and by their incestuous relationship with career federal workers. I groan under the tyranny of the progressive income tax and its burden on the free lives of Americans. But Americans must decide for themselves whether the drift from self-government has gone too far, or whether it needs to progress farther in the direction it has taken.

So I decided to join the conversation by describing my experience, my studies, and my return to the days of the nation's founders. It ranges from a lifetime of lessons and government promises to a review of the underlying ideas of our Constitution and its unique safety valve to save Americans from being overpowered by the federal government. There is a critical look at the oppressive tax system of today through the experiences of a paid tax preparer. The country's financial problems are examined by comparing the responsible operation of a small business to the irresponsible management of national revenue by elected representatives.

The sweeping claim of malfeasance in office is based upon the idea that elected representatives of the people have not upheld and protected the Constitution, and have failed to responsibly manage the country's treasury. More than a century of neglect has left us with a government that operates outside the boundaries of the Constitution by reading different meaning between the lines to suit its agenda. This method has permitted the implementation of countless under-funded spending programs until the national debt is bursting at the seams. It has created a bureaucratic class that seeks to sustain itself by controlling the very people it is supposed to serve. The ultimate fault, though, lies with us, the self-governing people.

In the end it is the challenge of a self-governing free people to choose and control the path of government. We are taught by our founding fathers that the Constitution is an active law that can change with each generation. Is it time for revisions? A list of ways to restore the people's authority is proposed for your consideration. Perhaps your generation is the one to change the course of American government and to restore individual liberty.

Join me in the following introduction to each section of the narrative, and continue with the conversation into the individual parts. Become immersed in the lessons of our fathers, and then see how modern leaders have ignored their advice. Notice how the good intentions of the last century have soured. See how the drift from the Constitution has left us with a stifling government and indescribable debt. Perhaps you, too, will come to agree that it has been one hundred years of malfeasance in office.

A LIFETIME OF PROMISES AND LESSONS LEARNED

My contribution to the conversation begins with a description of my experiences and lessons learned that have molded personal viewpoints. There is a short description of the impact of government and national events on my life from about 1950 to 2010. It ranges through periods of extraordinary protests, demonstrations, wars, inflation, and recessions. It makes up a lifetime of government promises.

In the course of everyone's life there are many lessons learned from study and experience. Mine are the result of school studies, military service, engineering training, and business experience. They include civics lessons that compare unalienable human rights with statutory rights vested by the government. Lessons on human nature include statistical methods for predicting the mix of honest and dishonest human behavior. There are ideas from John Adams to explain the human thirst for recognition, and Mohandas Gandhi's lesson for true, peaceful dispute. Other lessons range from basic economic principles to an explanation for why the government, or any organization, must continually monitor and manage its operations to avoid reverting to conditions of disorder.

Consider the actual effects on individual life in the description of a lifetime of government promises. Have the government programs during one lifetime been truly effective, or is it time to admit the failure of grand ideas? Discover the lessons learned and their application to the human experience and the pursuit of freedom. Are true human rights the unchangeable gift of nature, or are they merely the gift of a ruling class through changing statutes?

VIEWPOINTS

American history and the changes in government and society shape the discussion of viewpoints. I discovered that major changes steadily occurred in the last one hundred years to have a crucial impact on the development of American society. The country has slowly adopted the change from a predominantly self-governing society to a centralized government that dominates the people. This change has progressed for the last century, with three periods of monumental change that occurred roughly around 1913, 1935, and 1965. As a result of this evolution, America has become a hybrid society of dependent and independent citizens that have adapted into four classes. Today, there is a privileged governing class of people added to the three traditionally recognized classes of poor, middle, and wealthy.

Probably today few Americans would disagree with the view that the federal government is guilty of awful fiscal irresponsibility that has put the country in the terrible position of having to deal with an unimaginable debt. It is in direct contrast to the viewpoints of the founding fathers. They recognized the dangers of deficit spending and left following generations with ample advice and caution. But it was ignored by generations of political greed and mismanagement, and by a nation that learned to ask for favors from the government.

But what truly is the view of most Americans concerning the government and what it should provide? How do we answer questions concerning the strengths, fears, and needs of U.S. citizens? The founders dealt with these same questions when they were setting up the Constitution and the first government. America's truest strength has been in one another, our freedom, and the peculiar security of the Constitution. The people's fears and needs are based upon family, finances, and security. Virtually all other concerns are a mix or variation of these basic concerns.

Examine the narrative of our country's transition into a hybrid society with four classes. Is there really a ruling class in America? Are government's dependents really living under socialist rules? Are all of us in danger of surrendering all of our freedoms in exchange for the imaginary security of government handouts? Or, should we reevaluate the strengths of our people, our fears, and our needs in order to redirect the course of our self-controlled nation?

A LIST OF FAILURES

Unending reports of abused, inconsistent, and failed government programs started my efforts to learn how and why they occurred. The more I learned, the larger the list grew. In looking at the situation today with the large debt, abused social programs, and special favors for different groups, there is an overwhelming list of ineffective, insolvent, and mismanaged government programs. Examining the backgrounds of these programs exposes endless failures and bloated spending. In general, government programs benefit small segments of the population with special favors. Government tinkering with the nation's money is the primary type of intervention. Early instances include the mortgage, banking, and savings and loan businesses. It more or less started with the creation of Government Sponsored Enterprises to help

Americans buy houses. Eventually, the government tried to operate its own businesses such as Amtrak and the Postal Service.

Around 1935 the federal bureaucracy made a big entry into an experiment with social planning when it started the Social Security Administration. Extraordinary welfare programs followed until today the government hands out more money than ever before to create an entire society of socialized citizenry. One of the more powerful methods to implement social programs is through the progressive income tax system. This inefficient system has done more damage to individual freedom than perhaps any other change by the federal government. It requires about eighteen percent of the country's revenue to simply pay for administration of the Internal Revenue System, and the tax system is a prime cause for the growth of the lobbying industry with its waste and abuses.

Decide for yourself whether the long list of government programs is a list of failures. Notice the programs that are underwater today and have become anchors that are drowning the country's economic livelihood with them. Have these programs truly helped citizens and promoted freedom, or have they merely empowered a governing class that strangles true freedom? It's a long list of ideas that grows longer daily, and many more could be added.

OUR MUTUAL CONTRACT

The United States Constitution is our mutual contract for government by the people. A review of our national history gave me a renewed understanding of its meaning and a fresh curiosity about other forms of government. The influences of theories, such as communism and government by centralized authority, continually challenge the idea of a democratic republic, and we have allowed ourselves to drift somewhat from the pure principles adopted when the Constitution was formed. A fundamental question is whether Americans lost control of the government through manipulation by their elected leaders, or whether citizens intended a conversion to a centralized federal government. There is evidence that it may be a combination of both. But do Americans understand the basic differences between a self-governed people and a society ruled by a small ruling class? A study of the theory of government at the elementary level may help identify the distinction by starting with the theories behind the birth of our own government. The founding fathers' discussion with other great political philosophers during the period known as the Era of Enlightenment formed their great expertise in government theory, and this became the basis of the American Constitution. How and why James Madison proposed a system of self-government founded on public opinion and administered through a common law jury method is explained in a short examination of this historical period.

There are many variations and theories for types of government. Obviously, the American method is a system of self-government by the people. It is a democratic-republic where elected representatives administer the will of the people. Two competing theories are commonly practiced today: communism and centralized democracy. Communism is the ideal of a classless society with total equality controlled by the state. A centralized democracy uses a governing, or ruling class, to establish laws and distribute the wealth of the country among the people according to the conscience of the governing class. Right now, it appears like the U.S. is inclined toward becoming a centralized democracy, and it is important for all Americans to understand what may be the net result of such a system.

Join the brief excursion to the birth of our country's contract and laws. Consider the ideas of history's great thinkers and the discussions that formed the basis of our government. Rediscover the words of the unselfish founders and their plan for us. Compare the grand idea of a communist government with its modified version of central democracy. Is America chugging a path toward total rule by centralized government? Is it destined to surrender its republic to follow the centralized rule of a World Order?

HEDGING THE CONTRACT

Are our elected representatives truly working around the provisions of the Constitution? If so, why? Is it all a diabolical scheme to overthrow the government of the people; or, is it simply the result of ambitious efforts to help others while cementing professional careers?

A review of the Constitution and the ideals of its writers reveal the vast drift from its provisions that has occurred in the centuries since it was put to paper. The federal government, and its control of the people, has slowly grown until it approaches being a government by centralized authority. Our founders recognized this threat and wrote many warnings.

The important question is how America progressed toward becoming a centralized government. Was it constitutional? Was it a long-term plan? A review of the provisions of the Constitution and the history of change in America indicates that it is likely the result of simply working around the Constitution instead of taking the time and effort to confront the will of the people and change it according to their desire. All branches of the government have attempted to assume more control in the style of a centralized democracy. Generations of presidents have tried to impose their ideas on the country by using executive orders and lawmaking by board rule; it has grown steadily until it borders on dictatorship. The Supreme Court has assumed the role of lawmaking by interpreting the provisions of the

Constitution, instead of strictly ruling on its content; this activity is referred to as judicial activism and review. The legislative branch has enabled the hedging of Constitutional authority. Because it holds the ultimate power conveyed by the people, the Congress has the ability to restrain, or check, the other branches of government. Instead it has empowered rule by bureaus, presidential advisors, executive orders, and other methods to skirt the authority of the people.

Elected officials and career federal employees have banded together in a central culture with a devotion to power. In the central city their ideas are infected by party spirit and redirected in their search for favor. These forces combine into a smug idea that their centralized society knows more about government, more about life, and what is best for America's citizens.

The details of the abuse of our Constitution are astonishing. All of our country's founders feared and predicted it. They knew the fate of a self-governing people's Constitution rests with its citizens. Is now the time to restore the force of the Constitution through a tranquil revolution of legislative changes and amendments? Or, do the interpretations of past generations represent the will of the people today to put their fate in the hands of government?

GOVERNMENT CHAINS

My experience preparing tax returns for people of all ages and from different situations in life has given me detailed insight to the burdensome workings and inequities of the American income tax system. A short description of how the tax system works exposes the traps and burdens that are imposed upon honest, but unsuspecting, citizens.

The single biggest breach of American freedom occurred with the first great change of 1913 when U.S. citizens were chained by the government with a progressive individual income tax system. The American founders were against such a method for collecting taxes, and prohibited it in the original Constitution. It was authorized when the Sixteenth Amendment was adopted in 1913. Many Americans are surprised to learn the current income tax system was not authorized by the original Constitution. Most still don't realize it. This unwieldy system has changed taxation from a method for collecting revenue for operation of the federal government to a method used by the governing class to manipulate and control citizens.

Taxation should be restored to an equal system that is restricted to raising budget revenue. There should be no subsidies, no credits, no welfare plans, no energy favorites, no lobbyist incentives, or any other method of using taxation to influence social behavior. The tax system should be returned to supporting the original three purposes established by the Constitution:

provide for defense, insure fair trade, and maintain courts for fair and equal laws.

America was not meant to be a club with unequal members where anyone can join and live off the success of others. The tax system has caused a conflict between classes, and the clash is commonly magnified to advance the careers of professional politicians. The idea to "soak the rich" was proposed with the change in 1913, and it has become bigger than ever. But who are the rich? A review of the current tax system shows that it could be any average citizen under the right circumstances. Windfall profits and a confusing web of regulations entrap many unfortunate Americans, leaving them bewildered and in bondage. Is it freedom when the system causes the average citizen to hire a tax preparer to navigate it? This system has chained Americans to the government, and they groan under its weight.

The size and depth of the progressive direct tax system is remarkable. Review its fundamentals for yourself, and experience the fear it imposes on every citizen. See how Americans nervously face the annual period of reconciliation where many are caught in its bureaucratic trap and saddled with debt, while others revel in the unequal give-away game to enjoy huge gifts at the expense of fellow citizens. Notice how this system is used to control citizens instead of being strictly a method to fund government operations. Observe how the government uses "informational" reports, under the umbrella of filing taxes, to augment the controlling role of the tax system. The use of earned income credits and child tax credits are used for this purpose now, and the comprehensive new health care bill will require informational returns from each citizen to prove their compliance with government rules. Is it time to abolish this monstrosity and reverse the misdirected course set in 1913?

Fiscal Responsibility

Clearly the federal government has not maintained fiscal controls for the country. Almost every American knows the country wallows in oppressive debt. It is the result of one legislative plan upon another transferring benefits between segments of society and saddling younger citizens to pay for the benefits for earlier generations. As these programs have mounted, the size of government and its benefits have grown disproportionately until the business of government is about to fail.

Should the American government be operated like a nonprofit business? If so, then it has failed for decades to provide prudent stewardship of the nation's finances and resources. It has operated beyond its ways and means until it has accumulated a terrible debt. Can it be corrected? What should the federal leaders do? What do Americans want? Of course from a purely business point of view, it's an entirely correctable problem, although it may take a decade or more to sensibly restore the financial health of the country. But there will be the same difficult decisions that a business must face. Is it time to resize the government? Is it time to adjust government pay and benefits? Should limits be placed on social programs to keep them within affordable levels of the nation's productivity?

To better understand fiscal responsibility, the example of a hypothetical small business is used to describe profit planning methods and the pressures working against its plan to make a profit. How a typical business starts each year is examined, and then different problems are introduced which threaten its plan. These include material and labor inflation, energy cost, rising health care premiums, taxes, and the ever present pressure by foreign sources. It's a difficult thing to run a business and is filled at times with gut-wrenching decisions. When the business cost structure becomes too bloated to be sustained by its income, then business managers must often cut back or resize the operation.

Review with the hypothetical manager the stress of deciding how to adjust, if at all, to the pressures of business, and compare it with the review of the national budget plan. Look at how the national budget exceeds federal income year after year without responsible management to keep it within limits. Evaluate the categories of budget spending to see how the welfare giant has grown out of control. Compare the actions of a responsible business to the inactions of the irresponsible stewards of the country's business, and then consider the possibilities for controlling national spending.

The discussion of fiscal responsibility concludes by reviewing the idea that government can make jobs. Is it really possible? Or do jobs result from the natural industriousness of people and market dynamics?

How much longer can the country continue to operate in the red? How much longer can it borrow from other countries to provide handouts today that the children of tomorrow must repay? Or is it already too late to take corrective action to restore fiscal responsibility?

Study the basics of business management in the example. Familiarize yourself with the elements of good budgeting, and then compare it with the national budget plan. Look closely at the national budget, see where the money is over spent, and notice how government leaders fail to accept the responsibility for adjusting to pressures in order to preserve the Treasury. Is deficit spending a smart, sophisticated economic tactic, or does it threaten the country's stability and safety? When there's nowhere left to borrow, how truly secure are the promised handouts?

RESTORING CIVIL AUTHORITY

In a self-governing society it is the obligation of each person to decide the answers to the questions and pressures on government business. If America is to remain a democratic republic, and not a centralized democracy, then there are actions the people should encourage to restore civil authority within the provisions of the Constitution. There are almost two dozen ideas in the discussion that are meant to provoke thoughts on whether the government is due for changes; and if it is, ways for reasserting the people's control of the government. In order to aid in absorbing numerous ideas, they have been divided into four categories identified as Preserve Freedom, Temper Political Policies, Restrict Specialists, and National Concerns.

Although all of the proposals for a peaceful revolution are important, steps to preserve American freedom are considered the top priority. Until our freedom is safeguarded, it will be nearly impossible to make the other changes. It begins with four actions. The first is to repeal the Sixteenth Amendment. Second, balance the budget and retire the debt. Third, clarify federal government powers, and fourth, fortify the system of checks and balances.

No other single provision of government is viewed as so wicked a challenge to freedom as the progressive income tax system established by the Sixteenth Amendment. *The Communist Manifesto* lists ten steps to establishing a communist government, and the second step is to establish a heavy progressive or graduated tax. The abuses of this unreasonable, burdensome system have existed long enough. Abolishing its grip on the people will not only restore daily freedoms but also eliminate many other political abuses that have grown up around it.

Deficit spending and the huge debt compose the second priority for saving American freedom. Two activities are responsible for the debt problem: wars and social programs. Probably the biggest contributor to the debt has been to pay for America's wars, and since World War Two it seems like the country has been perpetually embroiled in expensive conflicts. The cost for social programs is extraordinary, too. It is not only the cost of the actual handouts to citizens, but also the monumental administrative costs and huge expansion in the numbers of government employees needed to support social programs. In fact, it would not be surprising to learn that administrative costs, including less obvious buried costs, may be equal to or larger than the actual handout amounts, and it doesn't end with the federal government. Administrative monstrosities have invaded state governments until their social departments are huge, too. Balanced spending will restore stability, strength, and prosperity to the country. Instead of cowering near bankruptcy, America can be free to grow, produce, and compete with the rest of the world.

The third step to clarify government power will be difficult but necessary.

The argument over government powers is ancient. It can be traced to the period when the states were considering ratification of the Constitution. It continued through the first administration and beyond. The debate continues today on many subjects. For example, are the social programs of today truly Constitutional ideas or merely the result of executive and judicial activism? The Supreme Court ruled, through interpretation, that social programs fall under government powers to provide for the general welfare and to regulate commerce. Nevertheless, the argument about it continues to this day, because the intent of the architects of the Constitution doesn't seem to support the Court's interpretation. Probably the only way to settle the dispute, at least for one generation, is to modify the Constitution to specifically identify and answer these questions; that is, to amend the Constitution. Then the questions may be reviewed openly and approved by the people of the country, instead of nine academics. The commerce and general welfare clauses, and all federal powers, can be strictly limited by amendment, and if there is to be a provision for social welfare, for example, then there should be an amendment that specifically authorizes it.

By specifically defining federal powers with Constitutional amendments it will take the opportunity for interpretation out of the abusive hands of renegade executives, legislators, and jurists. Openness and order can be restored to the people.

But the decision should be in the hands of the people, not a small group of scholastic theorists trying to read their particular brand of meaning into the supreme law. Whether Americans choose to add or eliminate certain activities in the Constitution will be their natural right to choose. If future generations disagree, then it will be their choice to change the active law of the Constitution to accomplish their social needs.

If the tax amendment is repealed, budgetary restraints imposed, and government powers specifically identified, then the country may wish to take the fourth step to reinforce the system of checks and balances and to curb the natural inclination of each branch of government to assume more power. Specific provisions should be made to restrict the Executive Branch's use of executive orders, advisors, and bureaus to independently implement and enforce laws. Such activities threaten democracy with a dictatorial branch that skirts the legislature's authority if allowed. Special advisors, or czars, are set up without accountability to the people, but they add regulations and punitive controls on citizens. These actions are supported through the abusive use of executive orders. Such activities have converted America from control by the people to control by laws established by bureaus. Legislative or Constitutional controls should be used to preserve America's protection from dictatorial rulemaking by the Executive branch. The Constitution requires presidents to enforce the laws of the Legislature, not make laws. This must be reestablished as the fourth priority to preserve freedom.

After fundamental control of the federal government has been returned to the people by the actions to preserve freedom, then citizens can consider other changes. The second category for restoring civil authority includes measures to temper political polices. They range from abolishing career politicians to eliminating earmark legislation. Restrictions on career legislators will reduce their inclination to band together to ignore their constituents. They should be removed from the rolls as federal employees and restored to status as representatives. Term limits can be imposed to eliminate lifetimes of profiteering on the backs of the very people they have pledged to represent.

The third group of actions for restoring civil authority includes new restrictions on specialists. This includes the Supreme Court, government unions, and the Federal Reserve System. Today may be the time to consider new restrictions on the Supreme Court and its decisions. Most Americans today accept the decisions of the Supreme Court as final and binding, almost like the word of God. These same Americans may be surprised to learn that not all founders agreed with this idea. In view of the inconsistency and abuses of the last two hundred years of Court decisions, perhaps America is ready to authorize veto power on their decisions, and then establish term limits for justices. At first it may seem drastic, but truly it is not a new proposal. Returning to the ideas of the founders, America was meant to have self-government with laws established by the people, not a small cadre with untouchable power.

Now may also be the time to review the existence of government unions. Make no mistake, the right of private citizens to form unions and barter with private companies must be fiercely protected and preserved. It's a principal right to freedom. But public service unions result in extraordinary conflicts of interest and abuse of taxpaying citizens. Their dues are used to influence elected officials through political methods in order to obtain increased compensation, benefits, and favors. Instead, the laws of good people should adequately protect the livelihood and safety of public employees, not the extra cost and abuses of a public union system.

The last category for restoring civil authority addresses various issues of national concern for today's America. Modern Americans struggle to find answers for social insurance and welfare programs, for immigration threats, and for worries about energy resources and the economy. The monumental costs to maintain the country's social handouts must be limited. Clearly changes are needed not only to paid-in programs such as Social Security and Medicare, but also to welfare programs where the recipients receive benefits without ever paying into the system. Social Security and Medicare can be revised into needs-based programs to reduce the draw on these plans, while limits on welfare spending may be necessary to maintain budget targets.

Americans fear illegal immigration today, because it has grown so large. It's the result of malfeasance in office for decades through government's failure to enforce laws that have always existed. Enforcing existing laws will likely solve the problem. When the jobs dry up, illegal immigrants with no allegiance or loyalty to the United States will return to the first love of their homelands.

Perhaps the largest American fear today is the loss of jobs. Government leaders promise to make jobs. But can they really? Of course they can't. The U.S. powerhouse will return when freedom is restored and the bureaucratic system is pulled off its back. Nothing can compete with American ingenuity and productivity when the burdens of government are reduced and fair competition with the world is restored.

It can begin with a national energy policy that promotes sufficient research and development for all modes of energy production. Targeted subsidies that lead to dead ends and waste must be abolished. Everyone should share access to technological developments equally. A national research policy to be shared by all will unleash American genius and free market forces to produce new forms of affordable energy, and affordable energy has been the secret of one hundred years of American growth and prosperity.

A lot of proposals fill the plan to restore self-government. Many of them may seem obvious. Others may seem extreme. Consider and think about all of them, though. Return to the lessons left to us by the men and women who created America, and let your mind explore corrections for our problems and new options for self-government. Shall we shake off one hundred years of government interloping, or have we resolved to hunker down and hope for the best at the hands of the few?

OUR TURN

The Constitution provides common citizens with the unique power to reclaim their authority to direct government to follow their choices; the founders left us this legacy in Article Five of the Constitution. Common Americans can use the Fifth Article in a peaceful revolution, if necessary. If true representatives cannot be found to spearhead the people's desire to restore civil authority, then a Constitutional Convention may be necessary to wrest control from the governing class and restore self-government. It would be history making – the first time ever. But if our government has become uncontrollable, then perhaps it is time.

Today and now is the time for Americans to take their turn to reclaim the authority of the Constitution. It is time to end the mismanagement of public funds and the failure to support and defend the Constitution. Now is the time to diminish unchecked government control. The elected defenders of the Constitution have allocated and delegated Constitutional powers to individuals that have not been elected by the American people, have not been confirmed by elected officials, and as a result, are making rules and regulating lives without accountability to the true governors of freedom – regular citizens.

It is our turn to choose. It is our turn to decide if we want a government ruled by a small governing class that decides what is right for the people, or whether we want a government that manages the people's treasury and follows the Constitution in its responsibility to the people. If you are content with a nation that borrows from the future and elects individuals to decide how Americans should live their lives, then there is nothing for you to do. It is a natural progression for government to grow and assume more power until it directs citizens in their jobs, where to live, and how to live.

If you choose a plain, simple government founded in reason, then you must insist upon a return to a government of the people. It is time to insist upon a government that operates within the limits of its budget, and to reduce the number of federal employees to fit within reasonable limits of revenue authorized by the people. It is time to shake off the chains of the abusive progressive tax system to let Americans live free again. It is time to abolish a governing class by eliminating elected representatives as federal employees.

Whatever your belief, examine the success of decades of government programs. Look at the history of government expansion. Consider the impact of the current tax system. Decide if current fiscal controls are satisfactory. Make your own decisions as a voting American citizen.

CHAPTER TWO

A LIFETIME OF PROMISES

I GREW UP TRUSTING OUR GOVERNMENT. I applied for my social security number as required (it wasn't required at birth like it is today), registered for the draft (no longer a requirement for young men), filed my tax returns, and answered the call to military active duty when instructed. My life has been average, unremarkable. But a short description of some of my experiences with the government may illustrate the continuing growth of the federal government and its broken promises and unfairness.

Work, frugal living, church, and home were the lessons and values of my youth. As the years passed I began to notice that government rules constantly changed and seemed wrong. The government continued to make gifts to the deserving few, but it would both give and take away. It passed rules for housing and pension plans that completely flipped the ways people were living and doing business. As a result, the country assumed new values. Welfare and public assistance became normal with the birth of the Great Society, and Americans became a nation of debtors. Home mortgage gimmicks were accepted. The expectation of government support contributed to a transition to a more uncivil society.

Americans my age lived through the civil rights movement and the assailment of the evil white male. I saw military servicemen treated with indifference, followed by hatred, and thankfully returned to admiration. I dealt with the ravages of inflation, and the inequalities of changing tax rules. As a result of government action and inaction, I have lost faith in the U.S. government. I still love my country, though, and my personal experiences explain many of my views and lessons learned. The promises of my lifetime are likely promises made to you, too.

The Fifties

I was born at the end of World War Two so my early youth occurred during the fifties. My parents divorced when I was a toddler, so my grandmother and mother raised me. I was somewhat of a curiosity in school, because divorce wasn't as prevalent as it is today, and I really don't remember any friends with single parent households. My grandmother and mother both worked; granny was a practical nurse, and mom was a stenographer for a construction company. My grandmother owned our home and kept it through the depression while raising four children after she was widowed in 1928. These two women taught me to work, live within our means, go to church, and take care of our home. They felt sorrow for folks who received charity, and would never dream of accepting it themselves. There were no provisions for food stamps, housing assistance, or any of the programs that exist today. There was a county poor farm where folks could work and live in housing located on the county's farm property, and there was commodity food ration for folks who qualified.

In school each morning we pledged allegiance to the flag and recited the Lord's Prayer as part of our daily exercises. Our town was segregated. The blacks and whites had separate schools and separate facilities. Public drinking fountains were labeled white and colored, and the toilet facilities were usually marked men, women, and colored; I don't recall separate toilets for black men and women. Restaurants and movie theaters were segregated as well; the whites and blacks each had their separate places. My family taught me to treat the blacks with courtesy and respect as fellow human beings, but I was never encouraged to cross the color barriers in town.

Work, church, and family were the primary lessons, both in speech and by example. I walked home from elementary school each day and let myself in the back door with a key hidden for my use. Each evening we listened to the radio, or attended church on Wednesday evenings. A big change came in the early fifties when my grandmother bought a television set. It was common for aunts and uncles to visit and watch TV with us, although there was only one channel broadcasting for a few hours. When I was seven years old, my mother remarried. Her new husband traveled around the country working on high steel towers. He was a union ironworker and welder. I stayed with my grandmother while they traveled, so I could go to school. So, for most of my early youth, it was just my grandmother and I living together, going to work and school.

The late fifties brought TV newscasts of clashes over segregation. This was the time when there was terrible fighting in Little Rock over the admittance of black children in the high school. I didn't understand at the time what all the fuss was about. I couldn't see why blacks wanted to go to a white school, nor could I understand why the whites didn't want them to be admitted. It was really my first experience and awareness of the hatred that existed between the races. This had just never been evident in our home, so it was new to me.

THE SIXTIES

I attended high school in the early sixties. My mother and stepfather added two more children to the family and my grandmother remarried, so my mother stopped traveling in order to stay at home with her three children. Mama constantly urged me to plan for college, so we opened a college bank account and I began putting money aside for school. Like most boys of that era, a paper route was my first job, and later I graduated to sacking groceries. The summers after my last two years in high school were spent in a local factory. It was a union job, and there was no choice for joining, so part of each check went for dues, and I received my first experience with tax withholding.

True to my mother's urgings I started college. My parents contributed a good amount to supplement what I earned each summer and what I received from scholarships. A scholarship from the U.S. Army took care of tuition, books, and minor expenses, but it was necessary for me to work to make living expenses. I had a variety of jobs as a laborer, draftsman, and waiter. I landed a job working five nights a week, from 10 PM to about 3 AM, at a parcel service. It was another union job and it paid well above anything else I could get at other jobs. Each time we received a pay raise the dues went up, too. It was my second union job, and I learned a little about guaranteed pay, in particular for the drivers. Many of the tractor-trailer drivers hooked up and drove to their destination, then waited for a trailer to return to their home station. They usually sat in the break room until their trailer was ready, then hooked up and returned. If the whole shift took six hours, they were guaranteed pay for eight hours whether on the job or not.

It was a decade of turmoil that included the civil rights marches, the riots, and the demonstrations against the Viet Nam war. I was confused by it and searched for what to believe. I believed the black citizens should have equal freedom and rights, and was bewildered by the resistance to the ideals and provisions of our government. But I despised the destruction and violence that came with it. I understood the desires of those who set up resurrection city on the national mall, but was despondent at the destruction that remained after they left. I advocated equality, but was repulsed by some of the means used to justify their demands.

The middle sixties introduced me to the welfare society, the Great Society as it was called. The poor would receive money, housing, and food stamps. Housing projects were completed to provide decent housing for the underprivileged. It sounded like a good idea to me. I thought the poor deserved help to seek opportunities to grow and prosper. Little did I imagine that the new housing would be ravaged to become slums and drug houses, and that fifty years later the grandchildren of the first recipients would remain dependent on the government. In hindsight, I think it hurt more than it helped.

The Great Society brought with it a new health program called Medicare. I noticed the effect on my paycheck, but it was a small amount, and health benefits for the elderly seemed like centuries away for me. I paid little attention.

Like most citizens my age, I didn't escape the impact of assassinations and the Viet Nam war. First we lost our president, then Martin Luther King, Jr., and a short time later the fallen president's brother. I didn't understand what was happening to our country. Compared to the apparent tranquility of the fifties it seemed liked the United States was coming apart in every aspect of our lives. I was called to active military service in 1968. Generally soldiers were ridiculed and despised. I received my initial training at an Army post near Washington DC, and we were cautioned to stay out of uniform when going to town. There were riots and fires in Washington, and two Marine officers were killed while walking the streets in dress uniforms. It was a hateful time. In short order I was ordered to duty in Southeast Asia with the Corps of Engineers in support of combat forces. The majority of my service was spent building supply roads and facilities. Near the end of my tour my grandmother passed away, and I was called home for her funeral. I arrived at an Oakland Air Force base and was transported on a military bus with a busload of Marines to the San Francisco airport to catch a flight home. The bus route carried us through an area populated by demonstrators against the war. They attacked the bus by pounding on it, smearing the windows with manure, and shouting threats at us. It was a disheartening experience, and I felt disconnected from my country. Everywhere I went while in uniform was demoralizing, and to make matters worse, there was often commentary about the admiration and bravery of the draft dodgers that fled to Canada to escape service to the country. I wondered if I was wrong to serve.

The conflicting ideas in those days were that the Viet Nam War was immoral versus the need to stop communist aggression. The domino theory claimed that the communist goal was to rule the world by taking power in country after country against the free will of the people. Presumably, the purpose of the Viet Nam conflict was to take a stand against further aggression. The opposite viewpoint believed U.S. help was unwanted and only brought suffering and death to innocent people. Probably the worst strategic action made by American leaders was to win the war with a superior body count. Usually wars were won by taking control of land, facilities, and supply routes, then keeping them away from the enemy. But for some reason,

America adopted a strategy to kill so many of the enemy that they would become disheartened and quit the fight. As a result, U.S. soldiers would lose lives in a typical fight to claim a tactical site, claim victory by comparing enemy body count against America's losses, and then leave the site, which was routinely reoccupied by the Viet Cong. This philosophy to win a war simply by killing large numbers of people was a tragic mistake, and almost certainly an immoral one.

I really didn't know what to believe. The war was terrible for sure. Communist aggression seemed real, too. My choice was to fulfill my obligation to my American homeland despite the hatred of what seemed to be about half of its people.

THE SEVENTIES

After completing my military obligation, I started a career in engineering, and I married. Our country continued to change during this decade, and to throw off many of the values I had come to accept as a boy. I worked for three companies in this decade. My first job was building conventional and nuclear ordnance. It was controversial being associated with the Atomic Energy Commission, but the company I worked for was a huge employer in the small town where it was located, so there was little demonstration against us, but there was some. Later I changed jobs and was assigned to a uranium enrichment study group. My group spent several months in the National Nuclear Laboratory at Oak Ridge, Tennessee to learn the technology behind uranium enrichment using gaseous centrifuges. We experienced the first gasoline shortage crisis during this period, and it was during this training that I learned that several elements of our government had predicted and expected the petroleum shortage for decades. This was the first time I was aware of our government's failure to prepare, but at least now they were planning for the future of nuclear energy. We were supplied with charts forecasting the need for more enrichment plants and the world's uranium reserves. The costs for each centrifuge plant were enormous and beyond the investment capability of any single private company. In addition, the forecasts showed there would likely be a shortage of uranium by the turn of the century, and the disposal of mountains of nuclear waste was an unsolved problem at that time. It left me somewhat perplexed about whether this fuel source was right for the future. Pressure groups against nuclear energy would later contribute to a virtual abandonment of this energy source.

Each of the three companies I worked for during the seventies operated under contracts with union hourly workers. These were my first union experiences where I was not a member. My stepfather was a union worker that always spoke of their good. He felt his work was highly skilled, and only highly skilled workers could be admitted to the union, and as a result, they were the cream of the crop that deserved to have their wages and rights protected. Of course, I belonged to unions as a student. I reaped the benefits of higher pay, but I was somewhat put off by the requirement for union membership. Working as a young engineer with union craftsmen taught me some startling lessons. I learned that I must work well with the stewards or face a slow down of my projects. I would receive an assignment from my supervisor, and then it would be necessary for me to coordinate my plans with union leadership. If it didn't suit them, then it was necessary to balance their requirements with the company's in order to complete the work. I learned that a union contributes inefficiency to the cost of operations.

I was involved in several strikes during my career, and there was never any good that came from them, for either side. My first experience was a pretty hostile strike force. The workmen would block our entrance to work, crowd our cars on all sides and against the windshield, and they shouted threats. Management provided us with signs to put on our dash that read, "engineering" but it was little help. Some were unlucky because the mob damaged many cars. I was just starting my working life and had little money, and I just wanted to stay home, but management left no option; report to work or face termination. So, here we were, stuck between a requirement to work, and a mob trying to keep us out.

Strikes and slowdowns proved to be the ultimate demonstration of inefficiencies of unions. The striking workers would suffer lost wages that they would never recover, and the companies would suffer extraordinary operational losses. Friendships were destroyed. Engineers working in the factories built relationships with all of the workers, and many of them became close friends. But strikes caused tension, jealousy, and harsh words. Afterward, our work environment would return to one of cool courtesy, but the team spirit and friendship would be dissolved. There was substantial physical damage to company and personal property. I remember waiting one night with company managers for word on a union vote. A phone call informed us that the vote was for a strike. Within ten minutes of that phone call a piece of steel was hurled through one of the office windows and the picket line established. I couldn't understand why these individuals were allowed to break the law. I acknowledged their right to strike, but it appeared to me that many of the strikers viewed a strike as a right to damage property, commit assault and battery, and other felonies. My view on unions began to change.

THE EIGHTIES

We struggled with inflation such as I had never experienced before, and we became more aware of the IRA and 401(k), and watched the Soviet Union split. I sold my home and took a lower paying job in 1981 in order to move closer to my pre-school daughter. My mortgage on the old home was established at a modest interest rate several years earlier, but when I looked at buying a replacement home, the interest rates were so high, and my salary so reduced, that it was nearly impossible to buy a replacement. The sale of my home introduced me to the complexities and general unjustness of our tax code. In order to avoid paying taxes on the gain from the sale of my old home I would be required to buy another home of equal or greater value within a certain period of time. Inflation caused the increase in the sale price of my old home, so it wasn't a real gain, and of course, all replacement property had zoomed in price, also. As a result, I was faced with a larger mortgage at a higher interest rate for a similar property, so I was forced to rent. After the replacement time period elapsed I faced taxes on the inflationary gains, and at a higher-than-normal tax rate, because the capital gain was added to my income. This captured my interest in the tax code and the twists and turns that mire each citizen in its spider web. Today, if I had sold that same property I would have paid no taxes, because the current code ignores any gain less than $250,000. This was just a beginning lesson for me on the arbitrary and changing progressive tax code that is established by representatives with individual interests.

Another thing that became very noticeable during this period was the assailment of the evil white male. Males in general were mocked and belittled in everything from the news to TV shows, but the white male got the worst of it. We weren't sensitive enough. We were unfair to women in the workplace and at school. No one, it seemed, could succeed because of the repression by white males. This group caused racial bigotry and was blamed for slavery and the plight of minorities. The poor were stuck in the projects, couldn't get a decent job, were wallowing in drugs, and it was all the fault of wicked plotting and conspiring by the evil white male. I really began to feel negatively about myself. Personally I didn't feel like I conspired against any one, and in fact, most of my life I had felt like a salmon swimming upstream as I struggled to work and make ends meet. The bile spewed at us was as negative as the behavior toward soldiers during the Viet Nam era. The more I thought about it, the more I realized it just didn't make sense.

Just about everything I had learned thus far in my life was part of the great conversation from white males, and I thought many of their ideas were good hearted. Sure, the history of mankind is full of terrible things, and the white male contributed his fair share to hate, bigotry, and greed, but I began to realize that the negative things were a human fault that is not peculiar to white men. When I examined the philosophy, science, arts, and law that white males wrote about and implemented, it was obvious that these were good works. They brought us the great ideas such as calculus, physics, the Reformation, and a constitutional republic. These ideas evolved with our society in its hopes for civil rights and women's suffrage. I realized that none of these causes could have succeeded without both the initiative and consent of white males. The life style of preceding centuries included slavery and the relegation of women to homemakers, with white males establishing and dominating the business world. In the United States, I am certain that if white males wanted to control the lives of others, then the Constitution would have read differently, and there would have been no capitulation. Our country easily could have resembled life in other places where we see women and minorities still treated like property, but the white male population in general was repulsed by inequality and did not want the subjugation of their fellow citizens. It simply didn't make sense to me that the white male was so totally evil as others accused.

It was during the early eighties that I rediscovered George Washington, our great defender of personal freedom. He inherited slaves, and was a slave keeper. I have studied and tried to understand life in the eighteenth century and how this happened. I can only conclude that it was a part of society in general, not necessarily just the white male. Their writings clearly show their hopes for a future without slavery and with equality for all people to govern themselves freely. It has been said that the good and bad events of a person's life can be lined up such that all individuals have a good line and a bad line. Our hope is that our good line is the longer. I think George Washington's good line was extraordinarily longer than the bad. He established many precedents for governing our country, and he saved us from becoming a monarchy or dictatorship, or worse.

During the transition period after the Revolutionary War from a confederation of states to a constitutional union, there was confusion and attempts to grab power. First was a threat of a military coup to take control of the country, because military personnel had not received the pay they had been promised by the Congress. They were angry and wanted to take by force what they were owed, while establishing military rule in place of civil rule. How many times have we seen this happen in country after country? Cuba is a good example of a military triumph over a despot, only to replaced by another. George Washington reminded the Army of its duty and influenced it to moderate its conduct. As part of its plan to recoup what the country owed it, there was a proposal to make Washington the country's king. As we know, this man of colossal character, humility, and fairness would have no part of it. He told them he was not a king but was their brother. He saved us from the tyranny that would accompany an American king, and he established the first model of an American citizen-soldier for us.

When Washington was elected president he began several incredible precedents for our presidency that are accepted traditions and laws. After his election there was no established protocol for addressing the chief executive. Following models of our British ancestry there were many aristocratic suggestions such as, His Excellency. The first Senate suggested, "His Highness, the President of the United States of America and Protector of Their Liberties," but the House of Representatives settled upon President of the United States. Washington insisted that he be addressed as Mr. President and nothing more. In office he reestablished the idea of the citizen-soldier and the citizen-servant with the idea that he would serve his fellow countrymen and then return to the higher status of fellow citizen when his term was completed.

President Washington initiated the annual state of the Union address by our president, and limited term of service. Article II, Section 3 of the U.S. Constitution requires that the president shall from time to time give the Congress information on the state of the Union. There is no specified time period. Our first president decided upon once a year, and this has been accepted and repeated for generations of chief executives. The first president created the first self-imposed term limit. Many people in the country expected him to serve as long as he lived. This was not uncommon at the time, just as we often see men today take seats of power for their entire lives. Just as a new Congress of Representatives would be elected with frequency, he thought there should be a limit of service for the executive branch. He limited himself to two terms, and it was important to him that his countrymen choose another president while he was still alive. Succeeding presidents generally followed his example. A few thought about more terms as they were consumed by their own ideas of self importance and disregard for self-rule of the people, but for various reasons it was avoided until Franklin Roosevelt disregarded Washington's example. Of course today we have the Twenty-second Amendment to the Constitution that limits each president to only two terms, and so President Washington's precedent has become law.

During his service President Washington relied on the Constitution to guide his decisions and to protect its provisions. It was a vulnerable time for our new nation as it sought to understand the Constitution and the concept of republican self-government. There were attacks on the Constitution, and the Whiskey Rebellion in Pittsburgh against a new liquor tax had the potential for overthrowing the provisions and authority of the new government. Washington knew a minority of citizens could not be allowed to demand changes by force, so he personally led a militia to settle the argument without violence. The new president steered us away from debt and advised us against the accumulation of debt. He believed it was wrong to burden later generations with obligations that each generation should bear itself.

There was much more that this wonderful patriot taught us with word and deed, and there are plenty of examples in books and memoirs. He warned us against the two-party system. The Federalist and Republican factions that were formed plagued our first presidential administration, but Washington said he was a man of no party, and called party spirit a demon. He recognized that party spirit is human nature, but he feared the destructive influence of political parties. President Washington recognized that alternating domination of one party over another would cause vengeful attitudes and result in government not unlike a dictatorship.

The more I have learned about George Washington, the more my admiration for him has grown to hero status. Not only was he brave and courageous, but also he gave the last measure of himself to his God, family, and countrymen. He was the perfect example of the citizen-soldier, and citizen-public-official. Our public officials of today could use him as an example of their obligation to America and its people, and we could all use him as an example for daily life. His last wishes after leaving office were of peace for the whole world with everyone contributing to the happiness of mankind.

By returning to words and examples of great men of history, I began to accept criticisms of the white male as simply criticisms of bad human character. It really wasn't strictly limited to race or gender. While trying to sort truth from intolerance, I met a woman that personalized the ideas of self-government and individual freedom. At a time when I supervised a small machine design department I came to need a machine designer. This would be a person qualified to work under the supervision of a project engineer to design mechanisms and machinery layouts. We advertised for applicants and began the process of interviewing folks for the job.

One of the candidates was a lady who had recently emigrated to the U.S. with her family from the Soviet Union. She was married and had two children. When I reviewed her resume I noticed her education was roughly equivalent to a Masters Degree in Mechanical Engineering, so she was extremely overqualified for our job vacancy. I explained this to her. She acknowledged it, but said she needed work so our position would be satisfactory. In probing further I learned her husband was similarly educated in Electrical Engineering, and was looking for work, too. I noticed she had a very thick accent and was somewhat difficult to understand, so I figured both she and her husband were having difficulty finding technical employment to match their qualifications. This was often typical for new immigrants.

Their situation intrigued me. I knew enough about the Soviet Union of the day that highly educated technical people enjoyed a higher-than-average standard of living. They received high pay, better living accommodations, and other benefits. So, during my conversation with her I asked her why she chose to leave Russia for the United States. Her explanation was a powerful practical lesson about freedom. She said they moved to America for their children's future. In Russia, she explained, there was no guarantee for choice of profession or where to live. All youth were tested when they were growing up, and based upon their scores and aptitude the government decided what their profession should be. Even if a person wished to pursue higher education, it could be denied if the State decided their aptitude scores were not satisfactory. If there was no need for their assigned job where they wanted to live, then they could be transferred elsewhere in the country for the good of the State.

She said she and her husband wanted their children to have the opportunity to choose and achieve on their own. This really struck me. It was unimaginable to me that people could be denied the ability to choose their path in life, or to be required to live in a certain area. Of course I had read about restrictions by the State in communist governments, but her story truly brought it to life. The meaning of unalienable rights and self-government was magnified for me. It really brought home how a centralized government can impose restrictions on people's lives to serve the government.

About this same time, in the early eighties, we noticed companies beginning to change retirement plans. For years many companies paid for defined benefit pension plans for their employees. Workers stayed with the same company for most of their working lives, and then were paid a pension for life after retirement. But not all companies offered pension plans to workers, and it was common for folks without pensions to live on their Social Security checks during retirement. This is exactly what my grandparents did. They never worked for a company and were left to their own devices when they were too old to continue working. The Social Security payments were meager, and inflation left many of them living in poverty.

The Traditional Individual Retirement Arrangement, TIRA, was authorized in 1974 for workers without employment-based retirement plans. I hardly noticed it until 1981 when the Economic Recovery Act allowed limited contributions to a TIRA regardless of pension coverage. There were various phase-out requirements and adjustments in the following years until the major addition of the Roth IRA, RIRA, was started in 1997.

Another subtle change was made in 1978 when Section 401(k) of the Internal Revenue Code was added to be effective on January 1, 1980. Again, the common individual, such as me, paid little notice, but companies began to recognize the 401(k) as a way to reduce the high cost of providing a defined benefit pension plan. In the middle 1980s there were less than eight million 401(k) participants in a little more than 17,000 companies that had accounts worth a total of $100 million, but by 2006 there were more than seventy million individuals and 438,000 companies participating, and the total account value was estimated at more than $3 trillion.

Private companies found that supporting a 401(k) plan was cheaper than a defined benefit pension plan, so they started the transition toward expecting individuals to be responsible for their personal retirement. There would be a small amount of Social Security and personal 401(k) and IRA savings to be used for retirement expenses. Some companies would continue to offer a scaled down retirement plan to supplement retirement income, but many, especially smaller employers, completely phased out the defined benefit plan.

The major exceptions are governments and unions. These groups have not joined the transition from employer-sponsored retirement to a plan where the employee is more responsible for personal retirement planning. Our federal government, and many state governments, continues to support expensive plans through tax revenue burdens on the people. Many governments and large companies are restricted by out-dated union contracts that require continuation of defined retirement plans. The autoworkers have enjoyed extraordinary retirement benefits that the average American will never receive. Our federal government is no different. The automotive industry has suffered terribly as a result of high labor and benefits costs that have left them uncompetitive in the world market. Government workers remain a load for the people, too, but they may soon learn the problems of an uncompetitive nation in the world's open market.

The TIRA was big news in the eighties, with big government promises, the 401(k) began to transition into company benefits, and the Roth IRA and 401(k) would add complexity and confusion to the options for the common American. But we all began to become more aware and concerned over deficit spending by our government. The Social Security and Medicare systems became prominent in news and political rhetoric. We were told these systems would eventually run out of money to pay the retirement stipends, and that these programs, combined with welfare, had become major components of our national budget. A patch was made to Social Security that would phase in older age requirements for full retirement, but the government continued to borrow the excess Social Security taxes paid by its citizens for their retirement investment. It was during the eighties that I personally began to notice the mismanagement of our government funds, but like many of my friends, we complained and shook our heads, but let it continue.

THE NINETIES AND TWO THOUSANDS

During the nineties there were more changes and modifications to the IRA and 401(k) programs that have left most Americans bewildered. The Roth IRA, RIRA, was started in 1997 to allow U.S. workers to save for retirement, but without the tax deferment benefits of the TIRA. The hook was that all earnings on RIRA investments would be tax-free. In 2006, a comparable Roth 401(k) program was initiated for companies that chose to participate. It was during this time that I began to distrust the government retirement savings programs. The Roth 401(k) was scheduled to expire in 2010, but now has been extended, so who can plan or count on anything in the future? The other big attraction in the government IRA and 401(k) schemes was that when an individual retires, they likely would have income in a lower tax bracket, and thus come out with an even better benefit. But who can count on consistency from a government that does little planning and continually changes the laws and rules? Now we hear that the tax rates may increase in the future, so those who have saved during their lifetime may look forward to paying a higher tax rate than when they set aside the savings. Of course, they still have the benefit of tax deferral on the income while in savings. Nevertheless, the nineties left me with a skeptical attitude about government programs; they are continually changed to the point of being unjust.

As I neared retirement age, I decided to prepare tax returns for a major tax service company. I thought I could add a little extra income to my retirement years while completing seasonal employment for about 100 days per year. I took hundreds of hours of classes and have been preparing tax returns for about a decade. It has been both an education and an eye opener when it comes to the abuses the American people suffer under this oppressive system. The tax system is entirely disproportionate, inconsistent, and subject to abuses by the clever taxpayer. The IRS is ill equipped to keep up with the abuses of some folks. I have seen people walk in to have their taxes prepared that have not filed a return for five years or more. They were required to file, but somehow escaped the overseeing eye of the tax police. How fair is that?

It was during this period when I realized that some people simply aren't able to prepare even the simplest tax forms, and this is where I received the most satisfaction in helping these folks. The government seems to expect its citizens to be accountants or to hire one. Most people don't know how to keep records, and many don't want to do it; they just want to live their lives in peace. As a result, I have seen people subjected to terrible distress because they wind up owing thousands of dollars, just because they weren't aware of all of the provisions of a tax code numbering thousands of pages.

I have come to believe that it's disgraceful for a country of free citizens to impose a revenue system that causes many of its citizens to pay someone to prepare their tax return. Many of these people are the poorest working folks that receive the earned income credit, EIC, on their taxes. This program was meant to encourage low-income people to work for their welfare payment. It grew tremendously in the nineties with the welfare reforms. Now, paid tax preparers take hundreds of dollars out of these welfare checks as part of their services; and, the abuses are notorious. The IRS has begun leaning on tax preparers to check out EIC applicants to the point that tax preparation services are the new administrators of welfare and social services programs.

It was during the nineties when political dialogue turned to self-directed Social Security accounts. After my tax preparation experiences I became convinced that this is a poor idea unless there are controls. I have witnessed dozens of IRA and 401(k) accounts that have been drained in time of need, or just for some special treat, like a new boat or a trip. Also, it's common for people to turn to their retirement savings when they lose their jobs. As a result, a large withdrawal runs up their gross income causing increased federal and state tax rates, and a ten percent penalty is frequently added to their tax debt when they show up at the tax office. If they have also drawn unemployment benefits, then they owe taxes on that as well, and most don't have withholding taken out of the unemployment check, so there they are, vulnerable, out of work, needing money, but owing a big tax bill. Their retirement savings is gone. If the government ever decides to implement a self-directed Social Security feature it should be controlled, or we will have a full generation of people with empty retirement accounts.

The terrorist attacks in 2001 added to our concerns about immigration controls and secure borders, and like many Americans I was both directly and indirectly affected. I worked in a factory that employed seasonal workers, because about sixty percent of annual production was built in a four-month spurt. My company hired a temporary employment agency each year to screen, hire, and pay the seasonal workers; they worked for the employment company, not the factory. It was controlled chaos during the season, and a majority of the seasonal workers were Hispanics that didn't speak English. The employment agency used a bilingual representative to review their identification, but illegal workers bought fake social security cards and identification papers that were virtually impossible to detect.

Their scheme usually worked for quite a while, but eventually the Social Security Administration would notify us that there were names and numbers that did not match government records. The affected workers were notified, and each claimed there was a mistake and vowed to provide correct information. The deadline from the government was usually two weeks. Most of them continued to work for two weeks, but vanished after the deadline. I became friends with one of the workers that was caught and disappeared. I didn't see him for a few years, and then one day I noticed he was working at the factory again. I called his name to say hello. He whispered, "my name is Victor, now." He was illegal with new papers, and he was a good friend, but I never knew his real name.

The terrorist attacks indirectly affected me afterward when flight schools were closed while the government checked out foreign flight students that were in our country. I provided flight instruction at that time, and the flight schools were crippled by the shut down. Most of all I wondered why the government was placing additional burdens on us to verify citizenship. I was a flight instructor, not an immigration and customs specialist. Why didn't the government do its job to screen these people and follow up on their whereabouts in the first place? That was, after all, their job.

Like many Americans, the illegal immigrant problem was a rude awakening for me. The government wasn't verifying status adequately, nor insuring that companies were following immigration laws. Why didn't the government follow up on individuals with mismatched identification? Why was I required to verify my own citizenship periodically at work, thanks to the Patriot Act, but illegal residents continue to skirt the law? Why was a private flight instructor required to verify citizenship before providing flight instruction, but an illegal resident was not forced to show proof after a crime?

During the first decade of the new century I continued saving as I had throughout my lifetime. I paid income taxes, Social Security and Medicare taxes. I worked diligently, lived frugally, and stayed out of debt. My reward was continued slavery to the system that caters to others who chose not to work, not to live within their means, and not to save. Now that I have saved for years and built for retirement, my reward will be higher taxes, higher Medicare premiums, and continued support of the give-away programs created by a Congress out of control.

Those of us working in the great American industrial system experienced continued pressure on our jobs as a result of the migration of manufacturing to foreign suppliers. The company I worked for during my last thirteen years closed a dozen or more plants in the United States, and built replacement factories in Mexico, China, and other locations off shore. In 2008 we faced the granddaddy of all recessions and we are still trying to recover. The manufacturing jobs are gone, and unlikely to return. Labor costs when I retired were about a dollar an hour in Mexico, and about a dollar a day in China; these odds were virtually impossible for us to overcome. In the sixties, I think the country could have produced its way out of this recession in a shorter period of time. This was during a time when we generated a larger part of our real wealth. I think now, we are at a point where our country must redefine itself and resize spending based upon our new economic capability. Barring an international conflict or war, I believe our lost manufacturing jobs will never be returned, or at least it will take generations.

I transitioned into retirement at the end of the first decade of the 2000s, and my involvement with government rules and regulations was just as bewildering to deal with as tax law. I wanted to retire with private health care I would provide for myself and would avoid getting caught up in the Medicare system. My employers provided my health care insurance in some form during my working life, and I expected to buy my own after retirement. Unfortunately I suffered a bout with cancer in 2005 that would change my perspective. I learned that virtually no insurance company would insure a person convicted of having cancer; this was the infamous pre-existing condition clause. There is a high-risk pool in my state for persons in this category, and at the time it would cost about $12,000 per year for $1,000 deductible. This was about six times what I had planned to pay for a private policy. Obviously, my only economical choice was to continue working at a job I wanted to leave in order to continue my health care policy. So, I held on until I reached the age to enroll in Medicare.

As we reach old age we are faced with being our own insurance agent, and with dozens of options and choices. After I trudged through books on the subject, I finally settled on a Medicare Advantage plan that would offer the catastrophic coverage I wanted at a reasonable price. Naturally, about this time the new administration started the push for its new health care plan. Now, it appears if the plan is implemented as proposed, Medicare Advantage plans are likely to be phased out some time around 2014. So here we are. More government intervention with more intrusion into our private lives, and in the name of helping the deserving few who are unable to obtain health care. In addition, as a result of my lifetime savings and the fixed income it produces, I am faced with higher Medicare premiums.

Another change of rules by the government resulted in a set back for my retirement savings when General Motors filed for bankruptcy. Several years before this problem occurred I purchased corporate bonds from General Motors. Being a conservative investor, I always bought investment grade bonds, which have a lower risk of default by the borrower. The General Motors bonds were well rated, and I bought senior bonds. These senior securities have extra protection in case of default, because the bondholders are first to receive compensation in cases of bankruptcy and such. I received a steady income stream from my bond purchase for years, and then suddenly and swiftly General Motors filed for bankruptcy. I accepted it like a loss at the roulette table, but I expected to be first in line with the other senior note holders, to receive some return of the loan principal. Behind us, according to securities regulation, were the funds for retirement benefits for the autoworkers union. Who could imagine that the president and his administration would interfere to change the rules? How do you get a do-over of the rules after the bankruptcy? I expect I paid a premium for the security of a senior note, and now I was relegated to a position behind the union pension funds, because the government changed the rules. I felt cheated and that it violated the principle of "no ex post facto" laws set forth in the Constitution. I'm sure a lawyer somewhere figured out that it was legal, even though unethical. So, for years I held these essentially worthless bonds, receiving no income, while waiting for the final disposition from the bankruptcy courts. I can accept the loss from a soured investment, but not extra losses due to rules changes for privileged groups.

So who could blame anyone who has lived and worked in the United States during the last half of the twentieth century and the first ten years of the twenty-first for being skeptical about government and its programs? The laws and rules have been constantly changing and rewritten. The size of government continues to grow and swallow huge amounts of our national wealth and it's never enough. In order to pay for its lopsided programs our government has continually borrowed to cover its failed planning and control. Government intrusion in our lives grows continually as well. Who can blame a person of my generation for accusing our representatives of malfeasance in office?

CHAPTER THREE

LESSONS LEARNED

ALL HUMAN EXPERIENCE is filled with lessons learned during a lifetime. Sources of learning range from trial and error, success and failure, to education, to learning from the historical experiences of others.

About a dozen lessons have been selected as examples and explanations for basics of government, social behavior, and malfeasance in office. These lessons include application of mathematical and scientific principles to examine human behavior, the occurrence of natural changes, and the human endeavor to control economic actions. A few philosophical ideas are offered to help understand the individual drive to pursue public office, and the ideas that form the basis of the Constitution.

For many years scientists and mathematicians have used principles of their arts to help explain human behavior and experience. Laws of statistical distribution are mathematical concepts concerning highs, lows, and averages. Before formal theories were proposed, the country's founding fathers recognized these patterns in human behavior and the various types of personalities in society. Statistical distribution theories suggest that in every group there are a certain number of good and bad individuals, and honest and dishonest ones. Application of this idea to the government should alert every American to the idea that they must keep a sharp eye on government operations.

Laws of constant change and entropy are used to explain the founders' acknowledgement that society is constantly changing and the Constitution must be flexible to change with it. Furthermore, they knew that a self-governing people must participate in the government in order to maintain the security and order of the Constitution. In return, government must continually review its programs to maintain order.

Economic theory has become a significant element of American society today, and the government is continually attempting to control it. Simple ideas of economic real wealth, and ideas from the father of economics are used in elementary explanations of business. According to the most elementary principles of business, government cannot create real jobs, but it must be left up to the free productivity of society.

The difficulty of controlling the national or world economy is explained by the concepts of infinity of actions and available time. These ideas complement one another with the obvious idea that life is too complicated, with too many interactions to be ruled by bureaucrats. Available time suggests simply there is not enough available time in a lifetime to understand and control the intricacies of taxes, mortgages, the economy, and welfare. These ideas help explain why the more the government becomes entangled with individual lives the more the programs become so unreasonable and wasteful.

Turning to philosophical studies of government, there are three concepts that may be used to describe the thoughts and hopes of the founders. Nearly every American is familiar with the idea of unalienable rights; it's in the Declaration of Independence. But few understand the idea of statutory vested rights, and the difference between the two. These ideas are basic to the idea of free government, and building upon the ideas of unalienable freedom the framers of the Constitution built it upon the idea of public opinion. Public opinion, versus popular opinion, is the basis of self-government as envisioned by James Madison. The administration of a government ruled by the people, then, was established on the concept of people's law through a common law jury. This would be very different from bureaucratic, or elite, rule through board laws.

John Adams helped identify the motivation behind an individual's desire to run for office. He claimed it is part of the make up of every human in varying degrees. He called it the pursuit of distinction, and he wrote that every human being has an inherent need to be recognized in some way, and without it, a person feels a personal loss. When the pursuit of distinction through public office is combined with an ambition for profit, then a dangerous career politician is created. In order to maintain their station, they resort to social programs to encourage their constituents to retain them in office. By borrowing against the productivity of future generations to support the current individuals keeping them in office, they are able to satisfy the dual need for distinction and profit. This borrowing from new citizens to pay old ones can be described as a Ponzi scheme. It's illegal in the private world, but has been accepted as a government policy for social insurance.

Peaceful dispute was a lesson supported by colonial Americans as a way to balance the differing ideas of people. They knew there always would be factions in society, and that there was always a danger of tyranny by the majority. As a result, they favored controlled discussion and voting as a means for regarding the rights of the minority. Ideas from Gandhi and Martin Luther King, Jr. offer strong ideas on the regard for one another and discussing disagreements without violence or causing harm in any way to other human beings.

STATISTICAL DISTRIBUTION

Basic statistical theories revolve around concepts of distribution of events or variables. The German mathematical genius, Carl Gauss, taught the idea of continuous probability. It is one of the first distributions taught in elementary statistics, and it claims that as the numbers of random elements continue to increase, they tend to cluster around their average. When it is perfectly balanced and placed on graph paper, it takes the shape of a bell; so, many people refer to this as the bell curve. Figure 3-1 shows what a typical bell curve might look like if the heights of a group of individuals were compared.

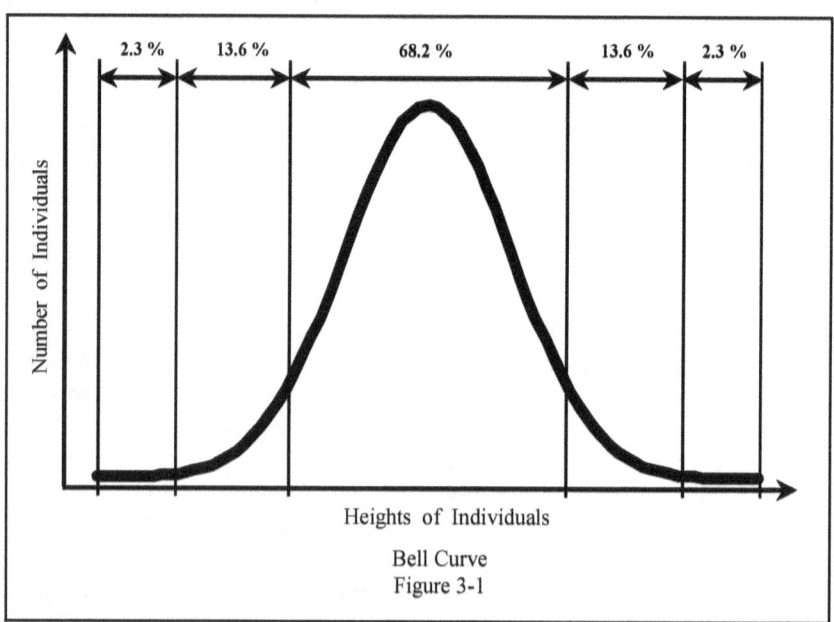

Heights of Individuals

Bell Curve
Figure 3-1

The highest point on a perfect curve represents the average height of the individuals. When everything is perfectly balanced, the properties show that about sixty-eight percent are in the middle close to the center. On each side, a little farther from the center, there are intermediate zones that are around 13.6 percent in size. Finally, about 2.3 percent of the elements are farthest from the center of the curve at the extreme ends.

Many students have dreaded classes where the teacher announces that the grades will be determined on the curve. The bell curve is generally what the teacher means. The teacher believes that all students fall in categories according to this distribution. After scoring the work of each student, the teacher will average the scores, and then establish letter grades based upon the approximate percentages shown in Figure 3-1. The middle sixty-eight percent of the class receive a C; the divisions on each side of the C zone receive a B or D, and the students with scores at the most extreme ends of the curve are awarded an A or F. Obviously, there are exceptions to every rule and theory, and this one is no different. When there are a small number of elements in the group, then the distribution won't look much like a bell curve, but as more and more elements are added to the group, it begins to take the shape of the predicted bell curve.

Social scientists have employed this idea for years in categorizing human behavior. It is not uncommon for human resource professionals to try to fit personnel ratings and pay raises into this distribution. The idea is that there should be a certain number of high performers and low performers, with everyone else filling out the middle. The military personnel system followed this same basic idea, and the top performers that would likely receive promotions in rank ahead of everyone else were often referred to as upper five-percenters.

Folks with just plain common sense have noticed examples of this distribution in human behavior. In just about every group or activity, there are a certain number of people that strongly support an idea and a similarly small group that strongly oppose the idea. The rest are in the middle and will go either way, and they usually follow the stronger of the two opposing groups. The same can be said of honesty or personal conduct. Some people are extremely honest virtually all the time; the standard statistical distribution would estimate about 2.3%. Average folks range from pretty honest to pretty dishonest, depending upon whether they think they will be caught. And, of course, the worst extreme is the criminal element that is dishonest virtually all of the time.

Bell curve categories are present in just about every activity in life. This distribution can be applied to abilities, competence, honesty, or just about any attribute for any group that may be examined. In a group of doctors, there will be a small percentage of really great ones and really lousy ones, while the rest are more or less of average competence. Even in the top levels of corporate management, where each officer has achieved the highest level of responsibility, there will be leaders, dissenters, and those riding the fence for survival. The same can be said for their honesty and competence. Some wound up in their job by some quirk of selection, and just shouldn't be there, and a certain number, about 2.3% on the whole, are selfish and dishonest. But there are extremely honest and accomplished business managers leading businesses today, and the middle group will follow the stronger example. If the dominant group or individual is a stinker, then the majority of the company top leaders, and the company at large, will follow along.

The learned and intuitive founders of America recognized this from their observations of the human condition, although Carl Gauss did not offer his theory until about the time of the first administration. Throughout their writings, men like George Washington, John and Samuel Adams, and Thomas Jefferson speak of the human capability for great good and great evil. Obviously, this is true today for the esteemed representative officers, judges, and federal employees. Apply this distribution to the House of Representatives, the Senate, the Executive Branch, or the Supreme Court, and these extremes will likely be found, whether it's a stance on an issue, their personal honesty, or how well they do their jobs. There will usually be small bunches within the group that are at opposite extremes, and the majority in the middle usually follows the more dominant personalities.

A variation of the standard Gauss distribution is developed when the quantities of elements grow exponentially. That is, when the relationship is the result of one quantity being raised to a power, or multiplied by itself a certain number of times. When this happens, the standard distribution becomes distorted such that it no longer looks like a bell, but more like the shape pictured in Figure 3-2.

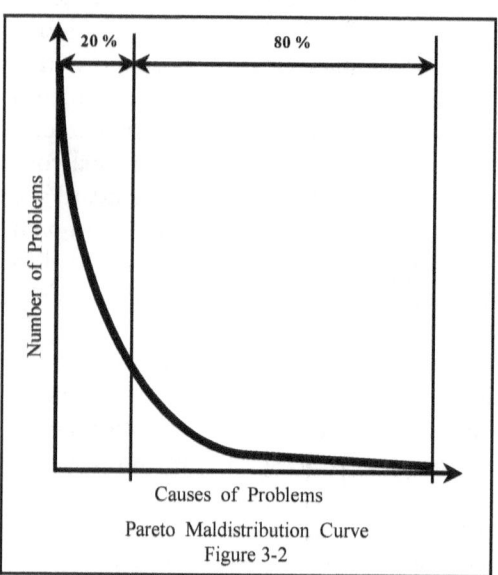

Causes of Problems
Pareto Maldistribution Curve
Figure 3-2

Vilfredo Pareto, an Italian engineer and economist, first applied this distribution to the study of wealth and economics. He discovered that in Italy eighty percent of the land was owned by only twenty percent of the population. As a result, the idea caught on that a few elements contribute to most of the cause, and it is commonly referred to as the Pareto Theory of Maldistribution. Today, technical analysts commonly use it to identify major contributors to problems, and this same 80-20 relationship is often identified; in other words, about twenty percent of the different causes of problems contribute to eighty percent of all problems.

Through the years, this idea has been used to describe a variety of theoretical explanations. It has been suggested that only twenty percent of the population controls eighty percent of the wealth, or that only twenty percent of the oil reserves contain eighty percent of the oil, and so forth. On the subject of human suffering, Pareto himself felt that the smarter and stronger take the lion's share and the weak starve. The same methods can be applied to prioritize work on some of the nation's problems, such as balancing the budget and spending.

Unalienable Rights versus Statutory Vested Rights

"All men are created equal, that they are endowed by their Creator with certain unalienable Rights." So states the Declaration of Independence. It goes on to list Life, Liberty, and the pursuit of Happiness. By unalienable rights, the Declaration refers to natural rights that cannot be changed or taken away from anyone. All people are born with the freedom to live their lives in the manner they choose – as wild or as disciplined as they wish. It also includes the freedom of the mind and conscience. No individual or government has the right to control or restrict the mind and thoughts of another. Consciousness is a gift of nature that cannot be repealed.

At the same time, governments may provide statutory vested rights. These rights may be offered, changed, or revoked according to the laws or dictates of the controlling authority. This may include minimum wage payments, pensions, health care, welfare, or other benefits from the people.

Political leaders often speak of rights, and it is important to distinguish between the two. Every American shares the natural and irrevocable birth right to freedom, but the receipt of statutory vested rights from the government are not the same for each citizen. Statutory rights are constantly subject to changes established by the prevailing governmental authority.

When Thomas Jefferson wrote, "all men are created equal," he knew every person was not born with the same abilities and opportunities in life. It's a natural observation that some people have greater physical or mental abilities than others. If any particular attribute of the human condition were statistically studied, a bell distribution would likely result where most of mankind would be about average, and some would be at either extreme. In addition, it can be seen that developed abilities are further influenced by environment and circumstance. Clearly, individuals born into privilege have more opportunity to improve their natural abilities.

Thomas Jefferson and others recognized the difference in abilities in people, but they further distinguished the natural equality of all to live their lives as free as they wish according not only to opportunities they receive, but also to opportunities they make for themselves.

All are equal in receipt of unalienable, irrevocable, natural rights to freedom, while some may receive variable vested rights established and controlled by governmental authority.

Public Opinion versus Popular Opinion

The ideas and concepts of self-government through public opinion originated in France in the last half of the eighteenth century. Prominent philosophers discussed public opinion during a period often referred to as the Era of Enlightenment. Strong communication was regarded as the foundation for government by public opinion, so the idea developed rapidly as printing was developed and began to supplement the spoken word.

The early French philosophers distinguished public opinion from popular opinion. They regarded popular opinion as a temporary sentiment of the people that is usually driven by the passions of immediate interests. Common examples include runaway inflation, jobs, and fear. If unchecked, popular opinion can develop into a sovereign rule of oppression. In the last century, the desperate popular opinion of the German people may have allowed the cruel and murderous Nazi regime to take hold.

Public opinion on the other hand, is described as a composite of passion and reason. It develops in time through communication, reason, and conformity of sentiment. It is a simultaneous communication between government and people to shape the national conscience and its desire for obedience; it occurs through consideration and maturing of ideas.

Public opinion depends on strong, efficient communication. Before printing, aristocrats and chiefs assumed the role of government and the people followed their will. Never before in history has strong communication been so enabled as today with books, papers, radio, television, and the Internet. When the colonialists were developing the nation's government, they used the printed word and town meetings to develop public opinion.

Ideas are distilled through layers of government to strain passion from popular opinion and refine it into public opinion. In the United States, this is accomplished by individuals from city to county, to the State, then to the House of Representatives, the Senate, the President, and the Supreme Court. Ultimately, public opinion becomes the true national authority and stability for a self-governing people.

James Madison, the primary architect of the U.S. Constitution, studied these ideas, formed his own concepts, and incorporated them into the early draft of the Constitution. He believed that over time public opinion would always seek right and justice. He recognized that it may err at times, but the people will soon correct it to a right path. The concept of statistical distribution and the bell curve can be used to illustrate President Madison's belief. The center portion of the bell curve, as shown in Figure 3-1, can be considered as the mixture of national beliefs that are distilled into the public opinion of common good. On either side of the bell's center there is a small percentage that might be considered as popular opinion. The voice on one side might be filled with hysteria or fear urging the nation to be severe. The opposite side could be stressing compassion or rescue. Both voices are heard, considered, and tempered until the national conscience is created in the middle of the statistical bell in the form of a considerate public opinion as Madison predicted.

As a result, public opinion is the basis for self-government as formed in the Constitution. The multi-layered system of government, and the federal government were set up to support public opinion. These ideas are the basis for the Constitutional provisions for free speech, free press, and free public discussion. The need for free and unrestrained communication must continue today with free radio, television, and Internet in order to continue the legacy of self-government by a free and just people through mature public opinion.

RULE OF PEOPLE VERSUS BOARD RULE

There is an important distinction between laws made by the people and laws made by a board of elite bureaucrats. The rule of the people is based upon laws established by the people and implemented through the common law jury system; these laws are formed from the people up. Conversely, board rule is set up under the authority of a central government that makes the laws, interprets them, and enforces them through punishments it decides are appropriate; such laws are formed from the government down. The fathers of the country recognized this distinction and purposely created a Constitution based upon the rule of people. As such, the national contract protects individual freedom in two ways: ability to change the Constitution, and the right to trial by jury. The authority of the people to change the Constitution is preserved in Article Five. It establishes the right of the people to require a Constitutional Convention to make changes through ratification by the States. Trial by jury is assured by Article III, Section 2, Clause 3 for criminal charges, and by the Seventh Amendment in the Bill of Rights for civil actions.

People's law in the United States is founded on the common law jury. The jury system is peculiar to this country with its safeguards against arbitrary judicial power; few, if any, countries in the world remain that utilize the trial by jury. When the American founders first set up the country's laws, the common law jury determined both the facts of the case and decided the law. The jury heard the attorneys' arguments on the law, and it was given advisory instructions on the law by the judge, but the jury was not bound by the judge's instructions. If the common law jury found charges in a case to be unjust or unconstitutional, then it could apply the law as it decided and find the accused not guilty. The jury could not repeal an existing law, nor injure anyone; only find in favor of the accused.

The founders believed the common law jury system was the people's ultimate defense against being overpowered by the government. Thomas Jefferson explained that the jury should decide both law and fact on any point of public liberty, and especially if a judge is suspected of bias. The common law jury system of deciding both law and fact remained in effect for the first one hundred years, until 1895 when it was changed to restrict the jury to only finding facts, and bound jurors to interpretation of the law by the court.

The use of bureaucratic laws has grown steadily in the country's history to accompany people's law. Bureaucratic laws are legally empowered under authority of laws made by the Legislative Branch. Today, bureaucratic laws include laws from boards and departments such as the Internal Revenue Service, the Environmental Protection Agency, and dozens more. In addition, the Executive Branch has used the executive order to add to its power as a lawmaker, too. A large part of these laws are reactions to solve problems with more rules, more bureaus, more administrators, and more waste. More dangerously, though, many of these boards have begun to write laws to support the policies and agendas of the bureaucratic leaders.

Board rules must be closely monitored and kept in check by the legislature, which is the true lawmaking instrument of the people. Board rules and executive orders must be curbed to protect the people. As soon as the right to trial by jury is lost, the destruction of the people's freedom to life and liberty begins. Mankind only remains truly free when required to obey the established laws of the people and not the arbitrary laws of a governing class.

CHANGE IS CONSTANT

There is a prime business axiom that every manager and worker must remember daily, if not hourly. It's simple: each business is constantly changing, and is either gaining ground or losing ground on competitors. The idea is that the markets continually change according to the rhythms of life and economics, and business methods must be altered and improved to adjust to them. The companies that stay fixed in their methods and outlooks are often left behind, and ultimately disappear. On any given day, a company may have a certain percentage of the market, but at any instant it may be gaining or losing ground. Without accepting the challenge to continually study, evaluate, and improve its methods and costs, stubborn companies will likely find themselves behind the others.

This is a good life example, also. It can be applied to job skills and personal relationships. Governments are subject to this basic idea of change, too. Governments receive money from the citizens for certain services, and their citizens expect it to be managed prudently. A city, state, or country may be in a leadership position for jobs, wealth, facilities, or beauty today, but at that moment it may be losing or gaining ground on the rest of the world. If it doesn't continue to assess the changing scope of its income and the needs of its community, then it will likely find itself in a different position in the future.

Most people born before 1950 have probably observed this principle in action. The look and needs of U.S. communities began to change with the development of the Interstate highways and shopping centers. A lot of cities did not adapt to the changes and were left with many social difficulties as a result. Large companies were unable to adapt to changing needs and interests of the public and were left behind. American automotive companies were absolutely arrogant and stubborn over changing needs and costs. They were constantly losing ground, but smugly ignoring it, until they found themselves in a difficult situation. Most have disappeared, the largest bankrupt.

The leaders of the United States should consider it, too. If the U.S. does not continue to keep competitive, then the national prosperity is threatened. America has thrived for decades, but in recent years it has not adjusted to the changes in the world, and right now it is losing ground. The federal government has committed to vested rights for its citizens that have been paid for from the grand years of prosperity. Now, the country is struggling to adjust to the changes, and it is important for leaders to realistically identify national abilities and adjust if the United States is to return to gaining ground.

LAW OF ENTROPY

There are several definitions or interpretations of the idea of entropy. Engineering students are first introduced to it in the study of thermodynamics. On an elementary level, entropy is defined as a measure of energy not available for work in thermodynamic systems. In other fields of study it is loosely associated with ideas of order and disorder, or chaos.

With a little imagination the idea of entropy can be applied to the observation of human behavior and the control of business systems. It can be recognized that energy and effort must be applied continually to maintain order and efficiency in any business activity. As soon as an activity is left on its own, it will degrade to a state of disorder, or chaos. A good example is military management systems. The superb military system requires continual review and update of unit policies and procedures. Everything in the military begins with directives and regulations from the Department of Defense to the Service Departments, such as the Department of the Army, for example. These regulations are further reduced in application to each successively smaller unit until it reaches the Company level. Unit commanders must keep the Standard Operating Procedures up to date, usually on an annual basis. Although military procedures are dutifully updated, there may be failures by personnel to comply, which are usually accompanied by problems. Unit commanders and supervisors must constantly add correctional effort, or energy, into the system to maintain order.

Private industry operates the same way. Business managers often direct subordinates to provide policies and procedures when there is a problem with a process or activity. They study processes and write volumes of procedures to correct and control processes. Often, though, the effort has little impact in the long run. A new written procedure usually is accompanied with explanation and training; so, things improve for a while. But after a period of time, people change jobs or departments, and there is no training plan for their replacements. Frequently the new people are completely unaware of the standard procedures, so they follow their own methods. As a result, the process reverts to its former unsatisfactory condition. The amount of energy put into the system was inadequate to maintain the higher order level of the new procedure and so the process reverts to its problematic state.

Any good military leader or business manager knows that in order to maintain maximum effectiveness it is necessary to have a vigorous program of periodic training and to constantly verify that all activity is accomplished as designed. Policies and procedures must be reviewed and practiced until all individuals understand their part and can effectively accomplish it. Managers must check and double check on a periodic basis that everything is correct. The best military units do this without failure. So do the best companies, but many companies simply won't allocate the time for training; it's looked at as too costly, and so all of the effort to develop procedures is wasted as well.

The law of entropy can be loosely adopted as a term to explain that effort, or energy, must be put into any activity to maintain order, or efficiency. If management is unwilling to enforce procedures, or provide reinforcement, then the activity will revert to a state of least resistance for all, it could be called a state of chaos.

The same can be said, then, of government controls. City, state, or federal governments can pass regulation upon regulation on its citizens, but if there are not adequate controls to maintain them, then it's just so much wasted effort. There must be adequate checks and cross checks to assure a program operates effectively. The more programs are added, the more checks are required to assure they are honestly administered. Unfortunately, the symptoms of inadequate control measures, such as welfare and Medicare fraud, are discussed daily in the news. It's the law of entropy in action. If there isn't enough energy to keep a program in order, then it will revert to chaos.

ECONOMIC REAL WEALTH

Sophomore engineering students are introduced to elementary economic ideas at about the same time as they study entropy. Early economic theory includes an introduction to concepts of wealth. Although there are not universally agreed upon definitions of wealth, elementary studies begin by dividing wealth into two categories; real and financial paper wealth. The difference is that real wealth may only be considered as actual physical assets, and paper wealth is essentially the selling price of an asset. Further, real wealth in the economic system occurs in only three forms: agriculture, mining, and manufacturing. Prosperity is maximized when the three forms of real wealth are balanced, but this should be a free and natural balance that is unfettered by artificial government manipulation. Admittedly a beginning economics class is limited in scope, but the idea of real wealth is an important concept that still can be applied to prudent management.

The manufacturing, agricultural, and mining might of the country during the past seventy years is undeniable. Its growth and prosperity has been built upon its great industrial capacity and natural resources. Nearly all Americans have felt the privilege of contributing to building the real wealth of the nation in terms of increased production efficiency in agricultural, mining, and manufacturing. Through their ingenuity and labor Americans have built the real wealth of their country and increased the standard of living for every individual.

Now, a part of its real wealth, at least according to the basic definition, is being diminished. Of course, this is the result of the great migration of manufacturing activities and oil production to other countries that has been in progress for the last forty years or so. The total effect of this departure is difficult to completely understand, but it has affected millions of U.S. countrymen, and it is probably the primary cause of the steady decline of the U.S. economy. No longer a nation of real wealth builders, Americans today consume more than they produce, and many have become government dependents instead of producing workers.

Infinity of Actions

Many of life's situations are so complex and interrelated that they become difficult, if not impossible to understand or control. This becomes evident when working in a modestly sized manufacturing operation. The business objective is to maximize efficiency and to maintain a competent, well-trained, and contented work force. This must all be balanced against continual changes in order bookings, raw material prices and delivery schedules, work force size and attendance, and dozens more variations on an hour-by-hour basis. Manufacturing managers are faced with a bewildering number of variables in their businesses, and infinite possible actions they may take. Daily life in a manufacturing operation produces similar patterns found in the national population.

In order to attempt to balance all of the considerations, analysts are taught to try to reduce the overall problem to simpler elements. Here is where the idea of the Pareto distribution may be employed. A manager tries to identify the few items that contribute most to the problem at hand, and then control them. In this way, the majority of the problem is held in check, while the remaining contributors to the problem may be considered impractical to try to control at all.

This is the idea of infinity of actions. It means that life itself is so complex that it is impossible to efficiently control all elements of its variability. It is contrary to the idea that governments can fairly and efficiently control the economy and people's lives. Although economists and legislators make many predictions and implement actions, it is likely that it is done using information based upon constantly changing conditions that cannot be collected quickly enough to fully know and understand. The huge number, or infinity, of considerations bearing on the public life potentially contributes to Congressional gridlock as the government tries to balance so many aspects of American life.

Available Time

There are an infinite number of good things a person may strive to do, but available time limits one's hope to accomplish only a few. This idea complements the idea of infinity of actions. Available time is the limitation on infinity of actions. Self-help commentary suggests there are generally three facets of life: family, work, and personal pleasure or hobby. At any given time there is only enough time to excel at two of the three. For example, if an individual is devoted to family and work, then there simply won't be enough time for fishing or golf. If a person takes enough time to do well at a hobby, and remains dedicated to family, then there likely will be a limited, or minimum, contribution of time to work.

It's an interesting concept. If not totally accurate, it seems plausible. When the idea is applied in conjunction with the concept of infinity of actions to the activities of government representatives, it is easy to see the difficulty these individuals face when they try to balance all the considerations for so many individuals and try to direct private people in their lives. Their biggest obstacle is their tendency to overreact to the latest headlines and make shortsighted decisions. After they finish congratulating themselves for their hard work to achieve equality for all, it is likely that the true best solution is simplicity of rules to avoid gridlock, and to leave the people to take care of their own problems.

PONZI AND PYRAMID CONFIDENCE TRICKS

There's a sucker born every minute. It's an old saying, and unfortunately almost all people have their own examples of falling victim to a schemer who preys on natural trust to skin the innocent. Two of the most common and persistent tricks are the Ponzi and Pyramid schemes. New variations of these gimmicks are born daily.

The Ponzi scheme is named for Charles Ponzi, an Italian immigrant to the U.S. over a hundred years ago. He didn't really invent the plan, but he was hugely successful with his version, and so later versions are generally described using his name. The reference to Ponzi schemes will be to investment plans where investors are paid from their own money or from funds received from new investors to the plan. The fund manager, or con man, collects the investors' money and uses the majority of it for personal purposes, then sends part of the money back to investors, telling them it is profit. In fact, more investors are needed to keep from running out of money. Inevitably, it all collapses when too many investors want all of their money back, or the fund manager can't bring in enough new investors.

Pyramid schemes are similar but are usually sold as business opportunities. The con man in this case appeals to folks who want to get rich quick, work at home, help mankind with a new health or beauty product, or some such group of vulnerable individuals. The con man doesn't pay the group from their own funds, but from the money their recruits collect themselves from people they, in turn, enroll in the program. Some folks truly have made a lot of money when they were first to sign up in the program, but when the program grows sufficiently large in popularity there simply aren't enough people to sustain the plan.

Most folks know about these schemes and how they work, but scams continue to flourish, and all Americans may be involved in one of the biggest Ponzi con schemes of all time. The U.S. government sold its citizens the

Social Security benefits plan. Many folks think they pay their entire lives into a retirement insurance plan. But a close look at this plan reveals that the benefits are paid from the investors' own funds and the investments of young, new members. The government denies that Social Security and Medicare are Ponzi schemes. Technically, they claim the programs are backed by government securities and good faith, so they aren't Ponzis. Nevertheless, these programs use contributions from the young to pay older beneficiaries, and the programs are running out of new investors and enough money to pay those claiming their benefits. The debts of one generation are put upon another. Of course, the program has teetered on the edge of failure for many years, and it is one of the prime examples of mismanagement and neglect by elected officials.

PURSUIT OF DISTINCTION

John Adams observed that all people seek distinction. He believed that all people, from every walk of life, carry a need to be approved of and respected. This idea, perhaps better than any other, helps explain the motivations that push men and women into politics and various other fields of endeavor. President Adams went on to explain that it is intolerable for people to know they have been overlooked.

The average citizen is driven by the desire for the distinction that wealth brings. Everyone has heard the description of America as the place of opportunity where anyone who works hard enough can rise to the top (become wealthy). This is the American Dream for many. It's part of the capitalist ideal. Entertainers want to be recognized for their great skill or ability, and wealth doesn't hurt, either. Educators want to be respected for their great understanding and genius.

Professional politicians may be the most dangerous, as a group, of all individuals seeking distinction. In general, more professional politicians seek office for the love of power and money than any other reason. Surely, these are the worst two reasons for pursuing public service, and the founding fathers warned Americans to be careful of this combination. Good representatives have been elected who want only the pleasure of doing good and serving, and their countrymen want to believe that most government people started with this aim. But when they become dependent upon public employment for their subsistence, and they feel the thrill of power when adoring crowds thank them for the latest benefit, then their passion for distinction has reached the dangerous point of no return, and they are lost to government instead of representation.

PEACEFUL DISPUTE

James Madison was the great genius behind the form of government the country has inherited. It was his hope that those following his generation and sustaining the Constitution would improve it and perpetuate it using amendments. In the beginning of the process for ratification of the Constitution, Madison thought a Bill of Rights was not necessary to protect against powers not granted in the Constitution. He feared that a list of enumerated rights might imply that other rights that are absent in the list are not granted. Nevertheless, after much discussion and writing, he authored the Bill of Rights.

Americans have carried his torch, and the provisions of the Bill of Rights, to protest and demonstrate. Perhaps the sixties generation has seen more public demonstrations than any before it. It's a wonderful thing for a people to be free to gather to review its government's activity and to complain. But folks get out of hand at times, too, and resort to violence and destruction.

This gift of free speech from the founders was meant to be peaceful discussion. They knew there would always be disagreement, just as there was vigorous disagreement among those of their generation. A discussion of malfeasance in office by elected and appointed officials must surely offer sharp criticism and ask for change, but always peacefully and within the wonderful provisions of the Constitution.

Mohandas Gandhi, the leader of the Indian Independence Movement, believed that the way to truth is through nonviolence. He thought there were many causes to die for, but none to kill for. It was his belief that only nonviolence leads to pure democracy. His ideas on civil disobedience inspired the activities of Martin Luther King, Jr. in his leadership of the civil rights movement.

Gandhi also thought it was wrong to cause discomfort, fear, or undue pressure on another living thing. For instance, it causes uneasiness when a line of demonstrators shouts at others, or even stands aggressively to block or restrict their pathway. Naturally, the demonstrators feel their cause is right, or they wouldn't take the trouble to come together to support their argument. But Gandhi implied that aggressive demonstration is a form of violence, and he believed it was the wrong thing to do, because it harmed others. Gandhi favored patience and tolerance, and he taught that there cannot be intolerance in the true spirit of democracy.

The Constitution offers Americans the opportunity for peaceful discussion of their differences, and the means to change the very laws by which they live. The Constitution leaves its citizens in charge, and when the American public believes adjustments are necessary, it can change things through peaceful demonstration and voting.

CHAPTER FOUR

VIEWPOINTS

FOR THE LAST FIFTY YEARS average Americans have neglected the politics and government of the country. Most were preoccupied with work and family, and had only slight passing interest in the affairs of government. Many still continue to vote and try to determine who would best represent their thoughts on efficient operations. Good luck with that. Their cursory assessment methods consist of a few editorials, interview shows, and debates when possible. Forget the distorted political advertisements. All of the degrading ads leave citizens wondering how any of the candidates could be worthwhile; they all appear worthless according to slick TV ads and defamatory stories.

The majority of Americans learn about new legislation the same way, from the news broadcasts, newspaper, and Internet. During the last half of the twentieth century the news was primarily from the three dominating broadcast networks, because this was before the deluge of information available today via cable and Internet systems. But these reports on new legislation usually provide part of the truth according to the slant of the source. Eventually the true effect of government intrusion into their lives becomes apparent through their paycheck, or new rules and regulations that restrict their private activity.

Older Americans have lived long enough to see government programs that are obvious failures, and it's difficult to understand why it isn't obvious to government regulators and other citizens as well. Prime examples are the welfare programs and housing projects that were begun in the 1960s that have cost so much, but have resulted in more poverty, substandard living conditions, and generations of people ensnared by government benefits.

These failed programs have given away a huge part of the national wealth that could have been used to improve the standard of living for more people by building the economy and jobs, and adding to the stability of the country.

Still the parade of abuses continues. The new health care legislation and continued debt spending above what the government receives from its citizens carry the country into more debt and even bigger government domination. Add to this the continued growth of the executive branch to include special advisors and individuals with no direct or indirect accountability to the people of the country. It's too much, and it's time for average Americans to speak up and become more involved.

When citizens decide to participate in guiding the direction of their government, it's important for them to study the state of America today, and to examine their fears and needs from their government. It's likely that the majority of Americans accept the idea that there are three classes in the country based upon economic status. But it's possible that in the last one hundred years the country has changed into a hybrid society with four classes.

The hybrid society consists of a subculture of government dependents living beside a free society. Those with the mental and physical ability, and the desire for independence, live somewhat free of the yokes of government, and they support the dependent group. The dependent group turns to government to provide food, housing, and medical care, while surrendering a portion of their personal freedom in exchange for perceived security. The dependent group is growing rapidly, and it has been estimated that forty-seven percent of American citizens pay no taxes into the treasury, but instead are supported by the free society. The combination of independent Americans who are forced to support the dependent group under the guise of a benevolent government has become a hybrid society, neither totally free nor totally controlled by government.

The long transition to a hybrid society with a large dependent group has resulted in the development of a governing class, or ruling class. These are the career politicians and federal employees that control the dependent class by spending the productive wealth of the working free class. The governing class has become a large and powerful part of American society, and unless the free, self-governing people of the country take steps to contain the government, then it is likely that a huge centralized government will be the eventual result, with no free society left in existence.

The change today is the result of drifting from the provisions of the Constitution for a hundred years or more, and decades of national fiscal irresponsibility. Before taking a stand, each American should review the strengths of the country and their personal fears and needs. The greatest strength of the country is the freedom of its citizens to choose where and how to live their lives. This great strength has resulted with a strong national defense, superior infrastructure, and exceptionally low cost and high standard of living.

America's fears and needs have changed little. The earliest Americans wanted strong defense and small government to leave them alone in their private lives. Today, a strong defense includes confronting the fear of being overrun by illegal immigration. In addition, most, not all, Americans are worried about the runaway debt that the governing class has permitted to grow to overpowering size.

The basic needs of the country are summarized in the Constitution by the twenty powers given to Congress. In addition to these, the needs for efficient and well-maintained infrastructure have grown with modern developments. In today's world, America's strength in its low cost of living is threatened by its need for low cost energy. As a result, the country needs a coherent energy policy that is free of subsidies and corporate favors, which only result in false starts and blind alleys in the search for alternatives.

FOUR CLASSES

It appears today that the United States has evolved from three into four economic and social classes. There are the three classic descriptions: poor, middle, and wealthy. Today a fourth can be added: the governing class.

Naturally, the greater one's wealth the greater the social networks and opportunities that are available to an individual. Wealthy children have more prospects for training on how to manage and direct their privileges in their different forms, and subsequently they are able to accumulate even more wealth.

The poor have the least amount of wealth and in the United States today generally receive some type of welfare distribution from the government. When the poor receive welfare assistance in its many forms, their wealth is usually limited by government regulations. In order to remain qualified for their assistance, they are not allowed to have more than a trivial amount of assets. When faced with the loss of benefits, many of them will not attempt to improve their economic situation, and so they are slaves entangled in the welfare system.

The middle class is the backbone of America. These individuals are focused on income to meet their daily requirements. Today, many in this classification are able to earn more than is needed for shelter, food, and clothing, and so they accumulate extras such as electronics, a larger home, cars, boats, and other unnecessary objects. Generally, the accumulation of wealth for these folks is in their savings for a rainy day, or retirement. It amounts to a home and a small amount for retirement income.

Now consider the governing class. They principally fit economically into the middle and wealthy classes, but how they obtain their wealth, and how they are affected by the rules of U.S. society are different. These persons have developed pay and benefits systems attached to the standard federal employees program, but enhanced further for their particular self interests. They have used the advantages of representation to develop their private interests while pretending to continue the liberty established by the Constitution. The people of the governing class, which includes all elected representatives, appointed bureaucrats, and the entrenched staff people that work and live in the center city of government, are removed from the daily struggles of American citizens. It appears they have little understanding of the total impact of their tax laws and welfare gifts on the lives of those they are pledged to fairly represent. The writing left behind by the nation's founders indicates they were completely aware of the danger of the evolution of representatives into a governing class. Human behavior was little different from today, and the early leaders cautioned of this problem more than two hundred years ago.

HYBRID SOCIETY

The founders of the Constitution originally intended for citizens to live in a free society. Their history included the flight of their ancestors from government tyranny. As a result, it was important to all of the states that the federal government should be limited in its role affecting daily life. They thought the union of the states should be to raise revenue for protection from foreign countries, to establish and maintain efficient communication, and for administration of the seat of government to establish equal rules of trade and commerce. Both their individual correspondence and the Constitution confirm that they wanted, and expected, little more from the federal government.

Today, though, the government has been transformed into a giant system with tentacles reaching into virtually every facet of daily life. It now provides housing, food, and income for a large part of the citizenry, and many of these folks pay no income tax into the system, but they do pay sales tax and other fees during the course of their daily lives. Robin Hood representatives frequently speak of taking from the rich and giving to the poor. They want to level the economic situation so that all are about the same, or virtually the same. Obviously, the counter argument is that this abuses personal freedoms, and these conflicting arguments have continued for ages.

After years of new government programs and class arguments the United States has developed into two societies. There is the welfare society, or something akin to a socialist existence, and there is the free society that contributes to the welfare society; that would be the counter culture that resembles a capitalist system. Those working in the capitalist industrial system for most of their lives tried constantly to be self-sufficient, provide for their families, and grow in the future. In return for honest work they received a paycheck that was reduced by a certain percentage to help sustain the welfare society.

So society today has evolved into two groups, or two systems, and it seems the governing class keeps these systems at odds with one another. The more that is poured into caring for the welfare and entitlement classes, the more these classes demand, and the more the governing class uses the conflict to maintain its own position in society. The net result is a hybrid society. It's a combination of many people living as free as they possibly can under the burden of a demanding tax system while trying to work to their potential (taxpayers), and a second society of citizens that is incapable or unmotivated to care for itself (non-taxpayers). The folks that are not able to provide for themselves, and the subculture of individuals that are able but don't choose to provide their own care, are more willing to give up liberty for security, even if it means stripping freedoms from the working group that provides the security.

The unfortunate consequence of a hybrid society is that both groups are slaves, trapped in servitude to the government. The pseudo-free element is buried in regulations, taxes, and government control of a large part of their private lives. Conversely, the socialized element has given up, surrendering their freedom for the pacifier handed to them by the governing class.

The crucial question concerning progression into a hybrid free-welfare society is where it should stop, or if it should stop at all. In the last one hundred years there has been an obvious transition to more welfare for the disadvantaged segment of American countrymen. How far should it go? Is there a stopping point, or has it already gone too far? By reading and digging deeper, the more a person may feel compelled to speak up.

FISCAL IRRESPONSIBILITY

In view of growing national debt accompanied by the expanding breach of American liberties it is apparent that the federal government has failed in its obligation of fiscal responsibility and adherence to the Constitution. They go hand in hand, but the apparent mismanagement of government funds that has left unimaginable debt is probably most responsible for an American awakening to determine what in the world they are doing. Responsible citizens know that debt ruins people, companies, and countries. It threatens the country's ability to defend itself and to prosper.

There is plenty of rhetoric defending debt spending. Some believe it's the way to grow and build the economy. Without a doubt, it's common for businesses to borrow to expand and grow, but if the growth plans are not fulfilled as expected, then companies find themselves in difficult situations. Often, a company must reduce its workforce and spending budget in order to survive to repay debt. But when liabilities exceed assets, the company usually is finished, and there is nothing more that can save it. Clearly, there is a limit to the debt that any individual or company can sustain, and it's all related to the proportion of income that the debt service requires.

Others believe in good planning and fiscal restraint to remain prosperous, and the early fathers of the country believed the same thing. Benjamin Franklin was an extremely successful businessman, and he thought the same ideas of restraint, self-reliance, and prudent budget management should be the course of American life and government. Franklin recognized that debt could threaten national security when he warned that when debt is incurred, then the debtor's liberty is lost to another. Thomas Jefferson believed the country could be improved without debt and he warned readers not to let the government load itself with perpetual debt. He knew that debt leads to oppressive taxes to carry the debt, and it would begin to threaten the very comforts and necessities of life.

Jefferson and others thought the people's finances should be clearly managed. He said the country's finances should be as clear as a bookkeeper's, so every person should be able to understand them and control abuses. Nevertheless, today's government has grown so large and unmanageable that many of the representatives and their staffs cannot adequately comprehend the interactions of programs and the resultant malfeasance that accompanies them. It has become an example of the Infinity of Actions previously discussed. There are so many programs, so many demands upon the system, and so many interactions, that it is likely too large to satisfactorily control. The result is extraordinary debt, fraud, and abuse. This result alone is a good argument against very large government.

OUR STRENGTHS

An endless variety of failed government programs and fiscal irresponsibility compels average Americans to turn a critical eye toward what they have observed. The United States is such a strong and free country. Conversely, fears remain, and common folks ask again, what do we want from government? Regarding life's fundamentals, Americans today have a lot in common with the families of the eighteenth century.

All Americans know the country is strong. Few are experts in government. Most understand the basics of the federal government and have read the freedom documents; namely, the Declaration of Independence and the Constitution. The vast majority has no doubt that the inherited love of freedom and self-government is the keystone of American national strength.

The great founding leaders referred to it as Constitutional supremacy. The ideas of liberty were developed as they studied and exchanged ideas about different forms of government. As a result, they established a contract with one another and set it to paper in a Constitution. The idea was that the Constitution would be a binding contract for self-government until changed by a majority, and this has become the foundation of the political system, which is the right of the citizens to make or alter their constitution of government. Americans cherish the idea that they are guaranteed authority to govern themselves through a system of representatives elected to uphold the system of laws established by the Constitution, but there is a sense of fearfulness that generations of careless elected officials have not safeguarded the provisions of this mutual contract.

Constitutional freedom delivers the overpowering strength of the country through the freedom to choose. Americans can choose to live where they please, pursue their personal wishes, and can elect to be a hard driving achiever or choose a life of simplicity. It's their choice. They cannot imagine being forced to live where they don't want to be, or required to work at an occupation that is not their choice. It's extraordinary that the majority of the world really doesn't have this privilege.

The U.S. defense system is second to none, and it has to rank as one of the country's titanic strengths. It includes technology, achievements in space exploration, and its manufacturing juggernaut. A strong defense has helped with international affairs, and to help others in their pursuit of freedom. Without a strong defense to protect the homeland and its Constitution, then the U.S. might simply have become part of a larger empire or world order.

The fabulous infrastructure that has been built in the United States has contributed to economic prosperity and bolstered defenses. This includes transportation, communication, energy, manufacturing, and public service systems. The country enjoys an economical system of roads, airfields, railways, and ports that rival any in the world. This allows movement of people, equipment, and products quickly and at a very low cost. Obviously, a strong and efficient transportation system must be maintained so the country can continue to grow and remain strong.

Communication includes the U.S. mail, telecommunications, and the Internet. Without strong communication ability, national defense could be jeopardized, but a strong communication system also is vital to all commerce, markets, and transportation. Americans can communicate with one another better than ever before, and this is critical to sustaining the Constitution. The developers of the U.S. Constitution considered communication to be a leading requirement for maintaining orderly self-government and civility. Modern communication methods with their speed and reliability offer new and greater support for the idea that strong communication is at the center of an unbiased system of self-government.

Low energy cost has been a major contributor to the economic success America has enjoyed. Its great reserves of petroleum, natural gas, coal, and other natural resources have given the country the luxury of comparatively inexpensive energy that is not shared by much of the world. Low energy costs keep product costs low, because manufacturing, agricultural, and transportation energy costs are a big part of the American cost of living. Although it doesn't seem like it at times, electricity and home energy costs remain a reasonable percentage of total household income for most Americans.

Services such as police and fire departments, insured banks, and courts of law are part of the public service infrastructure. A public service sector that can operate free of corruption is essential in maintaining a free government. Certainly there is corruption in public services today, but in comparison to most other governments, Americans enjoy reasonably honest public servants. The banks comply with regulations to insure the safety of money, and the courts protect citizens' property and liberty. It's somewhat difficult to bribe your way out of jail in America, and in general all must comply with the law or suffer the edicts of the court system. A corrupt government may be the single largest obstacle to prosperity in a country such as Mexico. It has bountiful natural resources, and it is presumably a free society, but it has not prospered like the United States or Canada. The degree of corruption in their country has been debilitating to commerce and general equality. Conversely, the Chinese system is filled with corruption and payoffs, but their economy is booming as a result of the U.S. rush to Chinese sources and markets. It is difficult to do business, obtain permits, and so forth in China without connections. Their economy, although called free, still is based upon bribes and payoffs in order to do business there. Obviously, the U.S. has its own system of union bosses and corrupt officials, but it is not generally an accepted part of American culture as it is in China. Right now, the huge and inexpensive Chinese labor force marginalizes the costs of corruption. Nothing stays the same, though. A business or country is continually in a state of gaining ground or losing ground per the lesson of constant change. Eventually, Chinese costs will rise, and their culture of extreme corruption could cause big problems in the far future.

Perhaps the most remarkable American strength is its low cost of living. An efficient infrastructure contributes to low cost of essentials such as food, clothing, housing, energy, and transportation. The working American spends a smaller proportion of income on these essentials than at about any time in history. Eighty years ago the average family couldn't afford to eat out or buy extras such as the latest gadgets. It took a large part of household income to pay for the essentials, such as housing, food, clothing, and energy. As the nation developed, people were blessed with more free time and opportunity to pursue education or enterprise. Today, Americans spend a modest portion of their income on the essentials, and the remainder is available for hobbies, luxuries, entertainment, and savings. The explosion of the fast food and entertainment businesses is beyond the imagination of early generations. Eating out may be America's main entertainment. In comparison to the rest of the world the low cost of living essentials in America may be at the top of its list of strengths. It has fired economic growth and inspired the genius and industry of its citizens. In summary, American strength starts with the rock of a Constitution supported by a moral people determined to minimize corruption. On this foundation a free and industrious society has built phenomenal systems of defense and infrastructure that has fueled an economy to support a low cost of living.

OUR FEARS

Probably the primary fear as a people is defense. The primary reason people band together as a country is for their common defense against invaders. This seemed to be the common theme for the first thirteen states. There were foreign interests adjacent to exposed borders, and the states bordering foreign territories were especially concerned about invaders. To be sure, the less exposed states knew that if a buffer state fell, they could likely be next.

A review of early commentaries by the founders shows how much they had in common with America today. The creation of a Constitutional Union for their common defense included two other fears of the people; debt and size of government. They knew they needed funding for defense, and for administration of the government, but they feared debt and its threat to prosperity. Many of the early leaders thought debt should be limited to supporting emergencies, such as defensive war. Government spending should be limited to income revenue during periods of tranquility, and when necessary to borrow money to support the defense of the country, then the debt should be paid within the lifetime of the borrowing generation.

The early colonial descendents especially feared the tyranny that could accompany a new government. They understood the search for distinction that drove many individuals to seek power and control. Ben Franklin and others left numerous commentaries about the ambitions of men and the love of power and money. He cautioned that honorable representative offices could become offices of profit.

Fears today have hardly changed, but there are perhaps a few additions. The threat of war against the United States is as great as ever, and with the added element of terrorism the country is as concerned about defense as ever. There are people in the world that want everything that others have, up to and including their lives. Most Americans understand that a strong defense and a desire for peace don't exclude one another, and their desire for peace must be supported by a strong defense.

Unfortunately the American forefathers' fear of runaway debt has become a great threat to the safety and prosperity of the country. As a result of a long list of government interventions and failures, America has evolved through several generations of government mismanagement until its national debt is so extreme that the country's safety and prosperity are in jeopardy. As a result, the debt has become one of the leading topics of public discussion and an enormous national fear.

Spurred by the massive debt the country faces, and fears, the loss of economic leadership it has enjoyed for many generations may be at hand. Economic leadership is an important part of national defense, too. If the U.S. is unable to grow and produce, then it won't be able to keep pace with growing technology and threats to peace. Many Americans may agree that the Soviet Union collapse was largely the result of its failure to keep up with the strong American economy. The United States produced so much real wealth to take care of its people, and to provide for a spectacular defense that no one could match it. Today, though, the U.S. is struggling, and must never forget it is constantly gaining or losing ground. Perhaps too much of its capacity to produce real wealth has been shipped to foreign shores.

Part of the great debt is the entitlement programs. They have become such a large part of the budget that they threaten extraordinary debt, reduced economic leadership, and ultimately national safety. The United States provides more income for nonworking individuals than ever before. The welfare, Social Security, and Medicare systems have become scams used by professional representatives seeking votes to advance their personal quests for power and income. The great dialog continues; how much of the productivity and wealth of the American people should be spent on entitlement programs? It has become a pressing national fear for both givers and receivers. Combined with the poor management by government representatives, it will likely continue to grow in concern.

A new fear for the country today is illegal immigration. For many years the constant stream of people illegally entering the country in order to work and receive benefits from the entitlement programs has been ignored. Everyone paid little attention. In fact, many large corporations pressured the government to turn a blind eye to employment of these people. In good times, average Americans also turned a blind eye to the influx. Many found amusement in it, but now, times are difficult, jobs are in short supply, and the debt continues to increase, until it has become a modern national fear. The current situation is not fair to the immigrants and it's unfair to working Americans.

In retrospect, today's fears and the fears of the founders are common. They feared invasion, debt, and big government. For the most part,

Americans today do, too. Modern additions to the list of fears are really forms of threat to national security. The debt, shrinking economic leadership, entitlement programs, and illegal immigration all threaten America's security and safety.

OUR NEEDS

If the idea is accepted that the government has produced failed programs that give away the country's wealth, and it has irresponsibly managed the public's funds, then it seems prudent to evaluate the true needs of citizens. Certainly people's needs include a system to alleviate our common fears, but there is likely more that is wanted from a federal government. Everyone has their own ideas, and it's easy to be swept up by the fads and promises of career politicians hoping to feather their caps. The nation's founders believed in changing needs and they left a framework for changing the government to meet the needs of its people.

The starting point is the Constitution and the twenty powers of government detailed in it. This list identifies the needs of the people from their government. It starts with the power to raise money, spend it, and borrow, because without revenue there can be no government operations. There is a clause establishing provisions for defense, communications, fair commerce standards, administration of the seat of government, rules for citizenship, and a system of federal courts and laws to implement the powers. It's a brilliant list of the needs from government that a self-governing people are willing to authorize in a federal system. Although many people believe it has changed somewhat over the last two hundred years, in truth it is unlikely that the roots of American needs have changed much.

The primary fear, lack of defense, is high on the list of needs. The Constitution guarantees federal protection for every state from invasion of its sovereign territory, and includes the power of the Congress to establish an armed force and declare war. Early Americans feared foreign invasion, and the Constitution guaranteed protection from this threat. Today, the government struggles to meet this commitment in its failure to control foreign immigration. The states with foreign borders feel a tremendous threat from this situation, but all of the states experience threats to their economy and personal safety from illegal immigrants. Not only the Mexican worker, but also foreign invaders who wish to harm America, have found it easy to walk into the country and cause it injury.

The founders recognized well-organized communication as essential to efficient government and commerce. Most of them understood that communication is an essential component of a democracy. They knew the ability to communicate across the large territories of the day was necessary for citizens to understand their government's actions and its impact on them. This was one of the primary arguments for a republic in lieu of a true democracy. The time lapse for communication across the large national expanse was impractical, and it prohibited direct contact by the citizenry with one another that is required on every decision in a democracy. They learned from the Revolutionary War how important speedy communication was to both government activity and war communications. Naturally, this was all done by mail and dispatch, and in order for it to proceed efficiently good roads along the routes were needed. So, the power to establish postal roads was granted in the Constitution to foster communication.

The remaining powers of the Congress that are named by the Constitution are little changed. The list of powers granted to Congress by the Constitution is shown in Figure 4-1 for reference.

But today, the needs of the country and society appear to have changed somewhat. There are remarkable new requirements for defense, infrastructure, and general science needs. One of the great national arguments is the amount that should be expended on defense. All of the founding fathers warned that the country must remain prepared, and if it does not, it will pay in blood. The world today is smaller and even more dangerous than the developing period of the country. A strong defense should include a strong space program and immigration controls. Without the ability to protect its sovereignty the country risks the loss of its freedom to choose and its homeland.

Obviously, the infrastructure requirement has been a fantastic expansion due to the growth in technology and prosperity. When the Constitution was launched there was no need to develop and maintain railroads, airfields, or power and communication distribution systems. It was somewhat limited to the early postal roads. Clearly the infrastructure is critical to defense and a competitive economy, and it is likely high on the list of priorities for the American people who send their tax payments to the government.

Today, numerous Americans probably believe an energy policy should be part of the national spending plan. Energy requirements have been in transition for about forty years. The American community has faced gasoline shortages and threats that its citizens are ruining the environment. Nearly everyone believes that oil reserves are limited and are tired of depending upon foreign sources. The majority of Americans understand that low-cost energy is a prime contributor to national strength, and agree with a priority in searching for alternatives. Some U.S. leaders want to increase the present cost through taxes and other mechanisms to manipulate people's behavior to cause them to switch to other forms of energy, but they admit that this will impose much higher cost; and, to be sure, higher energy costs mean a lower standard of living, at least during a long period of transition. Most citizens would prefer an energy transition policy without the artificial inducements

Constitutional Powers of United States Congress

Constitutional Article	Authorization
I.8.1	Lay and collect taxes, duties, imposts, and excises
I.8.1	Pay debts, provide common defense and general welfare
I.8.2	Borrow money on credit of United States
I.8.3	Regulate commerce (foreign nations, states, Indians)
I.8.4	Establish uniform rules of naturalization
I.8.4	Establish uniform laws on the subject of bankruptcies
I.8.5	Coin money, regulate the value thereof
I.8.5	Fix standards of weights and measures
I.8.6	Provide for the punishment of counterfeiting
I.8.7	Establish post offices and post roads
I.8.8	Secure copyrights and patents of authors and inventors
I.8.9	Constitute tribunals inferior to the Supreme Court
I.8.10	Define and punish piracies and felonies on high seas
I.8.11	Declare war and reprisals
I.8.12/13	Raise and support armies (I.8.12) and navy (I.8.13)
I.8.14	Make rules to regulate land and naval forces
I.8.15/16	Call (I.8.15) and organize (I.8.16) state militia to execute the laws of the Union
I.8.17	Exercise legislation over the seat of US Government
I.8.17	Exercise authority over federal lands purchased with consent of State Legislature for federal needs
I.8.18	Make all laws necessary for carrying into execution the foregoing powers, and all other powers vested by the Constitution in the Government of the United States, or in any department or officer thereof.

Powers of Congress
Figure 4-1

and interference by the government.

The needs of the self-sufficient American people make a short list. They expect to fund the government to raise revenue, provide for defense, communication, fair commerce and money standards, rules for citizenship, and a system of federal courts; and, if the costs for developing new energy sources are extraordinary, then some funding might be appropriated, as part of the list, to aid in research and development – not in forcing the public into an expensive and inefficient system. Government help on energy research that is available to all businesses would be equitable, but not subsidies and gifts to individual preferred business ventures.

The role of government has grown in another area over the last one hundred years or so, and that is in the area of public assistance. In the list of twenty powers established by the Constitution and referenced in Figure 4-1, there is really no provision for public assistance. Public assistance has grown through the broad interpretations of Constitutional references to commerce and general welfare. Today, the majority of Americans has grown up supporting or receiving some form of public assistance and most of the population has come to accept it as a government responsibility. Curiously, many of these public support programs are part of a long list of government failures. Some debate whether government should provide public help at all. The founders deeply believed citizens should be responsible for their own lives and for the freedom of life itself. It amounts to the regulation of individual consciences. Thomas Jefferson identified the individual conscience as a sacred unalienable right to be protected from government control. Slowly, America has evolved into the hybrid society that has decided it is the right of the majority to regulate the conscience of all individuals via a public assistance system.

It is difficult for many Americans to accept the public assistance programs as a role of government, but today a good number of fellow citizens rely on these programs in their daily lives. If a government role is accepted to mitigate disasters that individuals cannot guard against, then it should be identified and controlled. The problem with growing entitlement programs is mismanagement by a federal government that has given away more of the country's national production until it no longer can support it. A good analogy would be an individual that wants to help others but borrows money, that cannot be paid back, to give to others. Say a person earns $50,000 but wants to give away $75,000 each year, so $25,000 is borrowed. It continues every year until bankruptcy is required. The situation with government-aid programs has followed this same basic example until the debt created has grown to unmanageable proportions. Responsible governmental management requires that these programs be completely funded without borrowing. This fundamental error, continued for years, has put America in a terrible spot.

True national needs, then, are simple. Provide for the country as established by the twenty powers of government. Maintain and improve vital infrastructure. Establish an energy development policy for research and development of alternative energy sources, and provide the results equally to all Americans. Establish limits on the hybrid society that includes public assistance as one of its needs. Then operate within the limits of the nation's productivity and revenue.

CHAPTER FIVE

A LIST OF FAILURES

WHAT ONE INDIVIDUAL may consider a failed government program, another may believe to be successful. The programs in the following list are based upon two failures of duty by the U.S. Congress: failure to protect the Constitution, and failed stewardship of the national treasury. Through slick interpretations of the Constitution these programs were implemented by stretching the meaning of the commerce and common welfare clauses of the Constitution. Many argue they should be unconstitutional, others don't agree. In any event, these programs have been inadequately funded and managed, and have resulted in a massive assault on the U.S. Treasury. Give-away programs inflame the runaway national debt as the country continues to live beyond its means.

All failures have two things in common: they are inequitable, and they contribute to operating beyond budget spending limits. The idea of government social controls really picked up steam around 1900, and with it the idea of statutory vested rights. Gradually it was decided that all American citizens have the right to government-provided food, housing, supplemental income, and health care. This started the change in the government purpose of providing defense, fair commerce, and courts, to one of endless social programs.

The first major expansions were encroachments to regulate commerce and credit markets; these were the Government Sponsored Enterprises that began after the turn to the twentieth century. They have been used to regulate farming, banks, mortgages, and student loans, and they have drained the treasury until they teeter on the verge of bankruptcy. Building on Government Sponsored Enterprises, the federal government developed

Wholly Owned Government Corporations to add to its list of troubled assets. Familiar organizations such as the Tennessee Valley Authority, Ginnie Mae, Amtrak, and the Post Office are included in this classification of government programming. The Post Office was originally an independent government agency, but reorganization legislation in 1970-71 changed it. The Post Office has operated in debt and continues to borrow from the Treasury, but now has plans to cut its size and services.

In the thirties the government plunged into social programs as it continued its aim to legislate vested rights. Huge welfare programs such as Social Security, Medicare, Supplemental Security Income, Food Stamps, and Earned Income Credit were added to the list. Social Security and Medicare have been built on deception and hampered by poor stewardship. Welfare plans, with their supplements for the poor, have contributed to forty years of misery and despair for those caught in their trap.

Other failed programs include subsidies, education spending, and public broadcasting. Subsidies do little more than require the taxpayer to pay more for their products through hidden taxes, and they add to inequality. The Department of Education has squandered enormous amounts of money in a failed attempt to improve levels of educational attainment of America's children. The result has been a disaster. The federal government has no business in education, and if it were left to the states, then competition between them for jobs and prosperity likely would result in higher standards.

Unfortunately, the list of failures is a long one. It could be longer in the view of some individuals. Following is a brief description of some of the more notorious examples.

NATIONAL DEBT AND DEFICIT SPENDING

The U.S. national debt that has accumulated is a glaring example of malfeasance in office by the legislative and executive branches of government for more than a hundred years. There have been a few exceptions along the way, but by and large, this problem has grown with new programs as the American people have learned that it was possible to vote themselves benefits. So, a self-governing people must accept a large part of the responsibility, too.

Fiscal stewardship of the public treasury is established by Article I, Section 9, Clause 7 of the Constitution, which reads, "No money shall be drawn from the Treasury, but in consequence of appropriations made by law; and a regular statement and account of the receipts and expenditures of all public money shall be published from time to time." It was not the original intent of the founders to operate the government by borrowing money. Their letters and communications continually warned against building debt. Two successful businessmen of their time, Benjamin Franklin and Alexander Hamilton, wrote that debt was a threat to security and must be paid off by taxes. Benjamin Franklin believed debt must be paid off, and Hamilton agreed in the thirteenth volume of *The Federalist*, that it would mean less money would be needed from the people. Today, it would save a lot of tax money that is spent on interest payments.

In general, the nation's founders believed the government should only take on debt for emergencies, such as natural disasters, or for defense in times of war, and it should be repaid by the generation that borrowed the money. At various times in their lives Presidents Washington, Jefferson, and Madison cautioned against the dangerous practice of borrowing money. Washington wrote that nothing is more dangerous than borrowing money, because it soon becomes easy to do, so there is little thought to repayment, and soon the interest snowballs. Without a doubt, American society has completely ignored this warning for more than one hundred years. The government has implemented hundred of programs to spend money that can't be covered by tax revenues, and the number of new agencies and federal employees has begun to outgrow the private economy. It seems today that the government judges itself by the amount of legislation that it passes, rather than by stewardship of the Treasury and maintaining fiscal responsibility. The early leaders knew human nature; Madison wrote that government administration is more prone to passion than reason. Indeed, that is the great struggle today. One faction of society wants to distribute wealth equally, or somewhat equally, to all classes of people, even if there isn't enough money to go around, while an opposing faction wants to spend within the monetary limits of national revenue. Today, the dialog continues, and many folks favor a Constitutional Amendment to limit spending. Jefferson likely would have favored this, because he wrote that he wished for a single amendment to the Constitution that would prohibit the federal government from borrowing.

Modern Americans have forgotten or ignored these admonishments, though. The U.S. government has evolved into a great provider for many people, with many privileges and gifts for groups classified as eligible, whether there is enough money in the Treasury or not. At some point a "debt ceiling" was created to establish a line of credit to allow continued borrowing, and of course, this ceiling is raised on a regular basis until the national debt has become a major concern. Look how the debt has grown in Figure 5-1, which shows debt amounts from 1791 to 2006. The country started in debt as a result of Revolutionary War expenses. It remained about the same for about forty years, and then was nearly eliminated by 1835 under Andrew Jackson's administration. Then the debt grew substantially as a result of the Civil War, and again during World War Two. In addition to funding wars the debt has increased as a result of spending to support three great periods of expansion of government programs. By 2006, the debt exceeded eight trillion dollars, and only four years later it increased seventy-five percent to over fourteen trillion dollars. The government and its programs have outgrown the ability of working America to sustain them.

United States National Debt from 1791 to 2006					
2006	8.3 trillion				
2005	7.9 trillion	1985	1.9 trillion	1885	1.8 billion
2004	7.3 trillion	1980	930 billion	1880	2.1 billion
2003	6.7 trillion	1975	576 billion	1875	2.2 billion
2002	6.2 trillion	1970	389 billion	1870	2.4 billion
2001	5.8 trillion	1965	320 billion	1865	2.6 billion
2000	5.6 trillion	1960	290 billion	1860	64 million
1999	5.6 trillion	1955	289 billion	1855	35 million
1998	5.5 trillion	1950	257 billion	1850	63 million
1997	5.4 trillion	1945	258 billion	1845	15 million
1996	5.2 trillion	1940	42 billion	1840	3 million
1995	4.9 trillion	1935	28 billion	1835	33 thousand
1994	4.6 trillion	1930	16 billion	1830	48 million
1993	4.4 trillion	1925	20 billion	1825	83 million
1992	4.0 trillion	1920	25 billion	1820	91 million
1991	3.6 trillion	1915	3.0 billion	1815	99 million
1990	3.2 trillion	1910	2.6 billion	1810	53 million
1989	2.8 trillion	1905	2.2 billion	1805	82 million
1988	2.6 trillion	1900	2.1 billion	1800	82 million
1987	2.3 trillion	1895	1.6 billion	1795	80 million
1986	2.1 trillion	1890	1.5 billion	1791	75 million

Source: Bureau of the Public Debt
United States Department of the Treasury

US National Debt History
Figure 5-1

Throughout its history America has experienced an ebb and flow of the economy. There have been tremendous booms and dreadful recessions. Work was a pleasure when there was a lot of business, and frightful dreariness when trying to just survive. Modern business managers become over zealous with hiring and buying inventory during times of plenty, only to have to cut back during downturns. It is imperative for all businesses to operate at a size appropriate to the amount of available sales revenue. A common phrase used by managers during reductions in force is, "we must resize the company." This is the situation today for the country and its spending. Our economy and cost of living simply won't support the size of our federal government and its programs. Manufacturing has been reduced by the loss of millions of jobs to other countries, and millions more U.S. citizens are not working, so there just isn't enough money to continue to rely on a booming economy.

Instead of cutting spending to avoid increasing the debt, modern politicians want to depend on growth predictions for the economy. In other words, the plan is to grow out of debt. Their idea is that more income from taxes on more national production will make up the differences in the accumulated debt, and the country will just naturally produce itself out of debt. By claiming this for a plan to control the deficit, the career politician can avoid cutting government jobs and the benefits of the voters. Figure 5-1 shows how well this has worked. It simply piles the debt on the next generation while the irresponsible politician retires in luxury with a fat pension that continues to add debt for the people.

The truth is, the federal government is too large for the available revenue and needs to be resized. Just as private business must reorganize and resize according to its income, so must the federal government adjust its size, salaries, and benefits to operate within the boundaries of its income.

GOVERNMENT EXPANSION

Many government programs are operating unsuccessfully in debt. How did they start and how did they come into being in the first place? It's astonishing that most of these programs were created and implemented during three distinct periods of the nation's history; these were major expansions of government involvement in private life. The three periods can be grouped from 1913 to 1916, from 1932 to 1938, and from 1965 to 1975. Most of the troublesome government enterprises and programs were established during these time periods.

The administration of Woodrow Wilson was a period of substantial change in the way the government operated. In 1913 the Sixteenth Amendment to the Constitution was adopted and used to begin the system of income tax that exists today. Originally, this practice was unconstitutional and considered an intrusion into private life and personal liberty, but this all changed with this first great power grab. Also, in 1913, the Federal Reserve Act was passed that established the Federal Reserve Banking System. This would ultimately lead to deficit spending, printing paper money, and the tremendous debt that has been allowed to accumulate today. In 1916 the government of the Wilson era created the idea of Government Sponsored Enterprises. This has led to even more debt, false economy, and poorly operated government agencies; more programs, more employees, more cost.

Many people who inherit great wealth, or earn it with disproportionate ease, such as entertainers and professional athletes, have an overwhelming support for government gift programs. They seem to feel an obligation to the society that gives them a privileged lifestyle. This was true of the Roosevelt family. They had a wonderful history of generosity and sense of obligation to the less fortunate. This was apparently true for both Theodore Roosevelt and his cousin Franklin Roosevelt. Both men thought the government should do more, and Franklin Roosevelt made a huge expansion of this idea with his New Deal programs. He expanded the Government Sponsored Enterprise system established by Wilson and introduced Wholly Owned Government Corporations. Most of these agencies are financially troubled today and have left a terrible legacy of debt and responsibilities.

Franklin Roosevelt created the American Welfare State with the Social Security Administration, the crown jewel of government gifting. In the eyes of many, it was the beginning of a second Bill of Rights. It was thought that each citizen had the vested right to an education, a home, food, health care, and protection against monopolies. Unfortunately these ideas have become confused with the initial rights established by the U.S. Constitution. Natural human rights are unalienable, that is they are personal human birthrights, and no government has the right to limit or take them away – this is the guarantee of the Constitution of the United States. The rights to a home, and so forth, are vested rights that the government has decided are rights, but which can be taken back by the government, and often they are. For example, look at the problem with Social Security and its modifications; the rules change, the program is threatened, and countless young adults today fear this vested right may not exist when they reach eligibility. After decades of living with and expanding these programs, numerous citizens have confused the two types of rights. Many elected officials confuse this idea, too. There are a lot of politicians that do understand the difference, but nevertheless believe government should grant these vested rights and seek to do it regardless of their constitutionality or the country's ability to support them.

The third great expansion was started during the Lyndon Johnson and Richard Nixon era. In 1965 the Johnson Administration expanded the Social Security program by adding Medicare, Medicaid, Public Housing, and Supplemental Security Income. It was branded as "The Great Society," and it sounded okay to a lot of Americans. They saw nothing wrong with government giving a helping hand to those who had suffered misfortune, either by birth or fate. The economy was booming, so why not share? Still others opposed the ideas in the belief that these programs were not authorized by the Constitution.

Nixon continued the expansion by adding four more departments to the government payroll and funding another unsuccessful government owned enterprise – Amtrak. His administration saw the start of the Environmental Protection Agency, EPA, and the Occupational Safety and Health Administration, OSHA. Although the EPA and OSHA have not been useless, they have grown in power and regulating authority that result in more wasteful cost and a large federal payroll.

When examining the history of governmental agencies, corporations, welfare programs, and government subsidies, it becomes apparent most were established or expanded during the three periods of government expansion. Today, with the addition of the Health Care and Education Reconciliation Act, the country is on the verge of a fourth great expansion. Following is a list of some of the major failed programs, when they were initiated, and a brief history.

GOVERNMENT SPONSORED ENTERPRISE (GSE)

The long campaign to increase the size and reach of the federal government and its encroachment on the private lives of its citizens began long before the advent of the Government Sponsored Enterprise, GSE. In fact, it started with the first administration under George Washington when he signed a bank bill and established the principle of "implied powers," even though he thought it would be a temporary measure to ease the financial strain on the new Union. The use of implied powers continued in following administrations, but a very large expansion of the idea occurred in 1916 when Congress first established the idea of a GSE. The stated purpose for this intervention was to improve the efficiency of capital markets and to overcome market imperfections. It was thought that a financial intermediary was needed to improve the flow of credit on targeted sectors to make them more efficient and visible. As a result, the entire market system would adjust to this artificial influence. The government ignored the principle of infinity of actions when it launched these programs. The leaders and economists smugly thought they could completely understand the markets and manipulate them for the good, but the intricacies of economic markets are too large and interlinked for any individual or system to be able to artificially manage them. Adam Smith, the father of economics, recognized the problem of regulating commerce when he stated that only a part of commerce can actually be redirected, but it remains totally uncertain whether the effects of redirection will be better than if left to natural market forces. Every adjustment in one area causes unforeseen reactions in that market area, and many others as well. Yet even today, the government continues to manipulate the markets.

There is no specific guarantee of creditworthiness for a GSE, but they receive preferential treatment due to an implied guarantee that they are too big to fail. Despite the preferred treatment, the recent sub-prime mortgage crisis has forced the U.S. government to place Fannie Mae and Freddie Mac under its legal control.

FARM CREDIT SYSTEM – 1916

About the earliest GSE was the Farm Credit System. It was a lending cooperative that was initiated to provide loans to agricultural producers, rural homeowners, and farm-related businesses. It also established cooperatives for agricultural, aquatic, and public utilities. This was one of the government's earliest intrusions into credit markets, and the results have led to later abuses and skewed values in the credit markets.

FEDERAL HOME LOAN BANKS – 1932

In an effort to stimulate the economy during the great depression, this instrument was meant to provide stable, low cost funding for mortgage loans to small businesses, and rural and agricultural development. It provided for loans between banks and established twelve regional banks that are owned by some 8,100 owner-member banks. Today, the Moody's rating service estimated only four of the twelve regional banks may be able to keep required minimum capital levels, as yet another GSE struggles to operate efficiently.

FEDERAL NATIONAL MORTGAGE ASSOCIATION – 1938-2008

One of the two huge enterprises so often in news headlines, Congress initially chartered it in 1938 to purchase and secure mortgages. This is the Federal National Mortgage Association, FNMA, whose acronym is tagged with the nickname of Fannie Mae. It bought loans for cash or with mortgage-backed securities. At times it hedged cash flow by using derivatives, a risky method of paying only part of the value with the expectation that it will increase in value later.

In 1968 the association was split into private and public entities, and the public unit was called the Government National Mortgage Association,

GNMA, or Ginnie Mae, which became one of a new type of government entity called Wholly Owned Government Corporations.

There is not an explicit guarantee by Fannie Mae for private mortgages, but the reaction of the government to its problems implies the guarantee, because it is too big to fail. This huge corporation currently owns about ninety-six percent of home mortgages. It has suffered severe problems with defaults and other errors caused by aggressive lending, and in 2008 the corporation was placed under the legal control of the U.S. government to become another large part of our economy under government rule.

FEDERAL HOME LOAN MORTGAGE CORPORATION – 1970-2008

The second big newsmaker is known as Freddie Mac from its acronym, FHLMC. Unbelievably it was created in 1970 to provide competition with the monstrous Fannie Mae. Now the government intervention in the mortgage markets includes Fannie Mae, started in 1932, then split to create Ginnie Mae in 1968, and followed by the creation of Freddie Mac for competition. It was meant to further expand the secondary market for mortgages and market-backed securities by buying mortgages from Savings and Loans and other organizations. The dynamics and mismanagement of this involvement in a vital and complex facet of the economy has caused tremendous difficulties for many Americans. Older Americans recall the bailout of failing Savings and Loan institutions, and now the huge numbers of home mortgage failures. Much of this can be attributed to government interference with established and accepted loan practices by banking institutions.

In 2008, Freddie Mac joined Fannie Mae under legal control of the U.S. government, adding to the long list of failed government programs. It could be argued that these institutions, and their liberal and low-cost lending practices have benefited millions of low income Americans. Perhaps, but not if they cannot be properly managed without causing undue influence in the markets and costing the nation more than it can afford. In all probability the artificial manipulation of the mortgage markets has caused more harm and instability than benefit.

STUDENT LOAN MARKETING CORPORATION – 1972

The government decided to continue in the loan business by expanding its reach into loans for education. The Student Loan Marketing Corporation, SLM, or Sallie Mae, is a GSE created in 1972 to provide a federal guarantee of student loans. The idea, presumably, is to help more Americans achieve a higher education without the burden of having to work during their college years. Unfortunately, it has resulted with many young folks saddled with debt averaging more than $17,000. Most nineteen-year-old students have not developed financial skills to realize how much debt they accumulated until they receive the bill after they graduate, if they graduate. Many young people use these loans for living expenses, cars, and such, but never finish school. For many it is little more than a welfare plan that may have to be paid back, but in all likelihood it never will.

Like most government programs, there are targeted provisions with special privileges for certain groups. It's another part of the government role in manipulating civil behavior. If the new graduate serves for a period of time in certain fields or geographic locations the loan is forgiven. Many loans are never repaid, but hang over the head of the individual for years. Rather than helping, this institution preys on the student youth and has become usury in its practices and loan rate. It should be abolished.

In 2004 this institution was privatized and became a publicly traded business. It has been criticized for its collection and management practices. But the big blow may come from the Health Care and Education Reconciliation Act of 2010. This is the controversial health care bill that includes changes to education loan practices. Many Americans wonder what education has to do with health care, the practice of grouping different programs into one giant bill drives most citizens near apoplexy. Nevertheless, the new bill will end the program that subsidizes banks and other financial institutional loans, and instead allows students to borrow directly from the government at a lower interest rate. Also, it caps the payback amount to no more than ten percent of the individual's working income. Thus Sallie Mae is added to the long list of government's failure to develop well-managed programs and agencies, but instead infringe upon and damage the economy and personal lives. And it is just as likely that the latest provision for educational loans, passed under the health care program, eventually will be added to the list of failures.

WHOLLY OWNED GOVERNMENT CORPORATIONS

The GSE programs were joined by government-owned corporations, which were first developed by Franklin Roosevelt's administration. Three instances are worth briefly reviewing.

TENNESSEE VALLEY AUTHORITY – 1933

The TVA, or Tennessee Valley Authority, was started in May 1933 as a federally owned corporation with the objective of flood control and eventually hydroelectric power generation and water navigation. It has been estimated that the debt created to complete the project may have been about five times as much as the cost of the flood damage. Today, about eighty-five percent of TVA electrical power is generated by coal fired plants, not hydroelectric, and the largest part of water navigation traffic comes from barges carrying coal to the electric plants at a greater cost than rail shipment. It would be interesting to examine the business analysis that was used, if any, to justify government business ownership.

GOVERNMENT NATIONAL MORTGAGE ASSOCIATION – 1968

This is the GNMA, or Ginnie Mae, that was established as a split off of Fannie Mae. It was a Wholly Owned Government Corporation created with the transfer of mortgages from Fannie Mae to facilitate a secondary mortgage market. Ginnie Mae provides the only mortgage-backed securities that are officially backed by the U.S. government. It's an artificial interest rate subsidy that distorts market balance, and provides a pool of mortgage loans as collateral for Wall Street investors. These loans and subsidies are part of the spider web of debts and payments that make up the U.S. government's involvement in markets.

AMTRAK – 1971

The National Railroad Passenger Corporation is a government owned corporation created in 1971 and named Amtrak from the combination of America and Trak. The argument for its creation was the need for a rail system that would be comparable to the interstate highway system, and the airport system. The Amtrak board of directors is appointed by the president and confirmed by the U.S. Senate. Unfortunately, the government has again proved its inability to efficiently operate a business. It has never been profitable and continues to operate on subsidies.

AMERICAN WELFARE STATE

The majority of Americans probably acknowledge the existence of a social network of citizens that are supported by government welfare and become a component of a hybrid society. This is the American welfare state. It is a group of individuals that are completely dependent upon the government for their livelihood. This system of government support has continually grown throughout U.S. history, but from 1932 to 1975 it grew at an extraordinary pace. Rather than being a benevolent, helpful aid to citizens in need, it has left many unable to care for themselves and left them in bondage to the U.S. government.

The welfare system has resulted in government slavery for both those living within the system, and for those providing revenue to support the system. Those on the system must meet specific regulations and requirements in order to continue receiving food and housing supplements, medical services, and so forth. The other element of the hybrid society is a slave to the tax system to support the welfare state. Folks in the middle, meaning the working poor class and above, must work longer to achieve less while carrying the tax burden on their shoulders for their entire lives. Today America sags under the weight of these burdens while watching its government commit more support to the welfare system than it can produce, leaving the country more in debt each year.

The welfare system has essentially destroyed many poor cultures as they have changed their traditions and abandoned their moral values in order to appear to meet the government requirements for welfare benefits. Many become liars. They don't marry when it results in more benefits, and this usually results in a single-parent existence. Public housing has developed a reputation as an incubator for drugs, prostitution, and violence. The tax system has been pulled into the social system as the source for many credits for the working poor, and now has become an additional source of abuse and misrepresentations for those hoping to squeeze another dollar out of the welfare system. Today, the welfare system has become a way of life for the welfare society, and its recipients have taught their children to live within its boundaries. It has come to span generations, until now there are grandparents, parents, and children all living within the welfare system. They receive supplemental security income or public housing and food stamps. If they can qualify for Medicaid they receive routine medical care. If they don't qualify to be in the Medicaid system, then they receive free medical attention when they are ill. Of course, this all requires they remain in poverty, or lead the government to believe that is their condition. If they report too much income or worth they are stripped of benefits, so many have come to believe they aren't able to work, or don't want to work, and so they live in slavery to the system. They are trapped with no way up or out. Most despise the system and continually complain about its rules and encroachment into their private lives, and claim that what they receive just isn't enough.

There really wasn't much of a welfare system in the United States until the second third of the twentieth century. Folks in-need were helped by friends and family while some were relegated to a poor farm. Poor farms were usually working farms that included housing for their residents. These farms were a form of the English Poor House system and were administered locally by counties or townships. Residents were expected to provide farm labor to the extent of their ability. Generally, they lived in harsh conditions by today's standards, and this system slowly declined from 1935 to 1950 with the advent of Social Security.

From 1932 to 1975 welfare payments grew considerably faster than national production. Today it includes a smorgasbord of benefits including Social Security, Medicare, Medicaid, Public Education, and Earned Income Tax Credits. About five to ten percent of the public uses it in some form at one time or another, and roughly twenty percent of all citizens use Medicaid entitlements.

The Social Security Administration is the enormous giant of all programs. It includes Old Age and Survivors benefits, Medicare and Medicaid benefits, and the Supplemental Security Income programs. The Administration was formed in 1935 and curiously enough was composed of three people. Two trust funds were established: the Old Age and Survivors Trust Fund, OASI, for retirement benefits, and the Disability Insurance Trust Fund, DI, to provide benefits for disabled individuals. Nearly all Americans believe they are paying a percentage of their wages into a trust fund under the stewardship of the government that will provide a small retirement benefit when they can no longer work. In reality there isn't a trust fund at all, at least not in the sense that it is a fund with assets to pay income. Government lawmakers used the trust fund term in its rulemaking to segregate Social Security tax income from other forms of income tax. Government leaders often refer to the excess of the amount paid into the system, versus the amount of the benefits paid out, as the trust fund. For many years, the government collected more taxes for Social Security than it paid in benefits, and the extra was invested in U.S. Treasury Bonds. Then, if the Social Security Administration ran a deficit, it could redeem these U.S. Bonds. At one time, the Social Security Trust Fund Balance showed $2.4 trillion and Medicare roughly $380 billion. But the Congress has allowed itself to borrow and spend this surplus until there really is nothing left, so the system is operated from hand to mouth, so to speak. It's no secret today that the taxes of younger workers are used to pay the obligations promised to older individuals, disabled former workers, and Medicaid for America's underprivileged youth. Today, informed workers feel completely betrayed by the government when they learn it's one of the greatest Ponzi schemes of all time. How else could you view it? The government (con man) takes payments from new investors (young workers) and uses it to payout benefits to old investors (retired workers), without truly safe guarding it as promised. The government has used the excess collections, paid for decades by taxpayers, for other programs and purposes, similarly to the Ponzi con man using excess cash from his investors to finance a lavish lifestyle of yachts and mansions. It would be jail time for the perpetrators if it were a private enterprise.

Various depletion dates are often cited for the system's demise, but who really knows, or who can be trusted? A recent report from the Social Security Administration was that it would be out of money by 2042, but the Congressional Budget Office has estimated 2052. These are fluid dates and are based upon the performance of the economy. When employment is high then income can increase the pool. So what? Will it feel better to continue bilking more workers out of their money while continuing the legacy of mismanagement of this system?

This thing has grown out of control as more government programs add more people to the welfare state. As a percentage of Gross Domestic Product, it has been reported that the three big programs, Social Security, Medicare, and Medicaid, consumed about 8.7 percent of the national wealth in 2010, and is expected to grow to as much as eighteen percent by 2050. As the welfare system grows, and the population ages, the number of workers supporting each retiree decreases. In 1960 there were about 5.1 workers supporting each retiree, but only 3.3 in 2007, and by 2040 it is expected to drop to 2.1. In essence, the debts of preceding generations are piled upon current working folks.

When a lot of Americans discover the big con, they shrug and consider it their contribution to the livelihood of their grandparents. Granny had no fat corporate or government retirement plan, so they, like many others like them, lived on their Social Security payments when they were no longer able to work. But shrugging off the big con is a lax reaction. This abusive program should have been corrected decades ago. Americans should have been more active about it, but they droned on like good worker bees enslaved by the system.

In the eighties government representatives attempted to make a correction. Was it to stop borrowing the excess for other spending? No. Was it to cut spending or to stop adding more social benefits to burden the plan? No. Was it to reduce government spending to repay the Social Security debts? No. They decided to change the long-standing promises to the American people and increase the qualifying age for full retirement benefits. In other words, they revoked a vested right. The perceived reason was that the system was never meant to provide a complete retirement income for the public, and life expectancy had extended so much longer that the program needed change. But the real reason was malfeasance in managing the public treasury and trust of the American people. If the elected officials had managed this program like a true trust fund, and avoided including so many welfare additions through the years that draw further from it, then the system would be fine.

Today, the tunnel vision continues. Government leaders see no way to preserve the system except by defaulting on the promises to citizens. They want to sustain the con. Expect new rules, they say, like reduced benefits and higher retirement ages. Do they consider the size of government and the marvelous retirement plans government workers receive at the expense of the American people? Of course not, and it leaves a nation of disheartened youth expecting nothing but the burden of an extra tax their entire working lives.

The largest expansion of the Social Security system occurred with the Social Security Act of 1965, which led to the Medicare and Medicaid programs. President Truman was an early supporter of health care for elderly citizens that couldn't find affordable insurance. Often they were denied private insurance because they had existing health problems or just because of their advanced age. In honor of his efforts, the retired Truman was ceremoniously signed as the first enrollment.

The program falls under the administrative control of the Social Security Administration, and it has a similar trust fund with the same problems. Medicare costs have doubled about every four years from 1966 to 1980, and the trust fund is expected to be insolvent by 2019. Predictably, elected officials don't know what to do about it, so they do nothing. They "serve" the public, and then retire with honor to collect their accumulated service benefits. In 2010 another centralized health care program has been added to the drain on the system, but without a responsive effort to adequately fund the country's growing appetite for free programs. According to the Centers for Medicare and Medicaid Services, by 2019 the health care bill will increase expenditures on Medicaid and individual subsidies by about $165 billion a year while reducing Medicare expenses by about $125 billion each year.

Next came Medicaid. It was created for adults with low income and resources, for children, and for the disabled. It is a means-tested and needs-based program, as opposed to the disguise of social insurance. This program was put on the backs of state resources, too. Each state administers the program and provides up to half of the funding for this coverage.

Today, AIDS patients are considered disabled and receive Medicaid benefits. Nursing home coverage has become the fastest growing element of the Medicaid program; however, because the system is restricted to folks with low resources, many people transfer all of their assets to a beneficiary in order to qualify as low income and low resource. It has become a profitable industry for law practices that specialize in preparing transfer documents and providing court representation.

Another large arm of the Social Security Administration is the Supplemental Security Income (SSI) program. It became the responsibility of the Administration in 1973, and in 1974 it began providing stipends to people with low income, the aged, blind, or totally disabled citizenry. It is funded from the general fund of the U.S. Treasury, rather than the Social Security Funds collected separately. Here again a huge segment of law practices are dedicated to securing these payments for their clients. Daytime television is filled with advertisements by these law firms that will help individuals secure the "payments they deserve." If people believe they are qualified for Social

Security Disability payments and apply but are denied, they frequently contact one of these law firms. Many dedicated law firms employ former judges of disability cases. An appeal is filed, and it is not uncommon for the disability payment to be granted. In this case, the payment is retroactive to the date the applicant filed the original request. This can result in thousands, and often tens of thousands, of dollars of "back pay" awarded in a lump sum. The law firms accept these cases on a speculation basis, so they receive their payment from the lump sum award, and it is often a sizeable percentage of the award. So, a large part of these payments to the poor, aged, blind, and disabled go to the law firms. It's no wonder that many law firms specialize in these cases and practice nothing else except these situations. They have the inside knowledge on proper wording of the application, easy money. It's just another example of the inefficiency, unreasonableness, and waste of government programs gone wrong.

The government created another large program in the great expansion of 1965 when it authorized the Department of Housing and Urban Development, HUD. The idea was to provide public housing for the underprivileged having little or no income, or who were disabled in some way. Apartment buildings were constructed to provide a place to live for these folks, and they came to be known as "the projects." The problem developed when neither the government, nor the inhabitants of the projects, took care of the facilities. The people in this housing often were unemployed and living under one of the new welfare programs, and in their idle time, and with the pain of their disabilities, the inhabitants often turned to drugs, prostitution, and the accompanying violence. The term "projects" became a derogatory term. There are countless stories of difficult living conditions in the projects, with an occasional story of a triumphal escape from the projects and their ties to government support.

When the welfare state was proposed it was supported by a lot of American citizens. They thought many of the programs were needed to help individuals that were disadvantaged in some way, physically, mentally, or fiscally. Most supporters never dreamed that people would adopt it as a way of life and live in hopeless squalor without being able to lift themselves out of it. Today, many folks want to pour more of the national wealth into these give-away programs, but after more than forty years, it's hard to look back without seeing anything but failure in the effort. Some of the people receiving these benefits are truly needy, but many are not. The country needs an alternative to pouring trillions of dollars into a system that traps people, makes liars of them, and leaves them in despair with no hope for independence. Working Americans have changed their outlooks. The welfare plan didn't work. It's a poor idea as it stands today. The idea of the American welfare state needs to be completely rethought and changed.

U.S. POSTAL SERVICE

The U.S. Postal Service is the only independent government agency explicitly authorized by the U.S. Constitution. It was originally established before the Constitution was written. The second Continental Congress in 1775 set it up and appointed Benjamin Franklin as the first Post Master General. The leaders of the day recognized the need for swift and reliable communications, and postal service was the primary method of the time. The provisions of the Continental Congress were continued in the U.S. Constitution by Article I, Section 8, Clause 7, "to establish post offices and post roads."

President Washington established a position in the U.S. Cabinet in 1792. Generally the mail was delivered seven days a week until about 1912. As mail volume grew, deliveries occurred two to seven times a day, depending upon the region and amount of volume. Today, delivery is once a day for the most part.

A big change was implemented in 1970 with the Postal Reorganization Act that abolished the U.S. Post Office Department. It is generally accepted that this occurred as a direct result of the U.S. Postal Strike of 1970. It resulted in the postal service becoming another Wholly Owned Government Corporation; presidential appointees and the Post Master General control it. The Senate confirms the presidential appointees, and in turn they appoint the Post Master General, who acts as the Chief Executive Officer for the service. The Postal Service does not receive taxpayer money, but it borrows from the U.S. Treasury to fund its debt.

It is the only entity authorized to deliver to U.S. Mail letterboxes; all other delivery services must leave transmittals at the door. Now, with pressures from email and other forms of communication, the Postal Service is forced to change again with the times; this is not uncommon for any business. Slow to react and change, the Postal Service has been running at a deficit for many years. Like many other businesses undergoing changes, the Postal Service is having trouble pre-funding retiree health and pension benefits, and it has proposed cutbacks in personnel and the delivery schedule to five days a week.

The Postal Service is included with the list of government failures, because it has been slow to adapt and change, while piling up huge debts. Many question whether it is needed. Others think it remains an important part of the national communications infrastructure. There are still many regions and individuals that rely on it as the primary source of communication. Everyone doesn't use a computer, the Internet, cell phone, telephones, and so forth, so it appears at present to remain an important component of the total infrastructure, even though it demonstrates government's inability to operate a business, even a non-profit one.

SUBSIDIES

The long list of government subsidies includes obvious and not so obvious interference in daily business by the government. Subsidies have the effect of transferring income from the general taxpayers to the subsidy recipients. It includes mortgage rates, housing help, farms, food and energy products, and just plain paying people to be unproductive. Following are a few of the more notorious programs, and some of the more annoying ones. To dig into all subsidies would be a massive study in itself.

Farm subsidies are a good starting point. What could be wrong with farm subsidies? After all, farming has been the country's backbone for hundreds of years. In the thirties about a fourth of the country's population lived on about six million small farms, but today less than two percent of the people live on large farms that produce over seventy percent of agricultural sales. Today, the government pays about $20 billion a year in farm subsidies for the purpose of stabilizing farm income. In effect, income is redistributed from taxpayers to farm owners.

Corn crops receive the most subsidy payments. A large part of this is the result of the Energy Policy Act of 2005 that requires a minimum amount of ethanol, most often derived from corn, be blended into gasoline. But, these subsidies can reduce the nutritional value of meat, because subsidized corn can be cheaper than feeding natural grass to animals, and corn fed cattle have higher fat content. This interweaving of cause and effect spanning many unexpected consequences again demonstrates the principle of infinity of actions, and the folly of government interference in markets.

The list of agricultural subsidies is enormous, and today, the majority of them go to corporations. It includes grains, cotton, soybeans, dairy, peanuts, sugar, oilseeds, tobacco, wool, vegetable oil products, honey, and dozens more. Who can imagine what the proper price should be for these products, and how much they affect many other facets of daily life? One of the new items on the list of things that supposedly contribute to health problems is corn syrup. Scores of folks want more taxes on items that contain large amounts of this item, because it leads to health problems and obesity. Take a look at the ingredients of about any product at the grocery store; corn syrup is in about everything. It has become the sweetener and ingredient of choice because it's inexpensive compared to other ingredients, and this may be the result of the agricultural subsidy that lowers its true cost. Ironic.

When the word, bank, is associated with an activity other than money, it is an immediate alert that someone is receiving something for nothing. There are the infamous jobs banks established by many unions, and agricultural subsidies include the soil bank. What a waste of taxpayer money and unmerited payments to individuals for being unproductive. Most people living in the agricultural centers of the country know that farm owners can receive a rental payment from the government for agreeing to leave their farm acreage idle; in other words, for doing nothing. The convoluted reasoning behind this, including erosion prevention and price supports, is beyond belief.

Housing subsidies have proved to be ineffective and unequal for most Americans. This ranges from public housing to rental housing, and private homes. One of the most abusive of these programs occurred in the early seventies. Young workers struggled to save enough money for a down payment to buy a home. In those days, banks were the primary lenders and they required a down payment of about twenty to thirty percent of the mortgage value of the property. It would require years, if not a decade for average workers to save that much. But for qualifying low-income workers it was possible to live in a new home, because they received a subsidy from the government that allowed them to move in with no down payment, and on top of that, the government would pay over half of their monthly mortgage payment. Those who did not qualify were forced to continue trying to save a down payment for a home, while a portion of their income tax payment helped subsidize the gift to their coworkers.

The insult and injury became more infuriating when the subsidized homeowners would sell their homes at a profit and keep it, even though they had little or none of their own money invested in the home; it was from government payments. Many small communities sprang up just out of the city limits, because the funding was coming from the Department of Agriculture, so it couldn't be used for urban development. Finally, the government closed the loophole on the sale-of-home profits by requiring the homeowner to repay a prorated share. In the eighties, the prices on the homes in these subsidized communities were artificially inflated. This resulted, because the qualified buyers really didn't care what the mortgage payment would be, because the government would pay all but a small portion of the payment, according to their income. So, with no down payment, and a fixed percentage of their income for a monthly payment, they were able to offer virtually any price for the property, and did. Meanwhile, those who didn't qualify for the hand out struggled to buy a home with interest rates in the early eighties running as high as eighteen percent.

The latest interference in the housing market has been the First Time Homebuyers Credit that was offered to certain taxpayers. This was a wild program that included three different phases. The first phase offered first time homebuyers a $7,500 credit off their taxes to be repaid over fifteen years. Following right behind it was a second phase of the program that offered homebuyers $8,000 without ever having to repay it. The third phase included current homeowners. How fair is this program? Not only are unqualified taxpayers left out, but those who participated in the first phase, and must repay their no-interest loan, are flabbergasted to learn that if they had only waited a few months, they could have had even more money in the form of a gift. The tax code requires they own and live in their homes for a minimum period of time, or they may have to repay part or the entire gift. But, after the minimum period has elapsed, they can sell the property and keep the profit. They keep the gift from the taxpayers, and they keep the portion of the profit resulting from the taxpayers' gift. The taxpayers' contribution, in the name of economy stimulus, was wasteful, and the stimulus did virtually nothing for the housing market, but it successfully increased the debt for the children of the next generation to repay.

The interference in the free market system through mortgage subsidies may have contributed to more booms and busts in the economy than any other factor. The Government Sponsored Enterprises, Wholly Owned Government Corporations, and many banking programs that have been identified on the list of financially troubled failures are predominately low cost mortgage programs directed toward housing programs for low-income workers. On the surface these programs sounded high minded and benevolent. At some point in history, Americans and government decided that housing should be added to the list of vested rights, the revocable statutory rights provided by the government. The idea is that taxpayers that are earning more income than those below a government pre-determined income level will pay into the treasury, and then an army of government workers will distribute a portion of it to these mortgage subsidies. As already discussed, this leads to artificially inflated housing prices and artificial housing booms. In addition, the lending rules are relaxed and become more risky, so there are a lot of loans made to people that eventually are unable to meet the requirements of the debt service. This, of course, leads to foreclosures. This cycle has been repeated many times since the introduction of mortgage subsidies. Subsidized mortgages were a major cause of the depression in the thirties, the housing market problems in the eighties, and the bust in the first decade of this century. The government guarantees low-cost loans with reduced lending requirements, which leads to a boom and inflated prices. It is an induced boom that grows larger than the market can bear, and then there is a bust. Government reacts with new programs with lower requirements, and the cycle repeats.

The current housing crisis has been in deep recession for several years. The boom became so big that housing prices were extraordinarily inflated. Forty or fifty years before this crisis, a loan application required proof of income, a physical field check of the applicant's information and the condition of the property, and twenty to thirty percent down payment. When the boom element of the housing cycle really began to pick up speed, loan institutions began to accept an applicant's stated income, with no checks on the income statement, no inspection of the property, and no requirement for a down payment. Risk was at its highest level, beyond what a prudent banker would accept, but the loans were guaranteed, or had an implied guarantee, by one of the sponsoring government programs, and the mortgages were bought by investors who accepted the speculative risk. It became frenzied buying in many parts of the country where a seller would list a price, but the buyers would bid the price up beyond what the seller was asking. It was the boom of the low-cost housing projects of the eighties repeated and magnified.

Housing prices were rising so quickly that many folks decided to buy, and lie, in order to make money on the deal. A prospective buyer might state income of $200,000 while truly earning only $50,000 per year. There were no checks or verification of income required, only the stated word of the buyer, and loans were made with no money down. Some buyers expected the price of the home to zoom up by fifty percent or more in a year or two, and then their intention was to sell, take the profit, and use the difference as seed money to start a business. If they owned and lived in their home at least two years, the profit could be totally tax free up to $250,000 for single and $500,000 for married people. It worked for a lot of them, but those coming in at the end of the pyramid-style boom lost everything. The market crashed, loans came due, and these folks owned a home that was worth less than what they owed. On top of that, their falsified income was not enough to continue mortgage payments. They were out on the street so to speak. Not all of the foreclosures were caused by lies and speculation, but many were. Now the taxpayers of the country will pay even more for its government's interference as Freddie Mac and Fannie Mae take on these mortgages and appeal to Congress for help. In addition, some elements of the government want to provide relief from mortgage obligations and help these individuals escape with even more of the innocent taxpayers' cash. Until government learns that intrusion into markets is artificial, irrational, and causes problems to become even larger and more difficult to manage, these destructive cycles will continue.

SAVINGS AND LOAN INTERVENTION

Here again is an example of government incursion into the money and banking system. Government wanted to dictate lending rate controls instead of allowing the markets to seek the natural rates of demand. Government wanted more mortgages to be available again, so it imposed rate controls from 1966 to about 1979, and thus the problems began. For many years the Savings and Loan industry followed a set of standards for money and banking, but then the industry was deregulated to give Savings and Loan institutions the same capabilities as banks, but without the same bank regulations.

Predictably, this resulted in imprudent real estate lending practices. When the financial and real estate markets slowed down it became more difficult to qualify for a mortgage, so alternative mortgage types and interest bearing accounts were created. The same difficulties repeated until over seven hundred Savings and Loans failed, costing an estimated $160 billion, and taxpayers again contributed $125 billion.

ENERGY POLICY

Energy policy in the United State has been an on again off again effort. One of the largest problems was the gasoline shortage that occurred in 1973 as a result of the Arab oil embargo in response to the U.S. re-supply of the Israeli military. It was a difficult time for many citizens that resulted in long gas lines and demolished airline schedules. Many waited for hours to refuel their autos. In different areas of the country gas was available every other day, and many gas stations closed on Sunday. It required a lot of planning for those wanting to take an automobile trip. Gas prices jumped from about thirty-five cents to seventy-five cents a gallon as fuel supplies were diminished. Many Americans resented the wealthy Organization of Petroleum Exporting Countries, OPEC. It seemed like the Arabs controlled prices, the standard of living, and affected U.S. lifestyles.

The world petroleum shortage had been predicted decades earlier by studies of reserves and the prevailing technology to reach them. The problem became worse when the U.S. was involved in global conflicts. There was a shortage during the 1979 Iranian revolution, and in 1990 gas prices spiked for about nine months as a result of the Gulf War. As China and other countries begin to develop stronger economies, the demand for gasoline and oil continues to grow, and pressures in the twenty-first century have caused prices to more than double at times. The American government has worked on energy policies in fits and spurts, but as the oil supply problems have mediated for various reasons, the priority of an energy policy lost emphasis. Government priorities returned to give-away programs and manipulation of the national economy instead of developing a transition policy for developing energy sources. Elected officials felt a stronger need to promote give-away programs, redistribution of wealth some call it, because they believe that's how they are reelected, in support of their personal career plans.

Nuclear energy was a high priority for about twenty or thirty years. Many thought it would become the primary source for generating electrical power. Some of its drawbacks included safety concerns and what to do with acres of radioactive waste that remained from spent fuel materials. For more than fifty years scientists and engineers have searched for satisfactory solutions to the waste problem. Of course, there has been great resistance by much of the American public to the use of nuclear power plants, and when the problems at the Three-mile Island power plant materialized, the fate of nuclear power plants was sealed.

Today the outlook for petroleum products has changed considerably from the supply predictions of forty years ago. As a result of innovative technological advances in locating and extracting oil, there are more sources of not only oil but also natural gas and coal that were never before imagined. Technology advancements have also improved the way these energy sources are utilized to provide cleaner, more environmentally friendly consumption.

The enhanced ability to locate new energy sources and recover them from the ground has changed the market sources for U.S. petroleum. The majority of U.S. crude oil consumption, about fifty-five percent, comes from U.S. sources, and about thirty-five percent is supplied from sources in Canada and Mexico. Only about ten percent of the U.S. oil supply comes from the Persian Gulf region.

This is a surprise for a majority of Americans, because there always seems to be a spike in prices when there are problems in the Arab nations. This is not caused so much because the U.S. gets most of its oil from these countries, but because the oil market has grown into a global market with many more countries competing to buy it. Countries with growing economies need fuel, and today they are competing more than ever with the U.S. for a share of the oil. This means the total production of oil just about matches the growing demand, so when the oil supply from any country is interrupted, then world bidding on the remaining supply causes the price of oil to increase. A war in Iraq, an oil rig blows up in the Gulf of Mexico, a big storm shuts down an oil rig in Mexico, or any other type of production problem, will cause an increase in the price of oil in the U.S. and everywhere else in the world. It's fundamental free market supply and demand.

In the United States the search for affordable energy continues. There are hopes for alternatives such as bio-fuels, electric vehicles, and solar and wind power, but right now there is nothing more efficient than petroleum fuels, natural gas, and coal. It boils down to a term known as energy density, which refers to how much energy is contained per unit of fuel, such as a pound of fuel. Gasoline, for example, has an energy density more than eighty times the energy available in a lithium battery for an electric car, and it has a similar advantage over ethanol and the other biomass fuels. It's a large disadvantage that must be solved before an electric car, or burning corn fumes, can be considered as economical replacements for gasoline.

Unfortunately though, the U.S. does not have a resourceful energy policy to join the search for new energy sources. Politicians seeking office often think a policy is needed, businessmen are not so sure. So far, it has added up to little more than bursts of activity amounting to the tax credits and subsidies for favored companies. Instead of hiding cost under deceitful subsidies and rebates, maybe the government could support honest and equal programs to spread the cost of research that is too large and beyond the capability of the private sector to undertake.

INCOME TAXES

Control of taxes was of high priority to the creators of the Constitution; obviously it was an important factor in their decision to seek independence from Great Britain. The founders recognized the difference between direct and indirect taxes. They relied on the indirect taxes from duties and excise taxes to raise revenues to operate the government, and avoided the use of direct taxes for individuals, because it is impossible to fairly determine individual assessments. As a result, specific prohibitions against direct taxes were included in Clauses I.2.3 and I.9.4 unless they were evenly assessed according to the distribution of the population; it would be somewhat similar to the flat tax that is discussed today where everyone pays the same rate. Divide the needed revenue by the number of taxpayers, and that determines the rate. Nonetheless, the system used and abused today is unconstitutional under the provisions of the original Constitution.

All of this changed in 1913 with the adoption of the Sixteenth Amendment when the current progressive tax system was born. It's interesting to review its history. Initially the tax rate was seven percent for incomes greater than $500,000. Some folks insisted on a ceiling for the tax, but they were assured the country would never need more than the adopted seven percent; however, when the country became involved in World War One, the top tax rate inflated in 1918 to seventy-seven percent of income exceeding $1 million (about $16 million today). After the war the rate was reduced some, but during the depression the top rate was again raised to seventy-five percent in 1939 on incomes exceeding $5 million. During World War Two the rates were as high as ninety-four percent on incomes over $200,000. During much of the period from the sixties to the eighties the top rate remained seventy to seventy-seven percent, and as late as 1982 the government wanted fifty percent of earnings. In 2009 the top rate was reduced to thirty-five percent.

It didn't take long for states and cities to catch on to this idea of directly taxing income. So state rates have grown and added to the burden on the individual. A top-rate taxpayer in certain cities could see forty-five percent or more of their top income distributed to the governments. In reality, though, many of these folks avoid paying much of this by using various deductions, credits, and other deferment methods. For the average wage earner with no deductions or credits, just payroll earnings, it's real, and it's burdensome. For many, it inhibits their ability to save and remain out of debt, and it becomes a self-fulfilling system that ultimately leads them to dependence upon government programs.

The adoption of the Sixteenth Amendment and the authorization of the government to collect individual taxes may have changed American culture more than any tax system yet proposed. Instead of being used to raise revenue to operate the government, it has been modified and chopped up to manipulate the behavior of its citizens and the economy itself. Tax preparation is a terrible burden on the American taxpayer. It pre-supposes all citizens will operate in a money economy, all understand receipts, expenses, and profits, and all will keep reliable records. The tax system tries to make everyone into accountants. Unfortunately, none of this is true for the vast majority of U.S. citizens, and many citizens must pay a tax preparer to search through their records and attempt to recreate the events of the preceding year. Those who can afford it pay bookkeepers and accountants to keep up with it, but the reality is that most can't understand it regardless of their educational level. The original tax code of 1913 contained four instructions, but today it has grown to more than 4,000 situational directions.

It's abject slavery for the American public; citizens serve the system instead of the system serving the citizens. It's deplorable that a free government has developed a tax code that is so complex that most people must pay to have their income tax return filed. The tax preparation business has steadily grown since 1955 as more credits, deductions, and give-away programs have been added to manipulate the behavior of citizens. Many folks receive huge refunds, whether they pay into the system or not. Naturally, they don't understand the convoluted rules, and they want refunds in the thousands of dollars right away, so the fast money business has become a dominant part of the tax preparation business. The very people that the programs are meant to help give up hundreds of dollars to tax preparation companies to give them help and a fast turn around.

Today, the country's elected representatives, and social planners, are using the tax code as a mechanism to provide government-created vested rights to the public. It includes welfare help, housing relief, educational assistance, and health care programs. It is an unwieldy and growing monster.

The core question boils down to whether the governing class should use the tax system to manipulate the behavior of American citizens and punish those who don't fall in line with the preferences of government; or, should the tax system be an unbiased system strictly used to raise revenue to operate the government. Today, the tax system not only dips into welfare, housing, and health care, but also it is often used to influence folks in their choices such as energy use, smoking and drinking, marriage and children, and recently even buying a car or home. Dozens of tax deductions and credits are offered for special situations that the governing class has decided are in the best interest of its citizens. In reality, many taxpayers aren't aware of all the different tax programs, and many don't participate because they aren't aware of them. The system today is unfair.

Thomas Jefferson probably would not have supported the methods used in the tax system to control human behavior. He believed it was the duty of every individual to contribute to society's necessities, but explained that the people should not be burdened with oppressive taxes to support a list of civil objectives. Further, he thought it was wrong to force people to contribute money for opinions they oppose. How much simpler would tax payments be if they were simply limited to paying an equal share into the treasury? The founders established a fair system when the Constitution was written, but its Sixteenth Amendment has evolved into a cruel system.

Today the tax code is more inconsistent than ever before and growing more so with each new program from the government. The expressions on folks' faces at the tax desk when they learn they just missed a cutoff date, but their neighbor received a tax break a few days earlier is a great exhibit of an unjust system. Some folks walk into the tax office only to learn that because of a rule they were unaware of, they will be burdened with extraordinary tax debt. In most cases, these people weren't dishonest, they simply didn't know or understand the spider web of tax laws and nuances.

It is an enormous burden on senior citizens. Folks in their eighties and older are mystified and confused. They aren't able to keep up with the bookkeeping. They don't understand the maze of IRA and 401(k) rules. They can't begin to understand the annual changes of tax laws. So, they are relegated to asking for help, and in most cases say, "just take care of it for me." After they pass, the government requires one last tax return for the year of death.

Why should the common citizen be subjected to such terrors and burdens? Clearly the tax code has become one of the largest examples of legislative malfeasance that the governing class imposes on Americans.

Now, the government has decided to use the tax system to regulate health care. Actually, it already has for several years in the form of Health Savings Accounts, Flexible Spending Accounts, and Itemized Deductions. Many citizens, and probably imprudent legislators, are not aware that the tax code specifies what types of expenses are qualified for these tax advantages. The IRS code resembles a list from a health insurance company, so the government has already been deciding what type of medical treatments are "covered" under its program of tax breaks. Legislators irked the public as they argued the question of abortions during discussion on the new comprehensive health care bill, because abortion has been a qualified credit under the Health Savings Account for many years. It is covered as prenatal care, along with birth control pills and fertility enhancement treatments. So one group believes in government assistance in abortions and the other doesn't. At the same time, provisions in the new health care bill will require people to pay a "punitive" tax when using tanning beds, because artificial tanning might lead to medical problems. Abortions and tanning bed taxes are merely examples that demonstrate the efforts of a governing class to control its citizenry.

Is this really what Americans want from the tax system, or do they simply want taxes to be used to pay for defense, infrastructure, and other resources? The IRS was once compared to a secret police force with dictatorial power; now, under authority of the health care bill it will be checking individual participation in health care choices as well. Under provisions of the new health care bill, all citizens may be required to file an "informational" report, or return, with the IRS, even if they have no income or requirement to pay taxes. The informational return is to be used to prove they have health insurance in compliance with the law. It likely will lead to more traps for the common taxpayer and more oppressive situations.

After the Congress opened the door to direct taxes there has been piling on the dog pile by about every other state and local agency that can be imagined. Most states and many cities impose income taxes, and taxes on sales, real estate, personal property, phone fees, and more. Wages and salaries are reduced by federal, state, and local income taxes, and then what is left is further subjected to sales tax on virtually every purchase, on gasoline, on inheritances, and on about everything. If you don't spend the money, but save it, then the interest the savings earns is taxed, also.

Small, but heavily populated states, often have higher average tax rates than large, sparsely populated ones. With smaller size, fewer roads and public service areas to fund, intuitively it would appear that per capita taxes should be lower when expenses are spread among so many more taxpayers. The reason for their higher taxes is often the result of high welfare payments and large salaries and pension payments for government employees. Several of these states support huge populations of welfare recipients. Now these states are facing grave financial problems that may overflow onto other Americans. The ideas and examples from the federal government have spilled over into smaller governments until all are in debt and threatened by years of legislative malfeasance.

EXPLOSION OF GOVERNMENT PAY

Much of the discussion on containing government spending focuses on the colossal entitlement programs that have been created in the last seventy-five years. It's logical to examine these Ponzi-like schemes and modify them to make them as equitable as possible and to keep them within the limits of the nation's income. Sensible management is needed to reevaluate them. Naturally, many of the ideas, including limiting the benefits to lower income individuals, will not be equitable. Those who have been careful in managing their resources and saving for the future will have income from their savings and investments that the government will probably punish by reducing their benefits. Conversely, those who have recklessly spent everything and refused sensible planning for the future will have nothing and will be "rescued" by inequitable government programs filled with broken promises and deceptive rhetoric. It's like the fable of the grasshopper and the ant. The grasshopper fiddled around all day doing little, and the ant worked and saved in preparation for the turn in the weather. When the cold came, the grasshopper was left in despair. Today, the government will take part of the ant's hard work, and give it to the grasshopper because "he deserves it."

Although government statistics show the largest part of its budget is composed of Social Security and Medicare programs, in reality these programs are fully and separately funded by specific taxes into trust funds, and they have historically operated with a surplus. By definition, then, these programs do not contribute to the deficit. The true source of government debt is its size, compensation for its employees, failed programs, and non-paid-in welfare plans. When a private business experiences reduced profits it is usually necessary to evaluate spending and staffing. One of the most common problems in business is a bloated personnel roster. When business is good it is common for managers to offer little resistance to hiring new people, and the size of the operation grows under the perception that it will improve efficiency and service. A few years of this practice usually results in reduced profits, or when the economy takes a turn for the worse, then reduced profits become a glaring problem. The solution is to reduce the size of the operation, and analyze every on-going project to establish its effectiveness and profitability. The U.S. government is supposed to do this about every ten years, but the truth is that more programs are added than are cut, and the number of employees and agencies continue to increase. The point is that government should be sized according to its revenues and not to the latest rash of legislative programs. If the government were run like a business, then the number of employees (and agencies) and the size of the payroll would be limited to a percentage of actual revenue, and not unlimited in growth.

The size of government is only a fraction of the problem. Government employees receive disproportionate compensation when compared to the tax paying public. This is the result of giving the keys to the candy kitchen to the children. As a result, pay and benefits for government workers has grown disproportionately in recent years and the Cost of Living Adjustments, COLA, that accompany their pay and retirement situations are extremely excessive. When the government decided, under pressure from retirees living solely on Social Security benefits, to add COLA adjustments to Social Security recipients, COLA programs were also included as part of federal worker retirement plans.

Today, there are four different retirement arrangements available to government retirees, depending upon their dates of service. There is the Civil Service Retirement System, CSRS, plan that applies to folks hired prior to 1984. This plan was modified and replaced with the Federal Employees' Retirement System, FERS, for individuals entering service after 1983. When blended with Social Security benefits, there are various combinations to make up the four separate options. Depending upon the recipient's age at retirement and years of service, retirees under the older CSRS arrangement can expect the American people to support them for the rest of their lives by paying as much as eighty percent of their final pay.

Under the replacement FERS plan, a member of Congress with 30 years in Congress can retire at age 55 to receive forty-four percent of their pre-retirement earnings. If they elect to add the Social Security benefit, then they can receive as much as seventy percent of what they earned when they were actively working in Congress.

But it doesn't stop there, because their retirement benefit grows each year with a COLA adjustment. After a few years, government retirees (starting with eighty percent) often receive more than they earned when they stopped working.

Who in the private sector, other than some union programs, receive a retirement benefit like this? So average benefits for the Congress have grown to about $214,000 per year, which includes $174,000 salaries and $40,000 benefits. The average for non-congressional federal workers is about $70,000 compared to roughly $50,000 for private salaries. Private benefits average $9,000 for a total compensation of $50,000. When did this happen? It's the result of the same creep in hiring and increasing wages and benefits that businesses can get into with careless practices. In order to stop deficit spending, the number of government agencies, employees, and benefits need to be cut to reasonable levels. Government workers and representatives should not receive extraordinary pay and benefits at the expense of the taxpayer.

The idea of paying large salaries and benefits packages to Congress is not much different from huge salaries to officers of private companies. Legislators feign indignation at huge pay and bonus packages, and retirement plans, that corporate officers are able to arrange for themselves, while these same people are building huge programs for themselves. They appear jealous, while losing sight of their commitment to support the Constitution and represent the people.

IMMIGRATION CONTROL

With millions of illegal immigrants in the United States today it's impossible to conclude that the government has managed immigration laws carefully and responsibly. This lack of control has exposed the homeland to dangerous threats in many ways. It has contributed to successful terrorist attacks, drug smuggling, and of course, the overwhelming influx of counter cultural Mexican and South Americans that devour jobs and smother the welfare system.

How did this happen? There are many government laws to control immigration in the country, and for years there was nominal effort to enforce the rules. But many businesses wanted the cheap labor, so they pressured lawmakers to turn a blind eye to the problem while they paid minimum wages without benefits. So, for many years the government did not penalize employers, many of them agribusinesses, for violating immigration laws until now the problem has grown to unsustainable proportions. As a result, a new class and culture of people has developed that is captive to the system, or lack of a system. Many work without valid social security numbers and will undoubtedly become the next disadvantaged burden on U.S. society in the future.

It isn't just the Hispanic illegal immigrants, but also individuals from other parts of the world. As Americans learned after the attack on the World Trade Center, some of these people are not so much interested in working as they are in hurting the country and destroying its society of self-government.

Some of the current immigration laws are more faithfully enforced since the terrorist attacks of 2001. Responsible companies require new hires to fill out Form I-9, the Employment Eligibility Notification. They must verify they are U.S. Citizens or legal residents authorized to work in the country by producing a Passport, Certificate of Citizenship, Certificate of Naturalization, unexpired foreign passport, permanent resident card, employment authorization card, or reentry permit.

It is difficult to understand why all employers are not held to this standard. If Americans, born and raised in the heart of this country, who served its military, have obeyed its laws, and faithfully worked and paid taxes their entire life must show proof of citizenship, why isn't it required of all workers? Enforcement of this rule alone would be a powerful step in controlling the illegal worker problem. At the tax desk, identification is required before working on a tax return. For immigrants this means a valid green card or other form of identification, which U.S. immigration laws require them to carry. It's the law – they must carry a passport or required identification on their person at all times. Yet, illegal immigration advocates complain that it is discrimination to ask to see what the law requires; still, those who are no threat and have tried to build the country for a lifetime are required to comply.

U.S. borders today are open. It's the terrorist threat that is most troubling. They are mixed with the steady stream of lawbreakers, and they will bring trouble and destruction if left unchecked. The problem has continued for dozens of years, and our elected officials have argued about it for years. But almost none have had the courage to support existing laws at risk of losing a political career. This is a prime example of personal interest and pursuit of distinction overwhelming their obligation to the country, its safety, and its prosperity.

EDUCATION SPENDING

The United States spends more on education than ever before. Spending usually increases each year, and yet U.S. students are falling behind many other countries in educational achievement. The Department of Education is one of the newer government agencies established in 1979 and commenced operations in 1980. It employs about 5,000 federal workers adding to government payroll, benefits, and retirement plans. Its self-described purpose is to promote student achievement and global competitiveness. In view of the country's dismal educational record for the last thirty years it is difficult to conclude anything other than it is a failed program. In reality, the Department of Education probably isn't responsible for much of the degraded educational achievement, because the responsibility still remains mainly with state and local school districts. Much of the backward breakdown simply may be cultural evolution; that is, the majority of the U.S. population is disinterested in education compared to three or four generations ago. The welfare system may be the largest contributor to this demise, in combination with the relentless pursuit of leisure activities. Those on welfare have little incentive to improve, grow, or seek knowledge. The welfare lifestyle has evolved into a world of deception and complacency. It has been estimated that only five percent of the U.S. population is technologically literate. It seems the focus of American lifestyle today is on sports, movies, computer games, and recreation.

The main focus of the Department of Education has been directed at college financial aid, collecting educational data, and enforcing federal education laws. Rather than keeping college affordable, the college aid business has been a primary contributor to the extraordinary increase in college costs. It is similar to subsidized housing where individuals don't manage what is charged because there is a government program behind it. Many obtain grants and loans without regard to actual college costs. Tuition costs, teachers' pay and benefits, and campus building programs have disproportionately increased with the influx of government spending. In the last forty years the average starting salaries for new graduates have increased about five fold, while college tuition and fees are fifteen times higher or more. Major football coaches earn $2 million to $5 million and up. This is where the serious money is – and the true priority of the public.

The Pell Grants were initiated in 1965 under a bill sponsored by Senator Claiborne Pell. They are directed toward disadvantaged students based upon a financial needs formula. About six percent of today's students receive twenty percent of the money. High-priced national school networks, such as Phoenix, Everest, and Kaplan Universities top the list of recipients and have flourished as a result of the program. Unfortunately, many of the top receivers of government funds report low completion rates by their students.

Student loans also contribute to the high cost of college and drop out rates. Some students rely on them to finish school, but many others simply run up huge expenses without completing their program. All are saddled with large debts, and the colleges continue to raise rates because of the easy flow of government money.

The Department of Education does not show positive measurable results. If the program were part of a business operation, its future would be determined by comparing its effectiveness with the cost investment. Ineffective business programs and projects are routinely cut or discontinued when they are judged to be deficient in meeting their objective. It sounds like heresy to suggest that education spending be cut, but that appears to be the proper action for this wasteful and ineffective department of government. President Ronald Reagan quickly spotted this albatross in 1980 and pledged to eliminate the Department of Education, but the Congress stopped him. A financial evaluation of this department would likely show that the money saved by eliminating this department would pay for itself with little or no effect on education; in fact, it could improve college costs by stemming the flow of easy money. Serious, responsible, and dedicated students would replace those superfluously running up a debt that will never be repaid. The rest would be up to responsible parents and citizens to demonstrate a love for education and individual growth through a lifetime of learning.

GOVERNMENT SPONSORED BROADCASTING

Why is the government involved in broadcasting? There have been educational networks for decades, but where does the Constitution allow government funds to be expended on programming? The Corporation for Public Broadcasting was established by act of Congress in 1967 during the third great period of government expansion since 1900. Its lofty goals include strict adherence to objectivity and balance, but like any human endeavor there have been problems. There have been public radio programs that have assaulted certain religious beliefs, and political commentary that has been anything but balanced at times. Who decides objectivity and balance? The right to broadcast commentary and opinions is a guaranteed freedom, but not with support of the government treasury. Thomas Jefferson described the fundamental morality of the Constitution when he wrote, that it is sinful to force individuals to pay to support activities they believe are wrong. Isn't this what government sponsored broadcasting does? Americans have listened to or seen numerous opinion pieces they disagree with, but which have been sponsored with a portion of their tax dollars. It's appropriate for broadcasters to voice their opinions, but at network expense, not taxpayers'.

Both National Public Radio and the Public Broadcasting Service receive government funding through the Corporation for Public Broadcasting. Presumably they operate without airing commercials. Of course, as expenses grow the corporation has resorted to spot commercials. Really, there's not much difference in these commercials and those seen in private broadcasting. They just provide the commercials at the beginning and end of each program and present the program as being made by possible by contributions from the sponsors. The Congress appropriates roughly $422 million of tax dollars for the Corporation for Public Broadcasting. Getting out of the broadcasting business is the only way for the government to eliminate abuses, such as controversial commentary and opinions. Objectivity goes against human nature, and builds upon the idea of a governing class that understands everything better and knows best for the rest of the country. All public funding for these broadcasters should be removed. If they are able to survive on their own source of funds, so much the better for another voice in the great American debate. If not, it's the natural course.

GOVERNMENT SPONSORED HEALTH CARE

The idea of a national health care system has been discussed many times, but usually public opinion and the Constitution have prevailed. Recently, though, a colossal bill was passed without the complete understanding of the members of the House and Senate, and without the support of most of the American citizenry. The government has been in the health care business in various forms for many years. It has used the tax code where deductions for medical expenses have been allowed for decades, as long as the procedures and medications are on the "approved list" provided by the government and enforced by the Internal Revenue Service. In more recent years, the government has added patches in the form of tax deductions and credits, such as the Flexible Spending Accounts and Health Savings Accounts.

Now, the government has authorized a program with thousands of pages of unknown content. The bill was not created by Congressmen or their staffs, but by an independent group. There's nothing wrong with someone else creating the bill. The Constitution allows any private citizen to create a bill or amendment to the Constitution to be introduced in Congress; it's one of the wonderful rights of self-government the founders set up. The problem, though, is that the bill was passed in a rush without a proper review by the members of Congress to understand and digest the provisions of the bill. It was a terrible mistake of hasty legislation that Alexander Hamilton warned against. He thought prompt decision, without deliberation, circumvents full consideration necessary to check the excesses of the majority. In the common words of today, there's never enough time to do the job right, but always enough time to do it over.

And so the Congress has blasted headlong into a program with unknown costs and implications. Two versions of the bill are cited, but when pressed, the people in Congress have admitted that they have not read the bill, much less assimilated its effects and consequences. So whom can you believe? None is reliable and informed. In addition, now tax enforcement, that is, the Internal Revenue Service, will need more than 16,000 more agents to insure compliance, because the tax code is further complicated, and it encumbers the average citizen with more regulation of every day life. To add insult to injury, within six months of passage of the health care bill many privileged groups are receiving waivers to avoid participation in the health care program. How fair is that? It just exhibits and adds to the inequality of all government programs on the list of failures.

Within months the constitutionality of the entire program was challenged by various states. Ultimately it was upheld by the Supreme Court as one more example of the abusive use of the income tax system to herd Americans into their proper positions according to the ideas of central city bureaucrats The creators of the Constitution would have little doubt about it, and would find it an awful situation. The expansionists, of course, believe it to be a great social program that is the job of the government. Regardless of personal opinion regarding the program, the mess has been created via rapid and imprudent legislative malfeasance.

The list of government failures includes much more, but these are representative of wasteful and expensive plans that do little more than increase the size of the federal employment roll. Some folks may disagree with the list, and that is part of the great dialog. The list shows how the government has grown by adding program upon program that ultimately causes more problems for the economy and people than they help, and it exposes the three great expansions of government into society. These great expansions have left Americans with a Congress and Executive branch that judge their contribution to society by the quantity of legislation enacted, rather than by responsible management of the treasury.

CHAPTER SIX

OUR MUTUAL CONTRACT

THE UNITED STATES CONSTITUTION is the American agreement with one another to grant authority to the federal government to provide national defense, to fairly regulate commerce, and to install a system of courts to enforce laws. It is a free system of self-government through public opinion. This discussion of its provisions includes a brief background of its origins and a comparison of alternative ideals for government.

Thomas Hobbes, the early political philosopher, wrote that the theory of government is based upon three root forms of government: dictatorship, monarchy, and self-rule. He said all other forms of governments are merely variants of these three basic forms. A brief description of the theory of government will be based upon three prominent forms of government that are practiced today. This includes a democratic republic, where representatives are freely elected by the people; communism, where all citizens share equal statutory rights through service to the state; and centralized democracy, where elected rulers decide the degree of equality for all.

The American Constitution was born during an uplifting period of science and philosophy that is often referred to as the Era of Enlightenment. This era of new studies of philosophy and government lasted about one hundred fifty years when philosophers from different countries exchanged opinions and ideas on government. The American founders lived during this period and were active participants in the dialog. Ideas were bandied about, such as the political authority of public opinion, free speech, free religion, free markets, free assembly, the separation of powers, and equal rights for women and all races.

James Madison, often called the Father of the Constitution, studied and absorbed virtually all of the ancient and current writings of his time. Eventually he and the other founders of the country distilled the ideas to a government based upon self-government through public opinion refined by communication. In their plan, the power of the majority would be balanced to respect the freedom of the minority. The entire system would be based upon a common law jury system bound up in a Constitution serving as supreme law.

About fifty years after the Era of Enlightenment, the Communism ideal developed into a competing form of government organization. Communism founders envisioned a classless, stateless society with limits on citizens. Ownership of property would not be permitted, and there would be no inheritance or protection of the family unit. A progressive income tax would be used, and the state would run education and all production. Russian variants called for the elimination of factions; the minority must totally comply with the dictates of the majority. Chinese communist philosophy reinforced elimination of minority rights by its intolerance for free speech.

Centralized democracy, sometimes called social democracy, has developed for many years, and some Americans believe the United States has transitioned to this form of government. The ideal of this type of government is that government provides security for everything and relief from life's responsibilities. In order to achieve this, the people elect a central governing class and give it authority to control communication, transportation, education, the economy, and the degree of taxation and how it will be distributed. It is a government by the rule of bureaucratic boards, as opposed to the rule of common law by a self-governing people.

THEORY OF GOVERNMENT

There are many ideas about government and different theories on how it should work. Of course there are the monarchies and dictatorships that have been dominate forms of government throughout the ages. People have chosen kings, queens, and dictators, or had them imposed upon them, for as long as there have been historical records. Even today it is not uncommon to see a people revolt against its government in search of freedom or a new government. Unfortunately, after a successful revolt the leader of the cause often assumes power and will not relinquish it. The leader imposes personal ideals and beliefs upon the people, and citizens may be jailed, or worse, for their disagreements with the dictator. In many cases this may include religious beliefs for the country.

In addition to monarchies and dictatorships, there is the idea of government by the people. There are three prevailing ideas in various forms;

these are the democratic republic, communism, and centralized democracy.

The United States government is usually referred to as a democratic republic, or just a republic. It is based upon the profound idea that it is a natural right of people to govern themselves. As soon as an individual is born, each has rights established by nature. As surely as animals are born in the wild they are born with a right to freedom to live as they choose, where they want, to bring forth offspring, and to roam freely in their habitat. This is generally the way of nature except where man interferes with its freedom. These are the unalienable rights all mankind receives at birth, as opposed to vested rights, which are the revocable statutory rights granted by governments

The simplest form of self-government is a democracy where the people vote for each law and provision of government; the majority rules the decision. The minority must comply with the laws established by many. There are two limitations of a pure democracy that are often described. First, in a pure democracy the majority can become tyrannical and impose ideals and a difficult way of life on the minority, and, in effect, the democracy can become a sort of dictatorship. It has been said that hundreds of tyrants can be as repressive and cruel as a single dictator. The second limitation has to do with the number of people and the size of the territory that is governed. Imagine today if it were required that all Americans must vote on each element of legislation. Time for communication would be a problem, although today's technology makes fast communication possible, but even so, many people are not tuned in to radio, television, or the Internet. In addition, the physical size of the country is so large, spanning many time zones, that it further complicates the idea of all people voting on all issues.

Philosophers and students traded new ideas for government during a period of time often referred to as the Era of Enlightenment. The founding fathers and the creators of the U.S. Constitution participated in these discussions, and a modification of the idea of a pure democracy was developed. It addressed the democratic idea of all people voting on a subject by suggesting that representatives be elected by the people to represent their ideas and vote on their behalf. In addition, a balance of power was proposed where their elected officials could represent both the majority and the minority. Many governments since antiquity, from the Romans and Greeks, to the English Parliament, had tried these ideas in various forms, which evolved into the form of a democratic republic.

New ideas developed in the middle 1800s that were focused on the ideal of equality of vested rights among all people. Referred to by Karl Marx and Friedrich Engels as Communism, this philosophy is based upon the history of mankind as a clash of oppressed people versus oppressing people. It was their idea that this struggle between these two classes could eventually transform into a pure state of communism where there are no classes or state controls. In pure communism individuals must subjugate themselves to the good of the community at large. In this respect there are no unalienable rights for each individual; rather, all are given vested rights by the community so all may live equally. Marx and Engels believed the pure communist condition would progress through stages following the decline of capitalism and a transitory period of socialism where government is controlled by the working class of people.

A third type of government is more or less a blend of a republic and communism. It is often called centralized democracy, and many of the leaders today are inclined toward this form of government. In this form of government the idea of equality of all people remains; but, instead of self-government, an elite group of philosophers, educators and intellectuals, and political leaders decide the laws. In addition, this governing class decides what is equality for all. They award vested rights to those they decide deserve them. The crucial tradeoff in this form of government is security for people from birth to death in exchange for a reduction in unalienable freedoms. It is a seductive idea where the government will provide a job, food, clothing, housing, and medical care to all citizens during their lives. Everyone pitches in their earnings to be divided among the population according the decisions of the governing class.

It is both interesting and informative to take a closer look at how these three basic forms developed. The American government began to take shape during the Era of Enlightenment.

ERA OF ENLIGHTENMENT

The Era of Enlightenment is generally considered to have started in the late 1600s continuing through the 1700s. It involved writings and dialog from students of government in Europe and the American Colonies. Figure 6-1 shows a chronology of the lives of many of the participants. The figure displays their life lines and their prominent publications. Individuals from England, Scotland, France, Germany, and several other countries offered new ideas and commentary. It is not commonly considered to be a single movement or idea, because many of the concepts and theories are often contradictory. Instead, many of the participants in the grand dialog thought it was a liberation of the human mind from the authoritative doctrine of the day, and offered an opportunity for open discussion without secrecy.

Books on the subject suppose the dialog was a result of more reading activity. There were more book owners and more libraries than ever before in history. After about 1750 reading began to spread, which led to open discussions of philosophy, science, and politics among the public. In reality, the idea of public discussion was likely somewhat exclusive; that is, the access to books and libraries was probably restricted to elite scholars and those of some wealth. Nevertheless, it was a thrilling period of enlightenment that America's founders participated in, and it deeply affected their views of government and freedom.

The figures from the Era of Enlightenment offered new ideas that built upon the ancient principles of government described by the histories of the ancient Israelites, the Anglo-Saxons, Greeks, Romans, and the newer British Parliament. The creators of the U.S. Constitution were enthusiastic students of these early forms of government and relished the exchange of ideas with European theorists concerning the ideal form of government. The U.S. Constitution today is the result of these studies and dialog, and it is interesting, if not essential, to trace the origins of the ideas of the founding fathers and the evolution of American government.

Much of the early thought evolved from the ancient principles of government used by ancient Israelites and the Anglo-Saxons. Thomas Jefferson used the term, "ancient principles," early in his discussions of government. He discovered these principles during his early studies of Israelite society, and later noticed a close similarity of these ancient principles adopted by the Anglo-Saxons. Mr. Jefferson embraced these ideas and thought a return to these ideas for civilization was the right path for America. He adopted many of these principles in his wording of the Declaration of Independence. He starts with the main idea that all humans are born under the sacred truth that each has unalienable rights to life, to liberty, and to pursue happiness in their own way of choosing. The principles of government adopted by these early governments include the idea that no government, office, or agency has the right to exist without the consent of the free people and their representatives. Also, in the event of malfeasance or neglect by the government, such as its failure to protect individual rights, it is forever the right of a free people to regain control of its affairs and establish a form of government to serve them better.

Other government ideas from Greek and Roman societies were passionately studied during the Era of Enlightenment. Polybius was a Greek historian that offered ideas of political balance during the period about one hundred fifty years BC. He believed statesmen must be virtuous, and his ideas appealed to Marcus Tullius Cicero, the Roman philosopher, who built upon them with his ideas of statesmanship. Both of these men inspired the dialog of enlightenment, the American founding fathers, and the French Revolution. John Adams admired Cicero as a great statesman that fired his passion for freedom. Remarkably, Friedrich Engels, one of the founders of communism, despised the ideas of Cicero because Engels thought Cicero upheld the idea of republican democracy while forsaking class reform and the abolishment of land ownership.

The British form of government that operated during the Era of Enlightenment was generally admired by many of the idealists in their

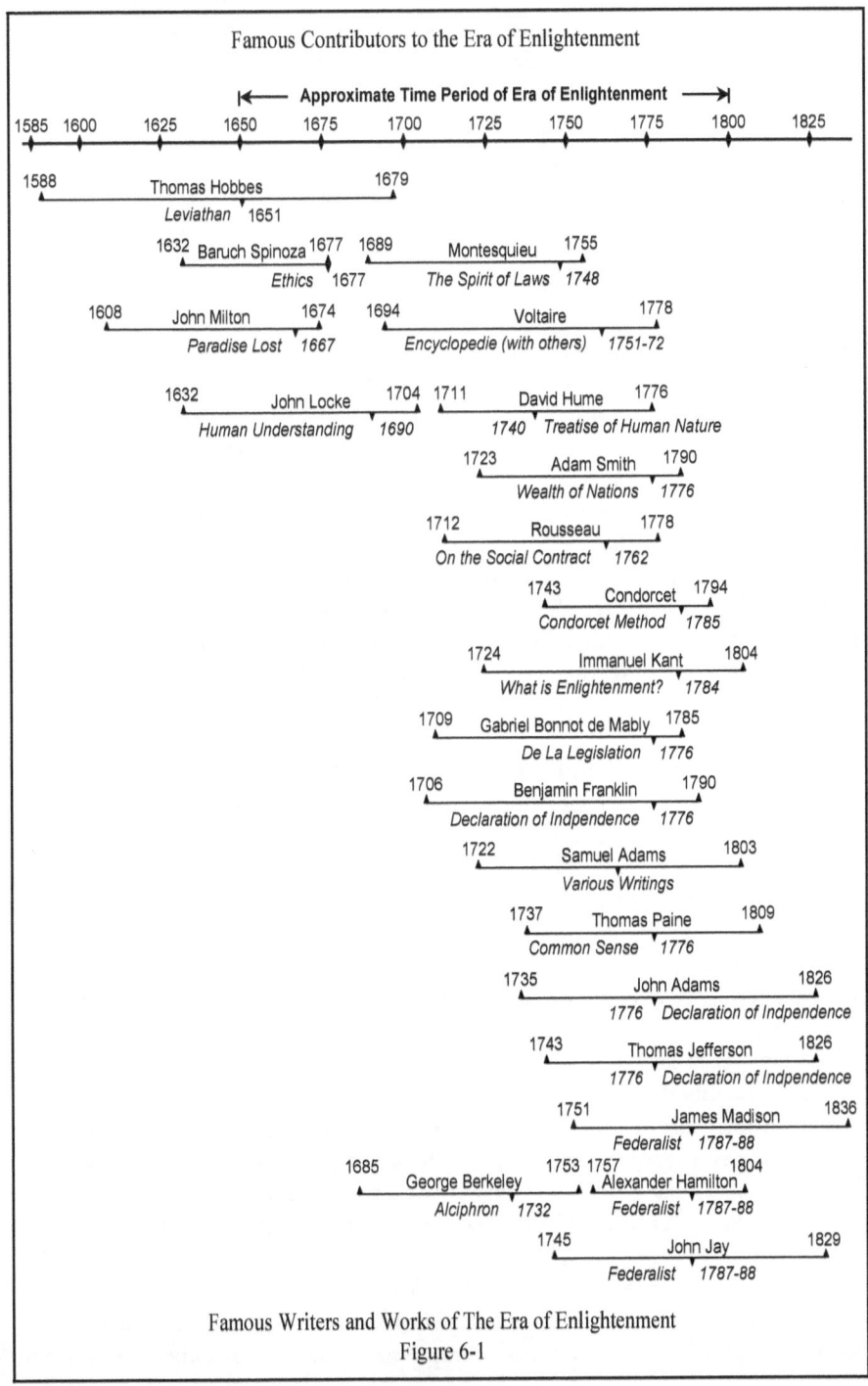

Famous Contributors to the Era of Enlightenment

Approximate Time Period of Era of Enlightenment

| 1585 | 1600 | 1625 | 1650 | 1675 | 1700 | 1725 | 1750 | 1775 | 1800 | 1825 |

1588 — Thomas Hobbes — 1679
Leviathan 1651

1632 — Baruch Spinoza — 1677 | 1689 — Montesquieu — 1755
Ethics 1677 | *The Spirit of Laws* 1748

1608 — John Milton — 1674 | 1694 — Voltaire — 1778
Paradise Lost 1667 | *Encyclopedie (with others)* 1751-72

1632 — John Locke — 1704 | 1711 — David Hume — 1776
Human Understanding 1690 | 1740 *Treatise of Human Nature*

1723 — Adam Smith — 1790
Wealth of Nations 1776

1712 — Rousseau — 1778
On the Social Contract 1762

1743 — Condorcet — 1794
Condorcet Method 1785

1724 — Immanuel Kant — 1804
What is Enlightenment? 1784

1709 — Gabriel Bonnot de Mably — 1785
De La Legislation 1776

1706 — Benjamin Franklin — 1790
Declaration of Indpendence 1776

1722 — Samuel Adams — 1803
Various Writings

1737 — Thomas Paine — 1809
Common Sense 1776

1735 — John Adams — 1826
1776 *Declaration of Indpendence*

1743 — Thomas Jefferson — 1826
1776 *Declaration of Indpendence*

1751 — James Madison — 1836
Federalist 1787-88

1685 — George Berkeley — 1753 | 1757 — Alexander Hamilton — 1804
Alciphron 1732 | *Federalist* 1787-88

1745 — John Jay — 1829
Federalist 1787-88

Famous Writers and Works of The Era of Enlightenment
Figure 6-1

discussions, including many of the American Colonialists. The British government consisted of three branches at that time: the monarchy, aristocracy, and democracy. This form of government was admired for its admission of representation of the people in the Parliament. The king functioned more or less as a permanent executive that, of course, inherited his authority from his birthright. The House of Lords was made up of appointments established by the king, and so long as each member did not displease the king, then he could retain his lofty position and often was able to pass on the position to his heirs as well. The House of Commons was composed of elected representatives of the people and was generally regarded as the most liberal idea of government in existence at that time. Of course, the American Colonies fell under the authority of this government, except they were not allowed representation in the House of Commons.

A good starting point for a review of political ideas during the Era of Enlightenment is the early writing of the English philosopher, Thomas Hobbes. His masterpiece, *Leviathan*, published about 1651, was an influential example of social contracts among people. He believed there were only three types of commonwealth, or government, namely a monarchy, aristocracy, or a democracy. He said all other forms of government are merely variants of the three forms he identified. When there is one person in power, he said, it is a monarchy. If an assembly of restricted membership is in charge, that is, every citizen is not eligible to be admitted to the assembly, then it is an aristocracy. Finally, if an assembly of unrestricted membership holds power, then it is a democracy.

It is interesting to note that Hobbes rejected the idea of separation of powers, such as the U.S. Constitution implements, and he favored censorship of the press and restriction of rights to free speech. He believed this was necessary to promote order. Thomas Hobbes believed monarchy to be the best form of government, because a monarch has a better aptitude for peace and security of the people.

Other political ideas from Hobbes included ideas on taxes and welfare. He believed in an equality of taxes that are not based on an equality of wealth, but on an equality of debt that each citizen owes for defense and maintenance of the law. At the same time, he favored a means of support for those citizens that were unable to take care of themselves.

In his discussions of human behavior, Thomas Hobbes warned about the human nature of politics. He referred to a kingdom of darkness, which was his label for secret groups working to deceive the public in order to obtain authority over all citizens. He warned that passion is usually more potent than reason.

Following Hobbes a few years later came writings from the Englishmen John Milton and John Locke. John Milton not only wrote the brilliant epic poem, *Paradise Lost*, but he wrote essays against the state-dominated church.

Milton was committed to republicanism, and favored government by an exclusive educated few in the cause of liberty.

John Locke is often identified as the father of classical liberalism. He wrote in support of his belief in the separation of the church and state, and the idea of the human right to hold private property. Locke's idea was that property precedes the government, so government cannot arbitrarily dispose of estates or seize property. Some two hundred years later, Karl Marx would disagree with this idea in his communist philosophy.

John Locke thought that a group of people could consent to be governed by surrendering certain natural freedoms in exchange for order and protection of the state according to the rule of law. He also warned that any government that rules without the consent of the people could be overthrown.

The American revolutionaries, and the Frenchman Voltaire, were heavily influenced by the ideas of John Locke. Many of John Locke's ideas can be found in the Declaration of Independence. Also, the later writings on freedom and republican government by Thomas Jefferson, James Madison, and Alexander Hamilton show the strong influence of John Locke on their ideas.

The great dialog on government included Scottish and Anglo-Irish authors. George Berkeley, an Anglo-Irish thinker, entered the early conversation and influenced David Hume, a Scottish philosopher, and Immanuel Kant, the German philosopher. Berkeley challenged the truth of mathematics in philosophy as a creation of the finite mind of man. He believed only the mind of God is infinite.

Adam Smith and David Hume were Scottish philosophers and early economists. David Hume believed true knowledge comes from evidence gathered by experience of the senses; he meant, ideas of philosophical thinking are creations of the mind and are not necessarily true or as true as actual experience. Immanuel Kant said this idea from Hume woke him from his acceptance of doctrine as absolutely true regardless of the evidence.

David Hume offered observations on the factions that develop among people. He thought the nature of man is the cause of faction that can be seen everywhere in different degrees according to the circumstances of society, and the most common cause of factions is the unequal distribution of property among society. His ideas on how to handle factions influenced James Madison in the design of the Constitution and can be seen reflected in Madison's writings in the tenth *Federalist* paper. Part of Hume's idea for equalizing factions was the idea of the separation of powers and to decentralize government.

Adam Smith is often called the father of economics and capitalism. He wrote the masterpiece of economic theory in 1776 titled, *An Inquiry into the Nature and Causes of the Wealth of Nations*. In this book, commonly referred to simply as *The Wealth of Nations*, Smith identifies the self-regulating nature of the marketplace as an important economic concept. He believed markets would always ebb and grow according to the laws of supply and demand and the productivity of the society. It follows from this idea that regulation attempts by a government usually results in false priorities and wildly exaggerated swings of the economy. He thought proper government expense should be limited to enforcement of contracts, to provide a justice system and national defense, to regulate banking, and to provide public goods, such as infrastructure. Smith saw public goods as items of such nature that profit could never repay the expense for their construction, such as roads, bridges, and harbors.

Adam Smith explained that in the capitalist society the individual may have a selfish motive for profit and riches, but the use of domestic industry and labor to achieve such goals also promotes the interest of society as a whole. In other words, the innovation and accomplishments of a capitalist endeavor also improves the social standing of the workers and society as well. In support of this idea, Smith believed in a progressive tax where the rich should contribute to public expenses in proportion to revenue. He looked at taxes as a badge of liberty, that tax laws should be transparent, and each individual should pay a certain, not arbitrary, amount.

Several French students of government participated in the great dialog during the Era of Enlightenment, and they had a great impact on the developing ideas of the creators of the American Constitution and ideas of liberty. In general the French authors submitted the idea that public opinion should be the political authority and is the basis of a stable government. James Madison and other contributors forming the Constitution recognized this important idea, and built the Constitution upon this principle of self-government of the people.

One of the earlier French theorists was Gabriel Bonnet de Mably. Written in the 1700s, his works contributed to development of both communism and republicanism ideas. He believed private property should be abolished, which became a primary idea of the communist movement, and he praised the ideas of Plato and his concepts of elitist control.

Mably also discussed the ideas of factions and differing opinions among the people. He recognized that individuals would be led to different opinions because of their differing interests, experiences, and passions. James Madison agreed with Mably's observations concerning human factions, and he tried to account for it in his ideas of equal government by the people by establishing a system of checks and balances.

Francois Arouet was the French author that was known by the penname, Voltaire. Ben Franklin was friends with Voltaire and undoubtedly exchanged ideas about freedom and self-government with him. Voltaire believed in classical liberalism, which at that time meant a belief in limited government and individual liberty, such as freedom of religion, speech, assembly, and free markets. Voltaire built on the economic considerations of Adam Smith. He sustained the ideas of free trade and religious freedom.

Jean-Jacque Rousseau, was born in the city-state of Geneva and also resided in France during part of his lifetime. Rousseau built upon the idea of classical republicanism and a social contract among the people. He declared that man is born free, but is chained in the world because one individual thinks of himself as the master of others. Although we are in competition with one another, he thought, we are also dependent on government to enforce the general will of all.

Rousseau believed the republican form of government could only work in small communities with small populations and small territorial size. He thought limited communication, among other factors, in a large society occupying a large area would make the republic ideal nearly impossible, so he favored city-states, such as the early Greek establishments and his own home city-state of Geneva. In fact, he thought the size of France itself was too big to have a republic. America's John Adams enjoyed the ideas of Rousseau, but he disagreed with the French author's belief that people are what the government makes of them. Instead, Adams thought government should be what the people make out of it. Thus was Adams' purpose of leadership and heritage of American liberty.

Baron de La Brede et de Montesquieu was known to early colonial leaders and referred to simply as Montesquieu. His ideas for a republic were extremely influential upon forming American ancestors' ideas of government and their development of the mechanics of the new Constitution. Montesquieu proposed the idea of two types of power: sovereign and administrative. He believed government should be set up so no man need fear another, so he favored the use of administrative power, composed of executive and legislative authority in combination with a separate and independent judicial authority. It was a radical idea that challenged the feudalistic structure that dominated Europe up to that time. Based upon this idea of administrative power, Montesquieu viewed government as a political arrangement based on rule of law. This idea left out the concept of public opinion as a consideration of government.

Montesquieu divided French society of the day into three classes: the monarchy, aristocracy, and common people. It is an interesting comparison to the British government of the time. He agreed with the idea of separation of governmental powers, and wrote against the idea of slavery. Many of these ideas and theories found their way into the hearts and minds of America's thinkers and leaders.

American leaders also followed the published ideas of the Marquis de Condorcet. Not only did he present concepts of liberty and morality, but also Condorcet had a leading role in the French Revolution in 1789. He believed in a liberal and free economy and free and equal education. In addition,

Condorcet saw freedom as equal rights for women and people of all races. His idea for these liberties was framed upon the contract of a constitution; he meant that a constitution would be the agreement among the people for establishing a free and liberal society. In his publication, *Idea of Progress* he presented his idea that expanding knowledge results in the justice of freedom, material affluence, and moral compassion. In other words, an educated public is best equipped to support freedom and prosper in society, as opposed to an ignorant society that is controlled by the elite few.

James Madison adopted Condorcet's comparison of public opinion with popular opinion as the nucleus of his plan for a constitutional government. Condorcet thought public opinion was the enlightened view of the public after discussion and consideration of differing ideas, while popular opinion is the short-term opinion of the most uninformed and miserable part of the public. He thought government should not relent to these short-term, popular ideas, but must follow the informed ideas of an educated public. James Madison would use this idea in his concept of self-government, the changing ideals of society, and the role of government in updating itself according to the ultimate rationale of public opinion.

During this wonderful period of exchanges of ideas the marvelous German philosopher Immanuel Kant offered his ideas for government, too. He believed a constitutional republic was the only way to end wars and create lasting peace in the world. Kant opposed the idea of a direct democracy, that is, a government where the people decide all issues directly through their votes. He thought this form of government would result in a form of dictatorship, because it would be a situation where all, who are really not quite everyone, would decide. Kant agreed with Hobbes' idea that there are three forms of government, monarchy, aristocracy, and democracy, but he felt a mixed form of these three types would result in the most ideal government.

These are just a few of the many European contributors to the grand dialog during the Era of Enlightenment, but these names are the ones frequently referred to in the writings of the founding fathers. Unforgettably, the early American leaders were right in the thick of the discussion, absorbing ideas of liberty and government and adding their own. America's list of contributors is long. At risk of leaving out great Americans without an exhaustive review, following are some of the early contributors to American ideas.

The Adams cousins, Samuel and John were consumed by the desire for freedom and self-government. Samuel Adams spurred the movement to split from the authority of Great Britain. He recognized that liberty is the gift from the Creator and it is placed on the heart of man by God. It is the crux of the idea that all men are created with equal unalienable rights.

Samuel Adams despised the rule of England, because he felt the British government took much without leaving a man to his own devices and the fruits of his labor. He thought the British tax not only attacked property but also the industriousness of people. It discouraged the will to get ahead, because he believed unfair taxes removed an individual's right to keep the results of his personal ambition and hard work, and to freely give according to his own wishes. None of this, Adams believed, should be taken from a citizen without individual consent.

The ideas of true freedom that Samuel Adams teaches is that rulers, or government should have little and the people should have much. There should be no inheritances or privileges for government servants. The government should promote an open world for genius and industry. This is the heritage of America, not the idea that government controls public genius.

John Adams and Samuel Adams spent many evenings discussing freedom and government. They served together in the early Continental Conventions of the Revolutionary War period. John would continue to serve with George Washington and later become the second U.S. president. Even today, his ideas fire the imagination and the passion for freedom, but much of what he wrote concerning the mechanics and pitfalls of a constitutional republic reveal the depth of understanding of human nature and politics that the founders possessed.

John Adams agreed with the idea that all men have equal rights under the laws of nature. But he also recognized that inequalities among men are inevitable. All humans are born with different abilities and interests, and live in different environments that provide different opportunities. Adams believed these inequalities in society would forever exist regardless of the form of government. He recognized that human beings were capable of both great good and great evil; it was a fact of history in his time that has been further confirmed since.

No person could be elevated above another without risk, Adams thought, and this led him to believe that a perfect legislature should be composed of a membership like a miniature example of the make up of the country. But he knew the power of this assembly must be checked to prevent tyranny and partiality of prejudice.

Adams warned of the human weaknesses of individuals elected to office, and he said to be ever vigilant of their activities. He wrote about the natural passion for distinction in all men and women. All people have this inherent desire to be approved and respected, and this can lead to official service for personal gain rather than representative service of the people. Most elected officials today appear more interested in their personal careers and distinction, rather than the desire to represent their constituents and to protect the Constitution according to the oath of office they have taken.

America's Constitution is a plain and direct document that establishes the limits of government and freedom beyond boundaries. This is a direct result of the ideas of the creators that is reflected in letters of John Adams. He told his fellow constitutionalists that government should be plain, reasonable, and easy to understand by common sense. When considering the voluminous acts and governmental regulations Americans live under today, it appears the focus on simple government and the ideas of this great thinker have been lost.

Both John Adams and Thomas Jefferson were great students of government theory and the philosophy of life. They were great friends, often with differing ideas, that corresponded through much of their lives. Jefferson studied the ideas of government from the earliest ancient theories and the ideas formulated during the Era of Enlightenment. He acknowledged that the Declaration of Independence was not an idea of new principles never before thought of. These ideas came from ideas he adopted from other writings. He thought it was meant to express the American mind of his time.

Jefferson not only studied current and historical ideas on government, but he spent two years studying Virginia laws to examine their effectiveness and further prepare himself for participation in the great debate of government form and function. Jefferson was the grand defender of self-government by the people given to them by the hand of nature that created mankind with a free mind. He believed common citizens were capable of understanding their rights and maintaining them, and he was firmly against any form of centralized government. He felt that a group of elitists would be just as oppressive as one dictator. But he also understood that it was unnecessary to expect each citizen to be qualified in every facet of government administration. He knew that each citizen would not be qualified to run the executive department or to write legislation, nor to judge a question of law. But he said in a government of the people, each citizen is qualified to choose the executive and legislators and to judge questions of fact in the form of juries. From these matters of fact decided by juries of the people, permanent judges could decide the law.

Thomas Jefferson fervently believed in a frugal and simple government. He warned against the increase in the numbers of public offices that can quickly increase beyond income. The purpose of government, in Jefferson's written thoughts, was to enforce the public's natural rights and take none away.

Jefferson believed in the right to own property. He thought all individuals should be entitled to the free exercise of their personal efforts and to the rewards of their efforts. Mr. Jefferson thought it was a violation of this original principle of nature to take from someone because the government thinks individuals, or their ancestors, have acquired too much, in order to spare others who are less successful or ambitious. These ideas followed from his belief in free enterprise. Jefferson believed there are four corners in the foundation of national prosperity: agriculture, manufactures, commerce, and navigation. He thought the conditions needed for prosperity should come from the freedom of citizens to manage their own affairs in their own way through their own skill and industriousness, and he cautioned against oppressive regulations and fiscal restraints of business.

It was Jefferson's belief that there are two basic differences on the idea of government. One group fears and distrusts the people and wants to take all power from them and give it to the higher or elite classes for sensible administration. The second group has confidence in the people as the most honest and safe method to preserve freedom. He taught that these two factions exist in every country, and where the people are free to speak and write, their differences will become obvious. The preferred method of handling factions, he thought, was to follow the will of the majority tempered with balances. He knew the majority may be wrong at times, but he had faith that they would be honest errors and would correct themselves in time. The philosophical balance of the power of the majority would depend upon a rightful and reasonable understanding that the minority have equal rights, too. Oppression results when the balance of rights is violated.

James Madison put it all together when he prepared the draft of the Constitution for consideration by the Continental Congress. Thomas Jefferson and John Adams were both in Europe when the Constitution was submitted for consideration. They wrote to America with their ideas and opinions, but it was a slow process, because it took about six weeks for a message to travel one way across the ocean in those days. Nevertheless, Jefferson sent shipments of books about government to Madison for his study and consideration when drafting the National Contract. These books covered ideas from the ancient authors and their ideas of government, to authors of the Era of Enlightenment. Madison poured over these books and ideas and made dozens of notes for reference in preparing the American Constitution. He put his own thoughts into many of the theoretical problems, and made an enormous effort to make the most of the great opportunity to start a government anew. Like many other founders of the country, he was a good man seeking to do good works for no personal gain.

James Madison condensed the idea of self-government into four basic ideas: the right to self-government, self-government by public opinion, refined public opinion through communication, and a balance of power to protect both the majority and minority. He started with the idea that people are members of the free community of mankind before they are members of a civil society. He believed that not even a majority has the right to dictate a person's belief, or disbelief, in God or nature. From this central idea he would build on methods to deal with factions and the majority.

Madison accepted the idea of most philosophers that differences of opinions will always exist and cannot be eliminated. Factions, he agreed, are the result of human nature and its ability to reason. People who are free to speak will form different opinions, which are the result of their interests and life experiences. So Madison relied on public opinion as the answer to balancing factions and the differences in the majority and minority. He believed communication was the method to temper the factional differences. Through free and efficient communication Madison was convinced that public opinion would always seek the stable and honest disposition of disputes.

Madison differed with Rousseau that a republic must be small, with a small population, such as a city-state. Madison thought small, free states could coexist under a federation through swift and free communication and public discourse. This is probably a contributing factor to establishing the Postal Service and Roads in the Constitution. The mail was the primary means of long distance communication during this era, and good roads and free waterways, and an efficient delivery system, were essential elements of a healthy republic of independent states.

The entire idea of following public opinion for the common good and protection of the minority was based upon communication and implementation of the idea of checks and balances. All founders knew this was essential, and it would ultimately result in the system used today for dialog, representation, and administration of the public's desires and freedoms.

AMERICAN CONTRACT – RIGHT TO SELF-GOVERN

America's system of government is based upon the idea that the only type of government that can be true to nature itself is a system of self-government. The founders accepted the philosophical idea that all humans are born with the equal and irrevocable right to live their lives in the manner they choose. This is the idea of the Declaration of Independence that affirmed, "all men are created equal." They recognized that there are different orders of men and women, all with different physical, mental, and spiritual attributes, and all with different opportunities based upon their environments. Still, all people are born with the right to their thoughts, the right to their conscience, and the right to live life their way; furthermore, each has the unalienable right to self govern, which can never be revoked by government, because it is a law of nature. If the people agree to confer statutory rights to citizens, such as food, housing, and an economic safety net, then it is the right of the people, not the government, to provide for this, but the people may revoke these statutory rights, because the people conferred them. These rights are far different from the irrevocable rights of nature.

With this fundamental idea established the founders began the discussion on the purpose of government. The original intent for a federal government was protection from other nations, preventing injury by one another, and to insure equal protection under common law for all. When the country was first established, many of the state borders were shared with other countries, and the citizens of this period feared intrusion or invasion by foreign countries. As a result, they saw the advantage of a federation of states that could be called upon to protect one another in the event of foreign difficulties. In fact, it is likely that most early Americans viewed the role of the federal government as primarily dealing with foreign concerns.

So the creators of the Constitution knew they must resort to some form of government to secure natural rights, but they also recognized that government could be a dangerous thing if it wrests control of people's lives from them. This led them to developing a Constitution intended to limit government intervention into the lives of individuals. Their idea was to prevent force, fraud, monopoly, and public indecency. Restraint of criminal activity by force, of course, was considered an important role of the government. Fraud and deceptive practices in the market place should be controlled by public laws. Destruction of free trade through monopolies, whether by large corporations or organized groups, would be a legitimate responsibility conferred upon the government. Finally, protection against public indecency could be subject to government laws. All of these duties are subject to changing ideas of society and to the rule of prevailing public opinion. The creators recognized this and left the people with the self-governing power to amend their Constitution.

AMERICAN CONTRACT – RULE OF PUBLIC OPINION

All people can never agree. It's simply the result of natural selection, environmental influences, and diverse interests of human beings. As people discuss their ideas and differences there are usually majority and minority opinions. Usually, though, most issues aren't as simple as majority and minority, they are usually clouded with many gray areas. When the outlooks of all citizens are considered, the picture might look something like the standard statistical distribution. (See Figure 3-1) There will be small groups that strongly favor or oppose a position, but the rest of the population likely will be scattered somewhere in the middle. Eventually people may splinter into factions created by their different passions. Many political philosophers recognized that a majority faction could be just as oppressive as a single dictator. There is evidence of this in the history of governments ruled by the church. The original founders wrestled with this idea and how to mediate its effects.

James Madison introduced into the Constitution the ideas of many philosophers during the Era of Enlightenment that public opinion itself tends to resolve itself to the right and fair solution. The government, then, should be tied to public opinion. This idea of government by public opinion refers to a continual refinement of trends and solutions through communication. It is the belief that the open and active dialog of the people will develop public opinion for the good of all. Public opinion may be wrong for a time, but through continued free discussion, factions may form and unite to discuss and refine it to resume a balanced course for all.

Communication, then, is the means for refining public opinion. It is the way to balance public opinion; the minority must have a way to defend itself. Refined, and changing, public opinion becomes the law. When public opinion is fixed, the government must obey it, and communication is the public check against government domination and oppression. America's contract with one another, then, is not a rigid rule of impersonal laws, but because its citizens' ideas of morality and law are forever changing, it is a continuous conversation with one another to protect the liberty of all by balancing the power of the majority.

Of course, communication can be disruptive and can lead to over zealous actions. It's like fire; it can be very beneficial or very destructive. The founders were quite aware of this trait of human nature. The discourse between factions during their lifetimes could be just as hateful as it is today. None of the early founders were strangers to the sting of half-truths and personal attacks. Even their most beloved and trusted President Washington did not escape the wounds of personal attacks. When he governed with decisions that displeased certain factions, he heard about it in less than courteous, often vile, comments. Nonetheless, the founders knew that free and open communication was absolutely essential to continuing development of public opinion and maintenance of liberty.

AMERICAN CONTRACT – SUPREME LAW

From the short review of the great discussion during the Era of Enlightenment it can be seen where the Constitution's creators received many of their ideas and added many of their own to develop the ideas of personal liberty enjoyed today. It was their task, then, to develop an American Contract – the Constitution of the United States, which would establish the power of self-government under the authority of public opinion refined by free communication, and balanced to protect the interests of the minority. The contract needed to be flexible to change with the demands of society and it should offer means of readdressing all issues as needed.

In order to provide for self-government, or government by the people, the role of government must be limited to prevent its eventual growth into a regime of dominion. The creators of the Constitution agreed that the people give the government the powers they wish for it to have, and not the right of the government to give people restricted liberty. As a result, the Constitution was established with specific governmental powers, and they meant for the government to have no more or less than what the people conferred upon it. They listed these powers in the Constitution and the specific first powers of government are shown in Figure 4-1 in the list of Powers of Congress.

Next, the ingenious founders of the Constitution provided a flexible contract to change with the demands of society. How far sighted they were to recognize that society and civilization would continue to evolve and change from what it was during their lives. Even more wonderful were their thoughts for future generations and the provision of a plan that could continue to support new and evolving ideas. They were sure their document was not perfect. There was a great deal of disagreement among them concerning the Constitution, but ultimately, through discussion they were able to come to a compromised agreement, and to provide a means for change. This is the genius of the provision for changes through amendments. This important idea, though, is that the people, through amendments, must agree upon desired changes to the provisions of the Constitution. In other words, if a government action is proposed that does not conform to the Constitution, then the people must agree to lawfully change it by amendment, rather than allowing ambitious elitists to work around it or ignore it altogether. This vital stipulation has been abused by generations of self-important representatives until the government by the people is in danger of being lost.

AMERICAN CONTRACT – BALANCE OF POWERS

Upon accepting the ideas that it is the primary right of humankind to self-govern, and that government must submit to the law of public opinion refined through discourse and reason, it was the task of the Constitutional Convention to decide how the power of the majority should be balanced in order to provide protection for the minority. It was a very real problem for the states with comparatively small territories or populations, because they feared they would not be equally represented in the government and might have been over powered by the larger states. If population were used to determine representation in the new government, then they were certain they would have little or no voice.

Through debate, dialog, and compromise, the ideas submitted by James Madison were modified to a form somewhat similar to what is used today. Madison devised an alternative to Rousseau's idea that a republic must be small in size, such as city-states, by proposing a limitation of federal power to a very few categories, and leaving the states' powers in the states' hands. This imaginative plan would allow the individual state to function effectively as a smaller, individual republic, but would rely on the federal government for defense and the limited functions set forth by the Constitution. Thus was established the first check of power between the federal and state governments through the concept of states' rights. The early elected officials fiercely protected states' rights, but clearly it has eroded in the last century.

Within the federal government itself, Madison proposed the famous separation of powers as discussed by many political writers in the world of his day. This, of course, ended up being the executive, legislative, and judicial branches. Law-making power was to be put in the hands of the people through their representatives in the legislature. It's an important and critical distinction to remember: the people make the laws. Here, the idea of public opinion trending toward the good of all was put into practice. But the problem of representation for the smaller states had not been solved; consequently, many of the smaller states were ready to leave the convention and the Union. Eventually, of course, a compromise was reached that introduced the Senate as the senior branch of the legislature. The idea was that each state would be authorized to have two senators for equal representation in the senate chamber. In addition, these senators also would be state representatives appointed by each state's own legislature. The senate became a strong protection against domination by the majority, it provided an equal voice for each state, and it further protected states' rights at the same time. It was brilliant.

The House of Representatives then became the representative of the people at large, and this was the heart of the idea of a democratic republic. James Madison thought a frequently elected legislature would remain most in agreement with the people and public opinion. Each state would receive a number of representatives in the house in direct proportion to its population.

With the modifications set to paper each state eventually accepted the provisions of the Constitution and officially joined the Union of the United States. While waiting for ratification of the Constitution, James Madison, Alexander Hamilton, and John Jay began writing the *Federalist*, which was a collection of articles explaining the intent and expected result from the new Constitution. In the thirty-ninth paper, James Madison further described the balance of powers for citizens. He explained that the House of Representatives is a national body, not a federal representation, that derives its powers from the people in the same proportion as they are in their state. The Senate receives coequal power of each state such that it is a federal body rather than national. The executive branch is a mixture of national power, determined by electoral votes, from the proportional representation in the House and coequal power in the Senate. Thus the government was intended to be of balanced and mixed character.

The final addition to the Constitution was the first ten amendments, or the Bill of Rights. The people of the states wanted these guarantees before ratification, but the conflict was resolved on the word and promise of George

Washington that each state could submit proposed Constitutional Amendments to the first Congress upon acceptance of the planned Constitution. James Madison personally accepted the task of resolving some 189 suggested amendments and combined them into seventeen. Eventually ten of these were ratified by the states to become the Bill of Rights that Americans enjoy today. Madison really didn't think a Bill of Rights was necessary, because he believed in the changing power of the Constitution, but he quickly and willingly complied with the will of the people. Today, the very first amendment guarantees freedom of speech, or free communication, and continues to be the heart of Madison's vision of a system of self-government through refined public opinion.

COMMUNIST IDEALS

During the Era of Enlightenment the exchange of ideas on the theory of government included many conflicting viewpoints. There were many voices against the ideas of a federal republic such as that implanted by the United States. Ultimately, the early countrymen established the democratic republic embraced by Americans today. About the same time the U.S. government was established, the French rose up in revolution against their monarchy and the fire for freedom was ignited. Unfortunately, it became an example of the brutality, imprisonment, and murder that can result from the power of an unchecked majority or absolute rule of elites.

In the latter part of the 1800s another turn on the idea of democracy was developed. Building upon earlier theories of government from enlightenment era philosophers, Karl Marx and Friedrich Engels developed the idea of a communist government, which would be the ideal of a classless and stateless society of equality for all. In 1848 Marx and Engels drew up *The Communist Manifesto* as a platform for the Communist League. It was followed in 1867 by the first edition of *Das Kapital* that laid out a theory of social struggle and the optimum form of government with no ownership of private property and equality among all mankind.

Marx built upon earlier ideas that the political history of humankind can be reduced to the simplest form of a struggle between two classes; specifically, the oppressors and the oppressed. He named the oppressors the capitalist or ruling class and the oppressed simply the workers. It was Marx's theory that the working class spends their entire lives working for the benefit of the ruling class. He believed the workers were completely exploited by the ruling class, and the more the working class worked, the more they became indebted to the ruling class, and the more affluent the ruling class became. Marx believed that capitalists must continually expand markets all over the globe, eventually drawing everyone into civilization and the menial tasks of labor. This included even honored occupations, such as physicians, lawyers, priests, poets, and scientists that would be turned into paid wage laborers.

The solution that Marx and Engels proposed was to equalize society through an evolution into an ideal communist society. In the communist society there would be equality among people without classes with no ownership of private property, and each individual's work would be a contribution to the good of the whole of society. In order to achieve the utopian communist government it would be necessary for society to work through different stages of development. He described transitions starting from early primitive tribes to capitalist and dictatorial societies of his day. From the capitalist state it would be necessary for the working class to revolt against the capitalist dictatorship and replace it with a working class dictatorship. Violent revolt would be likely and in fact necessary. Marx referred to this period of working class dictatorship as the socialism transition phase. About seventy years later the famous overthrow of the Russian monarchy occurred under the Marxist banner and the Soviet Union was born. After socialism has been well established it would evolve into the communist ideal of a classless and stateless society. Although it would be a stateless society it would still require an elite few to rule and maintain order. This seems to be a conflict in his definition of stateless and classless, because there would be an elite ruling class establishing state rule.

Some of the ideas of *The Communist Manifesto* conflict with the American ideals of today. Its ten steps to change to communism are listed in Figure 6-2.

The closing sentence of *The Communist Manifesto* reads, "Workingmen of all countries unite!" It would be necessary to abolish private land ownership and all rights to inheritance; middle class property ownership must be swept away and made impossible. The family must be abolished to stop the exploitation of children by their parents. A progressive income tax would be needed to level the income of all individuals. Universal education would be required under the close management of the state. In addition, it would be necessary to centralize and control all communication and transportation under state management. Finally, all means of production must be controlled and expanded by the state for the good of all. It is interesting that some of these provisions have been adopted by the U.S. government of today. America adopted the progressive income tax system about one hundred years ago, and it is used to both influence behavior of its citizens and to reduce rights of inheritance. Compare the communist ideals of centralized communication, transportation, and production with the ideas of American founders that free and rapid communication and transportation are chief requirements for the success of a self-governing people. Additionally, it was the American idea that free trade, or production, would result in raising the standard of living for all, as opposed to reducing the standard of living for some.

Ten Steps to Change to Communism

1. Abolish property in land and application of rents to public purposes.
2. Impose a heavy progressive or graduated tax.
3. Abolish all rights of inheritance.
4. Confiscate property of emigrants and rebels.
5. Centralize credit in State Bank with exclusive monopoly of capital.
6. Centralize communication and transportation in State hands.
7. Extend State ownership of factories. Cultivate wastelands.
8. Equal liability of all labor. Establish industrial armies, especially agriculture.
9. Combine agriculture and manufacturing. Gradually abolish distinction between town and country by more equitable distribution of population.
10. Free education for all children. Combine education and industrial production.

Source: *The Communist Manifesto*: Karl Marx & Friedrich Engels

Ten Steps to Communism
Figure 6-2

Vladimir Lenin built further on the concepts of Marx and Engels when he established the idea of democratic centralism about 1917. Lenin dreamed of a communist world where oppressed countries and colonies would unite to overthrow capitalism. Its replacement would be a democratic process that would honor free discussion and a unity of action. A central party was established and all members of the party were free to debate matters of policy and direction. But only party members were able to participate. When a majority decided the course of action after discussion, then the rule of the majority must be upheld. In general the party would operate as follows:

1. All directing bodies of party shall be elected from top to bottom.
2. Party bodies periodically give account to party organizers.
3. Strict party discipline and subordination of minority to the majority.
4. All decisions of the higher body are absolutely binding on the lower bodies and all party members.

In 1921 the tenth Party Congress passed resolution twelve that banned factions within the Russian Communist Party.

Compare the four steps for freedom of discussion and the absolute rule of the majority that are set forth in democratic centralism with the provisions for the balance of power in the system of government inherited in the United States today. A citizen must be a member of the Communist Party to be heard in the discussion, and the minority must completely comply in strict subordination to the majority. There are no means for dealing with ideas of factions; in fact, factions were banned altogether in 1921.

The next evolution of the communist ideal came from Mao Zedong in China and has been called Maoism. This movement took place in the fifties and sixties when Mao was established as the Chairman of the Chinese Republic. He built on the ideals of Marx, Engels, and Lenin with his Idea of Contradiction. Chairman Mao taught his countrymen that there is a contradiction in everything, and it is constantly changing toward domination by the subordinate class. He thought class conflict itself was a contradiction, and he focused more on an agricultural society than an industrial society.

Maoist society was built and maintained by a mass line, or a cadre, that was well trained in Maoist theories. Party cells were established throughout the country, and the cadre set up propaganda officers in each cell to supervise strict and fixed activity programs for its members and citizens. The ideas of the mass line established that no new ideas could be formed or discussed. There would be no rights for the minority and no dissenting free speech would be tolerated.

CENTRALIZED DEMOCRACY AND WORLD ORDER

The idea of a centralized democracy appears to have evolved from the early ideas of Communism and Maoism. It is sometimes referred to as social democracy. The main idea behind this movement is that government can offer security for everything in life from birth to death. Administration of such a program would be decided by the centralized governing class, which would be a dominant group of leaders who determine the proper distribution of benefits and security for all citizens.

The citizens of a centralized democracy must trade their freedoms for security. This form of government promises relief from the responsibilities of life; it promises, don't YOU worry. There would be security for everything including education, jobs, health care, and retirement. In order to provide this security, the governing class must have complete control of communication, transportation, education, and the economy. When a tax system is employed to fund the central bureau, then the bureau chiefs in power decide the degrees of taxation and how the funds will be distributed to the people.

As attractive as this form of government may sound, it assumes that all people have the same aims in life, the same thoughts, the same moral codes, and a common purpose. In reality, everyone knows this is false imagery. Some folks want to work hard and derive satisfaction from it, while others want to enjoy nature and a life of ease and observation. Some citizens want to be artists or musicians and others want to roam and see the world. Some people just want to stay close to their home and raise a family with the support of grandparents, aunts, and uncles.

The view of individualism is replaced with the conviction that all people have the same wishes or at least are willing to subvert the wish of the individual for the good of all. In this respect, socialism and pure democracy have equality as their common aim. A pure democracy promises equal liberty for all, and a social democracy promises equal restraint, and servitude to the government, for all. There will always be some who want to save their money for emergencies and those who will spend everything they have and more. It's human nature. These natural instincts must be eliminated in the central democracy.

There probably always will be people who are ready to trade freedoms for security. The early founders wrote about this segment of the population during their lifetimes. Each grant of security to one group causes insecurity for another group. In the central government all citizens must trade their own dreams and aims for the objectives decided by the state.

The idea that the government, or the ruling class, provides this security is a deception. The government produces nothing, but only divides the production of its citizens as equally as the central governing class determines is proportionate. The idea that a group of individuals can appoint themselves as having a complete understanding of life, and the economy, begins to fail when the concept of infinity of actions is considered. The operation of a modern factory was used to illustrate the concept of infinity of actions, and it can serve again as a comparison to the extraordinary difficulties when an elite few attempt to control the government. There is a never-ending aim to run it as efficiently and predictably as possible. But perfection is virtually impossible. Factory life is a small slice of the ebb and flow of society. Frequently, each day results in controlled chaos and reaction to new and unexpected problems. As hard as intelligent people have tried to figure out and offer solutions to running a factory, it has really never been completely figured out because of the infinity of actions in its operation. This example demonstrates the complexity of the larger reality of life. Look at the government today where too many programs cause confusion, overlapping duplication, and gridlock. No one person, or one group, possesses the ability to decide every facet of life and to provide equally and objectively for all. It is fundamentally impossible.

In order for a centralized government to function, it is suggested that security is provided through economic control and by restriction of personal choices and communication. Control of production and the economy is the ultimate control of human life itself, and thus it is essential to the smooth operation of a centralized government. Rule of people's law will be replaced by board rule. For example, agencies in America today, such as the Internal Revenue Service, the Environmental Protection Agency, and the Occupational Safety and Health Administration, would establish and enforce regulations to restrict human activity within guidelines and limits established by the central government. Individualism would be substituted by a system of regulations for maximum efficiency, and as society becomes more complicated, more restrictions would be needed to seek an average or normal for all.

Individual status and income will be established by the central government. In reality only the bureaucrats will be free to grow and achieve. The aim of the individual actually becomes an attempt to achieve a position of privilege. Ultimately, the control of individual destiny by the elite will lead to despair among the majority of humanity, because the doctrinaire elite may be as oppressive as the worst dictator.

Today, the concept of centralized democracy, or social democracy, can be seen spreading to the larger sphere of a world order where nations are replaced and a central group of individuals decide the rules of civilization for the entire world. It is usually promoted as a government of equality for all in the name of the working people. The working people become the class of privilege in this situation, and this appeals to jealousies of one group over another. There would be security for all, oneness for all, and equality for all.

Each American must decide what they desire, whether it is the democratic republic established by the earliest leaders of the country, a utopian communist government, or a centralized democracy. These are the variants of the three types of government described by Thomas Hobbes at the beginning of the Era of Enlightenment. The democratic republic is an assembly that is open to every individual, but the communist and centralized democracies are assemblies where not every person may enter unless they agree with ideals of the majority. The American founders warned that their formula for freedom through a democratic republic could be lost in a single generation. As soon as the people learn they can vote themselves benefits the government begins to grow and assume a greater role in individual daily lives.

CHAPTER SEVEN

HEDGING THE CONTRACT

THE CONSTITUTION HAS BEEN MODIFIED several times since the first States adopted it. There have been twenty-seven amendments. Seventeen amendments have been added since the first ten, which made up the original Bill of Rights. Actually, twelve amendments had been proposed with the first ten, but the States did not adopt two of them in 1791. Curiously, one of the two had to do with changes in salaries of Senators and Representatives, and it was ratified in 1992 as the twenty-seventh, and most recent amendment to the Constitution.

Changing the Constitution via amendment is exactly what the originators had in mind when it was submitted for approval. But the dispute of its provisions began immediately with the first administration. As factions argued over the role of government, the argument would turn to the Constitution for guidance. Each offered different interpretations of the meaning of the Constitution's wording. Slowly, federal leaders began to use interpretation, rather than clarification through amendments, to govern the country. This great conflict over the presumed powers of the federal government has continued to this day.

Both amendments and constitutional interpretation enabled the three big movements away from the original provisions of the Constitution. The creators intended for the Constitution to be changed using amendments. They were opposed to working around it by stretching its meaning. The huge changes in 1913 were the result of the Sixteenth and Seventeenth Amendments; the Sixteenth implemented the progressive income tax, and the Seventeenth changed the method for electing U.S. Senators. During the power struggle of 1936, Constitutional interpretation by the Supreme Court was needed to support the provisions of the New Deal and Social Security. Supporters claimed the general powers of Congress specified by Clause 1, Section 8, Article I of the Constitution permitted the federal government to take any action that provides for the, "general Welfare of the United States." James Madison believed this interpretation gave Congress boundless power.

In 1965, the interpretation continued with the welfare society and Medicare implementations. The disagreement continued over the constitutionality of the comprehensive health care bill. Not only was the general welfare clause invoked, so was the commerce clause. Clause 3 of Section 8, Article I is often called the commerce clause, which gives Congress the power "to regulate commerce." Supporters of the health care bill believe health care qualifies as both commerce and providing for the general welfare. Attorneys for the government added the position that the health care bill is merely an additional tax on the people. In the final analysis, the Supreme Court continued its record of massaging and hollowing out the Constitution to find a meaning to fit its purpose to uphold the Act. The chief justice thought it was reasonable to "construe" the meaning as increased taxes.

Hedging the Constitution is a disease in every branch of government as individuals attempt to support an agenda by working around the Constitution, rather than seeking to change it. The legislative branch has become a branch of federal employees instead of representatives, despite the objections of the American people when it was first proposed. Using legislative tricks and interpretation, legislators have used congressionally directed spending earmarks, hasty legislation methods to circumvent public opinion, and off-budget accounting tricks to muddy understanding of the national budget. Congress continues to manipulate budget accounts and raid trust funds in order to sustain their creations for the "general welfare."

The executive branch is guilty of trying to impose its will on the country using a combination of executive orders and board rules to control Americans. Executive orders have become a means of establishing laws without working through the Congress, and special advisors are used as a means of executive legislation by proposing controls to be implemented by executive orders. Bureaucratic federal departments have become institutions to set laws and prosecute citizens and companies. Even when an agency's proposals are unsupported by the Congress, it may use a combination of enforcement actions and inactions to suit its departmental agenda.

Even the judicial branch has become comprised of activists with political purposes. Loyalty to the Constitution has been lost as result of its ideological splits. Judges are guilty of having made rulings to carry out public policy, rather than basing its rulings on the Constitution proper. This dangerous practice has resulted in a tendency for the group to become authoritarian rulers through their activism.

The assault on the Constitution does not end with the power struggles between the branches of government. Corrupting influences such as the two-party system, lobbyists, and targeted subsidies constantly challenge the provisions of the Constitution, and often lead to measures to work around it. The lobbyist problem has grown to extraordinary proportions as each group petitions the Congress for subsidies and special treatment. Much of this activity is enabled by the progressive income tax system. It would do much to reduce lobbyist activity and corruption if this abusive tax restriction on American freedom were eliminated.

Unfortunately, today, the measure of a good Congress has become the amount of legislation that it passes. Instead, perhaps it should be how well it has managed a responsible budget and defended the Constitution.

CONSTITUTIONAL INTERPRETATION

No sooner had the Constitution been accepted and the first presidential administration begun before pressures to interpret the wording of the Constitution started, too. According to the law of entropy, unless effort is made to stay within the limits of the Constitution and follow its provisions, the Nation will gradually drift away from it and its ingenious plan. Thomas Jefferson recognized this when he explained that liberty will yield to government during the natural course of time. Per his prediction, for more than two hundred years now, all three branches of the Government have twisted the meaning of the Constitution by reading new meaning into the plain words established the authors. James Madison left an explanation of his original intent in the *Federalist* and other writings. But even this guidance by the Constitution's primary architect has been ignored or buried for social aims.

The immediate conflict began with the clauses in the Eighth Section of the First Article of the Constitution. Right away, the argument began with what powers does the Constitution (and the people of the Country) confer upon the federal government. It came to a head with Alexander Hamilton's proposal for a national bank. A bill to implement a national bank passed both the House of Representatives and the Senate and was submitted to President Washington for signature. And so the debate grew stronger. President Washington was uncertain about the constitutionality of the bill, and asked James Madison for his opinion about it. Both Madison and Thomas Jefferson opposed the bill, because they thought it authorized bankers to issue money for the United States, which was outlined in the Constitution as a Congressional authority.

But Alexander Hamilton sponsored the bill and urged the President to approve it. President Washington had tremendous admiration for Hamilton and his judgment. Hamilton served with President Washington during the

Revolutionary war and distinguished himself as a courageous and excellent officer and soldier. He displayed outstanding heroism, and Washington relied upon him through several desperate engagements during the war. Also, Hamilton gained respect as one of the most successful businessmen in the United States.

The constitutionality debate focused on the First and Eighteenth Clauses of Article I, Section 8 of the Constitution. Recall that the First Clause includes the statement that the powers of Congress include the power to "provide for the common defense and general welfare of the United States." The Eighteenth Clause is the reputed "implied powers" clause that states that Congress may "make all laws which shall be necessary and proper for carrying into execution the foregoing powers." President Washington trusted Alexander Hamilton with full confidence in his loyalty to the country and his understanding of finances. Because the country was strained with the heavy debts from the Revolutionary War, and because President Washington viewed the implementation of a national bank as a temporary measure, he accepted the idea of the implied powers of Congress described in Article I, Section 8, and Clause 18 of the Constitution and signed the bill into law.

Thus began the idea of Constitutional interpretation that has continued to this day, and the accompanying conflict of ideas of government's role in American lives. Alexander Hamilton believed government should control the people. He seemed to favor a government similar to Great Britain's where the welfare of the people was decided by the elites, which included the Monarch and the House of Lords established by heritage. Alternatively, James Madison drafted the Constitution on the belief of a government controlled by a free people exercising self-rule based upon public opinion, communication, and a balance of power. Similar debates and efforts at interpreting the meaning of the Constitution have continued throughout United States history.

The drift from the Constitution has really been allowed by its citizens, the free people of the United States. Americans have not paid close attention to the activities of the government, and they have let it grow so large that it is virtually impossible for anyone to comprehend, much less the private citizen. The rule of infinity of actions becomes more prevalent with each new government bill, agency, and overlapping legislation. The Congress itself doesn't really understand all of the interactions and duplications.

Americans have allowed continued interpretation of the Constitution and the growth of government. At some point the American people learned to vote themselves benefits. It started with government subsidies and programs intended to help its citizens. Farmers got on the subsidy bandwagon; various industries and banks received mortgage guarantees; and common citizens enrolled in social security and welfare. Elected officials quickly learned that the way to continue their appointment in office was to direct more of the nation's wealth to their constituents. Today, it seems the country wants socialist spending for every facet of its citizens' lives, but minimalist libertarian taxes. For certain, it can't have both. If the huge social programs of today are to be continued, the country will need a much higher tax burden upon the American people and the American economy.

Individual responsibilities don't end with the vote. This has been the mistake of many sincere American voters. They dutifully examine the candidates as well as they can in this era of slick TV ads and half-truths, and then they vote. Afterward, they make the error of placing too much trust in those in office to do the right thing for the country. James Madison guided against this when he reminded citizens they couldn't rest easy in the belief that elected officials would morally discharge their duties. The extraordinary example of an American citizen who followed Congressional activity can be found in the story of Horatio Bunce, who lived during the 1800s and was a constituent of Davy Crockett's congressional district. It's a revealing story about the duties of citizenship.

Horatio Bunce was a rock-solid example of the backbone of the country's citizenry. He farmed and kept a close watch on the activities of the government. Citizen Bunce refused to support Crockett in his run for reelection, because Crockett supported a bill for relief to victims of a fire in Georgetown, and Horatio Bunce believed this was an unauthorized misuse of public money. Mr. Bunce went on to admonish Crockett for his actions, because he thought the public treasury was not the Congress's money to give away. Today, it is common to see public money spent on disaster relief, and even harsh criticism of executive administrations that are judged too slow in providing aid to victims. Obviously this idea conflicts with the belief of Horatio Bunce, but the main idea of his story is that all citizens must remain as vigilant of government activity as their workdays will allow. Following is a reprint of the remarkable story of Horatio Bunce and Davy Crockett as told by Crockett.

NOT YOURS TO GIVE

Taken from: *The Life of Colonel David Crockett,*
compiled by Edward S Ellis (Porter & Coates, 1884)

One day in the House of Representatives, a bill was taken up appropriating money for the benefit of a widow of a distinguished naval officer. Several beautiful speeches had been made in its support. The Speaker was just about to put the question when Crockett arose:

"Mr. Speaker – I have as much respect for the memory of the deceased, and as much sympathy for the sufferings of the living, if suffering there be, as any man in this House, but we must not permit our respect for the dead or our sympathy for a part of the living to lead us into an act of injustice to the balance of the living. I will not go into an argument to prove that Congress has no power to appropriate this money as an act of charity. Every member upon this floor knows it. We have the right, as individuals, to give away as much of our own money as we please in charity; but as members of Congress we have no right so to appropriate a dollar of the public money. Some eloquent appeals have been made to us upon the ground that it is a debt due the deceased. Mr. Speaker, the deceased lived long after the close of the war; he was in office to the day of his death, and I have never heard that the government was in arrears to him.

"Every man in this House knows it is not a debt. We cannot, without the grossest corruption, appropriate this money as the payment of a debt. We have not the semblance of authority to appropriate it as a charity. Mr. Speaker, I have said we have the right to give as much money of our own as we please. I am the poorest man on this floor. I cannot vote for this bill, but I will give one week's pay to the object, and if every member of Congress will do the same, it will amount to more than the bill asks."

He took his seat. Nobody replied. The bill was put upon its passage, and, instead of passing unanimously, as was generally supposed, and as, no doubt, it would, but for that speech, it received but few votes, and, of course, was lost.

Later, when asked by a friend why he had opposed the appropriation, Crockett gave this explanation:

"Several years ago I was one evening standing on the steps of the Capitol with some other members of Congress, when our attention was attracted by a great light over in Georgetown. It was evidently a large fire. We jumped into a hack and drove over as fast as we could. In spite of all that could be done, many houses were burned and many families made houseless, and, besides, some of them had lost all but the clothes they had on. The weather was very cold, and when I saw so many women and children suffering, I felt that something ought to be done for them. The next morning a bill was introduced appropriating $20,000 for their relief. We put aside all other business and rushed it through as soon as it could be done.

"The next summer, when it began to be time to think about the election, I concluded I would take a scout around among the boys of my district. I had no opposition there, but, as the election was some time off, I did not know what might turn up. When riding one day in a part of my district in which I was more of a stranger than any other, I saw a man in a field plowing and coming toward the road. I gauged my gait so that we should meet as he came to the fence. As he came up, I spoke to the man. He replied politely, but, as I thought, rather coldly.

"I began: 'Well, friend, I am one of those unfortunate beings called candidates, and – '

" 'Yes, I know you; you are Colonel Crockett. I have seen you once before, and voted for you the last time you were elected. I suppose you are out electioneering now, but you had better not waste your time or mine. I shall not vote for you again.'

"This was a sockdolager. . . I begged him to tell me what was the matter.

" 'Well, Colonel, it is hardly worth-while to waste time or words upon it. I do not see how it can be mended, but you gave a vote last winter which shows that either you have not capacity to understand the Constitution, or that you are wanting in honesty and firmness to be guided by it. In either case you are not the man to represent me. But I beg your pardon for expressing it in that way. I did not intend to avail myself of the privilege of the constituent to speak plainly to a candidate for the purpose of insulting or wounding you. I intend by it only to say that your understanding of the Constitution is very different from mine; and I will say to you what, but for my rudeness, I should not have said, that I believe you to be honest. . . But an understanding of the Constitution different from mine I cannot overlook, because the Constitution, to be worth anything, must be held sacred, and rigidly observed in all its provisions. The man who wields power and misinterprets it is the more dangerous the more honest he is.'

" 'I admit the truth of all you say, but there must be some mistake about it, for I do not remember that I gave any vote last winter upon any constitutional question.'

" 'No, Colonel, there's no mistake. Though I live here in the backwoods and seldom go from home, I take the papers from Washington and read very carefully all the proceedings of Congress. My papers say that last winter you voted for a bill to appropriate $20,000 to some sufferers by a fire in Georgetown. Is that true?'

" 'Well, my friend; I may as well own up. You have got me there. But certainly nobody will complain that a great and rich country like ours should give the insignificant sum of $20,000 to relieve its suffering women and children, particularly with a full and overflowing Treasury, and I am sure, if you had been there, you would have done just as I did.'

" 'It is not the amount, Colonel, that I complain of; it is the principle. In the first place, the government ought to have in the Treasury no more than enough for its legitimate purposes. But that has nothing to do with the question. The power of collecting and disbursing money at pleasure is the most dangerous power that can be intrusted to man, particularly under our system of collecting revenue by a tariff, which reaches every man in the country, no matter how poor he may be, and the poorer he is the more he pays in proportion to his means. What is worse, it presses upon him without his knowledge where the weight centers, for there is not a man in the United States who can ever guess how much he pays to the government. So you see, that while you are contributing to relieve one, you are drawing it from thousands who are even worse off than he. If you had the right to give anything, the amount was simply a matter of discretion with you, and you had as much right to give $20,000,000 as $20,000. If you have the right to give to one, you have the right to give to all; and, as the Constitution neither defines charity nor stipulates the amount, you are at liberty to give to any and everything which you may believe, or profess to believe, is a charity, and to any amount you may think proper. You will very easily perceive what a wide door this would open for fraud and corruption and favoritism, on the one hand, and for robbing the people on the other. No, Colonel, Congress has no right to give charity. Individual members may give as much of their own money as they please, but they have no right to touch a dollar of the public money for that purpose. If twice as many houses had been burned in this country as in Georgetown, neither you nor any other member of Congress would have thought of appropriating a dollar for our relief. There are about two hundred and forty members of Congress. If they had shown their sympathy for the sufferers by contributing each one week's pay, it would have made over $13,000. There are plenty of wealthy men in and around Washington who could have given $20,000 without depriving themselves of even a luxury of life. The congressmen chose to keep their own money, which, if reports be true, some of them spend not very creditably; and the people about Washington, no doubt, applauded you for relieving them from the necessity of giving by giving what was not yours to give. The people have delegated Congress, by the Constitution, the power to do certain things. To do these, it is authorized to collect and pay moneys, and for nothing else. Everything beyond this is usurpation, and a violation of the Constitution.

" 'So you see, Colonel, you have violated the Constitution in what I consider a vital point. It is a precedent fraught with danger to the country, for when Congress once begins to stretch its power beyond the limits of the Constitution, there is not limit to it, and no security for the people. I have no doubt you acted honestly, but that does not make it any better, except as far as you are personally concerned, and you see that I cannot vote for you.'

"I tell you I felt streaked. I saw if I should have opposition, and this man should go to talking, he would set others to talking, and in that district I was a gone fawn-skin. I could not answer him, and the fact is, I was so fully convinced that he was right, I did not want to. But I must satisfy him, and I said to him:

" 'Well, my friend, you hit the nail upon the head when you said I had not sense enough to understand the Constitution. I intended to be guided by it, and thought I had studied it fully. I have heard many speeches in Congress about the powers of Congress, but what you have said here at your plow has got more hard, sound sense in it than all the fine speeches I ever heard. If I had ever taken the view of it that you have, I would have put my head into the fire before I would have given that vote; and if I ever vote for another unconstitutional law I wish I may be shot.'

"He laughingly replied: 'Yes, Colonel, you have sworn to that once before, but I will trust you again upon one condition. You say that you are convinced that your vote was wrong. Your acknowledgment of it will do more good than beating you for it. If, as you go around the district, you will tell people about this vote, and that you are satisfied it was wrong, I will not only vote for you, but will do what I can to keep down opposition, and, perhaps, I may exert some little influence in that way.'

" 'If I don't,' said I, 'I wish I may be shot; and to convince you that I am in earnest in what I say I will come back this way in a week or ten days, and if you will get up a gathering of the people, I will make a speech to them. Get up a barbecue, and I will pay for it.'

" 'No, Colonel, we are not rich people in this section, but we have plenty of provisions to contribute for a barbecue, and some to spare for those who have none. The push of crops will be over in a few days, and we can then afford a day for a barbecue. This is Thursday; I will see to getting it up on Saturday week. Come to my house on Friday, and we will go together, and I promise you a very respectable crowd to see and hear you.'

" 'Well, I will be here. But one thing more before I say good-by. I must know your name.'

" 'My name is Bunce.'

" 'Not Horatio Bunce?'

" 'Yes.'

" 'Well, Mr. Bunce, I never saw you before, though you say you have seen me, but I know you very well. I am glad I have met you, and very proud that I may hope to have you for my friend.'

"It was one of the luckiest hits of my life that I met him. He mingled but little with the public, but was widely known for his remarkable intelligence and incorruptible integrity, and for a heart brimful and running over with kindness and benevolence, which showed themselves not only in words but in acts. He was the oracle of the whole country around him, and his fame had extended far beyond the circle of his immediate acquaintance. Though I had never met him before, I had heard much of him, and but for this meeting it is very likely I should have had opposition, and had been beaten. One thing is very certain, no man could now stand up in that district under such a vote.

"At the appointed time I was at his house, having told our conversation to every crowd I had met, and to every man I stayed all night with, and I found that it gave the people an interest and a confidence in me stronger than I had ever seen manifested before.

"Though I was considerably fatigued when I reached his

house, and, under ordinary circumstances, should have gone early to bed, I kept him up until midnight, talking about the principles and affairs of government, and got more real, true knowledge of them than I had got all my life before.

"I have known and seen much of him since, for I respect him – no, that is not the word – I reverence and love him more than any living man, and I go to see him two or three times every year; and I will tell you, sir, if every one who professes to be a Christian lived and acted and enjoyed it as he does, the religion of Christ would take the world by storm.

"But to return to my story. The next morning we went to the barbecue, and, to my surprise, found about a thousand men there. I met a good many whom I had not known before, and they and my friend introduced me around until I had got pretty well acquainted – at least, they all knew me.

"In due time notice was given that I would speak to them. They gathered up around a stand that had been erected. I opened my speech by saying:

" 'Fellow-citizens – I present myself before you today feeling like a new man. My eyes have lately been opened to truths which ignorance or prejudice, or both, had heretofore hidden from my view. I feel that I can today offer you the ability to render you more valuable service than I have ever been able to render before. I am here today more for the purpose of acknowledging my error than to seek your votes. That I should make this acknowledgement is due to myself as well as to you. Whether you will vote for me is a matter for your consideration only.'

"I went on to tell them about the fire and my vote for the appropriation and then told them why I was satisfied it was wrong. I closed by saying:

" 'And now, fellow-citizens, it remains only for me to tell you that the most of the speech you have listened to with so much interest was simply a repetition of the arguments by which your neighbor, Mr. Bunce, convinced me of my error.

" 'It is the best speech I ever made in my life, but he is entitled to the credit for it. And now I hope he is satisfied with his convert and that he will get up here and tell you so.'

"He came upon the stand and said:

" 'Fellow-citizens – it affords me great pleasure to comply with the request of Colonel Crockett. I have always considered him a thoroughly honest man, and I am satisfied that he will faithfully perform all that he has promised you today.'

"He went down, and there went up from that crowd such a shout for Davy Crockett as his name never called forth before.

"I am not much given to tears, but I was taken with a choking then and felt some big drops rolling down my cheeks. And I tell you now that the remembrance of those few words spoken by such a man, and the honest, hearty shout they produced, is worth more to me than all the honors I have received and all the reputation I have ever made, or ever shall make, as a member of Congress.

"Now, sir," concluded Crockett, "you know why I made that speech yesterday.

"There is one thing now to which I will call your attention. You remember that I proposed to give a week's pay. There are in that House many very wealthy men – men who think nothing of spending a week's pay, or a dozen of them, for a dinner or a wine party when they have something to accomplish by it. Some of those same men made beautiful speeches upon the great debt of gratitude which the country owed the deceased – a debt which could not be paid by money – and the insignificance and worthlessness of money, particularly so insignificant a sum as $10,000, when weighed against the honor of the nation. Yet not one of them responded to my proposition. Money with them is nothing but trash when it is to come out of the people. But it is the one great thing for which most of them are striving, and many of them sacrifice honor, integrity, and justice to obtain it."

Horatio Bunce didn't let his civic responsibility end after he cast his vote. He monitored the activity of the government, and when he believed it strayed from the provisions of the Constitution, he resolved to remove the offenders with his vote. Citizen Bunce recognized the awesome power given to Congress by the people to collect and disburse money. Notice that this story occurred before the progressive income tax, so Mr. Bunce reminded Congressman Crockett that collecting revenue by tariff affected all citizens. This meant that giving charity to one meant taking from another that may be worse off. The evidence of this situation is apparent today at the tax desk when one citizen is seen struggling to juggle bills while meeting a tax obligation, but another pays no tax, receives an extra tax credit boost, and lives at a better standard than the low-income tax payer. Horatio Bunce knew there was no provision in the Constitution that gave Congress the right to give charity, and he recognized that charity opens the door for fraud, corruption, and favoritism. The story is an excellent lesson in civic responsibility for citizens and representatives alike.

Today, legislators and government officials have become federal employees rather than representatives of the people. They work for long personal careers with great pay and benefits at the expense of the people. They have learned to implement give-away programs to continue their tenure in office at the expense of their oath to "support and defend the Constitution of the United States." Many representatives started with nothing and ended with fortunes after a lifetime of public service. Benjamin Franklin recognized this pitfall from his experiences with European governments. He knew the love of power and money were two huge motivations of ambitious people, and when a public office allows this combination the government is corrupted. It's the old law of entropy again, where salaries get completely out of hand unless effort is made to keep them in check. Franklin said government salaries would be modest at the start, but there would always be many reasons for increases. Today, elected officials and support staffs receive extraordinary compensations and benefits at the expense of the common taxpayer. There are too many elitists with political and economic theories of how government should regulate daily life, but who have never worked in private society.

Because the government is filled with career politicians who are merely federal workers that make up the governing class, they have become a kind of aristocratic group that believes it knows what is best for the people and who are deserving of its favors. Instead of protecting and defending the Constitution against interpretation, the Congress has let the executive and judicial branches of government commandeer legislative power.

THE GREAT CONFLICT

The great conflict refers to the long history of disagreement over the powers of the federal government. The intent of the Constitution's draftsman, James Madison, is clear from his writing. In 1787, Madison and the other contributors to the creation of the Constitution carefully contemplated the powers to give to the government. A huge majority of the states and their representatives were afraid of a powerful federal government; they got a belly full of it from Great Britain, and were so fiercely independent that they didn't want it again. As a result, the Eighth Section of the First Article of the Constitution establishes twenty powers given by the people to the federal government. Also, the Ninth and Tenth Sections of the same article establish specific prohibitions of power of the federal government and the individual states. The authorized powers of government are listed in Figure 4-1, and the lists of prohibited powers are shown in Figure 7-1.

Prohibited Federal and States Powers

Limitation of Federal Powers

Constitutional Article	Limitations
I.9.1	Cannot limit States importing people until 1808.
I.9.2	Cannot suspend right to a hearing before imprisonment except for rebellion, invasion, or for public safety.
I.9.3	No legislative determination of a person to be a criminal without a trial.
I.9.3	Cannot pass a law enacted after an event and retroactively penalizing for it.
I.9.4	No head tax or direct tax unless in proportion to the census.
I.9.5	No tax or duty on any articles exported from any State.
I.9.6	No preference regulating commerce of one State over another.
I.9.7	No money withdrawn from Treasury without accounting.
I.9.8	No title of nobility may be granted by United States.
I.9.8	Government officers may not accept gifts, titles, or payment from foreign states.

Limitation of States' Powers

Constitutional Article	Limitations
I.10.1	No State may enter a treaty or authorize seizure of a foreign state, coin money, make coins, determine a person a criminal without trial, pass retroactive laws and penalties, impair contract obligations, or grant any titles of nobility.
I.10.2	No State may impose duties without consent of Congress.
I.10.3	No State may keep troops or ships of war, or make agreement with another state or foreign power, or engage in war, unless actually invaded, without the consent of Congress.

Prohibited Federal and State Powers
Figure 7-1

The conflict of understanding of Article I of the Constitution and the Tenth Amendment to the Constitution was immediate and ongoing through today. The primary interpretations for larger government have been focused on four clauses of Section 8 of Article I; specifically these are Clauses 1, 3, 17, and 18. The First Clause states, "The Congress shall have power to lay and collect taxes, duties, imposts and excises, to pay the debts and provide for the common defense and general welfare of the United States; but all duties, imposts and excises shall be uniform throughout the United States." As discussed previously, interpretation of the First Clause is focused on the authorization to "provide for the common defense and general welfare." The leaders of the early government left writings to explain that they meant this as a qualifying restriction on the use of taxes for the good of the nation as a whole without benefit to specific groups or individuals. Through the years, however, the interpretation of this clause has been molded to mean any program that Congress proposes that may benefit a certain state or class of people. The Supreme Court has largely supported this idea.

The Third Clause of the article of Congressional powers reads, to "regulate commerce with foreign nations, and among the several States, and with Indian tribes." The central focus has been the power to regulate commerce among the states. When this was written, the primary purpose of this clause was to prevent states from establishing regulations to promote their own prosperity by gouging another state and at the expense of the general welfare of the country at large. This could happen over control of ports or river ways, for example. The history of Supreme Court decisions, however, has resulted in an interpretation of commerce to mean every type of movement of persons or things whether or not for profit. It was decided that this means negotiation activity, intellectual exchanges, and every activity established in the course of doing business. Today, when this assessment of commerce is combined with the application of general welfare to individual states or classes of people, the Congress has been able to implement many of the failing government programs reviewed in preceding discussions. Social Security, Medicare, welfare, and many others have been decided to be within the authority of the federal government. Undeniably, some early citizens, such as Horatio Bunce, would not agree with the constitutionality of these programs; refer to thoughts on the Constitution in his story.

Clause 17 of Article I, Section 8 of the Constitution establishes the legislative authority of Congress to govern the seat of federal government; Washington, D.C., in other words. It also provides the same authority, "over all places purchased by the consent of the Legislature of the State in which the same shall be, for the erection of forts, magazines, arsenals, dock-yards, and other needful buildings." This one seems pretty straightforward, but as the country added new states the Congress did not allow them to take title to all public lands. Instead, it became national policy that each new state would acquire jurisdiction over these lands as fast as they were sold to private ownership. But the federal government has not complied with this policy. As a result, much of the land in the western states remains the property of the federal government, despite the fact that it is not used for the purposes identified by the Seventeenth Clause and without the consent of the respective state legislatures. Continuing the practice of broad appraisal of the general welfare clause, the federal government has retained authority over state properties to establish national parks and wilderness areas. The people of Alaska own only four percent of their land, Nevada less than fifteen percent, and Utah and Idaho less than thirty-five percent of the land within their state boundaries.

The technical writers of the Constitution added the Eighteenth Clause in Section 8 to authorize the Congress to enforce the Constitution. It allows Congress to, "make all laws which shall be necessary and proper for carrying into execution the foregoing powers, and all other powers vested by this Constitution in the Government of the United States, or in any department or officer thereof." James Madison explained that this clause provides the general authority to exercise the powers, given to the federal government by the states, in the form of the preceding seventeen clauses, without providing a detailed list of laws on every subject of the Constitution. Today, this clause is often referred to as the implied powers clause and has been stretched in combination with the interpretations of the First, Third, and Seventeenth Clauses to expand the powers of the federal government far beyond the scope of the twenty enumerated powers established in Section 8 itself.

The last part of the great conflict is focused on the last element of the Bill of Rights: the Tenth Amendment to the Constitution. It declares, "The powers not delegated to the United States by the Constitution, nor prohibited by it to the States, are reserved to the States, respectively, or to the people." It plainly establishes that states' rights and the rights of the people are first, and the states and the people limit the powers of the federal government. The combination of subsequent amendments to the Constitution and Supreme Court decisions has all but erased this last article of the Bill of Rights. The Supreme Court has interpreted federal rights to apply to jurisdiction of public morals, safety, health, and common good, stripping states' control of their own destiny. As a result, today the federal government regulates virtually every facet of daily lives, including encroachments into education, energy supplies, roads, and so on. This was the exact, primary fear of the first states when considering the Constitution for ratification. Once out of the bottle, this genie is uncontained.

Is the country on the wrong track? Is this the direction it should be taking? It's virtually certain the framers of the Constitution would not agree with the idea of a large federal government as it has developed today. Compare what James Madison, the primary architect, had to say about interpretations of the Constitution. He left a description for his fellow countrymen and succeeding generations in the forty-first publication of the *Federalist*. In this essay Madison describes the powers of government in six purposes: security against foreign danger; regulation of intercourse with foreign nations; maintenance of harmony among the states; certain miscellaneous objects of general utility; restraint of states from certain injurious acts; and, provisions for giving effectiveness to these powers. It's clear that Madison believed the powers of Congress were specifically limited to the twenty powers identified by Article I, Section 8 of the Constitution.

Later, when the first Congress began to debate the meaning and intent of general welfare in the First Clause of Section 8, Madison told the members that if Congress can apply general welfare indefinitely, then it might take everything into its hands, including religion, education, schools, regulation of roads, and everything down to the minutest policy. And yet, despite his warning, the government has inserted itself into all of these areas and more. Social-welfare legislation and government regulation has expanded the size and scope of the federal government to such an extent that taxpayers will soon have to pay more to support its employees and give-away programs.

GIANT STEPS

The federal government has chipped away at the power of the people since the first Congress, but there have been four giant steps to the federal takeover of power from the people. Three of these are the three major government expansions previously described by the list of government failures, which were the power grabs around 1913, 1936, and 1965. The fourth is the universal health care legislation and its use of the income tax system to force everyday citizens to file an informational tax return and to obtain health care insurance or pay a penalty at the tax desk.

Two amendments to the Constitution in 1913 established the groundwork for social legislation to follow. These, again, are the Sixteenth and Seventeenth Amendments. The Sixteenth Amendment established the progressive income tax system that has grown to dominate American lives today. The Seventeenth Amendment changed the office of U.S. Senator from an appointed office to the elective office that remains in use now. One good thing about these amendments may be that they demonstrate just how flexible the Constitution is, and how it can be modified according to the changing needs of society just as the founders visualized. It is not an outdated document, but an active, flexible contract between all Americans.

Because the founders distrusted the idea of taxes and its potential for invading individual privacy and freedoms, they carefully restricted the application of taxes. The methods and purposes for collecting taxes are established by three clauses of the Constitution: Clause I.2.3, Clause I.8.1, and Clause I.9.4. Clause I.2.3 is part of the Second Section that establishes the composition of the House of Representatives and how direct taxes would be determined. It states that both representatives and direct taxes shall be apportioned according to respective populations of each state. After this, when the general powers of Congress were established in the Eighth Section of the First Article, the very First Clause (I.8.1) establishes the power of Congress to collect taxes that are uniform throughout the country. Finally, in the Ninth Section of the First Article, the Fourth Clause (I.9.4) prohibits direct taxes unless collected in proportion to the census or an even method of enumeration. In summary, then, these clauses do three things: establish direct taxes according to population, authorize Congress to collect uniform taxes, and prohibit direct taxes unless in proportion to population. Clearly, the creators of the Constitution believed any type of direct tax on the American people should be even and equal among the population. This might be similar to the idea of the flat tax that is so often discussed today. In reality, though, the early federal government was funded through indirect taxes, such as tariffs and excise taxes, which could be compared to the idea of a fair tax that is proposed today from time to time.

By 1913, though, the country began to embrace certain ideas of social equality. Perhaps this was spurred by the communist ideals proposed by Karl Marx. Perhaps union movements added to the idea that the rich were using and oppressing the poor. Maybe it was a time of super fortunes and jealousy when Americans ignored the Constitution. In any event, class warfare was used for political aims of the dominant parties and elected officials of the time, and the idea to soak the rich became a popular topic, so the concept of a progressive tax to tax different incomes at different rates was borrowed from communist doctrine. Income taxes weren't exactly new. They were used to fund the Civil War, and another income tax law was attempted in 1893, only to be found unconstitutional by the Supreme Court. Some twenty years later the idea had become popular enough to ratify the Sixteenth Amendment and to collect taxes, "on incomes, from whatever source derived, without apportionment among the several States, and without regard to any census or enumeration." Thus, the progressive income tax in the United States began. It was a definite shift of the thinking of its citizens to a method of spreading the country's wealth more evenly among the social network of the population. It is interesting to find this change listed in the second step of the ten steps for changing to communism (See Figure 6-2) as established by *The Communist Manifesto* that says, "Impose a heavy progressive or graduated tax."

Also in 1913 the Seventeenth Amendment to the Constitution changed the method for selecting U.S. Senators. In its original form, Article I, Section 3, Clause 1 of the Constitution established the method for selecting Senators to be chosen by the Legislature of each State. This is a manifestation of the idea of a balance of powers both within the federal government and between the federal and state governments. As previously discussed, the House of Representatives was intended to represent the people at large through their direct votes, and the Senate was meant to provide a balance of this strong national power by acting as representatives of the states. This Senate of members appointed by state legislatures was meant to preserve the rights of individual states and to balance the strength of the federal government. With the change by the Seventeenth Amendment to the present method of popular election of senators, the entire Congress has been converted to a national house. This curbs the balance of power between the majority and minority, and it subjects America to the possibility of a majority tyranny the forefathers so anxiously wanted to avoid.

Of course, these two amendments can't really be counted as hedges to the Constitution, because they are legal changes implemented in the way the founders intended. But they are included as two of the major steps taken during America's history that have set the government in the direction of federal dominance.

The second giant step by the federal government to assume a stronger role in daily lives was supported by Supreme Court decisions in 1936. The Court finally settled the great disagreement over the meaning of the First Clause of the general powers section, which is to provide for the general welfare of the country. To be sure, the argument had continued for more than one hundred years since the first administration and the opposing constitutional interpretations of Alexander Hamilton and James Madison. Without question, Hamilton believed that any good cause for the country was within the power of Congress because this First Clause was a general grant of power to Congress. As previously reviewed, Madison felt this viewpoint would authorize Congress to delve into every area of individual lives. In 1936, the Supreme Court ruled that the First Clause of the general powers section is a separate and distinct power from the other nineteen listed in the section, and therefore, Congressional power is limited only by the requirement that its programs provide for the general welfare of the United States. Well, that was it. The door was officially opened to allow the federal government to set up infrastructure programs, social programs, national parks, and any federal program limited only by the imagination of the governing class. In rapid succession it was decided that building infrastructure was simply regulating commerce as provided in the Third Clause of general powers. Federal land banks were established under the interpretation that they fall under the authority of the war powers granted to Congress, such as in the Eleventh Clause of the general powers section; even though, the Seventeenth Clause of this same section specifically restricts federal ownership of federal lands to the applications listed, and only with approval of the respective state.

With the door open to Congress for providing for the general welfare of the American public, a huge social-welfare program was born with the Social Security Act. This was originally sold as a plan for individuals to pay the government for old age assistance when they were no longer able to work. Legislators led taxpayers to believe that more social security taxes would be collected than would be paid out. Citizens thought the surplus would be used to fund the program for their future. Unfortunately, the government did not hold any of the excess payments in reserve, but instead borrowed the money for different uses, such as new give-away programs. It was as brilliant a Ponzi scheme as ever devised. The federal government collected from new investors (taxpayers), and spent the money on other things instead of holding it in trust. It worked well until there were not enough new "investors" to sustain the system. Now it threatens to drag down national prosperity. Many other programs were implemented in the 1930s to advance the general welfare under New Deal programs that let the government slip into private lives.

Giant step three occurred from about 1965 to 1974. It started with the Great Society programs that implemented social-welfare, Medicare, and eventually Supplemental Security Income, and Medicaid. The social-welfare program was meant to give unfortunate individuals a way to secure meaningful work or go to school to improve their situation. There would be housing, food assistance, medical assistance, and money for other expenses. Few imagined that once these folks qualified for these benefits, they would be content to receive them throughout their lives and into subsequent generations. Medicare was meant to provide old age health insurance for folks who could not qualify for health insurance due to conditions of ill health. It also was based upon the Ponzi principles of social security, and now it too, suffers from a lack of new investors to continue to support the scheme.

Following the social programs of the sixties the government began to establish the idea of control by government agencies with the advent of the Environmental Protection Agency, the Occupational Safety and Health Administration, and others to join the Internal Revenue Service. These government agencies are authorized to establish and enforce regulatory rules that have the power of law, and so the migration to accept both the rule of law established by the Congress, and board rules of government agencies, has continued to expand. Congress has delegated its lawmaking authority to these agencies, and it has subjected American citizens to the domination of board controls.

The assault on the Constitution continues today with the fourth giant step in the form of the push to universal health care under controls of the federal government. A lot of folks are willing to surrender personal freedoms for the security of government-supported health care. All should remember though, the government can withdraw statutory rights, as many individuals are learning during current talks of revising the Social Security and Medicare programs. Like all bills intended to help a certain segment of society, it will help some, but hurt others, and not just the wealthy, in the process.

Although the challenge of the constitutionality of the health care bill was lost, the great struggle between federal authority and individual rights continues.

INTERPRETATION VERSUS AMENDMENT

The last one hundred years has seen the U.S. government move to one of Constitutional interpretation, instead of Constitutional change. The mismanagement of Constitutional power has resulted in letting the Supreme Court decide, or interpret, what the Constitution means. Instead of settling disputes by amending the national contract, the government has added to the confusion and assumed greater federal power by avoiding changes and using obscure, and often contradictory, interpretations of it. Some people claim the Constitution is an outdated document that is no longer applicable today. Either these individuals don't understand the principle of change that is the heart of the Constitution, or they want to skirt around it, or abolish it, with the aim of increasing federal power or changing the American form of government altogether. Often it is people who would like to see the United States join a world community or world government, which would mean the Constitution would no longer be applicable. Instead, America would follow rules set by a world government.

When American citizens allow the government to interpret the Constitution to suit its own aims, instead of changing it by obtaining the approval of the people, then they give the government power without boundaries. This is the situation today. Rather than asking the people for larger power, the government has assumed it through interpretation by a selected few. The slippery elites in all branches of government have inconsistently interpreted the Constitution to suit their individual agendas, often reversing course, instead of relying on the will of the people, and public opinion, to make changes to the national contract when necessary. When left to the interpretations of career leaders, the idea of self-government is lost and the people are left exposed to the domination of a large federal government, regulation by agencies, and intrusion into private lives and dreams. Power is given to these central rulers to decide who deserves, who does not, and how the resources of the nation should be allocated. Thomas Jefferson left this lesson for posterity when he told the country that its core security is the written Constitution, and it should not be made a blank piece of paper by working around it with interpretations. He wanted American descendents to continue on the principles of the Constitution instead of deviating from it for what pleases a controlling few. He believed America should follow its provisions or amend it.

The wonder of the Constitution is that it leaves it to the voters to decide. It is the decision of public opinion and the people that should make the laws, not a group of theorists who believe they can handle the infinity of actions that affect the world condition, and can decide what is best for everyone else. Naturally, the world has changed considerably since the Constitution was developed, and American society is vastly different from the founders' world.

But the idea that people can self-govern themselves in order to seek freedom is not outdated, and perhaps is stronger than ever. The dialog should continue, and if the American people decide that government should provide for the poor, give disaster relief, set aside land for national parks, or other programs, then let it be cleared up with Constitutional changes to authorize these powers, but do not continue with the idea of letting nine judges decide what powers may be allowed, often giving federal authority unlimited power.

LEGISLATIVE HEDGING

Perhaps a slow evolution of the legislative branch in three areas has allowed the confusion involved in interpreting the Constitution. The members have become nothing more than federal employees instead of representatives, they have allowed the use of legislative rules to supersede the Constitution, and they have circumvented fiscal responsibility with inadequately funded programs to assure their reelection and continuance of their individual federal careers.

In reality, many career politicians rely on high pay and benefits as federal employees. They share benefits programs with the federal employee system, which in itself seems to be somewhat of a conflict of interest. The pay and benefits for legislators have expanded from a stipend for public service to large salaries with benefits far in excess of what is available to the average American. Figure 7-2 shows the steady increase of legislator salaries and a short list of other federal benefits they enjoy.

Benjamin Franklin worried about this situation. He did not want the Congress to have the power to set its own pay, because he knew the salaries of British officers were enormous, and he feared that this could eventually happen in the United States. Franklin knew that when a post of honor also becomes a place of profit it would corrupt those who seek it. He believed that those who serve for little salary receive the greatest the honor, but he knew rising salaries would be a perpetual problem. In his wisdom he understood the law of entropy. Without consistent management Congressional compensation would be unchecked. John Adams believed that to preserve the integrity of the office of public servant, they should never depend upon public employment for subsistence. Of course, Americans have allowed the government to morph into a system of federal employees that do indeed allow their careers to affect their decisions. It is amusing to observe these individuals congratulating themselves for their public service while taking a huge piece of the treasury for their personal gain. Many of these treasure hunters complain of the benefits that corporate executives receive while chasing the same aims for themselves.

Congressional Annual Salaries

1815	$1,500	1925	$ 10,000
1855	3,000	1965	30,000
1865	5,000	1975	40,000
1871	7,500	2006	162,100
1874	5,000	2010	174,000
1907	7,500	2010	See Leaders Salaries

Congressional Leader Salaries: 2010
  Speaker of the House of Representatives: $223,500
  President pro tempore of Senate: $193,400
  Senate and House Majority and Minority Leaders: $193,400

Congressional Benefits

1. Salaries and fringe benefits are paid by federal government
2. Extraordinary retirement benefit from federal government
3. Special government life insurance with modest premiums
4. Special low cost government health insurance program
5. In line for high salaried federal job if defeated
6. Generous office benefits
      Special tax deductions
      Additional travel allowance
      Funded staff and assistants
      Free medical care at the Capitol
      Funded offices in Washington and at home
      Free mailing privileges for official mail

Congressional Salaries and Benefits
Figure 7-2

Legislative rules are used to make the process more efficient, or so ordinary citizens are led to believe. In reality, many of the rules of order have been created to benefit the specific needs of a party or cause. The use of legislative amendments and congressionally directed spending, or earmarks as they are often called, to direct public money to individual causes is infuriating to most Americans. Often these earmarks are attached as riders to a bill, but they have nothing at all to do with the primary bill under consideration. Slippery representatives attach these exclusive packages under the premise of negotiations; they tell their constituents, it is better to bargain for a vote to allow a special benefit for a small segment in order to pass the larger bill for the overall good of the country. How could this be providing for the general welfare of the people? Of course, they aren't kidding the American public, because people know this is just another excuse for continuing a career. Americans have complained about it for years, but the governing class does not acknowledge the objections.

Lately America has been subjected to hasty legislation and more modifications of rules to suit the objectives of those who are promoting legislation. Hasty legislation methods defeat the basic premise of self-government advanced by James Madison that public opinion will ultimately seek the right course of action through communication. By accelerating the acceptance of a bill without proper discourse the balance of power is circumvented. Alexander Hamilton said it best in the seventieth article of the *Federalist* when he wrote that seeking a prompt decision can often do more harm than good. It eliminates discussion that can spur deliberation on differences of opinion and expose the excesses of the majority.

Hamilton understood the central idea of balancing the tyranny of majority, but representatives today have lost this idea in their rush to cater to one group to advance their own careers while using legislative tricks and expedients to upset the delicate balance of power established by the American Contract. These individuals have pursued public office and taken an oath to adhere to the Constitution. Their first priority should be to uphold their oath of office. Each senator, representative, and judge takes the following oath of office; "I do solemnly swear that I will support and defend the Constitution of the United States against all enemies, foreign and domestic; that I will bear true faith and allegiance to the same; that I take this obligation freely without any mental reservation or purpose of evasion; that I will well and faithfully discharge the duties of the office on which I am about to enter." The Constitution is supreme. They have sworn to support and defend it, and the voters must hold them to it.

The primary responsibility of the Congress is to manage the public funds entrusted to it by the people. No debt may be paid and no new programs may be started without authorization of the Congress and approval of the President. But through the years the Congress has chosen a variety of methods to circumvent its responsibility for the budget in the name of efficiency. An example of this is the use of the Congressional Budget Office to estimate each government agency's fiscal requirements, which has the effect of reducing a close analysis of expenditures by the Congress. Instead of openly accounting for all federal funds the Congress has permitted certain expenses to be designated as off-budget items. It also has permitted some government agencies to spend the accrued interest on trust fund holdings without public accounting. In addition, the Federal Reserve is permitted to deduct expenses from its profits before returning all profits to Congress. The national founders believed the public finances should be clear and intelligible enough that anyone could understand it and identify abuses.

EXECUTIVE HEDGING

The executive branch has a long history of abusing power and expanding its reach into private life. Every president has wrestled with which executive actions are Constitutional. Many presidents have perverted the power of office in their belief that they understand what is best for the country, instead of following the will of the self-governing people. Theodore Roosevelt decided, for example, that the President could do anything not prohibited by the Constitution, rather than being limited only to the powers authorized by the Constitution, despite the provisions of the Tenth Amendment, which states that powers not delegated to the government by the Constitution are reserved to the people. His dangerous interpretation obviously opened another door to unlimited powers that should be closed and locked.

The growth of executive power includes expansion of the Cabinet and White House Agencies, departmental rulemaking, and abuse of executive orders. The expansion of the Cabinet has led the initiative to board rulemaking. Board authority is a principle of centralized democracy that has taken deep root in American government today. The Constitution was meant to establish a rule of law through the provisions of the Constitution. On the other hand, the rule of a board permits the board authority to do as it pleases, often without following due process of the law. The board becomes the judge, jury, and executioner. Citizens are bombarded today by agency and departmental rules that govern their lives. It includes agriculture, commerce, labor, education, welfare, transportation, and more. The remarkable growth of the number of Cabinet positions from the original four to today is shown in Figure 7-3 with a list of White House Agencies that interact with the various Departments of the Government.

Departmental rulemaking, or rule of board, has gradually increased for decades to the point that many of these departments are acting through the President in direct opposition to the directives of the Congress. Agencies such as the Internal Revenue Service, the Justice Department, and the Environmental Protection Agency have established and enforced their own rules. The Internal Revenue Service has variously been referred to as a police force capable of establishing guilt without trial and enforcing punishment. Even the nation's legislators have feared reprisal by the IRS at times. Now, the Environmental Protection Agency has chosen to enforce regulations, which in its judgment are for the good of the environment, regardless of the will of the Congress or the will of the people. This agency has limited all types of activity from drilling for oil to what types of energy can be used. All of this

Executive Cabinet Posts

1789 Department of State
1789 Department of the Treasury
1789 Department of War; 1949 renamed Department of Defense
1789 Attorney General; 1870 renamed Department of Justice
1829 Post Master General
1849 Department of the Interior
1889 Department of Agriculture
1903 Department of Commerce and Labor
    1913 Department of Commerce after Labor split off
1913 Department of Labor; split off from Commerce and Labor
1953 Department of Health, Education, and Welfare
    1979 Department of Health and Human Services after split
1965 Department of Housing and Urban Development
1967 Department of Transportation
1971 Post Office Department replaced by independent agency
1977 Department of Energy
1979 Department of Education; split off from HEW

White House Administrative Agencies

1. White House Office – President's personal and political staff
2. National Security Council – Key policy making of all foreign and domestic matters relating to national security
3. Office of Policy Development – Advisors on domestic problems
4. Office of Management and Budget – Aids President in developing the nation's fiscal policy and annual budget
5. Council on Environment Quality – Works with Environmental Protection Agency
6. Office of United States Trade Representative – Assists President on issues of foreign trade and trade negotiations
7. Intelligence Oversight Board – Monitors Central Intelligence Agency programs
8. Office of Administration – Service pool of clerical help, research assistance, and other requirements

Cabinet Positions and White House Agencies
Figure 7-3

activity is accomplished under the authority of board rule instead of rule of law established by Congress. The Federal Reserve is the central banking system established in 1913 in response to a series of financial panics. It is a mixture of public and private institutions used to supervise and regulate banking institutions. The Board of Governors are confirmed by the Senate, and Congress sets its salaries and maintains oversight, but the decisions of the Federal Reserve do not have to be ratified by either the executive or legislative branch.

Executive orders have become a method for the executive branch to join the lawmaking business. Congress authorized this practice with the idea that this power would be used by the President for administrative control of departments under their authority, not for passing regulations that affect American citizens. But the use, and abuse, of this delegated power has grown to the point that the executive branch may circumvent Congressional approval to issue administrative directives that have the full force of law. President Washington used executive orders in 1789, but the numbering system for executive orders was not started until 1907. As it might be expected, the growth of executive orders expanded enormously under the authority of Theodore Roosevelt and his idea that he could do anything not prohibited by the Constitution. For comparison, Grover Cleveland, who left office four years before Roosevelt's first term, issued seventy-one executive orders, but Roosevelt made 1,006 executive directives. It was the beginning of the idea that executive orders can be used to show the power of the executive office. But it's a dangerous way to get around the rule of the people and to impose the ideas of the governing class upon the public for their own good.

The use of special advisors to the president is an example of the use of executive power to establish policy by individuals with no accountability to the people. The people elect their legislators and the president. The Supreme Court judges and Cabinet members are appointed by the president and confirmed by elected senators. But special advisors are not tied directly or indirectly to the voters by confirmation of elected representatives. These offices are used to establish policy, author legislation, and influence agency rules, and the number of the offices is unlimited and uncontrolled by the Congress. The White House special staff has become a mini-congress working around the elected legislature and using board rule to implement its policies.

The group of special advisors used private organizations to write bills, such as the American Recovery and Reinvestment Act of 2009 (Stimulus Bill), and urged immediate approval by the Congress. Without question, it's completely within the authorization of the Constitution for private citizens to offer bills to the Congress, but the Congress erred in passing hasty legislation without taking time to absorb its contents and to adequately discuss and debate its effects, as meant by the creators of the Constitution. This stimulus bill contained numerous provisions for congressionally directed (earmark) spending. The Congress passed a bill from a private group without fully understanding its provisions and without fulfilling its primary responsibility to the American public. Today, the number of advisors has grown to about thirty people plus their attendant support staffs that are drawing upon the revenues from America's citizens without obligation or accountability to the people.

The power of the executive office has grown beyond Constitutional boundaries. The combination of executive orders, Cabinet expansion, special advisors, and board rulemaking has effectively resulted in two lawmaking and enforcement bodies. The power of this branch of government must be restored to the limits established by the Constitution if Americans are to maintain the delicate balance of power, and to avoid the oppression of an unaccountable separate arm of the government making rules without oversight of the legislative branch that represents the country's population.

Judicial Hedging

When the country's founders developed the idea of the national Supreme Court they believed a guardian of the Constitution was needed. The Constitution would be the supreme law of the people, and in order to protect it against violations by Congress, the President, and the States, the Constitutional architects established a Supreme Court to keep these branches of government within their assigned authorities. Their idea, of course, was that only the people could establish the laws through their representatives and the jury process. The Supreme Court, then, would be assigned the responsibility for insuring the laws were followed and rights protected.

The Supreme Court would have no right to make law, but only to follow the laws established by the people. The early founders lived in a time when judges often were removed by a monarch or other authoritarian methods if they did not comply with the wishes of government. This ability to control judges affected their activity and led to corrupt practices. In order to avoid this extraordinary influence on the guardians of the Constitution, the founders decided to establish an independent court of judges appointed to serve for life, and they set up the Constitution to prevent the compensation of judges from being reduced during their service. The majority of the founders, including John Adams, felt that these judges should be subservient to no one, so their rulings could be objective and without political pressures and prejudices that might slur their judgment. Not all agreed, though. Thomas Jefferson, especially, feared that appointments for life might cause the Court to become independent of the will of the nation. Also, he didn't favor the idea that their rulings could not be challenged or vetoed. It was his greatest fear that lifetime appointments and unchecked decisions could leave the country at the mercy of the singular authority of the small group on the Court.

Today, it could be argued that Jefferson's fears were somewhat founded. Lifetime appointments seem to have been balanced somewhat as a result of natural spacing of retirements so that one president can't appoint an entirely new membership, although Franklin Roosevelt tried to control the composition of the court by proposing the addition of six more members selected by him to support New Deal programs. But the lack of provisions for checks and balances on the Court's decisions has resulted in the evolution of its power to distort the original meaning of the Constitution. It started early during Jefferson's lifetime, he called it interpretation, or construction, of the Constitution. The practice grew into judicial review, through its power to declare laws void. Using this control, the Court can assume the authorities of the other branches of the government.

Jefferson's fears of interpreting the Constitution by squeezing its text, and inventing new arguments around it to conform to political policy have materialized. Today, it is called judicial activism. The Supreme Court has stated that many of its rulings were compelled to meet social needs and comply with established public policy. This is a dangerous assessment of the Court's role and power. It was not intended to carry out public policy. Slavery, for example, was once public policy. This is a case in point for why the Court should not be deciding social needs. Madison and others meant this authority to remain in the hands of the people through laws established by public opinion, not for a small, privileged group of lawyers to decide for them. This judicial activism has developed into administration of state schools, state prisons, and state employment practices.

Now the Court appears to be split between conservative and liberal ideals, with each generally appointed by the prevailing party membership of the appointing president. Their activism, instead of their loyalty to the Constitution, has resulted in both judicial legislation and judicial administration. Acting as the ultimate authority of judicial legislation the Court takes over the enumerated legislative powers of the Congress, and it further assumes executive powers when it exercises the idea of judicial administration.

CORRUPTING INFLUENCES

The first two hundred years of the nation's history shows the effects of the law of entropy, where it is the natural disposition of each branch of the government to assume more power, thus eroding the power of the people. Using methods of interpretation and political influence the government has circumvented the mutual contract and drifted away from self-government through laws established by public opinion. According to the principle of chaos (entropy), when the people fail to add energy and effort to maintain the Constitution, the country falls under the rule of the governing class, and each branch of the government competes for power and attempts to work around the Constitution as they try to impose their ideals upon the people, instead of following the will of the people.

Movement away from the Constitution is the result of the struggle for power and the corrupting influences that develop from it. Perhaps the largest corrupting influence has been the two-party system that has developed and controlled political choices since the beginning. A political party is really nothing more than a union, a group seeking privilege with the goal of imposing its views and ideas upon the country. Party histories are filled with stories of corruption, including paybacks and strong-arm methods by power bosses using their control of government to support their extraordinary lifestyles. The system of government today is at the mercy of the two major party unions. The parties select candidates for voters and encourage unyielding factions among the people. Nearly all of the founding forefathers opposed the party idea.

Benjamin Franklin reminded his colleagues that they were sent by the people to consult with one another, not to contend with each other. Party loyalty today is an absolute barrier to the nation's business. Loyalty, and faith and pride in their party are often more vital to their self-respect than consulting with the opposition for the good of the country. One hundred years ago it was not uncommon for delegates to the national party convention to have their official badges cast in gold and passed along in their wills. This fierce party loyalty has pervaded all levels of government and perverted sincere and trustworthy activity in deference to their pursuit of power and privilege. Today, as soon as one party holds the majority it strong-arms the other as much as possible. It becomes the tyranny of the majority instead of consideration for the minority in the balance of power. When the party power in government is closely matched, the American public is faced with stubborn gridlock, and the more that government authority is centralized, the split between parties is aggravated. The party system, especially the two-party system, may be the single most corrupting assault on the Constitution.

Professional lobbyists are another corrupting force that endangers the Constitution. Fortunately, they are exercising their right to petition the government as established by the First Amendment in the Bill of Rights. This gives any common citizen the right to submit a bill for consideration, and it should be forever protected. But the power of petitioning the government has been somewhat perverted by the use of professional lobbyists to influence government officials. Lobbyist activity has been additionally enabled by the progressive income tax system. Scrapping this tax system likely could reduce lobbyist abuses. There are more than 17,000 professional lobbyists in Washington, D.C. seeking to persuade representatives to support their aims. Naturally, money and privilege are used to encourage acceptance of their goals. This includes campaign contributions, free meals at high-end restaurants, use of skyboxes, entertainment events, and all manors of clever inducements.

Many lobbyists are former legislators, and it is not uncommon for lobbyists to write legislation. They receive enormous salaries as lobbyists, which catapult them into wealthy millionaires. It often is a status that they indignantly opposed as representatives, including sanctimonious positions against corporate executive pay and the rich in general. Some lobbyist firms even work both sides of an issue in order to force each opposing group to employ lobbyists. Although lobbying, or petitioning the government is the Constitutional right of every citizen, the professional business has stretched ethical limits and contributed further to the problems of stubborn factions.

The combination of government subsidies and entitlements with unlimited deficit spending has had inordinate consequences on the Constitutional system. For years now, elected officials have pushed to develop more programs to distribute aid and subsidies to those it has decided are the deserving few. As a result, the Congressional agenda has been one of passing more laws and more regulations, and it has become the measurement by which it judges its effectiveness. Politicians often boast of the accomplishments of a given Congressional session where many legislative bills have been made law, instead of how they have made the government more efficient or planned for the future. This drive to add more give-away programs has left America without a coherent national plan, and worse, as it piles program upon program, there are many duplications and wastes that are lost in the paperwork. Without a national plan there is nothing to measure against; this means a senator or congressman may introduce a bill for a pet project, and it may be considered without evaluating its effect on the overall national plan and its constraints. Then, after a new program is implemented, there are precious few updates or measurements of its effectiveness. This leaves the country with unmanaged waste and duplications.

The unlimited spending permitted by the government also enables its disjointed program making. In order to continue the free flow of money to give-away recipients and rich federal salaries and benefits, legislators borrow without limitation to pay the bills. They give money to citizens for housing, food stamps, and Medicaid, even though there isn't adequate revenue to cover the costs of the programs. So the country borrows money from other countries, and in addition, it sends borrowed money as aid to most countries in the world, many which hate the United States.

The government's spending addiction has a less obvious element set up by subsidies. Many programs discussed in the list of failures include

Government Sponsored Enterprises, Social Security, Medicare, and health care, all of this without apparent limits. Americans constantly are shown the tremendous costs of entitlement programs such as Social Security and Medicare, as though there is no way to control them, so the nation is told it must borrow the money to continue them. These programs continue without limits. What private business could continue to exist under these conditions?

The country's primary revenue source, the income tax, has been distorted to suit the irresponsible management of the nation's treasury. There is no apparent limit on what the government may decide to tax its citizens, and the politics of class warfare could easily result with the government commandeering nearly all of the income of the most successful citizens and businesses. The income tax system has been transformed from a source of national revenue into a give-away system for manipulating public behavior to suit the ideals of the governing class. There are benefits for education, energy-efficient home improvement, child adoption expenses, health care credit, and more. But a really big perversion was implementation of the earned income credit program. This was a transfer of the welfare program from the government's social agencies to the revenue system. Its inefficiency and abuses are extraordinary.

Without a national plan the government continues to grow in size and cost without limits or an organized plan for now and the future. The number of government departments and people, and their pay and benefits continue to grow without consideration of available revenue. There is no rational consideration for the nation's energy requirements. The government has rambled from one program to another to push people into energy sources it has decided should be the future, even at huge cost increases for the American taxpayer. Such cost increases dilute one of the nation's strengths – low cost energy. There is a current push to abandon oil and coal in favor of other sources, but where is the transition plan or calculated cost burden? The country's low-cost food supply is the result of modest energy costs, so the loss of oil will increase the cost of food production without a reasonable replacement. A national energy policy is needed that includes research and development of new energy sources, with a market-led transition to sources chosen by free and productive American citizens.

The entropic pressures on the Constitution have been titanic, especially in the last one hundred years. Each branch of the government has wrestled for more control of the people by constructing new explanations of the Constitution. These vacuum sweepers of power have accumulated more authority in the name of good causes that the governing class has decided are best for the people. Their hedging of the American Contract magnifies corrupting influences and distortion of the Constitution, losing sight of its intended protection of self-rule through public opinion and communication.

CHAPTER EIGHT

GOVERNMENT CHAINS

AS SURELY AS THE COUNTRY'S FOUNDERS believed the English tax imposed upon them was a form of slavery, Americans today are totally chained to the bloated and convoluted progressive income tax system they are compelled to use. Modern Americans serve the system instead of the system serving its citizens. The trials and tribulations of innocent American taxpayers are legendary. The system is burdensome, inconsistent, and filled with traps that devastate the lives of many citizens through no fault of their own other than the inability to understand the thousands of regulations, exceptions, and limitations.

In all probability, most Americans don't realize there are other ways to collect taxes without having federal fingers in every aspect of their income, and without the annual ritual of "reporting in" to the government. Because the current system has been in existence for one hundred years, today's citizens just don't realize that an original alternative existed. As a result, the tax system of today is more or less forced upon the people, instead of being chosen by the people to be the means of financing the government. Modern representatives seem to think they know what is best for the people, instead of listening to their constituents' choice of law. Given an alternative, it's entirely possible that the U.S. citizens of today are fed up with this burdensome scheme and would favor a less intrusive method.

In truth, the American forefathers never would have supported the assault of this oppressive system on personal freedoms. The authorization to collect taxes was meant to provide money to run the government, not to control the behavior of its citizens and take their personal fortunes. They described the two basic forms of taxation: the direct or internal tax, and the indirect or external tax. Direct taxes are imposed on a person, property, or income, while an indirect tax is levied against finished goods or work-in-process and is passed on to the consumer. The founders believed the direct tax method was impossible to fairly assess and collect, so when the Constitution was launched, the use of direct taxes was restricted to a uniform assessment for each individual. Today, through a Constitutional amendment, the inequitable direct tax system is used by the governing class as a form of control over American citizens in a similar manner to the monarchs of old. Unfortunately, the rule of infinity of actions restricts the ability of committee-rule to adequately assess all of the effects of this repressive tax system, and as a result, it has become an unmanageable monster.

Americans are bewildered by a tax system that leaves many of them with fearful anxiety. Who among the forefathers could have imagined that the country would create a tax system that hovers with a foreboding over the daily lives of a presumably free people? Because the system has become so complicated the majority of taxpayers are forced to pay a tax preparer or purchase computer software to help them through the maze of regulations and exclusion rules. Their anxiety level peaks during preparation of their tax return as they worry whether they will owe money they don't have. Many are left with substantial debt that must be repaid over time, with interest, and they are left disheartened and resentful. It is an absolute parallel to the strong-arm methods used by tyrannical tax collectors through history as they punished citizens for their inability to pay the imposed charges.

The burdensome system of today is filled with abstract accounting rules that can be a mystery even to accountants, professional tax preparers, and the IRS itself. Taxpayers must try to understand differences in deductions, credits, and exclusions. Most citizens are mystified by terms such as adjusted gross income, and they tense when faced with understanding the IRS term of tax liability, because it sounds to them like they're going to have to send in more. Hardworking Americans that save and invest for the future face boggling descriptions of depreciation, basis, capital gains, and more, that drain the joy out of their lives. The average American should be free to work, produce, play, live, and die without the weight of an oppressive government on their backs. One humorous commentary among those in the tax preparation business is based upon a play on the word, code, as used in the term, tax code. It jokes that it is called a code, because, "You can't read it. It doesn't make any sense. It's scrambled and nobody can figure it out." Of course the humor refers to rule upon rule with cross-reference to cross-reference and exception upon exception. It begins with the primary IRS publication for individual taxpayers. This guide has about 300 pages, and many of the sections in the publication refer to yet other publications on specific subjects that the taxpayer may need to work through the labyrinth of rules. Just the instructions for the basic Form 1040 are about 100 pages long, including tables. Even the taxpayer that successfully negotiates the gauntlet of rules to file a correct return is faced with burdensome recordkeeping. Many of the recordkeeping requirements are accounting rules that require the taxpayer to know when an item was purchased, for how much, and so on. The common citizen is not trained, and often is unable, to understand these abstract concepts, and so is relegated to paying for help. It's a pitiless restriction on freedom.

Every year leaves many citizens caught in traps of the system that leave them in debt. Often inadequate withholding due to their inattention or poor understanding causes it, or a mistake by an employer can cause it, too. Windfall income almost always causes a tax crisis for the receiver. Cashing an annuity or retirement plan, selling property, and other transactions such as winnings from the lottery, a game show, or gambling, can trigger an unexpectedly large tax event. One of the most insidious traps involves taxable unemployment benefits. Many Americans are unaware of the implications and are often brusquely informed at the unemployment office about possible tax problems. Those who receive the payment without withholding while they are out of work usually face a tax bill at the end of the year. Cancelled debt is just about as cruel. Consider the example of a taxpayer that is unemployed and unable to make car payments while facing repossession. The taxpayer owes more on the auto loan than the car is worth, so by negotiating with the loan company, a $5,000 balance due is reduced to $3,000, an amount the taxpayer can pay off from personal savings. At the end of the year, the taxpayer receives a notice of cancellation of $2,000 debt and must pay federal, and usually state, income tax on it.

The big change of 1913 has become a give-away game for many Americans as the means for raising revenue has been perverted into a method for bestowing vested rights. The distinction between unalienable and statutory rights is blurred by the idea of government-provided income, food, housing, health care, and retirement benefits. The progressive code uses the income of succeeding, or younger, generations to pay for the privileges of the current group of people receiving government payouts. States and local governments quickly dog piled on progressive income tax methods as they implemented their own direct taxes for a cornucopia of government programs. Now the new Health Care and Education Reconciliation Act of 2010, with its seven-year phase in will pile on more new taxes, new rules for individual lifestyles, new subsidies, and new traps for unsuspecting taxpayers.

The progressive income tax system used in America is based upon the idea of equalizing the classes. The more a citizen earns, the more the tax burden. Of course, professional politicians make it worse by inciting different class levels against one another using the old progressive tax battle cry from one hundred years ago to, "tax the rich." But even a citizen of modest income can be absurdly abused in this system of traps by becoming one of the rich for a year. This is often the result of windfall income.

Naturally, the idea of a progressive tax was repugnant to the founders. They believed every able-bodied person has a natural duty of contributing an equal share to the necessities of society. An amusing analogy might be the religious tithe encouraged or required by many faiths. It doesn't say support the church by giving ten percent of your earnings, unless, of course, you earn more than $10,000, you have children, deductible medical or business expenses, adoption credits, education credits, and other excuses, that reduce the amount of support you should give to the expenses of the congregation.

THE BIG CHANGE

Evolution of the tax system was briefly discussed with the list of government failures, but here are a few specifics on the transition. Initially the power and restrictions on taxation were established in Sections Eight and Nine of the Constitution. The often discussed general welfare clause from Article I, Section 8, Clause 1 of the Constitution authorizes Congress to "lay and collect taxes, duties, imposts and excises, to pay the debts and provide for the common defense and general welfare of the United States; but all duties, imposts and excises shall be uniform throughout the United States." Article I, Section 9, Clause 4 prohibits progressive taxation. It reads, "No capitation, or other direct tax shall be laid, unless in proportion to the census or enumeration herein directed be taken." These two provisions established by the founders make it pretty clear that they believed taxes should be equal among all citizens.

About seventy years later, though, the first income tax was authorized in July of 1861 to pay for the Civil War; it levied three percent of all income over $800. It was followed about thirty years later, in 1894, by a two percent tax on income over $4,000. This was needed to make up revenue lost through tariff reductions, which were a primary source of government revenue at that time. Though not popular, less than ten percent of American households earned enough to require payment. The following year, tax rules included taxes on real estate rent, interest income, and other types of direct tax. It was appealed, however, and the Supreme Court ruled that direct taxes had to be apportioned according to the Constitution. As a result, it was decided that equal distribution was impractical, so this ruling effectively prohibited tax on property.

But the big change came in 1913 with ratification of the Sixteenth Amendment to the Constitution. It allowed Congress "to lay and collect taxes on incomes, from whatever source derived, without apportionment among the several States, and without regard to any census or enumeration." And so the monster was born, and it has continued to grow until it is too big to effectively manage and has become an instrument for controlling citizens instead of a method of raising revenue for the administration of government. During World War Two, in order to support war expenses, the government implemented the idea of the pay-as-you-go system and withholding of pay. This 1943 rule deprives the citizens of their earnings before they are paid, and most taxpayers are completely oblivious to how much to withhold.

HOW IT WORKS

In order to understand the bias and many of the abuses of the current tax system, a brief and simple look at how the whole thing works is offered. The basic steps and layout of the Form 1040 tax return is shown in Figure 8-1 to help visualize the discussion of the process.

Everyone hears the terms, deductions and credits, but at the tax desk few taxpayers understand the difference. Simply stated, deductions refer to an authorized reduction of income, which in turn reduces the taxable income, but credits are the more powerful provision to reduce the total tax after it has been calculated. For example, compare a $1,000 deduction with a $1,000 credit for a taxpayer in the fifteen percent tax bracket. The deduction is subtracted from the taxpayer's reported income and is not counted for tax purposes, so the actual savings will depend upon the taxpayer's tax bracket level; in the example it is fifteen percent, so the taxpayer saves fifteen percent of the $1,000 or a reduction in taxes of $150. The $1,000 credit, though, is subtracted after total taxes have been calculated, and it reduces the tax due dollar for dollar, or $1,000. So, in the example, the same $1,000 deduction saves $150, while the credit saves $1,000. Obviously, the credits are generally much more powerful for the taxpayer. This distinction between deductions and credits will be necessary to understand the code as it is explored further. The most important concept of deductions and credits is to realize that these are gifts from fellow taxpayers. Every deduction or credit reduces the tax bill for one taxpayer, while those without these reductions pay more. The governing class utilizes these methods to manipulate taxpayer behavior to suit their ideas of who deserves a favor, or what type of car should be driven. This insidious manipulation of the country's revenue system is perhaps the most abusive and unjust of all government actions.

The first step for the taxpayer starting to work on the tax return is to decide filing status and number of dependents, if any, as shown in Figure 8-1. There are five filing statuses, and it can be a daunting and confusing chore for the taxpayer to decide theirs. The names for the filing statuses befuddle folks; for example, many believe they are the Head of Household, because they are the sole provider. It often isn't the case and causes audits. There are many rules and exceptions to deal with in order to establish filing status and

Basic Steps to Prepare a Tax Return

Step 1 – Determine Filing Status and Number of Exemptions

Step 2 – Add up Gross Income
     Wages
     Interest – Dividends – Capital Gains
     Business, Farm, Rental Income
     Pensions – Social Security
     Other Income (Unemployment, Alimony Income, Gambling, etc)

Step 3 – Subtract Adjustments and Deductions
     Health Savings Account – IRA Contribution
     Other Expenses (Student Loan Interest, Alimony Paid, etc)
   Adjusted Gross Income (AGI) is result of Step 2 minus Step 3

Step 4 – Subtract Personal Deductions and Exemptions from AGI
     Standard or Itemized Deduction
     Personal and Dependent Exemptions Deduction
   Taxable Income is result of Step 3 minus Step 4

Step 5 – Determine Initial Tax Liability
     Tax is based on rates for Taxable Income from Step 4

Step 6 – Subtract Credits from Tax Liability from Step 5
     Childcare Credit
     Education Credit
     Child Tax Credit
     Residential Energy and Other Credits

Step 7 Add Additional Taxes to total from Step 6
     Self-employment Tax (Social Security and Medicare)
     Penalty on Early Retirement Withdrawal (401(k), IRA, etc)

Step 8 Subtract Payments and Other Credits from Step 7 subtotal
     Withholding
     Earned Income Credit
     Additional Child Tax Credit
     Other Credits
   Result of Step 8 shows Refund or Payment Due

This illustration does not include all Form 1040 lines and items

Basic Steps to Prepare a Tax Return
Figure 8-1

who can be claimed as a dependent. It is impossible for many taxpayers to decipher the rules to simply determine their filing status. As a result, many people file the wrong status and claim too much or too little tax requirement. If they don't pay enough taxes, they receive a letter from the IRS demanding more. If they pay too much it is rare that the IRS identifies it and sends a refund, so the taxpayer pays more than the law provides.

After reading several pages of explanations regarding filing status and dependency rules, the taxpayer is ready to add up income in Step 2. But it isn't a simple task, because the Congress has identified different categories of income with different tax treatment; they refer to it as ordinary income and other rates. So, the taxpayer decides wages, which is usually simple and based upon a report from their employer on Form W-2, but even this report is a mystery to many taxpayers. Most don't understand the boxes and codes on the W-2 Wage Statement. In addition, there are income categories for interest on savings accounts, dividends from stocks, and capital gains on sales. The average taxpayer that asks for help has no idea of what a dividend or capital gain is or means, much less how to treat them differently from the few dollars of interest their savings account earned. If an individual is self-employed, there are categories for businesses, farms, rental income, and royalties from various sources. Older folks face different categories for private pensions, social security payments, and withdrawals from Individual Retirement Arrangements (IRA) and other retirement savings plans. The accounting rules for taking payment from an IRA or other retirement plan can be overwhelming, even for an experienced accountant; it's a hateful legacy for the elderly who are suffering from confusion or slow thought during their advanced years. They come to the tax desk asking preparers to just take care of it and leaving their trust in the preparer's hands. Is this the way free citizens should be treated, especially in their declining years?

After the taxpayer has identified all of the sources of income, they next enter the amounts on the proper lines established by the IRS report Form 1040 and its family of forms. Before entering values on Form 1040 for capital gains, social security, and other forms of income that are not categorized as ordinary income, the taxpayer must refer to other forms, worksheets, and more pages of instructions in order to determine the proper amount to be entered on the proper line of Form 1040. When the taxpayer has figured out all sources of income, then they are added together to establish gross income as shown in the second step of Figure 8-1.

After the total gross income has been determined, then the taxpayer may complete Step 3 to make adjustments to income in the form of various deductions allowed by Congress. Some examples are listed in Figure 8-1. Folks that are paying off student loans may deduct the interest here, and people that pay alimony may deduct the amount paid from their income. In addition, people paying education expenses and people contributing to a

Health Savings Account may deduct these expenses from income, but there are rules and restrictions that require more instructions, forms, and worksheets to determine the amount actually allowable for a deduction on the Form 1040. If the taxpayer contributed to an IRA, there are instructions and worksheets to determine whether there are limits on the amount of their IRA contribution. If they exceed limits, there could be strict penalties to pay. No wonder low income and poorly educated taxpayers avoid this program. There are many other types of deductions, but these are common and give an idea of how the taxpayer is drawn deeper into the spider web of rules, exceptions, and forms. After successfully determining the amounts allowed as adjustments to income and entering these amounts on the proper line of the reporting form, the taxpayer may add up these deductions and subtract them from the total gross income that has been calculated previously in Step 2. The reduced income shown in Step 3 is called the adjusted gross income, or AGI. Again, many Americans hear this AGI term often, but have no concept of the meaning. It's simply the total or gross income adjusted for deductions, but it may as well be a foreign language for many taxpayers; they just aren't accountants.

With the AGI determined, the taxpayer is ready to go to page two of the Form 1040, if required for their situation. This is Step 4 where the next thing the bewildered taxpayer must do is to subtract more deductions from the AGI amount. There are two deductions called the standard deduction and the personal exemptions. Both are actually deductions, the personal exemption meaning a certain amount is exempt from income tax. The deductible amount is based upon the filing status previously determined by the taxpayer, and for 2010 the standard deduction for a single person was $5,700, and for married people filing together it was $11,400. This means their first $5,700 or $11,400 is not taxable. Similarly, there are different standard deduction amounts for the other filing statuses. The personal exemption amount is income excused for each member of a household. In 2010 the amount was $3,650 per person. So, the single person receives an additional deduction of $3,650 and the married couple receives $7,300, or $3,650 each. When the amounts excused from taxes are added, the single person received $5,700 plus $3,650 or $9,350, and the married couple's deduction was $11,400 plus $7,300 or $18,700. As it turns out, these were the thresholds for filing taxes for these two filing statuses; this means, if individuals earned less than their threshold, they were not required to file a tax return. But many will want to file anyway in order to obtain a fat welfare refund despite the fact they don't any pay taxes at all.

To add to the confusion, the tax system allows the taxpayer to elect to use the standard deduction or to itemize deductions. A taxpayer may elect to use a standard amount that is based upon their filing status, such as $5,700 for single filers, and is equal for all taxpayers, or they may choose to deduct their actual allowed expenses if these expenses are greater than the standard amount. Because these actual expenses are reported item by item, the IRS refers to them as itemized deductions. Naturally, the itemized deduction form is long and detailed, and it is accompanied by page upon page of rules and exceptions that describe what Congress has decided are allowable deductions.

All taxpayers wonder about or are told that certain expenses are deductible. There are generally five circumstances that make it reasonable to file the itemized form. The most common is the allowance for mortgage interest paid on a home and second home, if the taxpayer is lucky enough to own two homes. This was a popular deduction for decades, but today it is less common, because the standard deduction has increased steadily, and mortgage rates have decreased. Of course, there is no point to itemizing deductions if the actual amount is less than the standard deduction; the taxpayer should select the larger of the two. For a married couple, it should be more than $11,400. More prosperous taxpayers have large mortgages and pay yearly interest of $20,000 and more. Obviously, they are over the threshold and this opens the door for many other forms of deductions, such as real estate tax, state tax, and gifts to charity. Folks with modest homes rarely have enough mortgage interest and other deductions that exceed the standard amount.

An important feature about itemized deductions is the inequity. In reality, the American people pay part of the mortgage interest for those who can afford to borrow large amounts. Consider the $20,000 mortgage interest paid by a married couple in a twenty-five percent tax bracket for an example. Also assume the real estate tax for this couple is about $4,000 a year, and they contributed $4,400 to charity. That's it, and it amounts to $28,400 in total deductions. This $28,400 is $17,000 above the $11,400 standard deduction and saves the couple, in the twenty-five percent tax bracket, $4,250. The government (their fellow citizens) pays this part of their mortgage interest, real estate taxes, and gifts to charity. Now consider their next-door neighbor that has saved a down payment for their home and has a smaller mortgage. They pay $4,000 in real estate taxes, too, and also contributed $4,400 to their church. But their mortgage interest is only about $2,500. Their deductions fall below the $11,400 threshold, so they don't get the extra deductions, and they pay part of their neighbors' mortgage, gifts, and taxes. If a single person owns a house in the neighborhood, they may get help for amounts above $5,700. Fair? Equitable? Soak the rich? Baloney.

Another extraordinary expense that vaults folks above the standard deduction is job expense paid out of their own pocket. Common jobs in this category are traveling salesmen and transportation workers such as truck drivers. The government allows a standard mileage rate for individuals who drive their own cars for business purposes at their own cost. Many of these folks can accumulate 50,000 miles a year and more, so this expense alone can add up to more than $25,000 per year. Truck drivers receive meal allowances based upon the number of days they are away from home. Over-the-road drivers are often away from home for 300 days a year, which can result in deduction amounts similar to a traveling salesman. These business deductions require yet another form and set of instructions. After the supplementary form has been completed the result is carried back to the appropriate line on the form for itemized deductions where more arithmetic is necessary to determine what portion of the expenses are eligible to be deducted.

Gifts to charity can exceed the standard deduction. Very wealthy people easily exceed the standard deduction, but it is not uncommon to see an average taxpayer receive a large inheritance and give $20,000 or more of it to charity. Although the generosity of these people is admirable, the government and fellow taxpayers contribute a portion of it for them when it is itemized.

Extraordinary medical expenses can bring tax relief above the standard deduction. But medical expenses have an additional bogey, or deductible, to exceed before medical expenses can be deducted at all. The floor, or deductible amount that must be exceeded is calculated at 7.5 percent of the taxpayer's AGI. This means that for an AGI calculated at $50,000, none of the medical expenses can be deducted until they exceed $3,750, so if the taxpayer has $3,751 of medical expense, one dollar may be added to the itemized amount. Most who qualify to claim this deduction have been very ill with ailments such as cancer or heart surgery.

The last of the five main reasons to itemize could be a casualty loss. This is usually a loss of property value as a result of an accident, natural disaster, or thievery. Many people are reimbursed by insurance for their losses, and so there is nothing to claim. For those that suffer large out-of-pocket losses the government allows them to deduct the loss that exceeds $100 plus ten percent of their AGI. Again, if this is their only deduction, they often need losses exceeding $20,000 or more, and it is somewhat rare.

None of the itemized claims are without bookkeeping and recordkeeping requirements. There must be receipts, logs, and records that the IRS may insist upon seeing if the taxpayer is audited. Itemized deductions are often a trigger for audit by the government, and if reasonable proof cannot be shown to the IRS agent, then the deduction will likely be disallowed and the taxpayer will owe additional taxes plus penalties for late payment, and interest on the amount due. Naturally, the IRS and the common taxpayer have different views of reasonable proof.

The incongruity of itemized deductions that should be remembered is that these expenses, losses, and contributions are partly paid by fellow taxpayers. When a celebrity or wealthy taxpayer avoids taxes with a huge charitable gift, it could be argued that other citizens gave part of it. When a huge mortgage and real estate taxes accompany the purchase of a luxurious home, it could be said fellow citizens pay the deducted amount. This is the imbalance of the method of taxation used today. The country's founders tried to avoid it, but the citizens of 1913 released the constrictor from its cage.

Now that the taxpayer has navigated the mystifying rules, forms, and calculations to determine filing status, dependents, standard or itemized deductions, and personal deductions, the job is about half complete. After all the deductions are subtracted from the AGI, the remainder is the taxable income. This is the amount that is finally used to calculate the taxpayer's tax liability in Step 5. Here is where the infamous progressive tax brackets are used. Many folks mistake the progressive system to mean that if their income is in the twenty-five percent tax bracket, then they pay twenty-five percent of what they earn in taxes. That is not strictly accurate. The progressive system is actually an average of different tax rates on different amounts. Look at the examples in Figure 8-2. It shows the different tax brackets for 2010 and the amount of taxable income that is taxed at that rate. So, all single taxpayers pay ten percent on the first $8,375 of taxable income (all married joint filers the first $16,750). This includes a wealthy entertainer or multi-billionaire, all pay ten percent at this level, and so on through each bracket. The next $25,625 (up to $34,000 single) is taxed at fifteen percent for all taxpayers. For a taxpayer in the $30,000 range the actual tax rate would be an average between ten and fifteen percent; for $30,000 taxable income it's about 13.6 percent.

2010 Progressive Tax Rates (Brackets)

Single Taxpayer			Married Joint Taxpayers		
Taxable Income			Taxable Income		
Over	Not Over	Tax Rate	Over	Not Over	Tax Rate
$0	$8,375	10%	$0	$16,750	10%
8,375	34,000	15%	16,750	68,000	15%
34,000	82,400	25%	68,000	137,300	25%
82,400	171,850	28%	137,300	209,250	28%
171,850	373,650	33%	209,250	373,650	33%
373,650	no limit	35%	373,650	no limit	35%

Tax Brackets and Effective Tax Rates
Figure 8-2

Examples of effective tax rates for a single taxpayer are shown in the second section of Figure 8-2. Both actual income and taxable income are shown. Remembering that a single person in 2010 was not required to pay taxes on the first $9,350 earned, the taxable income is reduced by this amount from the actual income earned. As a result, two effective rates can be considered: the effective tax rate on actual income, and the similar rate on taxable income. Using the same $30,000 taxable income example, the taxpayer would have actually earned $39,350 before the standard deduction, and the effective tax rate on actual income would be about 10.4 percent as shown in the figure.

Examples of Single Taxpayer Effective Tax Rates For 2010					
Income		Marginal	Actual	Effective Tax Rates	
Actual	Taxable	Tax Rate	Tax Rate	Actual	Taxable
$14,350	$5,000	10%	$503	3.5%	10.1%
24,350	15,000	15%	1,835	7.5%	12.2%
39,350	30,000	15%	4,085	10.4%	13.6%
59,350	50,000	25%	8,688	14.6%	17.4%
89,350	80,000	25%	16,188	18.1%	20.2%
109,350	100,000	28%	21,709	19.9%	21.7%
159,350	150,000	28%	35,709	22.4%	23.8%
209,350	200,000	33%	51,117	24.4%	25.6%
359,350	350,000	33%	100,617	28.0%	28.7%
409,350	400,000	35%	117,644	28.7%	29.4%
1,009,350	1,000,000	35%	327,644	32.5%	32.8%
100,009,350	100,000,000	35%	34,977,644	34.9%	34.9%

Note:
Taxable Income is the Actual Income after subtracting the amounts for Deductions and Exemptions. The Standard Deduction & Exemption amount for a Single Taxpayer in 2010 was $9,350, thus, when Actual Income is $14,350, Taxable Income is $5,000 ($14,350 - $9,350), and so forth.

Tax Brackets and Effective Tax Rates
Figure 8-2 (continued)

The examples in Figure 8-2 show the real mechanics and mystery of the progressive tax system for federal taxes; the taxpayer still must deal with state and local taxes. It shows that a person with a taxable income of $1 million is in the top bracket, but after averaging all of the smaller rates, the effective rate is actually about 32.8 percent (32.5 percent actual). Only when the taxable income approaches $100 million or higher does the effective rate become practically the top rate of 35%. Of course, few individuals with high incomes pay these tax rates. They seek all types of government subsidies and tax shelters, such as special farms or environmental preservation loopholes that afford them reduced actual tax payments. The alternative minimum tax plan was designed to avoid this situation, but Congress has provided plenty of new gifts to help the very wealthy avoid taxes altogether. Again, it is the average W-2 earner with no deductions or credits that proportionally carries the major tax burden.

Now that the tax liability has been determined, based upon the amount of taxable income, the taxpayer may review all of the give-away programs the government has established to help those it has decided deserve them; and, reductions may be claimed, which federal schemers use to maneuver taxpayers into its desired pattern of behavior These are the credits. Step 6 in Figure 8-1 shows some of the credits that can be used to reduce tax liability. For those who aren't eligible for any of the credit programs, they simply skip Step 6 and continue to the next set of instructions.

But for those eligible for credits it is time to read more instructions, and to start additional forms and worksheets to determine how much, if any, tax credit is permissible. There are two types of credits in the long list of credits that the government manipulates each year: assistance credits for disadvantaged or privileged individuals, and incentive credits designed to manipulate taxpayer behavior to suit the objectives of the Congress, the President, and various governmental departments. These would be credit for activity that has been determined to be proper behavior by the government. Usually, the credits are listed in order of preference and must be deducted in the order identified on the Form 1040. The sum of total credits in Step 6 may not exceed tax liability, that is, the credit total may not add up to more than the liability calculated in Step 5. As a result, few folks receive the full impact of these credits. Low-income folks have low tax liabilities, so they don't get much from these credits. For example, consider a single person who earns $11,000 and takes a college course. Their tax liability in 2010 was $166, so that is the credit limit for them in Step 6. But high-income folks are usually denied the credits altogether, so they can't use the credits, either.

Childcare credit is one of the first credits on the list. As the number of households with two wage earners, and the number of single parent households increased in this country, so did the need for childcare. The Congress decided that these households deserved help from the other taxpayers, and provided a tax credit for these situations. It's a graduated system depending on household earnings, but low-income individuals may have up to thirty-five percent of their daycare costs paid from the treasury. These folks usually don't receive the maximum credit, though, because again, their tax liability is very low, or zero, and this credit may not be more than their tax liability.

Education credits are next, and there is a baffling array of different types of credits. Taxpayers are faced with the decision to determine which credits they are eligible for and which will have the greatest benefit for them. In addition, there are deductions for education, too. Each of the different credits and deductions cover different types of education expenses, such as tuition, fees, books, room and board, and driving mileage. Certain programs are designed for the first two years of college only, some for all undergraduate years only, some for graduate work, and some for work-related school. Every program has its own set of rules and limitations. Usually, the credits are the most powerful, but in some cases it works out where a deduction program provides the best benefit. Most taxpayers can't figure out the differences, though.

Although politicians may crow about the need for education and what they have done to support it with these programs, in reality many Americans receive little or no credit for college costs, especially again, the low-income taxpayer that has little or no tax liability, and so the education credit is limited by these provisions. There are numerous major education incentives, depending upon what is available in a given year; these programs come and go according to the whims of Congress. The smorgasbord of programs and rules is confusing to most taxpayers, especially those of modest means, which presumably were the intended beneficiaries. Many households don't claim the credit at all because they are confounded by the rules for determining dependency and credit eligibility. High-income earners, generally starting at $60,000 for single and $120,000 married, can't take the credit at all.

How about a credit for saving for retirement? A lot of taxpayers are unfamiliar with this one. The Congress wants more Americans to save for retirement, so a credit is allowed for many retirement savings programs, such as an IRA or 401(k), and others. It's meant to help low-income taxpayers with their savings programs, so the government reimburses them for up to half of what they save. For example, if an individual contributes $2,000 to a retirement plan, up to $1,000 may be returned to them by this credit; they put in $1,000 and their fellow citizens contribute $1,000 to their retirement plan. Some folks get the fifty percent, but most don't, because the low-income requirements again result with a low tax liability that in turn limits the amount of retirement savings credit. Single taxpayers that earned more than $27,750 (AGI) and married taxpayers with a household AGI above $55,500 were ineligible in 2010.

Child tax credit is a big one for families with children. This program has been in effect since the early nineties to aid families with children. It provides a $1,000 tax credit for each dependent child in the household under seventeen years old, and it adds up significantly for large families. It's a gift from taxpayers with no children to those with children, because the governing class decided families with children were extra deserving. Low-income families often don't receive the full amount due to low tax liability, but the government, to make up the difference, added a second provision; it is called the additional child tax credit. If a tax liability is too low to allow credit for all of the child tax credit, then the difference may be added as additional child tax credit to make up the full $1,000 amount. As an example, say the tax liability in a given case is $400, so the child tax credit is limited to that amount, but the extra $600 might be claimed later, in Step 8 of the process, as additional child tax credit. More forms, more rules, and more calculations are required to decide. Very low-income families may not receive the entire $1,000, and high-income families are restricted by the amount that may be claimed. A single person's credit was reduced when earnings exceeded $75,000, and a married couple's phase out started at $110,000 in 2010. These aren't rich people, but hard workers such as pharmacists or department store managers. A single parent with two children that earns $115,000 is not considered deserving of government help.

After the credits that are restricted by the tax liability have been figured in Step 6, then the total tax is reduced by the amount of credits allowed. Next, comes a category in Step 7 called additional taxes that are added back on to the subtotal of total tax calculated in Step 5. The two most common taxes in this category are self-employment tax and the penalty on early withdrawals from a retirement plan. Self-employment tax is required for individuals with earnings that did not come from an employer, so Social Security and Medicare taxes were not withheld. It often results with the taxpayer owing a balance due. When an employer withholds Social Security and Medicare taxes from an employee's earnings, the employer pays a matching amount to the government. The total taxes for both employer and employee are 15.3 percent of earnings. When an individual is self-employed, such as a private daycare provider or a contract laborer, then the entire amount must be paid by the self-employed taxpayer, and it is assessed at this point on the return. There is an entire set of instructions and forms to be navigated to figure this tax. Imagine a day laborer attempting to decipher dozens of pages and forms in order to figure out how much Social Security and Medicare tax to pay. It's impractical. The government has lost touch with the people.

The penalty on early withdrawals from certain retirement savings programs, such as an IRA or 401(k), is usually ten percent of the amount withdrawn from the account. It's generally straightforward, for example, if $3,000 are withdrawn, then the penalty tax will be $300. There is a list of exceptions that the taxpayer may use to avoid the penalty, but few do this. Again, the governing class decides who deserves to be excused from this penalty.

After other taxes have been calculated in Step 7 and added to the running total of the tax calculation, the taxpayer has another long list of credits to consider in hopes of further reducing their tax bill in Step 8 as shown in Figure 8-1. These are the most powerful credits, because their amount is not restricted by tax liability like those in Step 6, and they can add up quickly. Naturally, the first items on the list are withholding amounts paid on account to the IRS during the year by the taxpayer. Following this is the big one for most low-income taxpayers called Earned Income Credit, EIC. This one causes individuals that are not normally required to file to submit a return in order to claim this credit. This credit was designed by the governing class to reduce the number of idle people on the welfare rolls and encourage them to seek employment. As a result, this social services function has been placed upon the taxpayer and at the paid preparer's desk. The 2010 credit was based upon four taxpayer categories: those with no children, one child, two children, and three children. The more eligible children in the household, the more earned income credit can be claimed. Taxpayers filing in 2010 with one child may have received up to $3,050 while those with three could have had as much as $5,666 added to their gift from their neighbors. For example, a single mother with one child earning $10,000 may have her income increased to $13,050 with the added earned income credit.

This credit brings taxpayers to tax preparation offices in droves, because the forms are extensive and filled with yet more rules and calculations. It is common for many low-income earners with no tax liability to walk out the door with a $7,000 refund or more. In states which also allow EIC and child tax credits, there is even more added to the reward. Tax preparation companies are not inexpensive, though, and it is common for a tax return with earned income credit, child tax credit, and additional child tax credit to cost more than $200. Naturally, most of the low-income folks don't have the money to pay the fees, so the tax services usually include holding the tax preparation fees out of the refund, at additional cost. Consequently, the government, in its benevolent decision to give away taxpayer money to these programs, has established a system where several hundred dollars of each give-away to help the deserving few also supports the tax preparation business, and hides its administrative costs.

But this is a very abused system filled with fraud and deception. It is not uncommon for unscrupulous recipients to visit different tax preparers until they learn the correct answers to qualify for the credit, and then make the final visit with half-truths to receive the credit fraudulently. For example, a savvy single parent with five children knows that only three of them can be used to claim the earned income credit. So, some of these individuals will provide information about the other two children to a friend or relative, or worse yet, will sell the information. The person receiving the information only needs to mislead a tax preparer by claiming the children are their own and lived with them all year, thus they can claim earned income credit, too. The whole system is a terrible burden on the IRS and the community of paid tax preparers. It has nothing to do with raising revenue for the treasury, but is a social give-away program that better belongs to the human services administrators.

There are many other credits. Taxpayers are nudged into making energy efficient home improvements; for example, if they purchased a wood burning stove in 2010, or new windows, they could receive fifteen percent of the cost from the national treasury. There are credits for a small number of home buyers that purchased homes during a short window of opportunity where their neighbors will pay as much as $8,000 of the cost of their home. If a family purchases a home just one day out of the window, they receive nothing. How fair is that to all concerned? On and on the credit list goes that includes adoption credits and credits for certain types of fuel-efficient or alternative fuel vehicles. The adoption credit includes some remarkable rules. It allows credit to the taxpayer for the expenses of adopting a child, such as legal fees, court costs, and so forth. But, if it is a special needs child, then the taxpayer may receive the maximum allowable credit, even though it is more than they actually paid. Many believe that anyone benevolent enough to adopt a special needs child deserves a little extra help. In some states, though, if the child is adopted through the state foster home program, then all children are considered special needs and the taxpayer receives the maximum amount. The full amount in 2010 was $13,170 per child. Curiously, this was recently increased under the authority of the Health Care Reform Act of 2010. Is this part of health care? Apparently it is, in the opinion of the governing class that decides who deserves special benefits and how much.

The taxpayer is ready to figure the last step in the tax preparation process by comparing total credits with any remaining tax in Step 8. If credits are more than the tax, there is a refund, but if the tax is a larger number, then a balance is due. Also, at this point the taxpayer can calculate the effective tax rate after all credits and deductions. By dividing the final tax number in Step 8 by the taxable income amount in Step 4, the effective tax rate can be seen. This rate will be less than the maximum tax bracket amount.

Examples of effective tax rates for a single taxpayer in 2010 are shown in Figure 8-2. It is estimated that about forty-seven percent of Americans have no tax liability whatsoever. Figure 8-3 shows a few examples of how this occurs.

The first set of comparisons show what taxes would be for low-income earners before they receive the special credits. It compares three situations in the column headings for single, married, and married with one child. If none of them received EIC or child tax credit, then the single taxpayer would contribute $166 to the U.S. Treasury, the married couple $333, and the couple with one child would pay nothing, because an additional $3,650 of their income is shielded from taxes, thus leaving them no taxable income.

The second set of examples in the figure compare the same three situations, but with EIC and child tax credits added. There's no change for the married couple with no children. They aren't eligible for EIC, and they have no children, so they still pay $333. The single taxpayer, though, if between the ages of 25 and 65, can receive a payment of $186 for EIC, which effectively wipes out the $166 that was originally due, so this individual walks out the door with an extra $20 in hip national bank (pocketbook), courtesy of fellow citizens.

Examples of Low-income minimal taxes BEFORE CREDITS for 2010

Tax Information	Filing Situations		
	Single & no children	Married & no children	Married & 1 child
Income	$11,000	$22,000	$22,000
Standard Deduction	- 5,700	- 11,400	- 11,400
Personal Exemptions	- 3,650	- 7,300	- 10,950
Taxable Income	1,650	3,300	0
Tax Liability	166	333	0
Tax Due, D or Refund, R	D 166	D 333	0

Examples of Low-income taxes for 2010
With Earned Income Credit and Additional Child Tax Credit

Tax Information	Filing Situations		
	Single & no children	Married & no children	Married & 1 child
Income	$11,000	$22,000	$22,000
Standard Deduction	- 5,700	- 11,400	- 11,400
Personal Exemptions	- 3,650	- 7,300	- 10,950
Taxable Income	1,650	3,300	0
Tax Liability	166	333	0
Child Tax Credit	0	0	0
Earned Income Credit	- 186	0	- 2,960
Additional Child Tax Credit	0	0	- 1,000
Tax Due, D or Refund, R	R 20	D 333	R 3,960

Low or No Tax Liability Examples
Figure 8-3

The real winners in the second comparison, though, are the married couple with one child. Because they have a child, they are eligible for both EIC and child tax credits, and it adds up to a $3,960 gift. One way to look at it is, it will take almost twelve low-income married folks, paying $333, to make up for the gifts to the other two credit recipients.

	Filing Situations		
	Single &	Married &	Married &
Tax Information	3 children	no children	3 children
Income	$22,000	$22,000	$22,000
Standard Deduction	- 5,700	- 11,400	- 11,400
Personal Exemptions	-14,600	- 7,300	- 18,250
Taxable Income	1,700	3,300	0
Tax Liability	171	333	0
Child Tax Credit	- 171	0	0
Earned Income Credit	- 4,491	0	- 5,666
Additional Child Tax Credit	- 2,829	0	- 2,700
Tax Due, D or Refund, R	R 7,320	D 333	R 8,366

Examples of Low-income taxes for 2010
With Earned Income Credit and Additional Child Tax Credit

Low or No Tax Liability Examples
Figure 8-3 (continued)

The powerful effects of credits for children are shown in the last example, where a single person with three children, and married couples with and without three children are compared. The same $22,000 income is used throughout, but look at the refund differences. These are examples of how nearly forty-seven percent of Americans do not pay income taxes.

It means that after standard deductions, exemptions, and minimal credits, almost half of taxpayers do not contribute to the necessities of American society. Rather, many of these individuals receive a gift from the treasury. Who then, are the rich that many citizens believe should support this abusive system? Well, the average family earning the average wage in America from strictly W-2 sources, but does not qualify for any deductions or credits, carries a heavy tax load for the country. The very wealthy employ a menagerie of tax specialists to minimize their tax liability, and the lower-income taxpayers pay nothing, so the middle folks with nowhere to hide wind up remitting a large amount of their paycheck to the federal treasury. Is it fair? How can it be?

The governing class uses the system to support their pursuit of distinction by claiming to equalize benefits for all, but the law of infinity of actions limits their ability to understand or manage this tangled jumble of credits, give-away programs, favors, and the never-ending unattended consequences and harm inflicted upon innocent citizen taxpayers. The governing class spews rhetoric claiming vested rights for the disadvantaged while stepping on the unalienable rights of others, and the resulting Ponzi effects result in more waste, more deficits, and continued fiscal malfeasance.

TRAPS

When the government employs a tax code with so many rules, preferences, cross references, and exceptions, it establishes a veritable quick sand of traps for unsuspecting citizens. The burden of a heavy tax due may be caused by inadequate withholding, windfall income, retirement savings rollover procedures, unemployment compensation, cancelled debt, or a last minute government give-away such as the recent making work pay credit set up in 2009 and 2010 to stimulate the economy.

Inadequate withholding bites more taxpayers than probably any other reason for a tax due. Remember, the insidious practice of withholding started in 1943 that continues to rob Americans of their pay each pay period. There are forms that company workers must fill out when they start work, but few understand the form, and most forget what they have submitted after a year or so.

Self-employed workers most often have nothing withheld, and do not make estimated tax payments, so all of their tax comes due when they file. In addition, self-employed workers must remit Social Security and Medicare taxes at this time. Unlike the individual employed by a company where the company pays half of these social taxes, the self-employed must contribute twice the amount, because there is no employer contribution. As a result, an additional self-employment tax of almost fifteen percent must be paid when the return is filed.

Taxpayers with children have large deductions from income and up to $1,000 per child for child tax credit. When the child turns seventeen, the child tax credit is gone, and if the taxpayer fails to adjust the withholding, then a large tax may be due. Similarly, when the child turns nineteen, the deduction for a dependent is lost, unless the child stays in school. If their child stays in school, the taxpayer continues to receive the dependency deduction AND a large credit for education expenses, so the withholding continues unchanged for years. But, when the child graduates, all of the deductions and credits are gone, and if the taxpayer has not adjusted withholding, a sizeable amount will be due. Often, low-income taxpayers have little or no withholding, are surviving on the extra taxes saved from the child in school, and when the hammer falls after graduation, they are saddled with a tax bill they can't pay.

Sometimes the employer makes a withholding error or fails to comply with the taxpayer's instructions. Each year, it is not uncommon to see wage reports of withholding of zero, or nearly zero. The result can be a disaster for a taxpayer that must pay an entire year's taxes at the end of the year, but has spent it all to live on, and is now in debt to the government.

Another withholding problem occurs when both spouses in a household are employed. Naturally, the employers have no knowledge of the separate income, so they withhold taxes at the rate for the earnings of their employee. When the incomes of each spouse are added, however, the tax rate for the household income may be higher than each individual's income considered separately. For example, imagine a taxpayer earns about $80,000 per year, and the spouse has a part-time job earning around $10,000 per year. The taxpayer's highest tax rate is twenty-five percent, and withholding on this amount might be about $7,700. The spouse's minimal earnings alone would not be taxed, and often these part-time jobs result in no withholding at all. But, the spouse's income must be added to the taxpayer's income to determine total household income of $90,000, so the actual tax liability will be in the $10,200 range, leaving a tax payment due of about $2,500. In effect, the withholding on the part-time job should have been based upon the household income to avoid a large tax due. Taxpayers can make proper adjustments to avoid this situation, but most really don't understand the arithmetic and the potential trap.

Windfall income often occurs when taxpayers receive lump-sum distributions from annuities or retirement plans, or when they hit it big in the casino, lottery, or TV game show. Tax withholding is required for these situations, but often it is not enough, because the windfall withholding does not consider other income the taxpayer earns, nor is any penalty considered for early withdrawal from a retirement account. In virtually all cases, the applicable state tax is ignored for withholding, which can leave a sizeable state tax bite, too. In addition, the taxpayers do not receive enough counseling when they receive these distributions, so when they must settle at tax report time, the amount due can be substantial for the common wage earner.

Here is a tragic example of what can happen to taxpayers in these situations. Consider a married couple with a modest household income of about $39,000 a year; one is a school janitor, and the other is a hospital cook. For years this couple worked everyday, raised a child, and set aside a small amount each month in annuities. After the child left home, and the taxpayer turned sixty years old, the couple wanted to buy a home for retirement. Also, the husband suffered a severe illness that involved surgery and a lengthy hospital stay during the tax year. Their part of the medical bill was $22,000, so they wanted to use part of the annuity distribution to help with it. They were told there would be no penalty when the annuities were cashed, because the taxpayer was over the minimum age of fifty-nine and a half. This was true; there would be no penalty. So, the couple took lump sum distributions totaling about $260,000. It's typical to withhold about twenty percent for federal so that's what the couple did. They allowed $52,000 withholding for federal taxes, and added about $8,100 extra for the state's tax share. After federal and state withholding totaling $60,100, they would have almost $200,000 left. The couple thought $60,100 was a lot of taxes, and that they should be covered, so they paid cash for a new home and paid off the medical bills. The following year the couple visited the tax preparation office with their papers. Look at the pitiful situation they faced as shown in Figure 8-4.

Usually, this low-income couple received a modest refund of about $400 in a normal year, but with the Making Work Pay Credit of $800 under the economic stimulus plan, they would be eligible for a $1,216 federal refund and $1,247 total when the state refund is added; this is shown as Case 1 in Figure 8-4. This year though, with the extraordinary medical expenses, they could have itemized their deductions and received over $1,500 extra, or $2,809 in refunds from federal and state tax. This example, with the extra deduction for medical expenses is listed as Case 2 in Figure 8-4.

But as soon as they took the $260,000 lump-sum annuity they joined the rich-for-a-year club. As so often is heard in tax discussions, many politicians want to soak the rich to give help to those low-income families that deserve help. So, for one tax year, this couple became one of the rich and were vaulted into the second highest, thirty-three percent, tax bracket with a total gross income of $299,000, and the "soaking" began. They lost their deductions for medical expenses, because no medical expense deductions are allowed until expenses exceed 7.5 percent of gross income. Without the windfall income, 7.5 percent of the couple's $39,000 income is $2,925, so they could have deducted $19,075 for medical expenses. This would be the $22,000 they paid out of pocket, minus the $2,925 limit. When their $900 withholding for state taxes is added to the $19,075 allowed for medical, then total itemized deductions from their income would be $19,975. But, when the windfall is added, 7.5 percent of the $299,000 is $22,425, which exceeds their total medical expenses of $22,000, and so they are unable to deduct anything for their medical expenses, because they are the rich.

As it turned out the extra $60,400 was not enough to cover their total tax liability for federal and state taxes, and this unfortunate family was faced with a bill for an additional $23,006 for the year.

Example of Windfall Trap: Based on 2010 Tax Rules

Example of married couple, both aged 61, with no children

Case 1: shows typical of an ordinary year for the couple
Case 2: shows ordinary tax year with surgery medical deduction
Case 3: shows effects of lump-sum annuity distribution

Tax Information	Case 1 Typical Regular Earnings Standard Deduction	Case 2 Typical Earnings with Medical Deduction	Case 3 Windfall Earnings with No Medical Deduction
Filing Status	Married	Married	Married
Tax Form	1040EZ	1040	1040
Wage Income	$39,000	$39,000	$39,000
Windfall (Annuity) Income	0	0	+ 260,000
Total Annual Income	39,000	39,000	299,000
Standard Deduction	-11,400	0	-11,400
Itemized Deduction	0	-19,975	0
Personal Exemptions	- 7,300	-7,300	-7,300
Taxable Income	20,300	11,725	280,300
Regular Tax Liability	2,211	1,173	70,280
Alternative Minimum Tax	0	0	+ 84
Total Tax Liability	2,211	1,173	70,364
Withholding Credit	2,627	2,627	54,627
Making Work Pay Credit	800	800	0
Total Credits	3,427	3,427	54,627
Under, U or Over, O Paid	O 1,216	O 2,254	U 15,737
Penalty	0	0	+ U 207
Federal Amount Due, D or Refund, R	R 1,216	R 2,254	D 15,944
State Amounts			
State Tax Liability	869	345	15,954
State Withholding	- 900	- 900	- 9,000
State Under, U or Over, O Paid	O 31	O 555	U 6,954
Penalty	0	0	+ U 108
State Amount Due, D or Refund, R	R 31	R 555	D 7,062
Total Federal and State	R 1,247	R 2,809	D 23,006

Windfall Tax Trap
Figure 8-4

Look at what happened in the example Case 3 in Figure 8-4. Of course, they under paid total tax for the year, because all of their income, including the $39,000 would push their earnings from the fifteen percent bracket they were accustomed to, into the thirty-three percent bracket, and they only had twenty percent withheld on the annuity distribution. In addition, the extra income pushed them into the parallel tax system called the Alternative Minimum Tax system. This added insult to injury for an extra $84 to "keep the rich from taking extraordinary deductions to escape taxes." The ultimate tyranny occurred in the form of penalties. The couple did not meet the pay-as-you-go requirements established by the federal and state rules; this was caused because the total withholding for the year was too low. As a result, penalties of $207 and $108 were added to the respective federal and state amounts due.

This example closely parallels actual cases. It could be said they should have known better, or they should have found an advisor. They thought they did when they cashed out their annuities. This situation occurs all too frequently. It usually results with tears and desperation. They said they were told there would not be a penalty, because the taxpayer was over fifty-nine and a half. That was true, but their wages jumped into the thirty-three percent tax bracket, too, and they simply didn't have enough withheld to cover the total liability. The unfortunate couple didn't have the money to pay the tax due. Basically, they had two choices: enter an installment payment plan with the IRS and pay additional fees and interest, or mortgage their home to pay the tax due. This couple decided to mortgage their home and pay off their tax bill. They paid a big penalty for their venture into the realm of the rich for one year, because the current tax system was set up to redistribute their windfall to other citizens that the governing class decided deserved it more. Their reward for working and saving for a lifetime was that a huge part of it was swept away by an unfair and unequal system to reward some individual that chose to work part of the year and to loaf part of the year, because there would be extra earned income credit at tax time. Or, perhaps it paid part of a movie star's contribution to charity.

The same situations develop when folks take money out of their deferred retirement plan for one reason or another. It often occurs when a person changes jobs or is laid off. The employer curtly tells them it must withhold twenty percent of the lump sum out of their retirement plan. Most people mistakenly believe this withholding will cover them. One of the worst traps occurs when an employee wants to rollover, or transfer the lump sum payment to another deferred account to avoid immediate taxes and continue saving without the tax burden. The tax rules allow this, but the transfer must occur within sixty days. So, consider the example of a taxpayer that had $80,000 set aside in a 401(k) fund. A check was received for $64,000, after $16,000 (20%) was withheld by the company and sent to the IRS. The taxpayer saved the nest egg over fifteen years and had no other savings set aside. About two weeks later, the taxpayer took the check for $64,000 to the bank and put it in a tax-deferred IRA, but the bank informed the unsuspecting taxpayer that the entire $80,000 must be deposited in the rollover transfer, or else the $16,000 that was sent to the IRS as withholding would be taxable. Of course, the taxpayer didn't have $16,000, because the IRS withheld it. The taxpayer is faced with two choices: borrow $16,000 to put in the IRA, or pay federal and state taxes on it. Most wind up paying taxes plus the ten percent penalty assessed for early withdrawal of retirement funds. The penalty alone is an extra $1,600, and many of the taxpayers caught in this trap wind up with tax owed at the end of the year to both federal and state governments. Why must the average American citizen suffer these traps?

The unemployed taxpayer is generally caught in a similar tax trap. With high unemployment rates, there have been a lot of cases somewhat like the following example. A corporation is forced to cut deep into its workforce with layoffs because of the severe economic recession. Many of the workers had been with the company for twenty years or more, and had enjoyed participation in the company's 401(k)-retirement plan. There would be unemployment benefits, but a lot of the folks had sizeable mortgage payments, real estate taxes, and a child or two in college. Unemployment pay simply wouldn't be enough, so these workers began to withdraw from their 401(k) accounts for living expenses. Some of these families would have to live off their unemployment benefits and retirement savings for a year or more. But their desperation would be met with a sizeable tax bill, because both the unemployment benefits, and the distributions from the retirement savings are taxable income. In addition, the distributions from retirement savings would be penalized an extra ten percent. The lucky ones authorized a little withholding to offset the year-end tax bill, but most were living on a minimum amount and did not have any withholding whatsoever. So, assume a family received $8,000 in unemployment benefits for the year, and withdrew $40,000 from their 401(k) account; this would give them about $48,000 to live on for the year, which was just shy of what they normally received in take-home pay. Well, for a married couple, the taxes on the $48,000 would be about $3,557, the majority of it falling into the fifteen percent bracket. But there will be a $4,000 penalty for early withdrawal from the 401(k), which must be added to the tax due. The total bill would be $7,557 plus some penalties for no withholding. There is no Making Work Pay Credit and no Earned Income Credit, because there was no earned income. And this doesn't include the damages for the state. So, the couple draws out more from the 401(k), if they have it, to pay the tax due to the federal and state governments, or they begin installment payments to pay their debt to their government. Of course, the governing class believes it's only right that these taxes should be redistributed to more unfortunate and deserving citizens. Here is a great example of a system that is so convoluted and impossible to manage because of the infinity of actions, that it punishes its working citizens for prudent savings.

The cancelled debt trap causes some real surprises for folks. This situation can occur a number of ways, but the most common examples are car loans, credit card debt, and home foreclosures. It occurs when a bank or other credit company excuses debt. Recall the credit card debt example, where an individual owed about $5,000 to a credit card company, and finds it impossible to pay off. Maybe it's another layoff situation. So, they negotiate with the credit card company to pay $3,000 as payment-in-full, in exchange for the company excusing the extra $2,000. This triggers a taxable event and a surprise for the taxpayer at tax time. The $2,000 frequently must be treated as income, and taxes must be paid on it to both the federal and state governments. Of course, they didn't have withholding taken out, because they didn't realize cancelled debt would be taxed. At the end of the year they received a tax form from the credit card company that they didn't understand, and were thoroughly dismayed to learn there are taxes due. The same circumstances can apply to home foreclosures and car repossessions. The government has offered relief for a few years to families with debt forgiven as a result of a foreclosure on their primary home. It is a temporary exception that excuses the foreclosure as a taxable event. Naturally, there are extra forms and reporting, and many taxpayers have no idea of how to handle it. Again, the government wants them to be accountants with detailed records.

There are dozens of taxpayer traps, but here is a last one to demonstrate the combined adverse effects of hasty legislation and the infinity of actions. Congress proposed a quick-fix economic stimulus with the Making Work Pay Credit. This program contributed to the withholding problem on several occasions, especially in the first year. Most taxpayers didn't know about the credit or how it would work. It was meant to allow an extra $400 credit per taxpayer, and it was set up to distribute the money throughout the year in lower withholding, so taxpayers would receive it gradually. If one of the spouses worked at two different jobs during the year, then the $400 was allowed at each job. As a result, the withholding was decreased to allow $1,200 credit to the couple during the year, but at the tax desk, only the maximum $800 would be allowed, so several taxpayers in this situation wound up in this tax trap owing taxes. The Congress had no idea of the problems they caused taxpayers, usually the poorest, with its quick-fix gadget give-away plan.

Piling On

The tax structures of many states and municipalities are reminiscent of some corporate cultures in the U.S. It's common in corporate America for a large corporation to hold annual conferences for its executives. They will meet for a few days at a fine resort where there will be presentations and discussions, and certainly, golf or other recreation; often these recreational events are justified as team building exercises. Before long the individual division leaders from the group decide there should be similar activities for their circle of divisional leaders. As long as the money for events is set-aside in the budget, the events grow to include an outing for the marketing group, one for human resources, one for sales, and so on until about every group has a similar event. But it usually doesn't stop at the division level; it continues to filter downward to the individual company level of the corporation. In the end, the parent company is sponsoring dozens of retreats and conferences. The same disease has infected every level of the federal government as well.

This me-too behavior appears to be practiced by many of the state and local tax structures. Following the federal implementation of the progressive income tax many individual states decided to use similar systems. Today, most of the states in the union have a form of progressive income tax. Some are more extreme than others, and some don't have an income tax system at all, but raise state revenues through other methods. Naturally, every government, such as state, county, and city, require money to operate. But the addiction for always wanting more has resulted in piling on the taxes until virtually every penny earned and spent is taxed. In addition to state income taxes, many large cities impose a wage tax. Usually, everyone pays sales tax, and there are real estate taxes, property taxes on cars, boats, and other personal items; and, inheritance and estate taxes when the unfortunate taxpayer dies.

Sixty years ago a common sales tax was increased from about one percent to two percent. Today, sales taxes run seven percent, more or less. Why has the percentage increased? Anyone could see the cost of living and paychecks rising through the years. If an individual paid $3,000 for a car at two percent, then the sales tax would be about $60. If the same percentage were applied today, then a car bought for $30,000 would result in a $600 sales tax. The car price inflated ten times, but so would sales tax. Of course, this is not what has happened. If the percentage of sales tax has increased to seven percent, then the sales tax on the $30,000 car would be $2,100; so, instead of increasing government revenue ten times, it increased thirty-five times. How could this be? How did government spending grow so much?

But it doesn't stop with sales tax percentages. Real estate rates, property tax rates, and state income tax rates have grown, too. Some of the reasons appear to be the welfare costs, and the costs of the public service workers. Many of the states with high taxes follow the idea of taxing the rich to support the poor. Welfare payments, Medicaid, and other social give-away programs experienced phenomenal growth through the sixties and beyond, and with this growth it was necessary to hire thousands of government employees to administer the gift programs. As a result, the tax percentage for all taxpayers had to increase with it. Also, the public service workers in most states today receive better pay and benefits than ever before. It just isn't possible without an increased percentage of taxes paid by the working class. Many states permit their public workers to retire as early as their fifties, and often draw pensions with cost-of-living adjustments tied to them for life. Naturally, this means total pension payouts must continue to grow, and it becomes another government Ponzi scheme that must be supported by higher tax rates.

Another glaring example of the increased percentage of taxes is the Social Security and Medicare rates. These have grown steadily since these programs started and the government continued to perpetuate the Ponzi principle to meet these obligations. First, the Social Security plan was meant to provide a retirement income supplement for older folks who found themselves without adequate savings in their old age. About thirty years later the Medicare plan was meant to provide a way for older folks to obtain health insurance without being denied coverage caused by the infamous preexisting condition. But, like all government give-away programs, it is never enough. Before long, the programs were expanded to cover younger folks. Today, there is Medicaid for children and unfortunate adults, and disability payments administered by the Social Security Administration. Although not all of these plans are funded by Social Security and Medicare taxes, they are examples of ever increasing programs, costs, and tax increases.

At the tax desk there is often a complaint of double taxation on many situations; this is normally the result of misunderstanding the abstract accounting rules established by the IRS. There is one legitimate case of double taxation, however, and this occurs with corporate earnings. A corporation is normally taxed on the amount of earnings it reports. A portion of the remaining earnings may then be distributed as dividends to stockholders. Each stockholder, in turn, must remit taxes on these same dividends to the federal and state governments.

Now, there are proposals for new tax methods. It teaches Americans to never underestimate the creativity of the professional politician for ways to stick their hands in their pockets. The extraordinary debt the country carries today has left the government scrambling for ways to continue to pay for existing and larger give-away programs. There are proposals for an additional value-added tax. The founders may have approved of this method as a sole means for collecting taxes, but federal managers today mean it as an additional tax. Also, it is reported that some would like to apply a mileage tax to driving. This would both manipulate behavior by discouraging driving while raising revenue. What could be better in the mind of a professional spender of public funds? It isn't responsible management, but abusive mismanagement.

THE GIVE –AWAY GAME

It seems the majority of elected representatives believe they are sent to Congress to develop new programs, especially programs that benefit their respective districts. Instead of restricting their service to prudent management of public revenue in accordance with the provisions of the Constitution, it has evolved into a give-away game that squanders the public treasury and supports the personal aims of their own posterity. Today, there are more give-away programs than ever, and the list just keeps growing.

The Congress has developed the attitude of a governing class that sets itself apart from the common citizen and is appointed to decide what is right for average Americans. The governing class believes they are the ones who decide who deserves public handouts and who doesn't, and they decide what the national behavior should be. If they decide home thermostats should be set at sixty-eight in the winter, and if they decide no one should drive more than 8,000 miles per year, because they know what is best for us, then they introduce legislation for citizens' own good. If they decide people earning more than $250,000 per year should pay more taxes to help support those who are unable, or even unwilling, to earn a certain amount, then they set rules for equality. Only the governing class, though, can decide how much should be provided to the unfortunate few; but rest assured it will grow continually. A good example of this attitude can be seen in recent public remarks about taxes during the discussion over raising the top two tax rates. Some complained after the two tax rates were left at the same level, "You would think they would say thank you" for the tax breaks. Another annoyed self-appointed member of the governing class protested, "can you believe they want to give more money to the rich?"

Say thank you? Give money? These folks have forgotten that the treasury exists on money appropriated by citizens to operate the government to provide defense, fair laws, and fair trade. Instead of prudently managing the allocated funds for their intended purposes, they have decided it is their role to take as much as it wants from its citizens to redistribute it according to what the governing class decides is best for all. It's pretty close to the idea of centralized government, isn't it?

Many of the principles discussed as lessons learned come into effect over the tax table. Unalienable versus vested rights must be considered. Social programs are vested rights that are established by the governing class, and can be revoked by the governing class. During the discussions concerning many of these issues there are claims that every citizen has the right to a job, a home, enough food, and health care. These are not the unalienable natural rights of all individuals to pursue their own lifestyles. Indeed, most Americans do not want fellow citizens to suffer hunger, homelessness, and so forth, and for years they have allowed the government to develop programs to take care of this for them. Taxpayers sent in the taxes, and government established the programs. But there was a price. With each grant of power, the governing class grew and developed, and freedoms for the individual were eroded.

The ever-expanding growth of programs has become so large as to be unmanageable, following the rule of infinity of actions. The programs are overlapping, duplicated, and so complex that it has become impossible for the Congress, with all of its committees, to properly oversee and manage. Americans overlooked the Ponzi schemes implemented by government through the years, and the government continues to add more instead of fixing the ones that are already out of control. Remember, Social Security, Medicare, and other schemes are merely arrangements for taking money from one group to fund plans for another. But those representatives who depend upon the people to continue their personnel pursuits of distinction have not learned the lesson. The new health care bill of 2010 continues the traditions established by the great social programs of 1936 and 1965. It's another Ponzi program, too.

The growth of the numbers isn't the only added cost, though. Another less obvious cost is the growth of administrative costs for the programs. The costs for collecting and enforcing the income tax system itself are enormous. The number of IRS employees is about 100,000 souls, more or less. The Congress should evaluate the administrative costs of the income tax system in a manner similar to charities or mutual fund companies. When people donate to a charity, they want the biggest part of their donation to go to the cause they are supporting, and not to those employed by the charity. The same is true for investors in a mutual fund; they want their investment dollar maximized, and the administrative costs for running the fund minimized. As a result, many organizations and funds publish this information. The Congress should do the same to analyze the effectiveness of every program. The IRS and its administrative costs should be compared with the effectiveness of the income tax system altogether. Alternative methods for collecting treasury revenues may be less abusive and less expensive to operate and control. In the end, it may be possible to reduce the size of the IRS and many of the rules and regulations that are the direct result of this example of government by board rule, rather than rule of law.

HEALTH CARE – IT'S A TAX!

June 28, 2012 was another historic day for the U.S. in its record of Constitutional interpretation when the fourth great step away from Constitutional supremacy was sanctioned by the Supreme Court. It all boiled down to the same age-old arguments concerning the limits of federal power over the people as set forth in Eighth Section of Article I of the Constitution; specifically, the power to lay taxes and provide for the general welfare of the country (Welfare Clause, I.8.1), the power to regulate Commerce (Commerce Clause, I.8.3), and the power to make all laws necessary for carrying into execution the foregoing powers of Section 8 (Implied Powers Clause, I.8.18). For the first time since the 1930s and passage of the New Deal programs, the commerce clause was denied in support of this type of legislation. The High Court concluded that the mandatory requirement for all individuals to purchase health care insurance could not be considered commerce, because Congress does not have the authority for force individuals to engage in commerce in the first place.

The big surprise for a lot of people came when the First Clause was invoked, but not the general welfare portion of the clause. The Supreme Court decided that the requirement to have health insurance was simply a tax, and the Congress is given the power to lay taxes in Clause I.8.1, and to impose the taxes unequally in the form of the Sixteenth Amendment. The Court "construed" it as a tax increase on folks who elect to go without insurance, and there is no real "compulsion," because those who fail to pay the penalty can't be sent to jail, or have liens on, or seizure of, their property.

As a result, the one-hundred-year legacy of Constitutional interpretation is continued, and the idea of centralized government in place of self-government advanced in a fourth awful stride. It is continued under the authority of the Sixteenth Amendment; the greatest restraint on individual freedom in American history. This wicked amendment has enabled the federal government to move into every segment of American life, and has now enabled the government to force individuals to annually report to the government the status of their health care coverage, and to buy insurance or pay a penalty tax. Remarkable.

The combined health care reform acts of 2010 have pushed a lot of Americans into reexamining government growth and the original ideas of self-government established by the Constitutional founders. Tax preparers have been examining the provisions of this bill since passage, and new wrinkles are continually discovered. Unfortunately for taxpayers, much of this bill will be implemented through the income tax system, somewhat like the earned income tax credit program. It's another application of social programs through the tax system. The vast burden for administration and control of the health care program will fall to the IRS, and it has been projected that more than 16,000 additional IRS employees will be needed to manage it. Health and Human Services grants the waivers, but the IRS will use its powers of board rule to establish and enforce health care regulations, leaving the common citizen caught in more muck at the tax desk.

Although it may seem unusual to have the IRS in the health care business, it really isn't, because the organization has been in the health care business for some time already. As previously explained, for decades taxpayers have been able to take extra deductions for medical expenses, but only medical expenses allowable by the tax rules; in other words, the government decides, much like a health insurance company, what is a covered medical expense and what is not. Many tax preparers were entertained during the debates over the new health care bill and provisions for abortions; those for versus those against. Should citizens be compelled to subsidize a procedure they are against? The amusing thing for tax preparers is that abortions have already been subsidized by the tax system for many years. As previously explained, legal abortions, birth control pills, and fertility enhancement plans are all eligible itemized deductions, as well as authorized expenditures under the Health Savings Account and Flexible Spending Account plans. In other words, individuals who have an abortion may receive a tax deduction on it.

Flexible Spending Accounts and other pre-tax methods and allowances for health care premiums have been used for several years, and reported to the IRS. Fortunate taxpayers who can pay their part of health care premiums through their employer do not have to pay any tax on pre-tax premiums. Also, taxpayers can place money in a Health Savings Account, HSA, to use the money for eligible medical expenses, but there are plenty of traps here for the unsuspecting taxpayer, too. There are more forms and paperwork to be submitted to the IRS so they can monitor citizens to insure they do not cheat. If the HSA money is spent for unauthorized uses, then there are more reporting requirements, and of course, penalties to be paid. More taxpayers try this program each year, and many become disillusioned and drop out.

Many purists view the use of the tax system to implement health care programs as a complete misuse of the tax revenue system and that health care belongs elsewhere. It merely expands the traps for taxpayers and confounds the system with abstractions and abuses. Nevertheless, the Health Care Reform Act of 2010 continues this misapplication of the revenue collections system to operate a social program. Figure 8-5 lists many of the tax implications that have been discovered in the health care act that are due to be phased in over at least seven years. It will continually grow and consume taxpayers in its grip of control.

Two interesting effects on tax laws were experienced in the first two years. For the 2010 tax year, the rules and amounts for adoption credit were changed. The maximum adoption credit was increased and provided with

Key Provisions of Health Care Reform Acts for Individuals

2010   Adoption Credit increased and fully refundable.

2011   No over-the-counter drugs qualify for reimbursement by Health Savings Account or Flexible Spending Account.

Penalty for use of Health Savings Account money to pay for nonqualified expense increases from 10% to 20%. Example for a $1,000 purchase it increases from $100 to $200.

2012   No new changes in 2012.

2013   Maximum contribution to Flexible Spending Account reduced by half from $5,000 to $2,500.

Itemized deduction threshold increased from 7.5% of AGI to 10% for years 2013 – 2016.

Medicare tax increases on earned income over $200,000 for single and $250,000 married from 1.45% to 2.35%

Additional investment income tax levied on single taxpayers earning $200,000 and $250,000 married at 3.8% of net investment income or AGI threshold paid on tax return.

2014 and later years

Tax penalty of $695 for failure to purchase health coverage to be phased in from 2014 to 2016 in changing amounts. Individuals who are without health care insurance for less than 90 days may claim an exception to the tax penalty. A premium subsidy for household incomes below 400% of poverty level can be used to reduce the premium, but must be reconciled on the tax return. NOTE: 400% of poverty level for a family of four in 2009 would be $88,200.

Households whose insurance costs are more than 8% of income are exempt from the tax penalty.

Tax penalty cannot be offset by other credits.

An information tax return must be submitted to the IRS to verify their compliance with the insurance requirement.

Key Provisions of Health Care Bill
Figure 8-5

relaxed rules for recovering the credit. Many tax preparers wonder what this has to do with health care, but there it is.

In 2011, it was reported that about eighty IRS agents would be needed to monitor the compliance of tanning salons with the new health care provisions. The bill imposes an additional tax on the use of tanning beds, because the governing class decided the use of these beds harms personal health, so it is their role to discourage people from using them by using the tax revenue system to increase the cost and thus manipulate personal behavior.

Other provisions of the health care bill involve ways to raise money to pay for it; another way to say it is there will have to be subtle ways to increase taxes. The first of these methods is to reduce the tax benefits for Health Savings Accounts, Flexible Spending Accounts, and itemized deductions for medical expenses. First is a much larger penalty for use of HSA money on ineligible expenses starting in 2011; it doubles from a ten percent penalty to twenty percent. In 2013, there will be several tax changes to redirect money to the new health care bill. The maximum allowance for FSA contributions will be halved from $5,000 to $2,500 in that year. Also, the threshold for itemizing medical deductions will be increased to ten percent of the AGI. For example, this means a person earning $40,000 and previously not able to deduct any medical expenses until they exceed 7.5 percent of their income, or $3,000, will have a new threshold in 2013 of expenses at ten percent, or $4,000. It's a diabolical way to nudge citizens in the direction set by the governing class.

Taxpayers with higher incomes will be required to chip in more money to pay for the new health care bill. What is higher income? It works out to about $200,000 for a single person and $250,000 for a married couple. The rich-for-a-year couple in the example in Figure 8-4 would fall into this category. High-income taxpayers will be required to pay higher Medicare taxes, and an extra investment income tax. The Medicare tax increases to 2.35% on the high-income earnings from 1.45% on earnings below the thresholds. Additional investment income tax of 3.8% of higher earnings will be implemented. This one will likely catch a lot of retired taxpayers who have saved a lifetime for retirement, but are rewarded by another dip into the fruits of their savings. Would the annuity payment for the couple in the Figure 8-4 example require another 3.8 percent and 2.35 percent for investment income tax and Medicare tax? The rules aren't published yet, but a good guess would be, probably.

Following is a summary of tax increase measures in the two bills.

Broaden Medicare tax base for high-income taxpayers: 210.2 billion
Annual fee on health insurance providers: $60 billion
40% excise tax on health coverage above $10,200/$27,500: $32 billion
Annual fee on manufacturers and importers of branded drugs; $27 billion
2.3% excise tax on certain medical devices: $20 billion

Raise itemized medical deduction limit from 7.5% to 10%: $15.2 billion
Reduce contributions to FSA in cafeteria plans to $2,500: $13 billion
Other revenue tax gadgets: $14.9 billion

Rules for failure to obtain health insurance start in 2014, and naturally, the tax system is used to punish citizens for failure to fall in line. There is a tax penalty, with rules and exceptions, which is scheduled to start at about $95 in 2014 and grow to nearly $695 per person by 2016. But the rules are confusing and complex, and will probably cause more traps for citizens at tax time. There are exceptions, of course, and families with household incomes below 400% of the poverty level may receive a government subsidy for health care insurance premiums; 400 percent of the poverty level was about $88,200 in 2009 for a family of four, so those with total income below $88,200 will receive some sort of subsidy to pay their health care premiums. The basic health care cost limits for low-income taxpayers are shown in Figure 8-6.

Maximum Out-of Pocket Payments Under the Patient Protection and Affordable Care Act

Federal Poverty Level	Maximum Premium as % of Income	Maximum Annual Premium by Family Size			
		1	2	3	4
100%	2.00%	$ 217	$ 291	$ 366	$ 441
133.00%	2.00%	$ 288	$ 388	$ 487	$ 587
133.01%	3.00%	$ 487	$ 656	$ 824	$ 992
150%	4.00%	$ 650	$ 874	$ 1,099	$ 1,323
200%	6.30%	$ 1,365	$ 1,836	$ 2,307	$ 2,778
250%	8.05%	$ 2,180	$ 2,932	$ 3,685	$ 4,438
300%	9.50%	$ 3,087	$ 4,152	$ 5,218	$ 6,284
350%	9.50%	$ 3,601	$ 4,845	$ 6,088	$ 7,332
400%	9.50%	$ 4,115	$ 5,537	$ 6,958	$ 8,379

Source: Annual Update of HHS Poverty Guidelines

Maximium Out-of-Pocket Payments
Figure 8-6

It shows the maximum a family would pay according to its size and where it falls on the federal poverty line. The example, then, for the family of four having $88,200 household income, shows the maximum health care premium of $8,379. Fellow taxpayers who do not qualify will make up the difference.

The next question is will they buy the insurance or pay the penalty. Will a family of four pay an insurance premium of over $8,000, or just go without and pay the projected penalty of $695? Probably some will and others won't. If they can't afford the insurance, obviously they will pay $695 more in income tax; this will help pay for those who take the subsidies. The real question is should they be forced to make this decision?

In addition, there will be a potential trap at tax time, because when the tax return is calculated, if it turns out that the taxpayer received too much or too little subsidy then it will have to be resolved at the tax desk. This could happen easily during a tax year, because family sizes notoriously change throughout the year due to separations, marriage, and divorce. If the taxpayer received too small a subsidy payment, then there will be a refund, but if their projections were too large, then the taxpayer will have tax due to settle too large a subsidy.

Naturally this program will exclude some individuals from the rule altogether. Native Americans and prisoners will be exempt. Also, very-low-income families may be excused when their health insurance costs are more than eight percent of household income. This means if a family earns $20,000 in a given year, eight percent of income is $1,600. If health care costs are $1,800, then the family is exempt from the penalty. Who decides the definitions of income, the cutoff points, the percentages, and the amount of penalty? It is another example of the governing class deciding who deserves help, who does not, who should pay, and how the country's revenue should be redistributed. Even citizens who are not normally required to file a tax return may be required to file an information return to verify that they are in compliance with the health care bill. How do you like that? People will be required to check in with the IRS to verify that they are following government controls.

After examining the twists and turns, traps and pitfalls, arbitrary qualifications and cutoffs of this program, could the principle of infinity of actions be more evident or clearly demonstrated? Is the overconfidence of the federal government's idea that it can fairly, evenly, and efficiently administer and manage this mishmash ever been more obvious than with this perversion of the tax code?

The health care insurance rules for businesses are even more difficult to interpret than the rules for individuals. Figure 8-7 lists their key provisions. Employers with more than forty-nine employees will be required in 2013 to provide health insurance to their workers, and the penalty for noncompliance is expected to be $250 per worker per month. Smaller employers will receive tax credits for providing health care insurance to their employees. But the number of employees in a business fluctuates; so formulas and calculations will be required to determine the average numbers and effects for the year.

Key Provisions of Health Care Reform Acts for Businesses

2010   Small Business Health Care Premium Credit for employers with less than 26 employees and payroll less than $50,000 credit up to 35% of health care plan increases to 50% after 2013.

        Very small employers with less than 11 employees and Payroll less than $25,000 may get 100%.

        Sole proprietors, partners, and S Corporation shareholders are not counted as employees.

        Excise tax of 10% on indoor tanning procedures, with some exemptions for medical purposes.

2013   Employers must report the amount of health insurance premium paid per employees on W-2 as nontaxable benefit.

2014   Employers with more than 49 employees REQUIRED to provide health care coverage AND PAY 60% of premium.

        Penalty for not providing required health insurance is MONTHLY excise tax of up to $250 per employee.

        Calculations are extensive to determine average number of full-time employees, seasonal workers, and payroll.

        Free-choice voucher must be offered to employees with household income at 400% of poverty level, or less, if health plan exceeds 8% of household income. NOTE: 400% of poverty level for a family of four in 2009 would be $88,200.

2018   Nondeductible excise tax on high-cost health plans of 40% of coverage exceeding $10,200 for individuals and $27,500 for family coverage.

Business Provisions of Health Care Bill
Figure 8-7

It will be one more government imposition of another difficult facet of business operations for managers to consider and balance. In addition, in 2018, there will be a hefty excise tax on comprehensive high-cost health plans. Government has defined a high-cost plan in the health care bill.

The health care bill is impossible for Americans, or Congressional lawmakers, to digest. Its size is extraordinary and filled with more give-away plans, more traps, more piling on, and more burden on the common American. It will be virtually impossible to control equally. The discussion of it has focused on the effects for individuals, but the additional burden and costs for businesses are staggering. It means more paperwork, more restrictions, and more intrusion by the IRS into private lives. But it's under the authority of the governing class and its ceaseless effort to control the citizens of the United States.

BREATHE FREE

The description of the tax code and the examples of traps and abuse are a very small part of the entire problem. With its tens of thousands of pages filled with cross references and exceptions, the income tax system oppresses its citizens more than the heavy taxes opposed by the colonialists of 1776. America's forefathers understood the dangers of oppressive taxes, and that's why they left little doubt in the Constitution that there was no room for progressive direct taxes. They knew the unlimited power to tax the people would evolve into a control system for an elite class of governors. Thomas Jefferson wrote about the problem, saying it should not be the intention of government to burden the people with oppressive taxes to provide benefits for the idle, or for a list of vested privileges. Unfortunately, starting with the big change of 1913 and early efforts to use national revenue for social purposes, the governing elite has established a system that is completely contrary to Jefferson's ideas of preserving freedom and self-government.

The original tax system was meant to be a source of operating revenue for the federal government. If it had remained this way, it's entirely possible that the U.S. wouldn't be facing the debt difficulties of today, and the country probably would be even more prosperous than it has become. Instead, one hundred years of tax evolution has resulted with the use of tax revenue as a source of redistribution of earnings and a way for the governing class to manipulate Americans into following the path that it has decided is best for all. No longer operating as representatives of a self-governing people, charged with stewardship of the public treasury and effective management of a small federal government with specific responsibilities, elected officials have become career-minded opportunists who have established themselves as a governing class above the common citizen, and who believe they know best.

The progressive income tax system in use today beautifully serves their purposes to control the American people and to steal their freedom.

A progressive tax system divides the country. It incites class warfare. Those without become jealous of those with plenty, and they learn to vote themselves benefits from the treasury; soon another group wants to join in the treasure hunt. Instead of each person fulfilling a natural duty to contribute to the operational necessities of government, it has become a society that wants some citizens to contribute more than others.

There is fanciful rhetoric from some elements of the governing class that tax reform is needed. It needs to be simplified, they say, and many of the deductions and abusive credits should be eliminated. But this has been tried many times before. Tax brackets are changed, deductions eliminated, and so forth, but as long as a progressive tax system exists, the governing class, with its limited imagination, will only let it creep back time and again.

The only solution is to close down the system and return to the way shown by the founders. This will remove the preparation burden on taxpayers and eliminate the need to pay for preparer services or software. In all likelihood the size of the IRS can be reduced substantially with a huge savings to the American Treasury. And at last, Americans can breathe free again.

CHAPTER NINE

FISCAL RESPONSIBILITY

IN ADDITION TO DRIFTING from their responsibility to work within the provisions of the Constitution, the Congress and President have failed in their duty to maintain prudent stewardship of the funds provided to the government by the American people. After a century of irresponsible spending, government representatives have left the nation with extraordinary debt that threatens American freedom and security.

The government is essentially a nonprofit business, and it is the responsibility of elected representatives to keep the business within acceptable limits of revenue and spending. When government commenced business it intended to raise only sufficient revenue to provide for defense, communications, fair commerce standards, administration of federal land, rules for citizenship, and a system of federal courts and laws. Today, however, it has added spending for human resources, and it is primarily this spending that has led to tremendous borrowing beyond the means of revenue provided by Americans.

Both private businesses and the government utilize similar management methods, but the difference is that the federal government has been allowed to operate at a deficit for too long. Running a business, nonprofit or otherwise, is just like balancing a checkbook; spending must not exceed deposits or there will be a problem. This is not to marginalize the tremendous job of running a business. Managers face a complex and intricate job to balance the pressures and difficulties that are faced, often on an hourly basis, to keep the business solvent. By examining planning methods and difficulties that accompany private business operations, and then comparing it with government planning and its problems, there may be deeper insights into and understanding of the debt problems of the country.

Private businesses usually start each year with a forecast of expected income and expenses. It is often referred to as the budget, or plan. No financial plan is perfect, though, and well-run businesses must adjust to variations, or pressures, on the plan that may threaten projected profits. Typical pressures on the business include falling sales, increased material and health care insurance costs, and higher taxes. Labor costs can easily get out of hand when sales fall off, so staffing levels must be closely and continuously monitored. The smartest businesses prepare alternative budget plans in advance, in order to be ready ahead of time for problems.

The federal government makes a national forecast or budget, too. Receipts are accounted for according to source categories and are classified as either trust fund or federal fund receipts. Receipts that are identified as trust fund money must be directed to the purpose identified; for example, taxes collected on aviation fuel and airline ticket sales must be routed to the aviation trust fund. Federal fund receipts are used for general purposes. The national budget is subjected to pressures similar to a private business. There might be unforeseen extraordinary expenses, such as a war, and income revenue may drop, especially when the country is out of work. The reaction to pressures on the national budget is obviously different than private business actions. The government borrows money without cutting costs and continues to dig a deeper hole. Private business can borrow, too, but it cannot print money like the government can, and eventually it must pay its debts or cease operations.

Spending in the national budget is referred to as outlays, and it has grown five percent or more, as a percentage of Gross Domestic Product, in the last ten years. There are many sources for the increase, including ten years of war spending, increased human resources spending, and growth in size of the federal government and its pay and benefits. The government has been forced to borrow to pay for human resource spending on welfare, food stamps, and other benefits for unproductive citizens. Despite reduced tax revenues, hiring in the federal government continues its expansion, and pay and benefits are inflated far beyond the averages of private citizens performing similar functions.

Proposed cures for the country's financial difficulties include raising taxes to cover the revenue shortfall, and creating jobs to add new sources to the revenue stream. Although simple on the surface, raising taxes may hide problems and work in reverse. Raising taxes is similar to raising prices in private business. Raising prices does not correct a bloated cost structure, but adds to it, and ongoing inefficiencies in the operation are not addressed, because they are masked by the glut of new income. The problem for private business occurs when the competition stays lean and does not follow the price increase, so the result can be lost sales, followed by even larger decreases in revenue. The same is true for the United States. Like it or not, the United States is a business that is in competition with the other countries of the world. Increasing taxes increases prices and leaves America's products expensive as a result of an inflated cost structure.

The second solution offered is to make jobs by offering tax incentives and make-work projects to keep government workers on the payroll. The laws of market supply and demand suggest that government cannot make jobs at all, because increasing the government payroll simply adds more cost for taxpayers to bear. If the economy is weak, and people are out of work, more jobs cannot be created out of thin air. Tax incentives and subsidies merely mask the cost of products and pass it on to the tax-paying public.

Following are examples of private business planning and pressures, with a comparison to the actual national plan for 2010 and the perceived pressures on it. Comparing these examples with the government effort to make jobs may help explain the failure of generations of career politicians to properly manage the nation's business.

BUSINESS PLANNING

Most profitable businesses make a financial plan, or budget, ahead of time for the next year, and then manage it as the year unfolds. If the company wants to earn a net profit of say, ten percent, then total costs and taxes cannot total more than ninety percent of its sales or revenue. It's easy to state, but the continual pressures of rising costs and unforeseen problems can make the job one of the most difficult to accomplish successfully. In addition to making a plan for the next year, many businesses will forecast finances for a more distant future of three to five years ahead. Businesses that do this will spend a lot of time trying to predict future income and what costs will be required to support the objectives.

The first thing business planners need to know to start the budgeting process is the expected amount of gross receipts. This is usually sales and miscellaneous income such as interest or other contributors. A simple business example is shown in the "Base Plan" column of Figure 9-1. In order to keep the example simple it is assumed the business is engaged in some form of manufacturing, and the number of budget items has been limited by lumping them into broad categories. An actual business budget, certainly, would have many more entries and items to be controlled by company management. At the top of the budget plan, then, gross receipts of $10 million for the small business has been predicted.

The next thing to figure out in the business plan is the cost of material and labor needed to actually produce the product. Usually, accountants classify these costs as direct costs as shown in the first column named, "Base

Plan," and they are limited to the amount of materials that are actually used to make the product, and to the labor costs that are spent on the people who convert the material into the finished product. The materials may include wood, metal, plastic, and hardware for durable products, food ingredients for food products, thread and cloth for textile products, and so on.

Company Budget and Contingency Plans						
	Dollar amounts (shown in thousands)					
	Base Plan		Sales Up 10%		Sales Down 10%	
	Dollars	% Sales	Dollars	% Sales	Dollars	% Sales
Gross Receipts (Sales)	10,000		11,000		9,000	
Direct Cost						
Direct Materials	5,500	55.0%	5,995	54.5%	4,995	55.5%
Direct Labor	960	9.6%	1,008	9.2%	816	9.1%
Total Direct Cost	6,460	64.6%	7,003	63.7%	5,811	64.6%
Indirect Cost						
Salaries	320	3.2%	320	2.9%	288	3.2%
Expenses	200	2.0%	210	1.9%	190	2.1%
Health Care Premiums	288	2.9%	288	2.6%	288	3.2%
Pension & Benefit Plan	192	1.9%	192	1.7%	192	2.1%
Total Indirect Cost	1,000	10.0%	1,010	9.2%	958	10.6%
Gross Profit	2,540	25.4%	2,987	27.2%	2,231	24.8%
Administrative Cost						
Salaries	600	6.0%	600	5.5%	600	6.7%
Expenses	200	2.0%	200	1.8%	190	2.1%
Health Care Premiums	36	0.4%	36	0.3%	36	0.4%
Pension & Benefit Plan	48	0.5%	48	0.4%	48	0.5%
Total Administrative Cost	884	8.8%	884	8.0%	874	9.7%
Operating Profit	1,656	16.6%	2,103	19.1%	1,357	15.1%
Income Tax	662	6.6%	841	7.6%	543	6.0%
Net Profit After Tax	994	9.9%	1,262	11.5%	814	9.0%

Company Budget Plans
Figure 9-1

The hourly rate for the craftsmen, and the number of people needed for the year, are used to determine the direct labor costs in the budget. Fringe benefits, such as health care insurance, vacation leave, retirement plan, and other benefits are not usually included in the direct cost for producing the product.

Business planners often utilize information from forecasting services, vendors, and labor surveys to calculate the expected costs for the next year. Material costs are perpetually subjected to inflationary pressures, and many forecasting services analyze the emerging markets to provide subscribers expected future costs. Also, vendors are consulted and contracts considered in determining the cost of materials and parts needed for the product. Labor costs are often decided by surveying the prevailing labor costs in the surrounding community and the national average, or, by its union contract when applicable. In order to remain competitive, each business must decide where the wages of its labor force will be in the range of the survey. Based on this information, pay increases will be forecast and worked into the direct costs of the budget.

In the Base Plan of the example, all costs are displayed as a percentage of gross receipts. This is but one of many measurements that are commonly used by managers in the budgeting process. The Base Plan example shows direct costs to be about 64.6 percent of the gross receipts. This is not an uncommon situation. For some businesses it may be much less, and for others it may be more. Usually, when direct costs are a lower percentage of gross receipts, the fortunate company makes a larger profit than those with high direct cost percentages. Strong competition is often the cause for the higher direct cost percentages, and companies in these situations must watch every penny in order to remain viable and competitive. Companies with lower direct cost percentages are frequently the ones that offer higher pay and great benefits, and these companies can continue to operate in this manner as long as they enjoy operation without stiff competition. When faced with the strong competition from a company offering a similar product at a lower price, then company profits may suffer and costs must be cut in order to compete and survive.

The next cost category that must be considered in the example is listed in Figure 9-1 as indirect cost. This usually includes the salaries of the support staff, such as supervisors, material handlers, and schedulers, and other expenses such as heating and lighting, work gloves, safety glasses, and supplies. Depending upon the business, these costs can be minimal, or they can be a major part of operational costs. In addition, the costs for the fringe benefits of the direct and indirect workers are often included in the accounting for indirect costs. The costs for health care premiums, pension payments, and other benefits costs are listed in the base company example. Although there will usually be many other accounts for indirect costs, the example is limited to a few categories to keep it simple. Nevertheless, the total indirect cost as a percentage of gross revenue could be considered somewhat representative for a typical small company. In this case the indirect costs are 10.0 percent of sales, and when both direct and indirect costs are added together to total 74.6 percent, practically three-fourths, of income has been spent on direct and indirect costs of getting the product ready for market. It is common at this point to subtract direct and indirect costs from gross sales revenue to determine a gross profit amount. In the Base Plan example there is a little over $2.5 million, or 25.4 percent left to work with. Many companies strive to achieve gross profit percentages of thirty-five or more. The higher the gross profit number, the more the company has to work with for other expenses and reinvestments in the business.

The next group of costs to consider is classified in the example as administrative cost. These costs usually include the salaries for the company sales staff, accounting, personnel, and the office of the chief executive. In addition there will be expenses for travel, office supplies, and other general expenses, and the costs for the fringe benefits for these individuals will be included in these accounts. Often referred to as Selling, General, and Administrative costs, these costs are as important to control as the direct and indirect costs of the operation. In the example, these costs use up another 8.8 percent of gross receipts to pay for administrative salaries, expenses, and benefits. After administrative costs are subtracted from the gross profit the difference is often called the operating profit of the company. In the example an operating profit of $1.656 million representing 16.6 percent of gross receipts is left.

One final deduction remains in the form of income tax. Naturally the income tax rate can vary considerably from company to company and from state to state. Depending upon circumstances, it can vary somewhat from year to year. In keeping the example simple, an income tax rate of about forty percent for federal and local taxes was used. As a percent of gross receipts, the governments take about 6.6 percent of the company's sales. With this final deduction, the base company is left with a net profit after tax of $994,000, or 9.9 percent of gross receipts. Ten percent profit would be considered poor for many companies, and is often referred to as a "low margin business." Companies seeking to attract investors with high growth rates and dividends would attempt to improve this number considerably, or they might consider selling the operation altogether. In very competitive, low margin, markets, the ten percent profit would be considered good. It's interesting that the major oil companies report less than ten percent. In fact, many manufacturing and retail businesses often achieve less, in some cases much less. Companies with low margins of less than two percent, such as food markets and certain retail businesses are often called "penny profit" businesses. So, it's a matter of the type of market and business, and the higher the profit, the more the company can afford to provide for its employees, and many do. When the margins are very tight, then pay and benefits are usually much more tightly controlled. That's why pay and benefits vary among businesses. It isn't that some companies are cruel or cheap. It's usually a function of profit margins dictated by market competition. When competition and margins are tight, a company simply can't survive if it offers high pay and benefits.

The final profit isn't usually put in someone's pocket. In order to remain competitive and combat the assault on rising costs, a sizeable portion of profits is put back into the business for efficiency improvements such as machinery and equipment that reduce company costs or improve quality.

Many well-managed companies don't stop with preparing a one-year budget. Good planners know from experience that the best business plans often don't last past the first quarter of the business year. In today's world there are many pressures on the business plan, such as rising material costs, added freight costs, or increased taxes. Also, the national economy may enter a period of boom or bust, or the company may have a new product that sells much better than expected when the original budget was planned. Rather than waiting to see how things work out, savvy business planners usually have contingency plans they can rapidly turn to during changes. They recognize the law of constant change, and may build hypothetical financial statements with lower or higher sales assumptions, with increases in material cost, or a variety of challenges that might occur during the business cycle. Just to demonstrate the effects of varying sales, two contingency plans are compared with the Base Plan in Figure 9-1. One example, in the center column, anticipates a ten percent increase in gross receipts and the other plan, in the right column, shows an adjustment for a ten percent reduction of receipts from the base plan. Compare the plan labeled, "Sales Up 10%," ($11 million). The company planners decided to meet the increased sales demand with overtime. They could add more workers, and would certainly have to do so if the product demand increased much more. Of course, more direct material would be required for more products, and there will be more indirect expenses for the cost of keeping up the operation during overtime hours. By restraining hiring and keeping a tight control on costs, the company would be able to squeeze out a little more profit and pay more taxes. In the end, the net profit might increase to 11.5 percent.

On the flip side, for "Sales Down 10%," the company may have to slightly reduce the number of direct and indirect workers in order to maintain a profit that is consistent with the Base Plan objective of 10 percent. Naturally, materials cost may be reduced, but due to the reduction in buying volume, the material cost per product will not be as efficient, and as a result, the material percentage of gross receipts may increase about a half percent to about 55.5 percent.

The sales reduction will mean a cut back in hours for direct and indirect workers. Probably a short workweek will be used, or there could be lay offs. But if action is not taken quickly, predictions for a modest profit could quickly become a loss. In the "Sales Down 10%" example, direct labor and indirect salaries are reduced.

After considering the effects of reduced sales, the company's managers don't want to reduce the administrative work force, because salesmen are needed to pursue more sales, and human resource and engineering folks will be needed to support the work force it will retain. But belts will be tightened to cut expenses and reduce administrative cost about $10 thousand.

Lower operating profit means income tax is reduced, and the net profit is cut from $944 thousand to $814 thousand, or about 9.0 percent of gross receipts. The company's base plan goal of 9.9 percent won't be achieved, but it will live to fight another day, and more aggressive action may be required in future years if sales remain low. Some companies immediately implement more drastic reductions in order to report the same 9.9 percent of the base plan. Others may take no action, especially those with weaker business discipline. When a company doesn't react, its profit will be further reduced and may even result in a loss. Many companies do operate this way and often fail. The example company has a base plan and contingencies, and is ready to quickly react to the pressures of trying to achieve its objectives.

ADJUSTMENTS TO PRESSURE

The pressures on a company to meet its profit objectives are numerous and continuous; every day usually brings new challenges for management. A casual observer might wonder why not just raise prices? Sometimes this may be necessary, but sometimes it can be a trap for a manager that is not careful in considering this option. The danger in arbitrarily raising prices to meet profit objectives is the inevitable loss of sales. There are dozens of cases where very successful companies believe their superior position in the market place will support price increases. It might work for one year, or a few years, but eventually their cost structure becomes too hefty, and the company realizes it has lost sales to a leaner and more aggressive company. It's the old adage again, the company is constantly gaining or losing ground. Unjustifiable price increases often result in a disguised situation of losing ground.

Suppose two competing companies with similar cost structures are facing an increase in cost of their primary raw material. One company considers the situation and decides the only alternative is to raise prices. Their competitor examines their operation and product design, then decides to implement a cost reduction program to offset the added cost for raw material, and so they are able to hold their selling price and quality. In short order the company that increased its prices begins to lose sales to the company that kept prices constant. Before long, the company that raised prices must retract its price increase, and now it is stuck with lower profit margins and has fallen behind its competition.

Continuing with the example company, consider the effects when it is subjected to pressure from labor, materials, health care, taxes, and falling sales. There are dozens more pitfalls for any company, but these five examples will provide good discussion of the pressures of running a business. Labor costs continually exert pressure on the business, but it is important for business managers to keep the costs of wages and salaries under strict control or risk limiting business growth and profitability by letting these costs grow too quickly. One of the most common complaints from workers is about pay, especially when the company has enjoyed a profitable year. Many workers believe they should receive not only regular pay increases, but also large pay increases when the company has reported strong profits. A lot of managers want to share the good fortune, too, but when they fall victim to the trap of making extraordinary pay increases with each successful year of profits, the next thing they find is that their pay structure has inflated in comparison with their competition. As a result, they have to raise prices or cut profits in order to continue business, but if their competitors have a lower cost structure due to lower average pay, the company with the higher wages usually loses sales. It can take years to correct a fat pay scale, but if action is not initiated, the company could find itself weaker, up to the point of going out of business.

So what can a company do? It must rely on its wage surveys of the country and their local area, and keep their pay structure in line with prevailing wages. Holding pay scales in line with the going rates applies to both hourly and salaried personnel. Contrary to popular belief, a year with spectacular profits does not mean management receives huge pay increases. To make it right, many companies today will set aside a portion of profits to be shared with the workers. When the company enjoys a good year, employees may receive a generous bonus, or portion of profits, based upon their years of service and pay grade. Conversely, when times are more difficult the portion of profits may be slimmer. Most American workers understand that it takes the efforts of all members of the company to be successful, and they understand it is reasonable to share profits throughout.

There is an ominous labor pressure from foreign countries, though. The difference in the standard of living in the United States and other countries is so large that it is impossible to compete with the lower labor and wage rates; at least, no one so far has figured out a way to offset these costs. Early labor pressures on American companies began in the late seventies and early eighties. Each year companies were faced with competition using Mexican labor. Their labor rates were barely a dollar an hour, and average U.S. workers earned seven to fifteen dollars an hour for similar work. Many companies turned to automation in an attempt to reduce the labor content in their product. For example, if a machine could do the job of ten people, but only required one operator, then seventy dollars an hour for ten workers would be reduced to seven dollars for one. Assuming the foreign operation still used ten people at a dollar an hour, the foreign cost would be ten dollars an hour and the jobs could remain in the United States. This worked for a time, but soon American companies began building new factories in Mexico and other countries, and set up machinery and equipment with U.S. technology. Eventually, the rush to Mexico and places south became an avalanche, and companies began closing plants and laying off U.S. workers. Those laid off were told they would need to retrain themselves for jobs requiring greater technological skill. It really hasn't worked out that way, though, because the U.S. companies are transferring their technologies and training foreign workers, too, so even jobs requiring higher skill and advanced knowledge are migrating, too.

The changes in China opened the door to stronger pressures on both U.S. and Mexican labor. Many Asian operations paid about a dollar a day to their workers. This was less than an eighth of the wages of new prosperity in Mexico. It didn't take long for U.S. companies to continue the transfer to Asian companies, and to build Asian factories. The arithmetic was somewhat simple. If the product had high labor content, sold a large number of units each year, and was small enough to ship at low enough cost, then it was a candidate for Asian production. High labor content is necessary to maximize the savings on labor; for instance, if a product required eight man-hours to build, then it would cost a dollar for direct labor in Asia versus something like $120 for U.S. labor, giving a savings of $119 per piece.

If one thousand units would fit in a shipping container, it might cost about fifteen dollars per unit for shipping and to pay tariff fees, so the total savings would be about $104 per piece, not counting reduced material costs. When high volumes of say, 100,000 units per year are needed, then the savings for a company are substantial. Figure 9-2 compares the base company example with comparable "Asian Labor" to do the job.

Asian materials are typically cheaper than in the United States; it has been estimated at $880 thousand less in the example ($5,500 − 4,620). The difference in direct labor rates of about $950 thousand ($960 − 10) is substantial savings in the example comparison. There are additional costs such as profit and administrative costs if there is an Asian intermediary, and of course, tariffs and shipping reduce the direct cost savings some as shown in the figure.

But there are additional savings at home, too. The support staff won't have to be as large, so company overhead can be reduced somewhat. The number of supervisors and schedulers can be reduced, because the workforce at home is minimal or nonexistent, and the administrative staff can be cut back. Less people result in a reduction in health care premiums and retirement and benefit costs. As shown in Figure 9-2 the net profit is almost doubled for the base company.

When American company managers are faced with a business analysis like the comparison of Figure 9-2, they often still resist the change and struggle to justify keeping the operation at home. No one really wants to make the change. Contrary to what many people may believe, most company managers want to keep jobs at home and keep Americans employed. Early in the trend many companies simply refused to make the change and hoped for the best. Tremendous cost reduction programs were initiated at home to support the struggle to compete with the unbalanced labor differential. But when their competitors made the switch, the loyalists were forced to follow suit in the new rush.

Many companies remain in the U.S., and some of them are faced with the opposite problem; higher labor costs and inefficiencies of union labor. Unions are not necessarily bad, and at times they are useful in keeping management honest. Today, though, with all of the federal occupational and labor rules, most companies and managers have been trained to treat the labor force properly and to provide a safe and comfortable working environment. Industrial engineers learned long ago that the better the working conditions for its workers the better the efficiency and productivity of the operation. The primary disadvantage of union labor to a business is the inherent inefficiency of the whole system. It begins with wages that are inflated by union dues. The company actually pays the union the dues in the form of wages, so this extra cost is added to the labor cost structure. Just about every time workers receive a pay increase there is an increase in union dues. Corporate cost structures are swollen further by the additional time and personnel required for union supervision and management. Most unions require stewards and chief stewards to watch over the operation and consult with union members. In some cases these individuals work on the job part time and conduct union business part time. Some contracts require union funds (from union dues paid by the company), be used to pay for the time spent on union business, but in many situations the company pays the wages for both the steward and worker while they consult in a private area provided by the company. The result of this situation usually means extra workers to cover the time lost while union workers are conducting union business. Also, because unions believe company profits should be shared with workers in the form of higher wages, ballooning pay rates may creep into the cost structure. Figure 9-2 also compares the example of the base company using union workers under the "Union Labor" heading. There are more workers in the example, and the union wages are figured about fifty percent higher than the base company wages to cover union dues and wage creep. In the example the net profit is reduced by nearly forty percent from $994 to $595 thousand.

	Effects of Labor Pressures on Company Budget					
	Dollar amounts (shown in thousands)					
	Base Plan		Asian Labor		Union Labor	
	Dollars	% Sales	Dollars	% Sales	Dollars	% Sales
Gross Receipts (Sales)	10,000		10,000		10,000	
Direct Cost						
US Direct Materials	5,500	55.0%	200	2.0%	5,500	55.0%
US Direct Labor	960	9.6%	48	0.5%	1,584	15.8%
Asia Direct Materials			4,620	46.2%		
Asia Direct Labor			10	0.1%		
Asia Admin & Profit			232	2.3%		
Tariff			238	2.4%		
Shipping			204	2.0%		
Total Direct Cost	6,460	64.6%	5,552	55.5%	7,084	70.8%
Indirect Cost						
Salaries	320	3.2%	240	2.4%	320	3.2%
Expenses	200	2.0%	140	1.4%	200	2.0%
Health Care Premiums	288	2.9%	48	0.5%	312	3.1%
Pension & Benefit Plan	192	1.9%	32	0.3%	208	2.1%
Total Indirect Cost	1,000	10.0%	460	4.6%	1,040	10.4%
Gross Profit	2,540	25.4%	3,988	39.9%	1,876	18.8%
Administrative Cost						
Salaries	600	6.0%	500	5.0%	600	6.0%
Expenses	200	2.0%	200	2.0%	200	2.0%
Health Care Premiums	36	0.4%	30	0.3%	36	0.4%
Pension & Benefit Plan	48	0.5%	40	0.4%	48	0.5%
Total Administrative Cost	884	8.8%	770	7.7%	884	8.8%
Operating Profit	1,656	16.6%	3,218	32.2%	992	9.9%
Income Tax	662	6.6%	1,287	12.9%	397	4.0%
Net Profit After Tax	994	9.9%	1,931	19.3%	595	6.0%

Company Budget with Labor Pressures
Figure 9-2

This high labor cost compared to the competition puts extraordinary pressure on the company to try to overcome the disadvantage. Compare the three scenarios of Figure 9-2 and consider management pressures and decisions.

Union inefficiencies don't end with dues and more people, though. Union operations typically are slow to react to changing market conditions. Contracts often don't allow company managers to make swift decisions to meet a crisis or take advantage of an opportunity, because they are restrained by contract provisions and must consult with union officials first. This can slow down reaction time until the situation becomes hopeless while a faster moving company captures the advantages that might be available. Contingency adjustments, such as increased or decreased sales, may be prohibited by strict union contracts.

And then there are the strikes and constant tension that generally infect a company with a union contract. When unions first started many years ago it was probably an admirable cause. The country didn't have the labor laws of today, and many company managers were selfish, cruel, and greedy, so early union movements were somewhat honest and noble. But soon the greed was transferred to union bosses and members who wanted to control companies without the responsibility of reporting a profit or without the risk of losing money. The last half of the twentieth century has seen unions convert from wanting appropriate treatment and wages, to seeking power, privilege, and greed. This seems to fit most union objectives today. Union members want to be treated special and feel superior to nonunion workers, and they want to direct management actions instead of following management decisions. There's an old principle of military leadership that says, "you have to be a good follower to be a good leader." This principle has been lost on most union operations. And the greed factor has grown so large that the more concessions they receive in pay and benefits, the more they want.

The true character of a union is exposed when the terrible expense and effects of a strike are considered. Figure 9-3 shows an example of the losses for a company afflicted with a strike; compare results under the "Base Plan" and "Year of Strike" headings. This example assumes the union members struck for more pay and lower health care costs. The sample strike lasted about three months; and, in the end, the average wage was increased about fifty cents an hour in the first year, and the company's portion of the health care premium was increased by $500 per employee. Naturally the company elected to increase the health care premium amount for all of its employees, which added to the overall cost structure for the future. But look at the losses during the year of the strike. Sales (Gross Receipts) dropped forty percent from $10 million to $6 million because of the work stoppage, but net profit was cut by about three-fourths from nearly $1 million to only $236 thousand.

Effect of Union Strike on Company Budget

	Base Plan		Year of Strike		Year After Strike	
	Dollars	% Sales	Dollars	% Sales	Dollars	% Sales
Gross Receipts (Sales)	10,000		6,000		9,000	
Direct Cost						
Direct Materials	5,500	55.0%	3,135	52.3%	4,995	55.5%
Direct Labor	960	9.6%	600	10.0%	1,000	11.1%
Total Direct Cost	6,460	64.6%	3,735	62.3%	5,995	66.6%
Indirect Cost						
Salaries	320	3.2%	320	5.3%	320	3.6%
Expenses	200	2.0%	160	2.7%	190	2.1%
Health Care Premiums	288	2.9%	312	5.2%	312	3.5%
Pension & Benefit Plan	192	1.9%	192	3.2%	192	2.1%
Total Indirect Cost	1,000	10.0%	984	16.4%	1,014	11.3%
Gross Profit	2,540	25.4%	1,281	21.4%	1,991	22.1%
Administrative Cost						
Salaries	600	6.0%	600	10.0%	600	6.7%
Expenses	200	2.0%	200	3.3%	200	2.2%
Health Care Premiums	36	0.4%	39	0.7%	39	0.4%
Pension & Benefit Plan	48	0.5%	48	0.8%	48	0.5%
Total Administrative Cost	884	8.8%	887	14.8%	887	9.9%
Operating Profit	1,656	16.6%	394	6.6%	1,104	12.3%
Income Tax	662	6.6%	158	2.6%	442	4.9%
Net Profit After Tax	994	9.9%	236	3.9%	662	7.4%

Dollar amounts (shown in thousands)

Company Budget with Strike Effects
Figure 9-3

The lost profit will set back investments in company projects, such as expenditures to improve efficiency and products, and efforts to meet debt obligations the company may have. In addition, the company likely will not recover all of the lost sales. Customers are not pleased when the product is not available, and once they switch to a competitor it is extremely difficult to win back their business. The full impact of the lost sales is shown in Figure 9-3 under the "Year After Strike" where sales are still off about ten percent at $9 million and profits remain off about one-third at $662 thousand because of increased costs for labor, materials, and fringe benefits. The sample company profit is well below its goal.

The quality of the labor work force is usually diluted, too. Many workers can't afford to live on union stipends during a strike, and the best workers want a job, so they find new work during the strike and are lost to the company. But the unspoken result of most strikes is hard feelings that remain between union members and company management. Almost all strikes seem to be viewed by union members as a license to commit a felony. They destroy property, intimidate salaried workers, and grow angrier at each passing day of demonstration. Salaried workers are required to continue working or lose their jobs, but union members don't usually respect their right to continue working. In today's environment most salaried workers are instructed to refrain from doing most union jobs during a strike to respect the union's right to strike, but the respect frequently is not mutual. Union members block entrances to the property, damage private vehicles and property, and threaten those that have to continue with their jobs. Often these daily confrontations result in name calling and worse. After the strike is settled, the tension remains, and it takes years for the bad blood to be erased, if ever. Old friendships between hourly and salaried workers are usually lost.

The net result of a strike is a loss for both the company and the workers. The gains in wages and benefits resulting from a strike are usually offset by the lost wages during the strike that may take years to recover. The company's losses are large, too, and it must take action in the future to restore its percentage of profit. Figure 9-4 shows what a company manager might do to restore profits. It compares the "Base Plan," the "Year After Strike" changes, and "Strike Adjustments" a company may need to make to restore its profit level.

Despite strong efforts to improve sales, the company remains at about ten percent of its historic revenues. As a result, it adjusts company size to correspond with current sales. Not only the direct and indirect labor force size is reduced, but also the number of administrative workers is cut. In addition, administrative expenses are reduced in an effort to restore the profitability of the company. Although profits are improved to $866 thousand, the net profit remains over twelve percent less than the previous history of the base company. The company has been crippled and will probably continue to struggle for years to come. The increased labor costs may plague the company if its competitors do not raise their labor rates. If the competitors retain labor costs at market averages, but reward their employees through bonus plans or profit sharing, they will likely enjoy the advantage of a lower cost structure and the ability to offer products of equal quality at a lower price.

Nevertheless, the union has achieved its goal of more pay and more power, but in the long run it may have achieved the goal of causing the company to consider off shore alternatives, or worse, to cease operations altogether.

Adjustment of Company Budget After A Strike						
	Dollar amounts (shown in thousands)					
	Base Plan		Year After Strike		Strike Adjustments	
	Dollars	% Sales	Dollars	% Sales	Dollars	% Sales
Gross Receipts (Sales)	10,000		9,000		9,000	
Direct Cost						
Direct Materials	5,500	55.0%	4,995	55.5%	4,995	55.5%
Direct Labor	960	9.6%	1,000	11.1%	850	9.4%
Total Direct Cost	6,460	64.6%	5,995	66.6%	5,845	64.9%
Indirect Cost						
Salaries	320	3.2%	320	3.6%	240	2.7%
Expenses	200	2.0%	190	2.1%	190	2.1%
Health Care Premiums	288	2.9%	312	3.5%	312	3.5%
Pension & Benefit Plan	192	1.9%	192	2.1%	192	2.1%
Total Indirect Cost	1,000	10.0%	1,014	11.3%	934	10.4%
Gross Profit	2,540	25.4%	1,991	22.1%	2,221	24.7%
Administrative Cost						
Salaries	600	6.0%	600	6.7%	500	5.6%
Expenses	200	2.0%	200	2.2%	190	2.1%
Health Care Premiums	36	0.4%	39	0.4%	39	0.4%
Pension & Benefit Plan	48	0.5%	48	0.5%	48	0.5%
Total Administrative Cost	884	8.8%	887	9.9%	777	8.6%
Operating Profit	1,656	16.6%	1,104	12.3%	1,444	16.0%
Income Tax	662	6.6%	442	4.9%	578	6.4%
Net Profit After Tax	994	9.9%	662	7.4%	866	9.6%

Company Budget with Strike Adjustments
Figure 9-4

	Effect of Increased Fuel Cost on Company Budget Fuel Costs Doubled					
	Dollar amounts (shown in thousands)					
	Base Plan		Fuel Increase		Price Adjustments	
	Dollars	% Sales	Dollars	% Sales	Dollars	% Sales
Gross Receipts (Sales)	10,000		10,000		10,630	
Direct Cost						
Direct Materials	5,500	55.0%	6,050	60.5%	6,050	56.9%
Direct Labor	960	9.6%	960	9.6%	960	9.0%
Total Direct Cost	6,460	64.6%	7,010	70.1%	7,010	65.9%
Indirect Cost						
Salaries	320	3.2%	320	3.2%	320	3.0%
Expenses	200	2.0%	190	1.9%	190	1.8%
Health Care Premiums	288	2.9%	288	2.9%	288	2.7%
Pension & Benefit Plan	192	1.9%	192	1.9%	192	1.8%
Total Indirect Cost	1,000	10.0%	990	9.9%	990	9.3%
Gross Profit	2,540	25.4%	2,000	20.0%	2,630	24.7%
Administrative Cost						
Salaries	600	6.0%	600	6.0%	600	5.6%
Expenses	200	2.0%	200	2.0%	200	1.9%
Health Care Premiums	36	0.4%	36	0.4%	36	0.3%
Pension & Benefit Plan	48	0.5%	48	0.5%	48	0.5%
Total Administrative Cost	884	8.8%	884	8.8%	884	8.3%
Operating Profit	1,656	16.6%	1,116	11.2%	1,746	16.4%
Income Tax	662	6.6%	446	4.5%	698	6.6%
Net Profit After Tax	994	9.9%	670	6.7%	1,048	9.9%

Company Budget with Fuel Increase
Figure 9-5

Imagine yourself with the job of balancing labor pressures and holding company profits. What would you do in such situations? Ruthless managers run through the organization with a paring knife. Timid managers won't face the problem and let the business slowly deteriorate. Judicious managers protect their workforce while looking for clever ways to balance the pressures. In a statistical distribution, the numbers of even-minded managers are in the center of the curve. (See Figure 3-1)

One of the major contributors to material inflation is fuel cost. Consumers notice that about every time gas prices increase, so do the prices on store shelves. When the cost of fuel increases it usually results in both higher freight charges and facility expenses for a business operation. Heating and cooling expenses are increased, and material costs increase as material suppliers pass on the higher costs of fuel.

An example of this problem is shown in Figure 9-5 under the "Fuel Increase" heading, where the cost of material increases about ten percent to over $6 million. In an effort to hold the price of its product, company management cut back on indirect expenses to about $190 thousand but still lost about a third of its profit as it dropped to $670 thousand. What would you do about higher fuel costs? Would you raise prices, cut jobs, pay less for employee health insurance, let profits suffer, or something else? Ultimately, the company in the examples decided to adjust its prices to counteract the increased fuel cost and return the profit to a similar percent of sales as the base plan. In the end, the consumer pays for higher priced fuel through price increases as shown under the "Price Adjustments" heading in Figure 9-5 as higher Gross Receipts.

Another pressure a company is likely to face is higher health care costs. Figure 9-6 shows an example of an increase in health care premiums of about eight percent under the "Health Increase" heading. It affects both indirect and administrative costs. This is not atypical, and often today the jump is much larger each year.

In the example case the net profit was reduced about $16,000 to $978 thousand, and the company was able to absorb it, but if it continues to rise, the company will have to make adjustments to protect its survival and profitability. Companies face two prospects usually: cut its share of the premium, requiring each employee to pay more for health care, or raise the prices of their products. Aggressive companies establish cost reduction plans to offset these costs, but often cannot keep pace with increases.

One important cost that companies must consider is the income tax they must pay. Large companies are often criticized and targeted for not paying enough tax, and this line of thought is frequently used in class warfare rhetoric. Many Americans believe companies should pay more tax so individuals can pay less tax, or receive a larger hand out if they are on the government dole.

Effects of Increased Health Premiums on Company Budget
Health Care Premiums Increased 8%

| | Dollar amounts (shown in thousands) | | | |
| | Base Plan | | Health Increase | |
	Dollars	% Sales	Dollars	% Sales
Gross Receipts (Sales)	10,000		10,000	
Direct Cost				
Direct Materials	5,500	55.0%	5,500	55.0%
Direct Labor	960	9.6%	960	9.6%
Total Direct Cost	6,460	64.6%	6,460	64.6%
Indirect Cost				
Salaries	320	3.2%	320	3.2%
Expenses	200	2.0%	200	2.0%
Health Care Premiums	288	2.9%	311	3.1%
Pension & Benefit Plan	192	1.9%	192	1.9%
Total Indirect Cost	1,000	10.0%	1,023	10.2%
Gross Profit	2,540	25.4%	2,517	25.2%
Administrative Cost				
Salaries	600	6.0%	600	6.0%
Expenses	200	2.0%	200	2.0%
Health Care Premiums	36	0.4%	39	0.4%
Pension & Benefit Plan	48	0.5%	48	0.5%
Total Administrative Cost	884	8.8%	887	8.9%
Operating Profit	1,656	16.6%	1,630	16.3%
Income Tax	662	6.6%	652	6.5%
Net Profit After Tax	994	9.9%	978	9.8%

Company Budget with Health Premium Increase
Figure 9-6

	Dollar amounts (shown in thousands)					
	Base Plan		Tax Increase		Tax Adjustments	
	Dollars	% Sales	Dollars	% Sales	Dollars	% Sales
Gross Receipts (Sales)	10,000		10,000		10,170	
Direct Cost						
Direct Materials	5,500	55.0%	5,500	55.0%	5,500	54.1%
Direct Labor	960	9.6%	960	9.6%	960	9.4%
Total Direct Cost	6,460	64.6%	6,460	64.6%	6,460	63.5%
Indirect Cost						
Salaries	320	3.2%	320	3.2%	320	3.1%
Expenses	200	2.0%	200	2.0%	200	2.0%
Health Care Premiums	288	2.9%	288	2.9%	288	2.8%
Pension & Benefit Plan	192	1.9%	192	1.9%	192	1.9%
Total Indirect Cost	1,000	10.0%	1,000	10.0%	1,000	9.8%
Gross Profit	2,540	25.4%	2,540	25.4%	2,710	26.6%
Administrative Cost						
Salaries	600	6.0%	600	6.0%	600	5.9%
Expenses	200	2.0%	200	2.0%	200	2.0%
Health Care Premiums	36	0.4%	36	0.4%	36	0.4%
Pension & Benefit Plan	48	0.5%	48	0.5%	48	0.5%
Total Administrative Cost	884	8.8%	884	8.8%	884	8.7%
Operating Profit	1,656	16.6%	1,656	16.6%	1,826	18.0%
Income Tax	662	6.6%	745	7.5%	822	8.1%
Net Profit After Tax	994	9.9%	911	9.1%	1,004	9.9%

Effect of Increased Taxes on Company Budget
Taxes Increase 5%

Company Budget with Tax Increase
Figure 9-7

The truth, though, is that companies don't pay income tax at all; it is incorporated into the cost structure, and tax increases are usually passed on to the customer.

Figure 9-7 shows the impact of a five-percent increase in income taxes. It compares the "Base Plan" to the result of the "Tax Increase" and to defensive "Tax Adjustments" that are likely. Company profits are reduced by the 5% added tax requirement ($745 - $662) of $83 thousand more paid to the government. But the prudent managers of the sample company likely will not allow operations to continue with the lower profit percentages. They may attempt to offset the tax increases with cost reduction programs, or they may decide to decrease the size of the company work force causing jobs to be lost. In the example the company chose to raise prices of their products (Gross Receipts) to offset the increased taxes, and ultimately the company profits increased slightly at the expense of consumers. Customers pay the taxes, not the company. Often, though, the tax increase is met with a combination of actions with both company layoffs and the consumer sharing the cost of higher taxes.

Of course it is obvious, after considering the different budget examples, that taxes are merely one element in the cost structure of a company, and the higher the taxes, the higher the company's expenses, and the more difficult it is for the company to compete. About forty or fifty years ago many states realized this problem and offered low taxes as an incentive for companies to relocate to their area. These states profited from more jobs for their citizens and a better standard of living from their productivity. Thus the great migration began and a boom for many shrewd southern states. These states offered lower labor costs, too, and so the example base company might benefit from lower taxes and labor costs as shown in Figure 9-8 with net profits almost one percent better on the same Gross Receipts.

The company is more competitive with lower labor cost and taxes, the state enjoys added income from a new business, and employees have money from their new jobs to spend in the community. This leads to more jobs, housing growth, and general prosperity.

The same scenario applies to the country as a whole today. The federal and state governments can continue to raise taxes on companies, but it hampers competitiveness with foreign operations. The clever actions to attract businesses during the migration of operations to the southern states should be further considered today as U.S. businesses struggle to compete with foreign companies. By lowering its tax structure and other operational costs, the U.S. may be able to bring jobs and prosperity home.

But today, U.S. companies battle extra costs of taxes and regulations from OSHA, EPA, and others. The result is lower company income and a corresponding reduced amount of taxes paid. Some elements of government want to increase taxes in order to offset the lost government income. As seen in the preceding examples, more taxes and regulations simply increase the cost structure for companies and make it more difficult to compete.

Effects of Lower Taxes and No Union on Company Budget
Taxes Decreased 5% and No Union Costs

	Dollar amounts (shown in thousands)			
	Base Plan		Lower Tax & Labor	
	Dollars	% Sales	Dollars	% Sales
Gross Receipts (Sales)	10,000		10,000	
Direct Cost				
Direct Materials	5,500	55.0%	5,500	55.0%
Direct Labor	960	9.6%	960	9.6%
Total Direct Cost	6,460	64.6%	6,460	64.6%
Indirect Cost				
Salaries	320	3.2%	320	3.2%
Expenses	200	2.0%	200	2.0%
Health Care Premiums	288	2.9%	288	2.9%
Pension & Benefit Plan	192	1.9%	192	1.9%
Total Indirect Cost	1,000	10.0%	1,000	10.0%
Gross Profit	2,540	25.4%	2,540	25.4%
Administrative Cost				
Salaries	600	6.0%	600	6.0%
Expenses	200	2.0%	200	2.0%
Health Care Premiums	36	0.4%	36	0.4%
Pension & Benefit Plan	48	0.5%	48	0.5%
Total Administrative Cost	884	8.8%	884	8.8%
Operating Profit	1,656	16.6%	1,656	16.6%
Income Tax	662	6.6%	580	5.8%
Net Profit After Tax	994	9.9%	1,076	10.8%

Company Budget with Lower Taxes and No Union Costs
Figure 9-8

Each day, companies commonly face all of the pressures that have been outlined, and more. It is a continual balancing act as managers battle increased costs of labor, materials, benefits, taxes, and more all at once each year. Put yourself in the position to decide the course of action to remain profitable. What would you do? Would you cut back by reducing expenses and labor forces? Would you increase prices at the risk of losing sales and eventually have to cut back on company expenses anyway? It's a difficult job to manage a company that must contend with business pressures, continually gaining ground or losing ground on the competition; successful companies monitor every change and consistently gain ground.

Most companies are managed throughout by working Americans that are trying to do the right thing and to contribute to their communities. Companies aren't filled with greedy fat cats as characterized by the class-warfare dialog often used to demonize business. Of course every company has greedy people, both managers and labor. In most cases it probably follows the lesson learned from the law of statistical distribution. There is a small percentage of greed, but the majority of companies are decent, honest, hardworking Americans that have achieved their position in the company through merit.

THE NATIONAL PLAN

Similar to a private business or a nonprofit organization, U.S. leaders develop a national financial program each year that includes a forecast for several years into the future. The national budget is similar to the example business plan that has been reviewed. Figure 9-9 shows budgets for 2009 and 2010 as published by the Office of Management and Budget, OMB, in its "Historical Tables, Budget of the U.S. Government" for fiscal year 2011.

The national plan closely resembles a nonprofit budget that includes operating cost for labor, material, facilities, and interest on loans. The remainder is used for services to the people in the form of defense, infrastructure, and give-away programs. Contrary to a private nonprofit business that must balance its budget by spending no more than it receives, the national plan includes provisions to borrow more than it receives in order to meet its spending plan. When the country borrows money each year it is added to the total debt that is owed. This debt continually grows as more is borrowed each year, and today the U.S. owes about $16 trillion.

The budget is laid out similarly to the example business plan in Figure 9-1. The receipts in the national budget compare to the gross receipts in the private business plan, and total receipts are further divided into nine categories as shown in Figure 9-9. Following receipts are national outlays, which compare to private business expenses such as direct, indirect, and

	The National Budget					
	Dollar amounts (shown in billions)					
	2009			2010 Estimated Budget		
	Dollars	% Total	% GDP	Dollars	% Total	% GDP
Gross Domestic Product	14,237			14,624		
Receipts						
Individual Income Tax	915	43.5%	6.4%	936	43.2%	6.4%
Corporate Tax	138	6.6%	1.0%	157	7.2%	1.1%
Social Insurance & Retirement	891	42.3%	6.3%	876	40.4%	6.0%
Excise Tax	62	3.0%	0.4%	73	3.4%	0.5%
Estate and Gift Tax	23	1.1%	0.2%	17	0.8%	0.1%
Customs, Duties, & Fees	22	1.1%	0.2%	24	1.1%	0.2%
Federal Reserve Deposits	34	1.6%	0.2%	77	3.6%	0.5%
Allowances	-	0.0%	0.0%	(12)	-0.6%	-0.1%
All Other	18	0.8%	0.1%	18	0.8%	0.1%
Total Receipts	2,105		14.8%	2,165		14.8%
Outlays						
National Defense	661	18.8%	4.6%	719	19.3%	4.9%
International Affairs	38	1.1%	0.3%	51	1.4%	0.3%
General Science, Space & Technology	29	0.8%	0.2%	33	0.9%	0.2%
Energy	5	0.1%	0.0%	19	0.5%	0.1%
Natural Resources and Environment	36	1.0%	0.2%	47	1.3%	0.3%
Agriculture	22	0.6%	0.2%	27	0.7%	0.2%
Commerce and Housing Credit	292	8.3%	2.0%	(25)	-0.7%	-0.2%
Transportation	84	2.4%	0.6%	106	2.9%	0.7%
Community and Regional Development	28	0.8%	0.2%	28	0.8%	0.2%
Education, Training, Employment, & SS	80	2.3%	0.6%	143	3.8%	1.0%
Health	334	9.5%	2.3%	372	10.0%	2.5%
Medicare	430	12.2%	3.0%	457	12.3%	3.1%
Income Security	533	15.2%	3.7%	686	18.4%	4.7%
Social Security	683	19.4%	4.8%	721	19.4%	4.9%
Veterans Benefits and Services	95	2.7%	0.7%	125	3.4%	0.9%
Administration of Justice	52	1.5%	0.4%	55	1.5%	0.4%
General Government	22	0.6%	0.2%	29	0.8%	0.2%
Net Interest	187	5.3%	1.3%	188	5.0%	1.3%
Allowances	-	0.0%	0.0%	19	0.5%	0.1%
Undistributed Offset Receipts	(93)	-2.6%	-0.7%	(80)	-2.1%	-0.5%
Total Outlays	3,518		24.7%	3,721		25.4%
Surplus or (Deficit)	(1,413)	-67.1%	-9.9%	(1,556)	-71.8%	-10.6%

Source: *Historical Tables, Budget of U.S. Government, Fiscal Year 2011*
Office of Management & Budget. Washington

The National Budget
Figure 9-9

administrative cost.

There are twenty standard reporting categories of outlays as shown in Figure 9-9 that include expenses, services, and handout programs. The twenty outlay categories are subdivided into various uses and accounts according to long-established definitions as shown in Figure 9-10. The numbers at the left of each functional category are account numbers used to track receipts and payments for that purpose.

Of course the national budget doesn't show a profit; presumably the objective is to break even each year. In place of profit the terms surplus and deficit are used; that means, when the government takes in more than it spends there is a surplus, and when it spends more than it receives, then it is called a deficit. The budgets for 2009 and 2010, shown in Figure 9-9, show results that are typical for most of the last fifty years; spending in 2009 exceeded receipts by more than $1.4 trillion, and when this budget was published it was estimated that 2010 spending would be over $1.5 trillion in the red.

Figure 9-9 includes an item that is not part of the private business budget example, the Gross Domestic Product, or GDP. The GDP is a measurement of the economic output of the country, in other words how much wealth is created each year. There are a number of different ways of figuring this GDP number. There is the product approach, which is considered the most direct method that simply adds up all of the output of the country. The income method limits the calculation to the sum of all producers' income. A third method is the calculation of expenditures, which adds private consumption, gross investments, government spending, and net export values after subtracting import cost. Economists and theorists can worry over the advantages of each method. For purposes of the country's budget, the OMB uses an adjusted figure.

The OMB calculates an adjusted GDP in order to allow a common comparison of data for current and prior years. The idea of calculating the percentage of GDP received and spent for government use is similar to a private citizen determining how much of their income will be spent for a home, clothing, and so forth. Figure 9-9 shows the GDP for each year and the percent of GDP for each category. In addition, there is a column that shows the percent of total receipts or of total outlays for each item in the budget. For example, individual income tax receipts are 43.5 percent of all receipts and 6.4 percent of the total GDP of $14.237 trillion for 2009. The figures for 2009 show total receipts were about 14.8 percent of national productivity for the year, but total outlays were 24.7 percent of GDP.

The majority of government receipts are from individual income tax, corporate income tax, and social insurance and retirement tax commonly known as Social Security and Medicare.

National Budget Functional and Sub-functional Categories	
Functional categories	Sub-functional categories
050 National defense	Department of Defense Military; Atomic energy defense activities; Defense-related activities
150 International affairs	International development & humanitarian assistance; International security assistance; Conduct of foreign affairs; Foreign information & exchange activities; International financial programs
250 General science, space and technology	General science and basic research; Space flight, research & supporting activities
270 Energy	Energy supply; Energy conservation; Emergency energy preparedness; Energy information, policy, regulation
300 Natural resources and environment	Water resources; Conservation and land management; Recreational resources; Pollution control and abatement; Other natural resources
350 Agriculture	Farm income stabilization; Agricultural research, and services
370 Commerce and housing credit	Mortgage credit; Postal Service; Deposit insurance; Other advancement of commerce
400 Transportation	Ground transportation; Air transportation; Water transportation; Other transportation
450 Community and regional development	Community development; Area and regional development; Disaster relief and insurance
500 Education, training, employment, and social services	Elementary, secondary, and vocational education; Higher education; Research & general education aids; Training & employment; Other labor services; Social services

National Budget Functional Categories
Figure 9-10

It's interesting to note that the government primarily operates on money from individuals who make income tax, Social Security, and Medicare payments; this is quite a change from the way the government operated during its first hundred years. Other receipts include excise taxes from various sources including penalties paid on early retirement withdrawals, estate and gift taxes paid by individuals who give away large amounts of their personal wealth, customs and duties on imports, and deposits from the federal reserve

National Budget Functional and Sub-functional Categories (continued)	
Functional categories	Sub-functional categories
550 Health	Health care services; Health research & training; Consumer & occupational health & safety
570 Medicare	Medicare
600 Income security	General retirement & disability insurance; Federal employee retirement & disability; Unemployment compensation; Housing assistance; Food & nutrition assistance; Other income security
650 Social security	Social security
700 Veterans benefits and services	Income security for veterans; Veterans education, training & rehabilitation; Hospital & medical care for veterans; Veterans housing; Other veterans benefits and services
750 Administration of justice	Federal law enforcement activities; Federal litigative & judicial activities; Federal correctional activities; Criminal justice assistance
800 General government	Legislative function; Executive direction and management; Central personnel management; General purpose fiscal assistance; Other general government; Deductions for offsetting receipts
900 Net interest	Interest on Treasury debt securities; Interest received by off-budget trust funds; Other interest
920 Allowances	Varies by year
950 Undistributed offsetting receipts	Employer share, employee retirement; Rents & royalties on Outer Continental Shelf; Sale of major assets; Other undistributed offsetting receipts

National Budget Functional Categories
Figure 9-10 (continued)

bank system. Allowances are generally accounting transactions from one government account to another, are common to both receipts and outlays, and may show a negative adjustment in some years. Finally, the other category obviously includes all other forms of receipts.

In addition to allowances, there are undistributed offset receipts accounted for as outlays. These are receipts from government sales and other activities as described in the functional definitions in Figure 9-10. Functions may include postage sales, fees collected from national parks and recreation areas, interest income, and sale of government land.

Remember, Congress and the OMB separate the budget into two fund groups: federal funds and trust funds. The law requires separate accounting categories for trust funds, which limits their receipts and outlays for specific purposes. Trust fund by this definition does not mean the same thing as a private trust where ownership of funds and assets of an individual may be held and managed by another. Federal trust funds are only a means of identifying income and outlays for specific purposes. The largest trust funds are retirement and social insurance funds such as civil service and military retirement, Social Security, Medicare, and unemployment benefits. The transportation trust fund is also a significant designation to support highways and aviation components of national infrastructure. For many years Social Security and Medicare receipts from worker and employer payments have exceeded the payouts. Unfortunately, instead of protecting the surplus, and perhaps earning a little interest on it, Congress has stripped the surpluses to spend on other projects and programs without looking ahead to future requirements for these trust fund programs. The obvious result is that increased Social Security and Medicare outlay requirements will soon exceed the income receipts, and the government may soon default on another of its promises to the people who have paid into these accounts for their entire lives. Just like a Ponzi schemer, instead of investing the surplus, Congress elected to fritter it away on itself and new programs while using the payments of new and young taxpayers (investors) to pay those collecting from the system. And, just like Ponzi schemers, the government has run out of enough new investors, so the promise is fading.

The second fund group is federal funds. It is simply defined as all funds not specified by law as trust funds. This group includes provisions for the Postal Service.

Most studies of the national budget include a comparison of the amount received and spent as a percentage of the GDP. The portion of national wealth that is spent on government operations and programs is an important consideration for each American citizen. If citizens pour all of their productivity into the government then the nation's ability to grow and prosper will be stripped away. It would be similar to a business that fails to invest some of its earnings in development and productivity improvement. Very soon it would be far behind its competition. On the other hand, if a very small proportion of the country's productivity is allocated to the government, then government programs must be cut back; however, many economists believe that leaving a large portion of what Americans produce in their own hands will assure the continued legacy of growth, prosperity, high standard of living, and personal freedom. Figures 9-11 and 9-12 show a history of America's national plan for the last fifty years.

The National Budget - The Last Fifty Years

	Dollar amounts (shown in billions)					
	1960	1970	1980	1990	2000	2010E
	Dollars	Dollars	Dollars	Dollars	Dollars	Dollars
Gross Domestic Product	519	1,013	2,724	5,735	9,821	14,624
Receipts						
Individual Income Tax	41	90	244	467	1,004	936
Corporate Tax	21	33	65	94	207	157
Social Insurance & Retirement	15	44	158	380	653	876
Excise Tax	12	16	24	35	69	73
Estate and Gift Tax	2	4	6	12	29	17
Customs, Duties, & Fees	1	2	7	17	20	24
Federal Reserve Deposits	1	3	12	24	32	77
Allowances	-	-	-	-	-	(12)
All Other	0	0	1	4	11	18
Total Receipts	92	193	517	1,032	2,025	2,165
Outlays						
National Defense	48	82	134	299	294	719
International Affairs	3	4	13	14	17	51
General Science, Space & Technology	1	5	6	14	19	33
Energy	0	1	10	3	(1)	19
Natural Resources and Environment	2	3	14	17	25	47
Agriculture	3	5	9	12	36	27
Commerce and Housing Credit	2	2	9	68	3	(25)
Transportation	4	7	21	29	47	106
Community and Regional Development	0	2	11	9	11	28
Education, Training, Employment, & SS	1	9	32	37	54	143
Health	1	6	23	58	155	372
Medicare	-	6	32	98	197	457
Income Security	7	16	87	149	254	686
Social Security	12	30	119	249	409	721
Veterans Benefits and Services	5	9	21	29	47	125
Administration of Justice	0	1	5	10	28	55
General Government	1	2	13	10	13	29
Net Interest	7	14	53	184	223	188
Allowances	-	-	-	-	-	19
Undistributed Offset Receipts	(5)	(9)	(20)	(37)	(43)	(80)
Total Outlays	92	196	591	1,253	1,789	3,721
Surplus or (Deficit)	0	(3)	(74)	(221)	236	(1,556)

Source: *Historical Tables, Budget of U.S. Government, Fiscal Year 2011*
        Office of Management & Budget. Washington

The National Budget - The Last Fifty Years
Figure 9-11

The National Budget - Historical Percent of GDP

	1960	1970	1980	1990	2000	2010E
	Dollars	Dollars	Dollars	Dollars	Dollars	Dollars
Gross Domestic Product (in billions)	519	1,013	2,724	5,735	9,821	14,624
	% GDP	% GDP	% GDP	% GDP	% GDP	% GDP
Receipts						
Individual Income Tax	7.8%	8.9%	9.0%	8.1%	10.2%	6.4%
Corporate Tax	4.1%	3.2%	2.4%	1.6%	2.1%	1.1%
Social Insurance & Retirement	2.8%	4.4%	5.8%	6.6%	6.6%	6.0%
Excise Tax	2.2%	1.6%	0.9%	0.6%	0.7%	0.5%
Estate and Gift Tax	0.3%	0.4%	0.2%	0.2%	0.3%	0.1%
Customs, Duties, & Fees	0.2%	0.2%	0.3%	0.3%	0.2%	0.2%
Federal Reserve Deposits	0.2%	0.3%	0.4%	0.4%	0.3%	0.5%
Allowances	0.0%	0.0%	0.0%	0.0%	0.0%	-0.1%
All Other	0.0%	0.0%	0.0%	0.1%	0.1%	0.1%
Total Receipts	17.8%	19.0%	19.0%	18.0%	20.6%	14.8%
Outlays						
National Defense	9.3%	8.1%	4.9%	5.2%	3.0%	4.9%
International Affairs	0.6%	0.4%	0.5%	0.2%	0.2%	0.3%
General Science, Space & Technology	0.1%	0.4%	0.2%	0.3%	0.2%	0.2%
Energy	0.1%	0.1%	0.4%	0.1%	0.0%	0.1%
Natural Resources and Environment	0.3%	0.3%	0.5%	0.3%	0.3%	0.3%
Agriculture	0.5%	0.5%	0.3%	0.2%	0.4%	0.2%
Commerce and Housing Credit	0.3%	0.2%	0.3%	1.2%	0.0%	-0.2%
Transportation	0.8%	0.7%	0.8%	0.5%	0.5%	0.7%
Community and Regional Development	0.0%	0.2%	0.4%	0.1%	0.1%	0.2%
Education, Training, Employment, & SS	0.2%	0.9%	1.2%	0.6%	0.5%	1.0%
Health	0.2%	0.6%	0.9%	1.0%	1.6%	2.5%
Medicare	0.0%	0.6%	1.2%	1.7%	2.0%	3.1%
Income Security	1.4%	1.5%	3.2%	2.6%	2.6%	4.7%
Social Security	2.2%	3.0%	4.4%	4.3%	4.2%	4.9%
Veterans Benefits and Services	1.0%	0.9%	0.8%	0.5%	0.5%	0.9%
Administration of Justice	0.1%	0.1%	0.2%	0.2%	0.3%	0.4%
General Government	0.2%	0.2%	0.5%	0.2%	0.1%	0.2%
Net Interest	1.3%	1.4%	1.9%	3.2%	2.3%	1.3%
Allowances	0.0%	0.0%	0.0%	0.0%	0.0%	0.1%
Undistributed Offset Receipts	-0.9%	-0.9%	-0.7%	-0.6%	-0.4%	-0.5%
Total Outlays	17.8%	19.3%	21.7%	21.9%	18.2%	25.4%
Surplus or (Deficit)	0.0%	-0.3%	-2.7%	-3.9%	2.4%	-10.6%

Source: *Historical Tables, Budget of U.S. Government, Fiscal Year 2011*
Office of Management & Budget. Washington

The National Budget - Historical Percent GDP
Figure 9-12

The first table, in Figure 9-11, shows the budget table in dollars, and the table in Figure 9-12 shows each category as a percentage of the GDP. In general Americans have contributed about eighteen to twenty percent of GDP to government receipts while spending has been about two or three percent more than what was received; thus the debt has grown as a result of deficit spending year after year.

The years 2000 and 2010 are distinctly different from the preceding ten-year intervals. In these years the national GDP really slowed in growth; it grew about seventy percent from 1990 to 2000, and less than fifty percent from 2000 to the estimate for 2010. In the preceding thirty years the national productivity about doubled during each ten-year period. In 2000 a large percentage of GDP was contributed to the government while defense spending was much lower and social spending remained about constant. This resulted in an unusual period of surplus. The growth of national productivity has slowed considerably by 2010 as a result of economic weakness and unemployment. As a result Figure 9-12 shows the contribution to the federal treasury from individual income taxes paid by working Americans has dropped in 2010 (6.4%) to levels even lower than 1960 (7.8%) as a percentage of GDP.

Looking further at receipts, it's interesting to observe in Figure 9-12 for 2010, that Social Insurance and Retirement receipts, primarily Social Security and Medicare taxes, are about an equal percentage of GDP as individual income taxes. It's the only time in the chart of the last fifty years that Social Insurance and Retirement receipts have been a nearly equal portion of GDP as individual income tax payments.

Slowing GDP causing reduced receipts is a terrible combination, but government hasn't slowed in its spending. Projected total outlays for 2010 are about a fourth (25.4%) of national GDP, which is larger than any percentage in the chart. Social Security (4.9%) and Medicare (3.1%) costs each grew about one percent from levels in 2000, but the cost of wars and income security grew substantially more. Defense spending, at $719 billion is about double the spending before the terrorist attacks in New York and Washington. Income security spending, such as welfare and food stamps, consumes over two percent more in 2010 than it did in 2000 by increasing from 2.6% to 4.7%. As a result, the deficit for the year 2010 is expected to be extraordinary in comparison with preceding years, jumping to the 10.6% double digit.

As shown in Figures 9-11 and 9-12 the primary source of government receipts for the last forty years has come from individuals in the form of the individual income tax, Social Security, and Medicare tax. In 1960, before Medicare was passed, most government income was drawn from individual ($41 billion) and corporate income tax ($21 billion) revenues for a combined total of about $62 billion.

By 1970 though, the combination of larger Medicare and Social Security payments had propelled Social Insurance and Retirement taxes ($44 billion) into a major revenue source, until it is was about half as much as the individual income tax category, and more than the corporate tax contribution.

But income taxes have not always been the source of receipts for the government. From the beginning of the Republic until the Civil War started, the federal government mainly relied on customs and duties to supply about ninety percent of its receipts with supplements from sales of public land. Indeed, prior to passage of the Sixteenth Amendment to the Constitution in 1913, income taxes did not exist or were of little consequence, but by 1930 the federal government relied on income taxes to supply about sixty percent of its receipts; the idea of progressive income taxes had become a colossal way to dip into the pockets of Americans. In the thirties the federal receipts were about five percent of the GDP, but it grew to more than twenty percent during World War Two. Federal receipts have hovered around eighteen percent for most of the last fifty years.

The failure of the federal government to manage the financial budget of the country while keeping within the means provided is one of the key elements in the argument accusing national leaders of malfeasance in office. The deficit has grown steadily for the last one hundred years or so, until the national debt threatens the country's ability to grow, prosper, and defend itself. America's financial security is threatened by the immense debt that has been permitted to accumulate by the stewards of the treasury. Some economists, and creators of sly schemes to enhance growth of the national economy by using the leverage of debt, believe a controlled amount of debt can be a good thing. But most early founders disagreed and advised of the traps of debt. Benjamin Franklin, the astute businessman and wise student of human nature, believed that public credit should be handled like private credit. He thought paper currency must be adequately funded, and debt must be paid off by taxes in a prudent and timely manner. Thomas Jefferson thought no generation had the moral right to accumulate greater debts than could be paid off during their own lifetime. Undeniably, the current debt faced by today's generation has been accumulated by the excesses of several preceding generations. Moreover, most of the early founders thought the only ones who profit from debt are bankers, investors, and politicians who are remembered for their generosity in spending borrowed money. How prophetic was this wise man's observation. Probably no single cause for the huge debt is greater than the continued spending by elected representatives to secure their personal careers, and the greed of private Americans with their hands out to the government.

The main contributors to deficit spending have been wars and human resources. The country has had to borrow money to conduct every war from the Revolutionary War until today. The country was swamped with debt after the Civil War. Later, World Wars One and Two left the U.S. with some of its largest debts. Within the last fifty years it has engaged in the Viet Nam War, the operation to save Kuwait, and the attacks on Afghanistan and Iraq among others. Referring again to Figure 9-11 it can be seen that the growth in spending for National Defense grew enormously during each of the war periods. Unfortunately, the U.S. has been involved in a conflict for part of nearly every decade shown in the chart. As a result of the Viet Nam engagement National Defense spending was seventy percent more in 1970 than 1960 as shown in Figure 9-11, and by 1980 it increased another sixty percent. This same pattern has continued during each war, and the current deployment of Armed Forces on two fronts has set new records for defense spending. American leaders continue to involve the country in these wars without making provisions for supporting them; instead, they have chosen to borrow the money. If the country is to carry on military actions, then it must raise adequate revenue to support them. The unquestionable consequence of raising taxes to pay for these wars is probable trouble for the national economy. An alternative would be to cut spending elsewhere without raising taxes, but this would leave many Americans without the safety net they have come to depend upon. But certainly the most favorable alternative is to stay out of wars altogether. The engagements in the Middle East have been long and expensive. U.S. leaders led America into a trap when they started ambitious and ill-advised projects the country couldn't afford.

The greatest expenditures from the national treasury can be categorized as spending on human resources. When the creators of the Constitution identified the purposes for government they listed defense, communications, fair commerce standards, administration of federal land, and a system of federal courts. Many American citizens, such as Horatio Bunce, understood this and fiercely protected their individual freedoms by keeping government out of their lives. (See *Not Yours To Give* in Chapter 7.) There were no provisions for the human resources that have grown to be expected in the last one hundred years. Human resource spending has grown with the three great expansions of government in 1913, 1936, and 1965-70. As previously described, these were the periods that marked the beginning of the individual income tax, the Social Security program, and the Medicare and Medicaid programs. The Social Security plan matured around 1982, and now a huge demand from the population bulge known as the baby boomers are expected to further strain the ability of the government to meet its promises to retirees. But there has been more expansion caused by the Great Society plan that includes Medicaid, food stamps, Supplemental Security Income, Earned Income Credit, Child Tax Credits, and other programs. In the end, a large part of the national wealth is spent on defense, human resources, and government administration, until there is little left for infrastructure and purposes that were originally defined in the Constitution. America has become a nation on the dole and perpetually at war.

The OMB has provided another way to look at expenditures that further demonstrates the spending on human resources. The chart is called Outlays by Super-function Categories; the spending for 2009 and 2010 are shown in Figure 9-13 for the super-function categories. The six super-function categories include three main types of spending: National Defense, Human Resources, and Physical Resources. The super-function categories reveal the evolution of government from providing the basics envisioned by the creators of the Constitution to a major role in providing human resources programs. Although defense spending, as shown in Figure 9-13, is a large element of government spending that was estimated to consume over nineteen percent of all funds to be outlaid in 2010, the spending on human resources is by far the largest category, scheduled to require over sixty-seven percent of total budget spending; that's about seventeen percent of the country's GDP productivity for the year. Physical resources, interest, and other government functions have each been allocated about five percent of total spending.

The human resources category includes Social Security and Medicare, of course. These programs were established in the thirties and sixties as programs where citizens support these programs by paying into these funds during their working lives. Both programs were originally designed as supplemental help for retired citizens; Social Security for income assistance and Medicare to help elderly citizens obtain health care when they could not qualify under the rules of private insurance companies. These two programs require the largest outlays of any human resources program, and they take up over thirty percent of total outlays for 2010 (12.3% Medicare and 19.4% Social Security).

The Social Security and Medicare programs could be further classified as paid-in programs; that is, the citizens that receive these benefits have paid in taxes throughout their working lives with the promise that they would be eligible for some return when they retired. Many Americans view these programs like an annuity or pension plan where they receive a return on what they have paid in. Of course, this is not strictly true, because the surplus money has long been swept away by the government for other spending.

There are other programs that could be considered paid-in plans, and these definitely were described to their participants as retirement plans. These include obligations to the Federal Employee Retirement and the Veterans Benefits and Services plans. Someone, either the employee or the employer has paid into these plans through the working years of the employee and they are offered as benefits.

The National Budget - Outlays by Super-function

| | Dollar amounts (shown in billions) | | | | | |
| | 2009 | | | 2010 Estimated Budget | | |
	Dollars	% Total	% GDP	Dollars	% Total	% GDP
Gross Domestic Product	14,237			14,624		
Receipts						
Individual Income Tax	915	43.5%	6.4%	936	43.2%	6.4%
Corporate Tax	138	6.6%	1.0%	157	7.2%	1.1%
Social Insurance & Retirement	891	42.3%	6.3%	876	40.4%	6.0%
Excise Tax	62	3.0%	0.4%	73	3.4%	0.5%
Estate and Gift Tax	23	1.1%	0.2%	17	0.8%	0.1%
Customs, Duties, & Fees	22	1.1%	0.2%	24	1.1%	0.2%
Federal Reserve Deposits	34	1.6%	0.2%	77	3.6%	0.5%
Allowances	-	0.0%	0.0%	(12)	-0.6%	-0.1%
All Other	18	0.8%	0.1%	18	0.8%	0.1%
Total Receipts	2,105		14.8%	2,165		14.8%
Outlays						
National Defense	661	18.8%	4.6%	719	19.3%	4.9%
Human Resources						
Education, training, employment, social services	80	2.3%	0.6%	143	3.8%	1.0%
Health	334	9.5%	2.3%	372	10.0%	2.5%
Medicare	430	12.2%	3.0%	457	12.3%	3.1%
Income security	533	15.2%	3.7%	686	18.4%	4.7%
Social Security	683	19.4%	4.8%	721	19.4%	4.9%
Veterans benefits and services	95	2.7%	0.7%	125	3.4%	0.9%
Total Human Resources	2,156	61.3%	15.1%	2,504	67.3%	17.1%
Physical resources						
Energy	5	0.1%	0.03%	19	0.5%	0.1%
Natural resources and environment	36	1.0%	0.2%	47	1.3%	0.3%
Commerce and housing credit	292	8.3%	2.0%	(25)	-0.7%	-0.2%
Transportation	84	2.4%	0.6%	106	2.9%	0.7%
Community and regional development	28	0.8%	0.2%	28	0.8%	0.2%
Total Physical resources	444	12.6%	3.1%	176	4.7%	1.2%
Net Interest	187	5.3%	1.3%	188	5.0%	1.3%
Other Functions						
International affairs	38	1.1%	0.3%	51	1.4%	0.3%
General science, space and technology	29	0.8%	0.2%	33	0.9%	0.2%
Agriculture	22	0.6%	0.2%	27	0.7%	0.2%
Administration of justice	52	1.5%	0.4%	55	1.5%	0.4%
General government	22	0.6%	0.2%	29	0.8%	0.2%
Allowances	-	0.0%	0.0%	19	0.5%	0.1%
Total Other Functions	163	4.6%	1.1%	214	5.7%	1.5%
Undistributed Offset Receipts	(93)	-2.6%	-0.7%	(80)	-2.1%	-0.5%
Total Outlays	3,518		24.7%	3,721		25.4%
Surplus or (Deficit)	(1,413)		-9.9%	(1,556)		-10.6%

Source: *Historical Tables, Budget of U.S. Government, Fiscal Year 2011*
Office of Management & Budget. Washington

The National Budget - Outlays by Super-function
Figure 9-13

But there are many other human resources programs where individuals receive benefits that neither they nor an employer have made contributions to the program. These are generally referred to as the welfare programs that include Medicaid, housing assistance, food stamps, and Supplemental Security Income.

Types of Human Resource Spending						
	Dollar amounts (shown in billions)					
	2009			2010 Estimated Budget		
	Dollars	% Total	% GDP	Dollars	% Total	% GDP
Gross Domestic Product	14,237			14,624		
Receipts						
Individual Income Tax	915	43.5%	6.4%	936	43.2%	6.4%
Corporate Tax	138	6.6%	1.0%	157	7.2%	1.1%
Social Insurance & Retirement	891	42.3%	6.3%	876	40.4%	6.0%
Excise Tax	62	3.0%	0.4%	73	3.4%	0.5%
Estate and Gift Tax	23	1.1%	0.2%	17	0.8%	0.1%
Customs, Duties, & Fees	22	1.1%	0.2%	24	1.1%	0.2%
Federal Reserve Deposits	34	1.6%	0.2%	77	3.6%	0.5%
Allowances	-	0.0%	0.0%	(12)	-0.6%	-0.1%
All Other	18	0.8%	0.1%	18	0.8%	0.1%
Total Receipts	2,105		14.8%	2,165		14.8%
Human Resource Outlays						
Paid-in Human Resource Outlays						
Social Security	683	19.4%	4.8%	721	19.4%	4.9%
Medicare	430	12.2%	3.0%	457	12.3%	3.1%
Federal employee retirement	118	3.4%	0.8%	121	3.2%	0.8%
Veterans benefits and services	95	2.7%	0.7%	125	3.4%	0.9%
Unemployment compensation	123	3.5%	0.9%	194	5.2%	1.3%
Total Paid-in Human Resource Outlays	1,449	41.2%	10.2%	1,618	43.5%	11.1%
Not Paid-in Human Resource Outlays						
Education, training, employment, social services	80	2.3%	0.6%	143	3.8%	1.0%
Health care services (Medicaid)	300	8.5%	2.1%	335	9.0%	2.3%
Health research and training	31	0.9%	0.2%	33	0.9%	0.2%
Consumer & occupational health & safety	4	0.1%	0.0%	4	0.1%	0.0%
Gen retirement and disability	8	0.2%	0.1%	8	0.2%	0.1%
Housing assistance	51	1.4%	0.4%	77	2.1%	0.5%
Food and nutrition assistance (Food Stamps)	79	2.2%	0.6%	99	2.7%	0.7%
Other income security	154	4.4%	1.1%	187	5.0%	1.3%
Total Not Paid-in Human Resource Outlays	707	20.1%	5.0%	886	23.8%	6.1%
Total Human Resources Outlays	2,156	61.3%	15.1%	2,504	67.3%	17.1%

Types of Human Resource Spending
Figure 9-14

Figure 9-14 shows a comparison of the split in human resources according to paid-in and not paid-in programs. This chart indicates that spending on programs for beneficiaries that have not paid into the system is over half as much in 2010 ($886 billion) as spending on participants that have contributed funds in advance of receiving benefits ($1,618 billion). The $886 billion and $1,618 billion are 23.8% and 43.5% of total government spending for 2010.

The National Budget - Social Income and Health

	Dollar amounts (shown in billions)					
	1960	1970	1980	1990	2000	2010E
	Dollars	Dollars	Dollars	Dollars	Dollars	Dollars
Gross Domestic Product	519	1,013	2,724	5,735	9,821	14,624
Insurance and Retirement Receipts						
Social Insurance & Retirement	15	44	158	380	653	876
Outlays for Social Security and Medicare						
Medicare (paid-in benefit)	-	6	32	98	197	457
Social Security (paid-in benefit)	12	30	119	249	409	721
Total Outlays for SS and MC	12	36	151	347	607	1,179
SS & MC Surplus or (Deficit)	3	8	7	33	46	(303)
Paid-in & Not Paid-in Benefits						
Outlays for Paid-in Benefits						
Medicare (paid-in benefit)	-	6	32	98	197	457
Social Security (paid-in benefit)	12	30	119	249	409	721
Total Outlays for Paid-in Benefits	12	36	151	347	607	1,179
Outlays for Not Paid-in Benefits						
Health (not paid-in benefit)	0.8	6	23	58	155	372
Income Security (not paid-in benefit)	7	16	87	149	254	686
Total Outlays for Not Paid-in Benefits	8	22	110	206	408	1,058
Total Paid-in & Not Paid-in Outlays	20	58	260	553	1,015	2,237
Surplus or (Deficit); All Social Outlays	(5)	(14)	(103)	(173)	(362)	(1,361)

The National Budget - Social Income and Health
Figure 9-15

Figure 9-15 takes a slightly different look at comparing paid-in and not paid-in plans. It shows the historical amounts for Social Security and Medicare paid into these funds by working taxpayers since 1960 (Insurance and Retirement Receipts). Naturally the amounts are quite low in 1960 because there was no Medicare program until 1965. The receipts are compared to the outlays for Social Security and Medicare and indicate that these old-age plans ran a surplus for most of the last fifty years; only in the estimates for 2010 do they start to show withdrawals greater than receipts; it's a substantial amount estimated to exceed $300 billion.

The second section of the chart compares the last fifty years of spending for paid-in Medicare and Social Security benefits with not paid-in health and income security benefits. The total for both paid-in and not paid-in programs is compared to Insurance and Retirement Receipts. When considered together, the outlays for both paid-in and not paid-in benefits have exceeded the Receipts from taxpayers in every year shown. Deficits range from $5 billion to more than $1.3 trillion.

The government outlays for free health and supplemental income assistance historically have been less than the amount contributed by taxpayers to the trust fund, but the amounts have steadily increased. By 2010, according to Figure 9-15, spending on not paid-in welfare programs for Health ($372 billion) and Income Security ($686 billion) will total over $1 trillion, which is expected to exceed tax receipts for Social Security and Medicare ($876 billion) for the first time.

Although the purpose of Social Security and Medicare payments may not have been intended to pay for all health and income spending, it indicates the strain that these extra programs have imposed on the budget. As the plan for the Great Society began to mature and more Americans decided this was the lifestyle for them, the deficits continued mount up. By 2010 it is expected that outlays for not-paid-in health and income benefits will be about ninety percent of paid-in Social Security and Medicare benefits. This has rocketed from the ratios of the last fifty years where not-paid-in benefits were typically about sixty to seventy percent of paid-in benefits. Despite the discussions of problems with the Social Security and Medicare trust funds, it appears a watchful eye should be kept on not paid-in welfare payouts as well.

It is, without much doubt, obvious that the federal government must borrow money to pay for the immense cost of the welfare programs, as certainly as it must borrow to pay for defense and other plans. As more is borrowed each year to pay benefits and support, the interest on the total accumulated debt continues to grow. It's estimated to consume $188 billion of receipts in 2010 (Figure 9-13). This leaves little of the nation's total receipts to be spent on productive programs for physical resources and running the government as shown in Figure 9-13; the $176 billion allocated is less than net interest paid. The spending on continuing to develop the country's physical resources and to promote efficiency in its systems and prosperity for the future has been slowly marginalized. The United States has evolved from a country that pays its way to a country that borrows to pay unproductive citizens.

The question for America is how should its resources be allocated and should it borrow money to pay for programs other than the extraordinary expenses for war engagements. The answer is to be found in the genius of James Madison and his confidence in the truthful justice of public opinion. Americans can weigh the consequences of deficit spending against the benefits for disadvantaged and unproductive citizens, defense spending, and the cost of government. There are only three answers for the astute business manager of a nonprofit business: increase revenue (taxes) to balance outlays with receipts; modify outlay programs to conform within the limits of receipts; or, some combination of each. For the last one hundred years or so the thrust of public opinion in the booming and prosperous years of American history has been to go along with plans of social planners to increase the size of government and its give-away programs. During this period it was probably the correct thing to do for the members of society that lived during these times. But they have left the current generation with programs that may no longer fit. It may be time to reevaluate and develop plans that fit the needs of the living generation, but do not place demands upon the generations of the future; it is for succeeding generations to freely decide their priorities. Public opinion today is without doubt different from that of one hundred or two hundred years ago, and the society of today is vastly different from the society of two generations ago that loaded it with unending commitments for human resource programs. This is the genius of freedom and self-government that allows the people themselves to decide and change according to the ideas of their generation.

MANAGING NATIONAL PRESSURES

As surely as the manager of any business must adjust to pressures, so must the elected legislators and the executive carefully adjust receipts and outlays. Just like a private business manager must adjust the size of the operation within the limits of current income in order to avoid losses, so must the stewards of the national treasury make similar adjustments. The pressures on the national plan are not uncommon with those of business, and similar corrective actions can be utilized. When a business is faced with reduced business or income, a responsible business manager will immediately direct evaluation of all costs, expenditures, and existing programs. This is what the Congress and President should do, instead of increasing costs during times of hardship.

The most difficult question the Congress and President face is whether the size of government is too large for the economy and the receipts it collects from the American taxpayers. In view of the long history of deficits that has been established, it appears that the size of government is too large to be supported by the current level of taxation. Additionally, it does not appear that Americans want to pay higher taxes in order to support high payments for human resources and defense, so something has to give. Just like the example business manager in Figure 9-1 must face adjustments when receipts are reduced, so good stewards of the federal treasury should make adjustments. The Congress should examine the size of government; meaning, the number of people and their benefit plans. Like a good business, the Congress should examine all existing programs and their effectiveness, and cost reduction programs should be implemented to pare costs and develop savings.

First the size of government should be questioned. Are there too many employees and can the number be reduced? The answer for any business, naturally, is that there can be layoffs and the operation should be reduced and streamlined. All businesses do this from time to time, at great benefit, and there is no reason that this should not be applied to all elements of the federal government. After building a structured plan to systematically reduce the federal workforce, the extraordinary expense of pay and benefits should be examined. Just like the private manager utilizes surveys to determine the range and averages for pay and benefits to determine a competitive rate for company employees, so should the federal government. Wage creep can lead to high costs in a company, and similarly, it should be controlled for federal employees. Probably few American citizens would approve of federal employees earning more than the averages for similar jobs, and many might expect that federal workers should earn below the average.

Certainly, the health care and pension plans for federal employees are extraordinary and should be adjusted to the average levels among the private sector. This means the amount they pay into the program, the amount the government pays into the program, the eligible retirement age, and the amount of the retirement benefit. For most of the twentieth century a lot of company employees expected to work for their company for most of their life and receive a defined benefit pension plan after retirement. Some employees paid into the retirement plan and others were fortunate enough to work for a company that paid the entire cost of the plan. Other individuals worked for many different companies during their working life and lost eligibility in retirement plans if not vested. Still others worked for small businesses that offered no retirement plan. It was the idea of Social Security to assist folks with little savings and little retirement income. Federal employees, on the other hand, have enjoyed generous retirement plans provided by the American people.

In the last twenty-five years, or so, of the twentieth century the trend among private companies offering defined benefit plans began to change. Workers became mobile and weren't staying with companies for life, and the costs of the defined plans became a burden on the competitiveness of private companies, especially when faced with increasing global competition where low wages and no retirement plan were normal. It was about this time that the Individual Retirement Arrangement, IRA, and the Section 401(k) programs were worked into company retirement plans. Strong private competitors decided that their employees should be personally responsible for their retirement situations. Many were told to plan on a retirement income to be supported from three sources: Social Security benefits, a modest company retirement plan, and the remainder from their personal savings. Each person should plan for a certain portion of their working income to be replaced by one or all of these three methods that are available to them.

Social Security was designed to replace a higher proportion of earnings for lower-paid workers than for higher-paid. Workers who have earned the least during their working lives may receive a benefit as much as ninety-four percent of annual earnings, and so they may be able to subsist solely on Social Security. High-paid workers who have paid the maximum tax rate into the Social Security fund will receive a much smaller percentage of the maximum taxable wage base, usually about twenty-six percent of their wage base. These workers will need personal savings to make up the difference during retirement, and a defined benefit annuity pension plan can help make up this amount. Defined benefit plans in the private sector are often designed to replace twenty percent or more of the worker's average pay. Practical companies, and companies in the most competitive markets, usually offer minimal retirement income supplements of twenty percent or less of their employees' base pay. Companies that enjoy high margin businesses may provide retirement plans to replace fifty percent of base pay or more, but generous retirement programs are often modified when strong competition is added to the market place, forcing high margins to more modest amounts.

In order to encourage personal savings, private companies have offered varying degrees of matching contributions. This move to personal responsibility for retirement has been a huge savings for companies, and today many companies follow this basic provision. Some companies don't offer a defined benefit plan at all, and others don't offer a 401(k). In these cases, the employee retiring from a company with no retirement plan must rely on Social Security and personal savings when they stop working.

And so this is the basic situation for all but the most profitable and generous companies in private business today. The federal government, however, has not followed suit. The initial pension system for federal employees was established in 1920 and has been modified several times through the years. Congress added its members to the plan in 1942 but it was repealed in response to adverse public opinion; nevertheless, with a few changes Congressional members were finally added to the program in 1946.

Four different retirement arrangements have been described that have been in effect for several years, and the most recent plan is the Federal Employee Retirement System. Government workers on this system accumulate retirement pay at a rate of about 1.7 percent for each of the first twenty years worked, and one percent for each year worked beyond twenty years; this means they will receive thirty-four percent of their highest average salary for three consecutive years worked when they complete twenty years of service, and about forty-four percent of their average salary for completing thirty years of service. For a member of Congress who averages $175,000 per year, the pension for thirty years of service would be $77,000 each year. In order to qualify for the program employees contribute eight-tenths of one percent of their pay and the government, or American people, pay eleven percent. This is an extraordinary benefit when compared to private plans or 401(k) plans. Initially, a lot of companies matched the employee's contribution to a 401(k) up to six percent, but with the turn down in the economy, many have cut their match to half the employee's, up to six percent, and quite a few more have suspended it altogether. This is a result of reduced revenues, but the government hasn't reduced the plan for federal employees at all despite reduced government revenues; they're in their own little world. The congressional plan is worse; members of Congress contribute 1.3 percent of pay and receive government contributions to their retirement plans at a rate of about sixteen percent of their salary.

The most fantastic feature of the federal retirement plan is the cost-of-living adjustment. If the Consumer Price Index increases, the pension pay out to retired federal workers increases also, although not necessarily at a matching rate. Very few defined benefit pension plans in the U.S. today enjoy this feature, and it certainly could not be considered average. Federal employees can retire with full benefits as early as age sixty-two with only five years service.

Health care coverage is similarly generous for federal workers and the Congress when compared to average plans offered in private business. Some of the basics of the Congressional health care plan include no waiting period and no precondition requirements. Up to seventy-five percent of the insurance premium is paid by the government. Congressional members have a choice of about ten plans in a national network of doctors and hospitals; their doctor co-pay is $20, generic prescriptions are $10, they receive free immunizations, and there is no coverage limit on the policy. It rivals the best private plans.

In addition to keeping the size of government within the limits of spending established by the people, and assuring that wages and benefits do not become extraordinary, Congress and all government agencies should continually evaluate existing programs and plans. A principle of good business management is to establish measures of effectiveness for every program and periodically evaluate it. Here is a lesson for legislators who focus solely on new programs and new spending, but fail to provide follow-up on their creations. As a result, the nation trudges on with many ineffective and overlapping programs. It is common in private business to evaluate duplicated inventory that accomplishes the same function, and then consolidate it to reduce the costs. This same method should equally apply to judicious management of the nation's business and its overlapping programs.

Ineffective programs should be discontinued. An effective program in private business must accomplish the objective, remain within its budget, and stay within time limits. Probably one of the major sources of ineffective or overlapping legislation occurs with congressionally directed spending, or earmarks. This legislation is often poorly conceived, and added as an amendment to other legislation that may have nothing to do with the subject of the earmark. No well-managed company would embrace hasty programs that are not evaluated within the overall company objectives. There are many arguments for continuing the use of earmark legislation, but the reality is that they likely cause more duplications and more harm than direct, well-thought-out legislation that suits the needs for the nation as a whole.

A powerful cost reduction program probably contributes more to the continued effectiveness and competitiveness of a private company. The most successful companies never forget they are always gaining or losing ground on the competition in the market place, and they rely on cost reductions to gain new advantages and maintain a lean cost structure for both new and mature products and services. Without this constant vigilance on cost, and an unceasing effort to reduce it, a company may soon find itself with a fat cost structure, loss of its share of the market, and years behind its competitors.

The federal government should follow this example in adjusting to national pressures. Like private businesses, the United States is constantly gaining or losing ground in its competition with other countries, too. Cost reduction programs may include projects to reorganize and streamline the government. The size and usefulness of each agency should be periodically evaluated and modified as needed to keep it effective. Periodic audits should challenge the number of people needed to sustain the objective for the agency, and continual surveys of wages and benefits should be used to avoid ballooning salaries and benefits. Congress should compare the administration of all programs at regular intervals to verify that they remain effective within the scope of their objectives and there are no overlapping programs that inefficiently duplicate their provisions.

All branches of government should be involved with proactive cost reduction programs aimed at reducing the prevailing cost of administration. Cost reduction plans should establish clear and measurable objectives with verification by accounting audits that the cost reductions have been realized. For example, if an element of the government establishes a cost reduction program, its effectiveness should be audited, and a reduction of spending must actually occur and be verified.

Many governmental managers want to turn to another plan, raise taxes.

Naturally, this is an option, but it could easily become an anchor on the American people and economy. An analogy for this action by private businesses would be to raise prices to offset reduced sales. It seems to be a simple and painless solution, but it can be a debilitating trap. In reality the company may be losing market share or the market is shrinking. In either case, if the company is competing with other companies that have learned to operate within lean limits, the company that raises prices to offset lost sales and to compensate for its heavy cost structure, may soon find itself continuously resorting to price increases. Eventually the problem snowballs, and in the long run the company may find itself unable to sustain its operation. This may be a large part of the problems faced by the American automobile industry. Costs grew, labor wages and benefits grew well above the prevailing averages for similar work, and after decades of expense creep, American manufacturers found themselves in a death struggle with the leaner and more reasonable cost structures of foreign car makers. The companies resisted change, labor resisted change, and in the end most of them lost. Their competitors offered lower-priced cars of equal value. American carmakers lost market share, and when they tried counteracting higher costs with higher prices, they failed. But this scenario is not limited to the automobile industry. The case histories of U.S. businesses are filled with similar situations. Many companies may have the good fortune to enjoy extraordinary profits as a result of a new and better product, but there will always be a competitor working to offer an equal product at a lower price. All companies must realize that they are continually gaining or losing, and must never relent in efforts to contain costs and keep their size within the limits of their business.

This same scenario clearly applies to governments and nations. The individual states of the U.S. have learned the importance of competing with one another to induce businesses to establish operations with them. So should the United States government and its leaders recognize the importance of competing with other countries for business and jobs. Raising taxes, like raising prices, only leads to the same inflated cost structure that drains more industry than can be sustained. In the long run businesses move away and national revenues are again threatened. It's an insidious and miserable cycle that can leave America far behind its competitors.

The correct action is to establish the size of the tax burden that the country can support and remain competitive, and then government tax receipts should be held within this limit. When the size of government is too large, then it should be trimmed, and cost reduction programs should be implemented with an objective to continually lower the tax burden, rather than opting to increase it. By treating the government as a business and keeping costs lean and competitive, then business in America will grow and prosper, and the American worker will grow and prosper, too. Which is better: increase taxes to support more idle American workers, or keep the tax burden modest and U.S. companies competitive so more Americans will be contently working toward independence and personal goals? The example of the last one hundred years demonstrates the truth of prospering business. All Americans, including the nonworking welfare recipients, enjoy a standard of living beyond any imagined even sixty years ago.

GOVERNMENT MAKING JOBS

The news is filled with political speeches that proclaim government actions are needed to make jobs. If the economic principle is accepted that states the three forms of real wealth are agriculture, mining, and manufacturing, then it's difficult to understand how government makes real jobs. In fact, government only consumes the wealth of the country. If the country as a whole were considered a business with the GDP as its total income, then the government is nothing more than a cost of doing business; it doesn't add income to the GDP. As the budget in Figure 9-9 shows, the government consumes a percentage of the nation's productivity. When the government claims to add jobs it usually means taking a bigger portion of national productivity to contribute a salary for a created, but unneeded, job; it's disguised welfare. To make matters worse, in today's environment, the nation borrows the money in order to sustain these jobs.

The government uses other tactics to create jobs besides hiring to swell its own ranks. There are tax credits, subsidies, and special deductions for businesses that wish to participate. Take tax credits for instance, using a program that was enacted in 2010, The Hiring Incentives to Restore Employment (HIRE) Act, also known as the jobs bill, offers an array of payroll tax breaks and incentives for businesses to hire unemployed workers. Like most government programs, it is filled with rules and exceptions for businesses to receive reduced taxes for hiring qualified people, meaning people out of work as defined by the regulations.

The tax break presumably helps the competitive position of participating companies, but it is an artificial cost reduction that is not likely to be sustained. In addition, the payment for the program only leads to higher government administrative costs and more money borrowed by a government that's underwater and unable to afford it. And so the circle goes; more borrowing, more expenses, and eventually higher taxes to pay for it, which in the end will likely lead to more layoffs.

But compare the effects on the example company depicted in Figure 9-1. If the company is properly sized to fulfill the requirements of its gross revenue, then additional people will only serve to inflate its costs. An analogy might be a shopper who spends $1,000 on an unneeded item because it was on sale for twenty percent off so they saved $250. In reality the shopper wasted $1,000. Similarly, a company that hires unneeded workers is getting a deal on the wages, but it is really adding costs to its structure, although at a lower rate. Naturally there are instances where a company may be on the fence when considering more workers, so the incentive might be enough to cause it to make the plunge; however, if the sales revenue are not enough to sustain the added work force, the company will be forced to reduce its work force in the long run, or suffer losses.

Many of government's actions to create jobs are directed toward the government sector itself. Although some government jobs may contribute to maintaining infrastructure, such as road repair, in reality the move is simply inflating the government cost structure, or budget, that has been established for this purpose. Instead of streamlining the government, it is adding bulk to the operation. As a matter of fact, many government jobs added in this manner will never be reduced, and the government just continues to grow and grow and consume the nation's wealth.

The reality is that government can never create jobs that will contribute to the nation's productivity and real wealth. The words of Adam Smith, the father of economic theory, were used in the explanation of the folly of governmental attempts to regulate commerce. More of his remarks are equally applicable to the idea of government-created jobs. In general terms, he explained it when he wrote that the number of workers that can be kept in employment must be in proportion to the employer's resources, such as capital and income. This means that for a society, employment can never realistically exceed society's production. No regulation or government manipulation of commerce can increase the job demand beyond what the capital and production of society can maintain.

In short, jobs are created or lost as a result of supply and demand in the marketplace, which is related to the real wealth created by the country. Government can't create this, and only does harm when it tries.

It should never be forgotten that government employment does not add productive jobs; they are a cost to the country. Remembering that the production of real wealth for the country comes from agriculture, mining, and manufacturing, then the results of these production efforts are used to pay government employees for their services. Consider the example of a manufacturing company. A maintenance worker may be needed to keep the place operating, but the maintenance worker does not actually produce the product; this individual is a cost of the operation. The same is true of adding government jobs. These folks don't produce a thing for the country, but a certain number of them are needed and should be recognized as a cost of running the country. Adding more bureaucrats, teachers, police officers, or other public service workers does not add jobs – it adds COST for taxpayers. Just like a private company must keep these support costs reasonable and in check, so should the federal government, instead of selling them to

Americans as jobs that have been created.

Real jobs are the result of providing a product or service at a strong value that leads to more sales and more revenue that require more individuals to keep up with demand. Companies won't hire more people just because government offers to pay part of new salaries. There must be a market demand to justify adding more people and cost to their budget structure. The jobs that have been lost to foreign sources are gone, never to return unless or until the situation is equalized. The only alternative is to develop new industry and new markets that need more people.

True tax cuts can help companies challenge both national and global competitors. No matter how disguised, government subsidies and job creation programs only add cost and size to government operations and continue to cripple the efforts of private citizens to compete on the world market, to grow, and to prosper. American achievement is not the result of government plans and ideals, but it is the result of American freedom to compete and grow despite government programs.

CHAPTER TEN

RESTORING CIVIL AUTHORITY

THE PURPOSE AND FUNCTION of the U.S. government has steadily changed during its history. The first half of its existence was based upon the views and aspirations of the founders that the government operates according to public opinion with the objective to restrain people from injuring one another. James Madison, the champion of government by public opinion, believed in active citizens constantly reconstructing and changing government with the changing times. The founders envisioned the Constitution as a document of active law that established the purpose of government to provide defense for all states, central services for commerce and physical resources, and unity in foreign relations. Generally, that was all that was expected or desired from the function of the federal government.

For the first half of its history, the government more or less was held to the original purpose. The second half of its history has been a steady change from a government ruled by citizens demanding minimal involvement in their lives to a government of charity controlled by a governing class. If this is the will of the people, then the founding fathers probably would have agreed with changing government according to public opinion, but they likely would have wanted it to be done within the provisions of the mutual contract, the Constitution. In other words, if the people want a centralized government to make life's decisions for them, and wants the government to cradle them in times of need, then they should insist that the Constitution be changed to provide for it. Such a change, if ratified by three-fourths of the states, would become the law of the land. One warning though, if such a change is made, the prevailing generation must be certain to retain the right to reverse the role of government. This is for the protection of succeeding generations that may have different views and ideas as dissimilar from today's people as today's society is from the people living two hundred years ago. It would be a dangerous change, because once the people are governed by a ruling class, it will be difficult, if not impossible, to wrest the power from their grasp. Even today it may be almost impossible to restore public authority.

Unfortunately, the evolution of government purpose has not been changed through open proposals for modification of the Constitution. Instead, it is the result of varying interpretations of meaning that has left the country with a tremendous split in the views of the people. It has been modified by the differing ideas of nine justices and renegade presidents, instead of being decided by the people. The will of the people of the current generation is the law, and it is their choice to decide the meaning of the Constitution in their times. Those in favor of social services and intrusion of federal authority claim it is authorized according to various and inconsistent interpretations of Constitutional meaning and authority. Those in favor of minimum government involvement in private lives declare the interpretations of the last one hundred years are largely unconstitutional. Although Thomas Jefferson probably would have disagreed with the spending on social services that has become such a large part of government operations today, he probably would have accepted it if the government openly asked for an enlargement of power, and received it through public support, instead of assuming it through interpretations. He explained the danger of changes through interpreting its wording. It could become a meaningless relic. Predictably, many leaders today assert that the Constitution is flawed and outdated, instead of realizing the adaptability of it.

Today, the United States operates closer to the centralized democracy form of government than the democratic republic principles the Constitution is based upon. Recall that both forms of government propose equality, but centralized government trends toward equal restraint, while the republican government aims for equal liberty of its citizens. The founders understood human nature and knew this trend toward government growth would be inevitable if not controlled.

The last fifty years of U.S. history have exposed problems with centralized government. As the government becomes more involved in the economy, business, and human services, the law of infinity of actions is manifested. The government is too large to comprehend. There are many intellectual studiers who believe they can understand and predict the infinite rhythms and directions of life, but in reality, they are overwhelmed by the infinite actions and interactions of changing society. That is why a pure democracy works best with local self-government where people guide the actions of the world with which they are familiar. In addition to its unmanageable size, government-imposed welfare has left a large sector of citizens in despair. Their place in life has been assigned by the government, not themselves. In a competitive society, the human spirit is not defeated, even if they are unsuccessful in a given endeavor, because they can look elsewhere to find their place in society. But when their opportunities in life are fixed by the government through welfare rules and regulations they are relegated to a life of hopeless dependency.

Now it is time to return to the Constitution through the civil power it provides. The Constitution is not a flawed document, but it is active law left to the country by the founders. It is time to return to the truest form of individual freedom that results from self-government by public opinion. There are many in the community today that do not believe in self-government, especially those caught up in the glorious idea of their own superiority. James Madison viewed it differently. He recognized that informed public opinion may lack the philosophical views of intellectuals, but it could be more effective in providing justice in everyday life. The founders knew there would be errors in public opinion, but not more so than the errors of a governing class, and public opinion errors would be honest yet destined to soon return to a right way. Their faith in this principle of human behavior resulted in the Constitution as their expression of public opinion.

Because of their faith in public opinion, the founders left their successors with the power and an obligation to change the Constitution to conform to the changes of society. Of course they knew society would change. Of course they knew innovations and the spirit of invention would change future ways of life from theirs. That was the whole idea of their Constitution. It was not to bind the people to never change, but to allow the people to change with the times and change their mutual contract with one another, too. The founders believed it was the duty of succeeding generations to improve and perpetuate the Constitution. George Washington explained that the Constitution is binding until changed by the majority when he wrote that our government is based upon the people's right to their Constitution, but at the same time, they are obligated to explicitly comply with the existing Constitution until it is changed by an act of the whole people.

It was the founders' vision that the people must redress the government when it oversteps its authority, and that when a fault is discovered in the Constitution it must not be perpetuated but corrected by amendment. As a result, they left the power of the government in the hands of the people when they established the Fifth Article of the Constitution. Article Five of the Constitution gives state legislatures the power to reverse Congressional or Court decisions. It leaves the power of the people, through two-thirds of the state legislatures, to call a convention for proposing Constitutional Amendments, and to ratify the Amendments when three-fourths of the states accept the provisions. A Constitutional Convention of state legislatures has never been convened in U.S. history, but if the election of representatives to protect and defend the Constitution is unsuccessful, then it may be time for the people to restore their civil authority using this mechanism.

In a free country the people must dare to change its general rules to bind the limits of every power of government. The people must boldly read, think, and speak up to reclaim the power of self-government. It is time to rebalance the powers of the three branches of government, to restore their mutual independence, and to correct the abuses that have occurred. This may require both legislative actions and Constitutional Amendments to reestablish the Constitution as the supreme law of the United States that all citizens can understand and depend upon as their truest form of security.

Restoring civil authority is the challenge for free Americans who want to reclaim their right to govern themselves. Following are viewpoints to stir new and old opinions for recovering total liberty. Condensed outlines of the ideas are illustrated by Figures 10-1 through 10-4. At the risk of becoming monotonous, duplication of parts of preceding discussions has been used to emphasize the reason behind each argument.

The discussion of proposed changes to restore the people's authority have been divided into four categories: preserve freedom, temper political policies, restrict specialists, and address national concerns. The great assault on personal freedom has been both deliberate and incidental. Generations of legislators, presidents, and justices have deliberately circumvented the Constitution by reading new meaning into it and adding presidential powers to make laws. In many cases their ideals were admirable, they wanted social improvements for the country, and at other times their actions were protective or self-serving. In order to enable their plans, the Constitution was legally changed by American society after the turn of the twentieth century to adopt a new system of direct income tax. These actions began America's slow creep into the acceptance of deficit spending. In order to reverse these trends, new amendments and laws are needed to repeal the progressive income tax system, require the government to operate within a balanced budget, to specifically define the enumerated powers of the federal government, and to eliminate the use of executive orders and special advisors for making laws.

In support of the rally to save personal freedom the country needs to revise its political system and policies. The first step of this initiative is to abolish career politicians who have caused the country's fiscal problems and its drift from the Constitution as a result of their personal aims. They should be removed from classification as federal employees, and then term limits imposed on their offices. Additional changes should include steps to eliminate earmarks, change campaign rules, and clamp down on the details of professional lobbyist activity. Revamping the country's political policies should include a review of the Seventeenth Amendment while redefining the enumerated powers established by the First Article. The goal would be to ensure States' rights according to the will of the people.

Various government specialists enabled the continued drift from

Constitutional authority, including the Supreme Court, government unions, and the Federal Reserve. The Supreme Court is often viewed as a sanctimonious and untouchable group. Within the provisions of the Constitution today, it is somewhat true. But the views of all of the founders didn't strictly agree, and it can be learned from them that it is indeed reasonable to further check its activity and balance its power. Term limits for justices and veto power over its decisions have been considered and suggested by great Constitutional minds as a means for subduing its natural tendency toward judicial interpretation and review.

Huge conflicts of interest have developed within government unions and the Federal Reserve. Unions have no place in government where they can contribute to the careers of the same representatives that determine union workers' pay and benefits. The Federal Reserve is a group of bankers and economists with finite minds trying to control the infinite workings of an infinitely complex economy. Its history is ripe with failures, while the net result is service of its own self-interests.

Many of the national concerns of today are the result of the government's failure to stay true to the Constitution. Essentially, national problems can be divided into two categories, human resources and physical resources. The challenge is to determine how to balance them. Human resources include concerns about social insurance, welfare, and immigration. Social insurance and welfare involve consideration of paid-in and not paid-in programs and the degree of investment in statutory rights according to the nation's conscience. Immigration can be reduced to an issue of following the law.

Physical resource problems include the economy, jobs, subsidies, and infrastructure. Dwindling appropriations for research and infrastructure, caused by the growing human resources beast, contributes to the crumbling of America's strengths and sources of prosperity. Economic problems are further magnified by the liberal and abusive application of government subsidies. The ultimate damage to the economy is caused by government interference with free markets, such as subsidies and human resource give-away programs, and the vast migration of American jobs to foreign soils. The loss of jobs is the country's lost ability to produce, and it likely will remain lost for an era, until the free market forces of supply and demand are naturally restored.

In the final analysis, the nation's concerns are caused by lost ties to the Constitution, and can only be cured by restoring Constitutional supremacy and fiscal responsibility. It's time for the people to bind its government according to the wisdom of the founders, and to correct the abuses that have developed through inattention and self-interest. It's time to reexamine the national character and the direction for public opinion of the living generation.

Preserve Freedom

The last one hundred years of the country's history have brought a ceaseless assault on the Constitution and the personal freedoms of the American people. It began with the abuse of executive power as presidents began to assume a law-making role without authority and acted without asking the most important question before any action, "is it Constitutional?" The next great theft of freedom occurred with ratification of the Sixteenth Amendment to the Constitution that permitted the use of a progressive income tax on Americans. Many people believe this action led to the greatest crisis in American culture than any other form of taxes. Following this, the country's leaders began to invent many forms of interpreting the wording of the Constitution in order to implement programs affecting every facet of a citizen's life. It ranged from subsidies and handouts to social insurance that could be used to insure the professional careers of the growing number of members of a governing class. Before long, the clever economists and professional politicians built debt upon debt to support their give-away habits until the country's security is truly threatened by inordinate debt.

These elements of political malfeasance go against virtually every idea and belief that the founders described in their work and writings. These abuses can only be corrected through Constitutional Amendments or legislative actions that will change the methods of taxation, balance the national budget, redefine the enumerated powers of government, and contain executive power within the limits of the Constitution. Figure 10-1 outlines these corrections.

Preserve Freedom – Repeal Sixteenth Amendment

The power to tax is necessary for the operation of any government, and so the creators of the Constitution established the authority of the federal government to impose taxes within specific limits. The original Constitutional restraint on its power to tax was limited to indirect taxes and equal assessment of direct taxes; and, the Congress was prohibited from imposing taxes on goods exported from any state. But this power to tax has severely abused American freedom with the adoption of the Sixteenth Amendment. It was a mistake and should be corrected. This has never been more evident as seen in the events connected to the health care bill, where the tax revenue system itself is used to compel citizens to comply with federal directions, or deal with the tax collector. Instead of an iron-fisted king directing his subjects to pay up or else, America has allowed central planners to do the same thing today. As surely as Americans decided the Eighteenth Amendment, passed in 1919 to prohibit manufacture, sale, and transportation of intoxicating liquors was a mistake, then repealed it in 1933 by passing the Twenty-first Amendment,

Americans today can reverse one hundred years of repression of the Sixteenth Amendment by repealing it in the same manner.

Restoring Self-Government by the People
Preserve Freedom

- Repeal Sixteenth Amendment – Draw on founders' wisdom
  - ✓ Return to a value-added or consumption tax method and tariffs
  - ✓ Eliminate oppressive tax burden and reduce size of IRS
  - ✓ Restore idea that all have a natural duty to contribute to treasury
- Balance the National Budget
  - ✓ Establish an annual spending limit as a percent of GDP
    - ▪ Establish absolute limits for each functional category
  - ✓ Set long-term plan to reduce size of federal government, salaries, and benefits
    - ▪ Study size and operation of all agencies, departments, and cabinet
      Eliminate ineffective departments and programs
    - ▪ Eliminate federal workers' life of privilege
      Freeze and adjust pay. Use termination and attrition to phase out jobs.
      Revise retirement age minimums to equal Social Security limits
- Redefine Government Powers
  - ✓ Amend Constitution to specifically define powers of federal government
  - ✓ Revise Articles I.8.1, I.8.3, and I.8.18
    - ▪ I.8.1: Limit general welfare as established by articles of Section 8
    - ▪ I.8.3: Define commerce as fair and equal conduct of business
    - ▪ I.8.18: Federal power strictly limited to provisions of articles of Section 8
  - ✓ Decide government role in providing social insurance
    - ▪ Define and add to Section 8 according to the will of the people
- Contain Executive Power
  - ✓ Restrict use of executive orders, board rulemaking, and special advisors
    - ▪ Confine use of executive orders to apply to executive staff
    - ▪ Limit authority of government agencies to make and enforce laws
    - ▪ Abolish use of special advisors and eliminate any lawmaking authority
  - ✓ Revise Constitution Section II.2 if required

Restoring Self-Government – Preserve Freedom
Figure 10-1

The graduated income tax system is a cruel burden and terrible abuse that was never intended by the creators of the country to be developed. The human mind is created free and should remain free without restraint. The use of a progressive income tax system has resulted in attempts to influence the mind and control behavior instead of being strictly limited to a purpose of raising revenue to operate the government, and it has left the nation with a complex, unequal, and hypocritical system that terrorizes its citizens.

The idea that every citizen should contribute a fair share to the necessities of societies was a common idea among the forefathers, and it is manifested in the limitation that all direct taxes should be assessed equally, as originally set up in the Constitution. It isn't hard to imagine that this idea follows naturally from the prevailing idea of tithing as a part of their religious beliefs. The idea is that all members should share equally in the support of the church, and the founders generally believed a similar idea applied as a duty for all citizens to support their government.

The current income tax system is an inefficient failure with many weaknesses. Its first inefficiency is the tremendous cost to regulate the income tax system and enforce it on American individuals and businesses. Recalling the discussion on the tax administration, there are roughly 100,000 people employed by the Internal Revenue Service, and it costs about $430 billion each year to operate the IRS agency. The estimated budget for 2010, as shown in Figure 9-9, anticipates receipts of about $2.1 trillion income taxes ranging from contributions by individuals and businesses, to collections for social insurance, excise and estate taxes, and duties. It's easy to see that $430 billion is almost twenty percent of the receipts for one year. Any serious business would be investigating ways to reduce or eliminate spending such an extraordinary percentage of its revenue on administrative and enforcement costs. Certainly, there is a more cost effective way to collect money to operate the government.

All tax systems have strengths and weaknesses, although it is difficult to identify the strengths of a progressive income tax system. It's weaknesses, however, are renowned. It invades the privacy of its citizens and resorts to intimidation tactics that have rivaled many of the world's special operations forces. The Congress provided authority for it to establish board rule, and many of its regulations have devastated private citizens without recourse of trial. Like many tax systems the pay-as-you-go income tax system results in an underground economy of cheaters that pay nothing as they work for cash without reporting it to the IRS. And, of course, there are the mountains of deductions and credits for jobs and people that have been identified by the government for special treatment. It ranges from homeowners receiving mortgage assistance to truck drivers receiving meal allowances while on the road. But the worst abuse, without question, is the subtle wickedness of manipulating honest citizens to do what the governing class has decided is best for them.

Repealing the Sixteenth Amendment will leave the country with the choices of the original dreams of the creators of the Constitution. The government would be forced to resort to excise taxes and duties, or income taxes at an equal rate for all American citizens. Federal excise taxes have been proposed under varying names such as a fair tax, a national sales tax, and a value added tax. Whatever the name or method, it amounts to a use tax that is imposed when something is purchased, and it would apply to all citizens for all purchases, unless there is a poverty provision that excuses certain citizens who have no income. This system could be employed further in the business world to eliminate the mounds of deductions and tax calculations needed to support tax reporting of business operations today.

The potential cost savings for implementing such a system are astounding. The size of the IRS would be reduced substantially, and Americans would save billions each year in tax preparation time and fees. Most of all, though, there would be a collective sigh of relief across the country as the oppression of the individual income tax system and its insane reporting requirements are lifted from the shoulders of weary Americans.

Some argue that a federal excise tax will be vulnerable to black market operations. What's new? For every system there will be cheaters and crooks. It's no different today, though, and the savings on underground labor will likely offset the losses of the underground black market economy. Others argue that enforcement against black market sales would be easier than trying to police the entire population of the country.

The federal excise tax, without an income tax provision, would free the savings and investment income of retirement accounts from the additional penalty on income from savings. This could result with inordinate prosperity for those so inclined to work, save, and invest for their future. The result would be long-term security that they built for themselves, and it would leave more money to be spent. There would be more demand for real goods and services that would promote economic prosperity, and increases in spending would add to the coffers of the federal government with more excise taxes.

The operation of the government without income taxes has been proven. The federal government worked this way for the first half of its history, and even today, there are nine individual states in the union that operate without an income tax system. Seven of these states, Alaska, Florida, Nevada, South Dakota, Texas, Washington, and Wyoming successfully operate with no income tax assessment whatsoever. Two states, Tennessee and New Hampshire, tax only intangibles. These states provide a lesson for the federal government and country that an oppressive and wasteful income tax system is not only not needed but also not wanted. Best of all, with the repeal of the Sixteenth Amendment, all states with progressive income taxes would be required to ditch their systems, too.

The alternative to the fair tax would be a direct income tax that is equally assessed for all Americans as originally provided in the Constitution. Today, it is sometimes called the flat tax system. Essentially it means that all American citizens would pay a certain percentage of their income to the federal government. Various figures have been discussed and often a percentage is discussed that would result in the same income for the government as it receives under the current system.

Basically, each citizen would be required to add up all income and then take a simple percentage for tax due. If it's a straight percentage, then everyone should come out even at the end of the year without owing or receiving a refund. It's conceivable that a system might be developed that would require no reporting at all. All deductions and special allowances would be eliminated. No more depreciation and depletion allowances, no subsidy grants, and no mortgage interest deductions, would be permitted. It would signal the end of child tax credits, alternative energy credits, education credits, earned income credits, and dozens more. If the people decide there should be help for people in certain situations, then the government can provide this help in other ways, but not by abusing and confusing the source of revenue.

The flat tax would be subject to abuses, too, as would any tax system, but it would offer simplicity. Ideally, the tax percentage would be deducted from all income subject to taxes. If successful, and it is somewhat unlikely that it would work perfectly, then no citizen would be required to file any kind of tax return to the government. Think of the freedom. The alternative would be a simple tax return consisting ideally of a single form. The taxpayer would add up income from all taxable sources and then calculate the tax due based upon the standard percentage. The return would be filed to receive a refund or pay any amount due. If desired, households with income below a certain level may receive tax forgiveness and owe nothing.

The flat income tax system would be superior to the progressive income tax laws in force today, but it still leaves the burden on the average citizen to periodically report to the federal government, and it remains vulnerable to similar abuses. Many Americans would still need help in determining their tax burden. Some are simply unable to maintain records and to figure out a percentage; and why should they be forced to do this? Hopefully, the system would be so simple that free help could be found to assist those in need, but the overpowering specter on all Americans would remain.

In the end, nothing could preserve American freedom more than the simple act of repealing the oppressive and abusive tax system established by the Sixteenth Amendment. Honest, hardworking citizens would be relieved of accounting and business responsibilities, and it would restore individual freedom in the United States as originally envisioned through the honesty and genius of its creators.

PRESERVE FREEDOM – BALANCE THE BUDGET

The growing and abusive tax system is no accident. It is the result of a growing government's need to sustain its demands and associated debt spending. In order for any government to support itself it must become oppressive and tyrannical. Instead of operating the nation within the limits of its income like a responsible nonprofit business, the country has allowed a governing class to grow that keeps itself in power by giving away a large part of the country's treasury. It is no secret that the debt has grown beyond bounds until it has become unmanageable and threatens to ruin the nation's security. Figure 5-1 shows the enormous debt growth from 1791 until 2006; from millions through billions to trillions of dollars owed. It continues to grow each year. The $8.3 trillion debt in 2006 in Figure 5-1 grew more than eighty percent in about five years to over $15 trillion. At the same time Figure 9-9 shows the GDP for the country, as reported by the Office of Budget Management, to be $14.2 trillion in 2009 and around $14.6 trillion for 2010. This means the country owes as much as it produces in one year. But instead of taking action to retire the debt, career politicians continue to spend more than the treasury receives; over $1 trillion a year more. This huge debt limits the nation's ability to spend money on the items of original government purpose, such as physical resources and protecting the states.

Raising taxes and giving government more money will not solve the problem. A judicious business threatened with such a large problem would immediately begin to evaluate the situation in order to identify causes and ways to correct it. Once the problems have been identified the business will develop a plan for corrective action. It isn't uncommon for businesses to find themselves in situations so extreme that it may require several years to correct; in other words, to correct it immediately could be such a devastating shock to the business that the plan itself could jeopardize operations. For example, it would be devastating to a business to immediately cut salaries in half. Instead, there should be an organized plan to bring salaries within reasonable boundaries over a planned period of time. The same is true today for the United States. A long-term plan for paying its debts and limiting spending to no more than annual revenues will be needed to prevent a huge shock for American citizens. There have been decades' worth of promises that should not be wiped out overnight, but phased out with new and judicious plans that will both pay the debt and restrict spending.

The prime question is what the country can afford and how it should be limited. One method would be to limit government spending to a fixed percentage of the Gross Domestic Product, GDP. For instance, if the limit were fixed at eighteen percent it would mean the government budget could not be greater than eighteen percent of what the country produces. If the GDP were about $15 trillion, then government spending would be limited to eighteen percent, or about $2.7 trillion. This would include a budgeted amount to gradually retire the existing debt of about $16 trillion that has accumulated through decades of inattention and malfeasance by hundreds of elected officials. Many representatives and government employees fear the loss of their jobs and careers, because corrective actions may cause adverse attitudes in their constituency. In reality, the American people can understand the concept of limiting the amount taken in from the public, and of spending only what is collected. It's basic to the lives of most Americans. Those who fail to follow this rule of life soon find themselves in the same difficulty the nation faces, debt and bankruptcy at the individual level.

When a business develops a long-term plan for correcting a problem it includes a system of measures and audits to monitor the plan's effectiveness. Similarly, this would be a part of the nation's long-term plan, too, if professional politicians could be trusted to follow it and honestly maintain it. History and common sense shows this would never succeed. Remember Thomas Jefferson's wish for a constitutional amendment to prohibit borrowing. Many of the early U.S. citizens agreed with spending within limits, except in time of war when the nation's security is threatened. Naturally, numerous modern economists and business leaders disagree with this idea and have filled the heads of the Congress with scholarly studies, predictions, and promises. "Debt is a good way to keep the economy growing," they say. But how accurate are these assessments, really? The law of infinity of actions comes into effect immediately when theorists try to explain the operation of the economies of the country and world. They begin with the idea that markets are trying to tell them something, and they wind up by examining a static picture of a world that wanders as a result of countless opposing forces. Truly, it is beyond current abilities to predict and control the infinite number of factors that affect the economy, jobs, and security. One thing is for certain, it will be difficult to go bankrupt if the country doesn't spend more than it takes in; Jefferson's common sense trumps the theory of debt spending. If a private business chooses to risk leverage and debt tactics to grow or multiply its earnings, then it is free to do so, but the welfare and security of the country should not be jeopardized by similar strategies. Rather, the hard work of its citizens should be the true and tangible source of its prosperity.

Should the country follow Jefferson's wish and adopt a balanced budget amendment? Plainly, something should restrain the professional legislators; they have proved they cannot be trusted to keep within limits. Whether it is done by amendment to the Constitution, or by legislative action, the result should be iron clad to limit the excesses of the federal government. First, maximum revenue, or intake from the American people, should be limited by some means, whether a percentage of GDP or an alternative method. Following that, the various categories of government spending should limited as a percentage of the total budget. For example, a maximum spending percentage should be designated for defense, physical resources, human resources, and administration of the government. These limits could be established according to government function as shown in Figure 9-9, super-functions as shown in Figure 9-13, or any similar manner that would limit and control legislators. Naturally, a provision for defense spending in time of war would be needed when the country is threatened, and the rules for such a provision should be similarly restricted against clever tactics and abuse, and a time requirement to repay any debt spending caused by war should be included, just as the founders of the Constitution thought should be the case. It's just wrong for one generation to become embroiled in an armed conflict, run up huge debts, ask for increased budget debt ceilings, and then leave the debt for their children to deal with.

The restriction of government income as a percentage of the country's productivity, and the further restriction of the government's administrative budget as a percent of the total budget will likely result in a plan to reduce the size and expenses of federal operations. Just like the private business that finds itself with an overblown cost structure and must implement cost reduction programs to correct the situation, so must the federal government. Common sense dictates that it can't just grow beyond its means, and continue with a high cost structure while the nation is bleeding. It's tyranny not unlike the heartless emperor that needs more money and takes it by crushing citizens while squeezing the last ounce of their livelihood from them. The U.S. government continues to grow and spend without conscience while the people struggle to find work and to pay bills.

Jefferson believed in cost reduction strategies for the federal government. In his second inaugural address, he reported that his first administration had reduced expenses, and eliminated useless offices, to enable the country to discontinue internal taxes and rely on taxes on incoming foreign goods as a replacement. So it should be today as part of the long-term cost reduction plan for the federal government. The operations of all agencies, departments, and cabinet organizations should be studied to identify ineffective and unjustifiable programs. The size of the presidential cabinet has grown substantially from four positions and a post master general to more than a dozen agencies as shown if Figure 7-3. The growth of an administrative staff is a typical problem faced by private business managers, and it must be periodically reviewed and pared. So should the size of the federal government.

A glaring example of an ineffective program is the Department of Education. This department was created in 1979 as a spin off from the Department of Health, Education, and Welfare with an aim to improve the educational status of Americans. As shown in Figure 9-11 spending on education has grown from roughly $1 billion in 1960 to about $143 billion estimated for 2010. The agency's spending has resulted in lower test scores and lower levels of educational attainment than ever before. This would be a red flag to a painstaking business manager who would want to know how much of this money went to schools and how much is simply swallowed by the costs of supporting an administrative bureaucracy. In all probability, the Department of Education should be eliminated altogether and the role of education given back to the individual states where it belongs in the first place. In today's competitive climate between states it is obvious that states that do not strive for educational excellence will be left behind. Certainly, no state wants this, and all will do what is right for the aims of their citizens.

The White House and its Cabinet departments should be equally evaluated and reduced. Figure 7-3 lists the White House Administrative Agencies and Cabinet Posts. The size and scope of each of these should be examined. It would be remarkable if the number of people and expenses could not be reduced.

All elements of the federal government must fall under the scrutiny of cost reduction studies, and these studies should be part of a continuing plan of periodic revue. When unhealthy private companies are subjected to the actions of a "turn around specialist," it is common for these specialists to dictate an immediate reduction in force to be followed by additional reductions after a more detailed study of operations. A common tactic is to reduce the work force by ten percent. In companies with swollen cost structures and failing sales revenue, it is unlikely that necessary personnel will be eliminated. The U.S. military is no stranger to these actions, and the federal government should be no exception. The cost reduction plan should call for the immediate reduction of the number of federal employees by ten percent, to be followed by comprehensive studies of each unit's operation and costs to determine practical staffing levels and expenses.

Pay levels and benefits, especially retirement and health care plans, should be reevaluated. Legislative action should limit the pay and benefits levels of government workers to the average of all workers in the country employed at a similar level of work and responsibility. This wage and benefit survey should be conducted annually and adjusted up, or down, as necessary to guard against the ballooning that has occurred in the last thirty to fifty years. Salary adjustments should be phased in during an established time period. Through a combination of freezes, reductions, and attrition, it will be possible to return federal salaries to the national average. Retirement plans for federal workers are beyond belief for most Americans. The contributions by the people to federal retirement plans are excessive and should be brought more in line with private industry and the country's averages. Of course, it will take years for these retirement plans to be modified fairly to levels on par with the country, because current workers have been employed with the retirement promises of Americans, and it should be honored. In the long term, though, new workers should be placed on pay, retirement, and benefits plans that are nothing more than the national average. The goal of government workers should not be a life of privilege at the hands of the people, but of steady service. If this doesn't seem right to them, then they should seek the pay and risk of working in the private sector.

The long-term strategy to balance the federal budget will require a creative and discretionary examination of all programs including the human resource programs such as Social Security, Medicare and Medicaid, and welfare programs. Subsidies should be evaluated and completely eliminated. All of this must be planned and implemented over time in a similar manner to correcting the paychecks of government employees. Promises have been made to many people, and they should be kept, because many people have organized entire lifetimes around these promises. But slowly, and surely, the government should phase out current rules and programs to be substituted with rational plans within the confines of what the country can afford.

Once the new plans and new rules have been established with a timetable, then the plan must be sensibly monitored and audited to assure its effectiveness. Just like any other plan or program, a cost reduction plan to balance the budget must be suitably checked with a skeptical eye and corrected where it fails to meet its objectives.

So, with a balanced budget amendment, or strong legislative action, in hand to establish income and spending limits for every element of the federal government, and with a long-term cost reduction plan in place to achieve its goals, then the country may take a large step toward financial freedom, independence, and prosperity.

PRESERVE FREEDOM – REDEFINE GOVERNMENT POWERS

Perhaps the biggest split among the citizens of the United States is the result of interpretation of Article I of the Constitution. It is primarily here that the fundamental powers of the federal government are established by the nation's mutual contract. There is one faction of the population that believes government should provide social programs, housing, food stamps, and other welfare programs for the less fortunate members of the society. Several presidents have stretched the boundaries of the Constitution in order to implement various social programs. Ultimately, the Supreme Court sided with this idea, largely under its interpretation of the First Clause of the Eighth Section of the First Article, where a reference is made to provide for the "general Welfare of the United States." Through this and the liberal interpretation of the clause to regulate commerce, the country has gradually progressed toward operation as a centralized government.

Conversely, there is an opposite faction of the country that believes the Constitution should be followed according to the guidance left by the founders in their explanations of where federal operations should be strictly limited. However, even many of these followers of the interpretation of limited government power have come to accept much of government's intrusion into the private economy and individual lives by the means of subsidy programs, welfare, social insurance, and so forth.

Although the primary architect of the Constitution, James Madison, probably would have objected to the ideas of social insurance, welfare, and the like, it is equally probable that he would agree to it if it were the demands of public opinion and the result of Constitutional changes. Welfare from the government simply wasn't an accepted idea during the first generations of the new republic. The perception and insightful understanding of life and human nature that the founders possessed resulted in a consummate understanding that the ways and needs of society constantly change and evolve. Naturally this is the original idea behind the active law established by the Constitution, and the provisions for change according to public opinion. It is the embodiment of common-law based upon the jury method.

Unfortunately, instead of addressing the differences of these two great factions directly, the elected stewards of the Constitution chose to interpret it to suit their individual preferences – not necessarily public opinion by majority. If the early movements toward a centralized government were brought before the people, and the Constitution amended to provide for a government role in private lives and business, then the constitutionality dispute could have been settled long ago. And, if society and the people change and evolve, then the Constitution should be modified accordingly. The regrettable result of this continuing argument over the meaning of the Constitution has grown into a huge and fractious split among America's citizens. The argument has been shaped into a battle between oppressors and oppressed, wealthy and poor, undeserving and deserving, and to its detriment, the argument is used to build careers and personal fortunes instead of serving as honest dialog.

Now the split is too big and still growing to the point that many Americans live in fear of a runaway government of unlimited power. Where does the interpretation end, they wonder?

There have been many presidents that believed if the Constitution doesn't prohibit an action then it is okay to go ahead and do it. This attitude could be interpreted as an indication of strong leadership and aggressive advancement of society. Unhappily such a single-minded approach has led to many unconstitutional actions and lawmaking by the Executive Branch, and it completely ignores the vital premise that the laws of a self-governing people are founded on public opinion.

The primary security of the self-governing American people is in the written Constitution, not by interpretation or constructions of renegade representatives, executives, or justices. So, it seems the only resolution of the problem of governmental powers appears to be basic Constitutional changes. A new Constitutional Convention is needed to resolve these problems for modern times. Of course it will be long. Of course it will be contentious. But it will be a free and honest discussion in the open, and it should result in answers to many of the arguments that have plagued Americans for at least a hundred years, or more probably, since the beginning of the Union.

Such a convention should start with the needs of the people to be provided by the government. Three of the elementary needs are identified in the Constitution and can be summarized as defense and security for all citizens, fair and legal commerce, and administration of the nation's business. These vital necessities are met with the twenty constitutional powers of the United States Congress authorized in the Eighth Section of the First Article of the Constitution, and listed for reference in Figure 4-1.

Defense and security for all citizens and states is found in several clauses of the Eighth Section of Article I that establish the armed forces, army, navy, and militia at that time. In support of this there is an authorization for the Congress to make war when necessary, and to punish felonies on the high seas. Naturalization and immigration controls were set up in the Fourth Clause. The purpose of this protection was not to prevent diversity; rather, it was meant to protect all states, particularly border states, against an influx of aliens with hostile viewpoints to the United States, or in such large numbers that would pose a threat to the individual states and the country. Finally, the post offices and postal roads were launched. The postal system could be considered both an action to protect the country with an efficient communication system in times of threat, and as a tool of infrastructure to promote commerce in times of peace.

Commerce clauses were included as a power of Congress to promote fair and legal commerce. The original purpose of the commerce clause should not be lost. This is where a century or more of interpretation has transformed the republic into a centralized federal government. In addition to the postal service provisions, various commerce clauses authorize the Congress to make bankruptcy laws, establish fair and stable money standards and punish counterfeiting, set up uniform weights and measures, and to secure copyrights and patents for the intellectual genius of it citizenry. It appears to be a stretch to include social insurance and other forms of human resource spending under the Constitutional provisions of the commerce clauses.

The third basic service permitted to Congress by the Constitution satisfies the need for administration of the nation's business. Here is where the original authorization is established to collect taxes, borrow funds, pay debts, and exercise authority over federal lands and the District of Columbia. With each new law and program, these clauses permit the Congress to permit new hiring and new regulations for adequate administration of their provisions. There is no doubt that the original idea of the founders was that each individual citizen would contribute an equal amount to the treasury in order properly fund and operate the federal government. Naturally, the Sixteenth Amendment reversed this idea with the new idea that citizens should pay according to their labor, industry, skill, and savings. Those who have acquired too much are expected by many today to pay not only a larger portion to support government operations, but also to spare others who are less talented or have not exercised equal industry and prudence.

Today, it can be argued that a fourth fundamental need has been added through interpretation of Congressional powers in this same part of the Constitution, or, conversely, that the Constitution has always made provision for social and economic programs. Predictably, the crucial question will be whether government has a mitigating role in the lives of its citizens, and if so, how much. This is a question for modern times, and for each generation to decide for itself. Without question, the American society of today is far different than that of colonial days, and it will be profoundly different in two hundred more years. Here again the power of the active law of the Constitution that can be changed and molded by the prevailing ideas of public opinion of the living populous may be used to change with society's needs.

There are theories and indications that a free society can establish communal action to mitigate disasters that individuals cannot guard against, such as earthquakes and hurricanes. Horatio Bunce, the American citizen from the Davy Crockett era that was described in the story told in Chapter 7, might not have agreed, but the government and people of today have come to expect it. The country has steadily added social programs, but the fear is that it could grow out of control. Financially, in fact, it has, and is one of the overpowering causes for the financial distress of the country in modern times. But the larger fear is that government will continue to dip its hand more and more into everyday life until it becomes a dictatorial centralized democracy.

If the country at large, in a Constitutional Convention, wishes to add social resources to the role of government, then it can be done with strict limits upon government power and ability. New laws to restrict it would provide some form of satisfaction for the faction favoring social intervention, and a measure of security for the faction that fears total government immersion into and control of American life. Changes or modifications to the First (Collect taxes), Third (Regulate commerce), and Eighteenth (Implied powers) Clauses in the Eighth Section of Article One are needed to clarify exact limits on the power of the federal government. The general welfare and commerce wording should be strictly defined with set limits established. If the government is to continue to provide welfare and social insurance for a segment of the population, then it should be added to the Constitution with controls as absolute as humanly possible. In addition, there must be no doubt that the power of the federal government is firmly limited to the powers delegated to it by the citizens of the country, nothing more.

It would be wonderful if the people's representatives could adequately address the confusion and interpretation that has developed through the years. Regrettably, the quest for power, party, and personal achievement will, in all likelihood, block any such effort to address the problems openly and honestly according to the law of the Constitution. There will be arguments that rules to restrict government activity will limit its ability to react to unforeseen developments. It shouldn't, if adequately drafted, but again, if there is a problem, the creators of the Constitution expected future generations to correct it.

If the elected and appointed officials can't, or won't, recognize the opinion and needs of a self-governing people, then the creators preserved the ultimate power of the people and states in Article Five. Any citizen can propose a bill or amendment. Similarly, the security of the people is in the Constitution. If two-thirds of both Houses won't propose the necessary Amendments, as provided by the Fifth Article, then two-thirds of the states should convene a Convention to propose the Amendments to the Constitution to settle the perceived discrepancies and interpretations; and, if satisfactorily in accord with the people's opinion of government, then the Amendments will be ratified by three-fourths of the States. The country, and its internal peace, is past due for these clarifications and changes.

PRESERVE FREEDOM – CONTAIN EXECUTIVE POWER

The growth of Constitutional interpretation by the executive branch of government has gradually threatened to replace the power of self-government with dictatorship. To be sure, the Congress still has control to check the power of presidential policies, but it has delegated much of its power to the executive branch until Americans today are controlled by board rules and regulations established by a small number of people. Worse, many of the individuals making the rules are neither elected nor confirmed by the Congress; that is to say, they operate without direct or indirect accountability to the people.

This situation has developed through the liberal use of board rules, executive orders, and a poor attitude toward the Constitution. Many presidents, in fact most, have trampled over the Constitution to some degree in an attempt to do "what is best for the country." Theodore Roosevelt was one of the most ardent. Remember, he believed the president could do anything the country needed unless specifically forbidden by the Constitution or Law. As a result, the power of executive orders was expanded to include laws affecting individual citizens, and there was an explosion in the number of issued orders during his administration. He did not believe he seized legislative power; rather, he thought he broadened the use of executive power.

This cancerous idea of a few individuals deciding what the country needs has grown until Americans today are faced with more rules established by boards of bureaucrats than ever before.

The engineer of the Constitution, James Madison, recognized the possibility of an imposter republican government that is driven by a private agenda while pretending to operate for the good of the country. In the thirty-ninth edition of *The Federalist*, Madison describes various applications of the republican term to different forms of government. He described the governments of the day in Holland, where no authority comes from the people, Poland, with the worst forms of aristocracy and monarchy, and England, with only one republican branch of its government. All of these governments called themselves republics. It has been just as easy, then, for generations of U.S. presidents to sell their brand of domination by a few elites as republican liberty for many.

The Second Section of Article Two of the Constitution establishes the powers of the President in only three straightforward clauses. The First Clause establishes the military authority of the office and civil duties such as administration of executive department heads, and granting reprieves. The Second Clause permits the president to make treaties with the consent of the Senate, and this where the responsibility to appoint Supreme Court Justices is created. The Second Clause further allows the president to appoint all officers established by laws of Congress, and it also permits the Congress to delegate lone presidential responsibility for appointing inferior federal officers without the requirement for confirmation. Here is where the license to add to the size of the executive branch has been exploited virtually unchecked. The Third Clause of Section II.2 simply lets the president fill important vacancies while the Senate is in recess; such appointments normally require the advice and consent of the Senate.

That's it for presidential power. There's nothing about rule of boards and agencies, or special advisors with powers to establish administrative laws. This has developed through years of Congressional grants and lack of adequate oversight until the executive branch has become the largest lawmaking arm of the federal government. This clearly violates the intent of the Constitution and must be reversed before the totalitarian actions of administrative law overpower freedom.

The President of the United States swears to uphold the Constitution and enforce its laws, not to make laws. Article II.1.8 establishes the oath. President Washington added the words, "So help me God," when he was sworn in, and this has generally been the tradition since. The executive does not swear to uphold only the laws that suit a personal agenda and ignore those that don't. This has become a growing problem for the country. A current glaring example is the laws for legal immigration. It is the constitutional duty of the president to enforce these laws. Sadly, many presidents have shirked this duty as a result of both political pressures and personal beliefs. But the Constitution is the only security of the American people, and as long as the laws are on the books, they must be enforced. No president can legally fail to uphold the law; it must be enforced until the law is changed. It is easy to see how the immigration problem has grown so large as those sworn to uphold the law of the land bury their heads in a bureaucratic quagmire.

The greatest threat to personal freedom by the growing power grab of the executive branch of government is contained in the use of rule by boards, special advisors, and executive orders. Acts passed by Congress that allow a board authority to legally establish what it pleases also open the door to authoritarianism and unchecked control of human behavior. There are two types of law: law of the people based upon the jury method and the people's representatives; and, board or administrative law based upon decisions by a select few individuals to decide what is best for all. The second is the ultimate defeat of the power of self-government by public opinion and people's law, and it must be checked if the country is to avoid the subjugation of bureaucratic rule by appointees.

Board rule today includes rule making by agencies such as the IRS, EPA, OSHA, Health and Human Services, and others. These agencies daily impose rules to control individual behavior and restrict personal freedom. Essentially, it's legal. But the use of Article II.2.2 by the Congress to use legislative action to grant these powers of board rulemaking have grown to overwhelm American life as each of these well-meaning lifetime government servants work tirelessly to protect and restrict citizens.

A more insidious method of rulemaking is the liberal use of executive orders and special advisors, commonly called czars today. Executive orders were originally used to control the activities of the executive staff itself. It generally stayed that way until the aggressive administrations of Theodore Roosevelt as he continued his campaign to see to the country's needs regardless of whether or not they were authorized by the Constitution. Remember, he issued more than 1,000 executive orders to demonstrate his independent power. Executive orders are never approved by Congress, but are published in the "Federal Register" and carry the same weight as any Congressional law. This has been compounded in recent years with the expansion of the use of the special advisors. These offices have become independent lawmakers with no accountability to the people, either through elections or advice and consent of the Senate. The country is now bombarded with more than thirty of these little dictators that decide what is the best policy for Americans and impose it upon them without restraint. Where could anyone find a better definition of centralized democracy or dictatorial authority?

It's time for Congress to stop the growth of centralized rule by bureaucratic boards. Legislative action is needed to restrict executive power and its use of administrative law and special advisors. The use of executive orders should be strictly defined and limited to administrative use for staff functions. The idea of using this power to impose laws on the people must be discontinued. Special advisors must be eliminated, period. There should be no office in the federal government that is not strictly controlled by the people through Congress. This is the function of Congress. This despicable idea got started more than forty years ago, and malfeasant Congresses have failed in their duty to protect the Constitution by allowing it to continue and flourish. Legislative action is needed to stop advisors now, eliminate this power and its rulemaking.

Finally, the Congress needs to review the mechanism of granting the rulemaking authority it gives to the different government agencies. Rulemaking especially, must be restricted and subject to review by the Congress, instead of allowing these bureaucracies to grow unimpeded. One sure way to assure oversight is to reduce the number of agencies. This will save money for the people's treasury and simplify the job of Congress in assuring that the freedom of the people is not injured.

Professional politicians in the Congress have permitted the runaway power of the executive branch. It can be ended just as simply when Congress accepts its constitutional responsibilities to check these abuses. If Congress will not respond to the demands of the people to eliminate a dictatorial executive branch, then the people can resort again to the use of Constitutional Amendments.

Temper Political Policies

The accepted political system in this country has grown into a huge network of professional politicians and lobbyists that are controlled by party unions that impede the exercise of self-government by public opinion. Many elements of the current campaign and legislative processes that are utilized by political insiders work against the grand idea of a government of the people. The political policies of today have resulted in the development of the professional politician and supporters that have become a governing class of individuals that have set themselves up for personal gain at the expense of the very people that have elected them to serve.

Changes to the system are needed to restore the power of the people in self-government. It should begin by abolishing the use of career politicians in the government. Instead of electing individuals that have become nothing more than federal employees, the country needs individuals that wish to fulfill the wishes of their constituency without making their personal goals their first priority. In addition, new legislative rules and laws are needed to limit the power of the two-party system, and to reform lobbying methods and abuses. Four steps to temper political policies are described, and Figure 10-2 summarizes the thoughts.

Restoring Self-Government by the People
Temper Political Policies

- Abolish Career Politicians
  - ✓ Require periodic recurrent training on provisions of Constitution
  - ✓ Remove elected representatives from federal employee status
    - Reduce compensation to a stipend equal to national average wage
    - Eliminate retirement and health care plans paid for by the people
  - ✓ Control reimbursements and expenses
    - All expenses limited to government per diem rates
    - Abolish gifts to federal officials
  - ✓ Impose term limits for Congressmen and Senators
- Curtail Abuses
  - ✓ Reform campaign rules. Limit spending and campaign time period
  - ✓ Regulate professional lobbyists. Abolish gifts to federal representatives
- Revise Legislative Methods
  - ✓ Abolish use of congressionally directed spending (earmark) legislation
  - ✓ Require a period for public comment before vote by House and Senate
- Reconsider Seventeenth Amendment
  - ✓ Consider returning selection of Senators to State Legislators
  - ✓ Provide protection of the rights of the minority and States

Restoring Self-Government – Temper Political Policies
Figure 10-2

TEMPER POLITICAL POLICIES – ABOLISH CAREER POLITICIANS

It is time, perhaps past time, for the country to take steps to eliminate the employment of professional politicians. The governing class has convinced a large portion of the population that candidates with extensive political experience are needed to run the government. The political history of the country, with its long list of failures and malfeasance, might serve as an argument against the idea of career representatives. Many of the wise founders of the country left admonitions against the election of individuals who pervert their office into places of profit. The founders knew there would be a ready supply of honest and reasonable people to occupy the posts of government if given a chance to serve. Unfortunately, the political party machines make this almost impossible today. Perhaps now is the opportune time to change current practices.

The purpose of legislators is summed up in the oath of office that each senator, representative, and judge takes without reservation. Their purpose is simply stated, "I do solemnly swear that I will support and defend the Constitution of the Untied States against all enemies, foreign and domestic; that I will bear true faith and allegiance to the same; that I take this obligation freely without any mental reservation or purpose of evasion;..." When these individuals fail to uphold the provisions of the Constitution, or try to evade its requirements, they are not fulfilling their duty. The nation's security is in the Constitution, and the people rely on elected representatives to be true to it. Anything else is dishonor.

George Washington understood the importance of a mutual contract when he wrote about upholding the Articles of Confederation that was the law of the land during the Revolution. He found every violation of a constitution as reprehensible and added that if it is defective then amend it, but do not ignore it while in existence. The importance of the Constitution is not diminished today. Americans should strive to elect only those who promise to follow the Constitution. If the people want to change it, then let them elect individuals who will endeavor to change it, but they must never deviate from it until it has been amended. This is the only chance the country has for stability and security.

The first question every individual in federal service should ask about every contemplated action should be, "is it Constitutional?" If it is not, then they are bound by oath to reject it in their support of the Constitution. The alarming truth, though, about the country's representatives is that many of them are not familiar with the Constitution, and some obviously have not read it recently. Here is where the first step can be taken in assuring the Constitution's provisions. Every Congressman, Senator, and other officers should be required to complete refresher studies on the Constitution each year before they are permitted to be seated in office. Recurrent training is required for most professionals to continue practice. Accountants, physicians, engineers, architects, tax preparers, and many others are required to complete refresher courses on a periodic basis in order to be permitted by governing authorities to continue practice. It would seem to be of even more importance for the actual people who swear to uphold the Constitution to be familiar and recently trained before voting on legislation and rules that may or may not conform with the country's peculiar source of safe haven.

After the first step of insisting that government officers be adequately trained and have a proficient understanding of the Constitution before being seated, the next question becomes whether or not the country really wants professional politicians. During colonial times and the earliest years of U.S. business, it was unfashionable for individuals to petition for office as it is done today. More frequently, the people wrote names on their ballots, and the person with the most votes was asked to accept the office. Early Americans believed those in public service should never depend on public salaries for their support. They thought they should have other, honest means of support first, and then they would be fit for additional service in public office. Naturally, there were subtle ways for those who would like to be elected to let it be known, but for the most part, the elected officials were true public servants receiving minor reimbursement for their time and expenses. Today, of course, public servants are actually career politicians with professional aims, goals, and personal profit at the forefront of their motivation to assume office.

The serious danger of professional politicians is the development of a ruling political class so entrenched in office that they come to believe they better understand what is right for the country, losing sight of the idea of a people's government. This has become more evident than ever before in the last decade or so. One political party obtains a majority, even a small, but controlling majority, and then takes a strong-arm approach to government, rather than acting like representatives sent to consult with one another on the nation's business. Driven by lobbyists and financial supporters, the party in power seeks to advance a one-sided agenda without consideration of the views and rights of the minority. The country recognized this problem with the multiple terms of Franklin Roosevelt and his executive lawmaking efforts and attempts to expand the size of the Supreme Court to suit his personal agenda. This resulted in the ratification of the Twenty-second Amendment to limit service in the office of President to two terms as it stands today.

One change to the current system to discourage career politicians would be to revise the compensation and benefits for Representatives, Senators, Judges, and the President. Elected representatives should not be treated as federal employees as they have managed to incorporate themselves through the years since 1946; prior to that time they were not included in the federal employee system. There should be no retirement or health plan paid for by the American people. It's a deceitful conflict of interest when elected representatives determine pay levels and benefits for federal employees in which they themselves are included. Individuals who wish to serve should be prepared to receive a stipend for service and expenses, and nothing more. Any retirement or health program for these individuals should be at their personal expense. This will return them to status as representatives of the people.

In addition, as representatives of the people their salaries should be slashed from high salaries to a modest reimbursement for their expenses. The base reimbursement should not exceed the average pay of all Americans. This would eliminate the perception of themselves as executives or someone with specialized expertise that should receive salaries commensurate with private managers. Figure 7-2 demonstrates the attitude of Congress at being federal employees with ever increasing annual salaries and benefits.

The final step in returning elected officials to servants of the people is to limit the number of terms any individual can serve in an office. This would support and augment the steps to remove them from federal employee programs. It is a difficult question, but it isn't a new question. It stretches back to the beginning of the Republic. George Washington thought it unadvisable to limit the term of the President. He thought there would be little danger of a corrupted individual being retained, and that limiting the term of a capable individual would deprive the nation of such services. Others, though, were more skeptical of allowing individuals to serve without limits. George Mason understood the nature of mankind to not only hold on to power as long as it can be retained, but also to increase it as much as possible. James Madison recognized that a governing class of society tends to form group opinions, such as is done in Washington today. He thought the pressures of party and politics could skew independent thinking, especially of new or weaker members who lack confidence in their own ideas and judgment. What an astute prediction he made of the situation today as Congressmen and Senators speak of co-opting new members to their prevailing ideas.

In more recent times, the situation during the long tenure of Franklin Roosevelt serves again as an example of the dangers when individuals are left in office for long periods. Sam Rayburn served as the powerful Speaker of the House of Representatives for seventeen years. He was dedicated to Roosevelt's governmental programs, and when combined with the Speaker's tremendous power to direct the legislative agenda and decide who was recognized to speak, it was extremely difficult for opposing views to be heard. Although many recognized this long-standing stranglehold on the Presidency and House as problematic, the Congress later acted only to restrict the term of service of the President. Limiting the term of offices for representatives, though, would reduce the possibility of a coordinated power hold on the Congress and the Constitution.

Another argument for term limits can be found in the tendency to accept long-standing repeated dialog as fact. It is not uncommon to observe this in academic fields. One writer may describe a hypothesis that another reads and includes in a following commentary. From writer to writer the observation continues until it may eventually be accepted as fact. Such may be the case with continual political discussions today regarding vested rights, such as social security, food stamps, home ownership, and health care. Many politicians today have come to accept these as factual rights without remembering the distinction between vested and unalienable rights.

The top executives of many companies have understood for many years the need for change. The most astute observers of this idea often will not hold the top position for more than about fifteen years. New ideas and directions are the lifeblood of healthy companies, and no single individual is so important, or so experienced, that they should remain entrenched forever. The same can be said for elected representatives. Individuals in power won't give it up, and Jefferson noted that many would remain even after they have become a dotard. How true. On more than one occasion one party or another has propped up an aged and obviously incapable Congressman or Senator in order to maintain their power bloc. Term limits would tend to break up party power blocs.

The number of terms in office for Congressmen and Senators should be limited in a manner similar to the President. If it was needed for the executive branch, it follows that it is needed for the legislative branch. The exact length of time should be earnestly evaluated and proposed as a Constitutional Amendment. It isn't a new idea, and service terms such as eight years for Congressmen (four terms) and twelve years for Senators (two terms) have been suggested. Self-important individuals will want to follow service in one house with service in the other; they could have political influence for twenty years. Let them, but with little pay or benefits. It is likely that a referendum initiated by the States will be needed, because it is equally unlikely that the elected officials themselves would support a measure of this sort.

There will be much argument against slashing pay and benefits and limiting length of service. A typical preparation today for public office includes a law degree. There will be strong argument that to get the best and most capable people will require competitive pay and political credentials. The forefathers couldn't disagree more. Benjamin Franklin said there would always be a supply of good men who were willing to serve. He said the less the pay the greater the honor. The argument against high pay requirements can be found in the abundant supply of firefighters, police officers, and military personnel that serve for love of country rather than love of power and profit.

It's time for a change. It's time to elect good people who are willing to serve at great sacrifice for a limited period of time in order to serve the people that elected them and to advance the idea of self-government through public opinion. It could be the virtual end of the governing class in America and the restoration of the great republican government.

TEMPER POLITICAL POLICIES – CURTAIL ABUSES

Political abuses and corruption are not new to modern times. From time immemorial, and even during the great period of construction of the nation's

Constitution, there have always been individuals seeking to find pathways to personal gain from prevailing laws and policies. There are those in constant search for power and wealth by using the political system. It would be easy to say it is worse today, but in all probability it isn't. The laws of statistical distribution likely apply to all eras. The percentages are about the same, so there are numerically more in each category in the larger population of today. But there may be ways to ease the effects of abuses through legislative actions and rulemaking. Three major contributors that restrict honest public opinion are the two-party system, campaign rules, and lobbyist activities.

The two-party political system sprang up almost immediately with the start of the first Congress, despite the dread of it by the early leaders and their admonishments of its problems. There will always be factions, because it is part of human nature. Thomas Jefferson noted in his writings that men are naturally divided into two parties that exist in every country where people are free to speak and write. James Madison tried to design a constitutional government to balance natural factions. So there will always be natural disagreement and differing ideas, which is a good thing as long as it isn't used to stifle opposite speech. Factions are like fire or water. It can be very beneficial and provoke growth, or when misused or out of control, it can destroy property, life, and freedom.

The individuals chosen to serve the people were sent to Washington to consult with one another in accordance with the provisions of the Constitution while serving as stewards of the nation's business. Today, this purpose has been all but defeated by the contentious struggle between the two parties for power and distinction. Two great parties under their leaders continually work in opposition to one another.

The political parties in power are really nothing more than two huge unions pursuing the primary goals of any union, which are power, privilege, and greed. These political unions select the candidates to be submitted to the voters, form platforms, and build careers that must be directed according to party loyalty if they are to be continued. The development of the governing class in the country is a direct result of party unions. Individual judgment is distorted by the influence of senior party union members on the weaker nature of new members and their stifling effect on new ideas by co-opting each party member until they all blindly conform. Just like any typical union requirement, committee chairmen and other party leaders are chosen by seniority, rather than by qualifications.

Party unions cannot, and should not, be eliminated, but it may be acceptable to temper their power, especially where it prevents public opinion to flourish. An important step would be the change to term limits and returning the role of leaders to elected representatives instead of federal employees. This should result with more individuals choosing to serve the country instead of setting up a career for personal gain. The continual supply of new people, new ideas, and new commitments to the country that are not so strongly tied to the party might loosen the stranglehold of party bosses and open parties to the ideas of consulting with others to serve America.

A second source of party power is established by campaign and election rules. In many areas of the country the party unions hold sway on how candidates for election are established. The parties establish who is ready for office and who will be presented to the people for vote. There should be no limitations on the number of candidates on the ballots. Election rules should ease the parties' grip on candidates.

Campaign contributions and election spending often serve to limit public knowledge of candidate qualifications and ideals and usually result in a winner being the one with the most money. More restrictions on campaign contributions should be implemented. There should be a spending cap on every campaign. It should be a maximum amount that can be spent by a candidate, so the playing field can be leveled; all would have the same spending limits. No direct contributions from government labor unions should be permitted. This aggravates the conflict of interest that exists when the employee can influence the employer by contributing to election coffers. The work of unions in the private sector, of course, is an essential freedom to be left alone.

Campaign time limits could help reduce the campaign-spending cap. There should be a strictly enforced time limit for active campaigning for office. A thirty or forty-five day limit for active campaigns would be a welcome relief to both candidates and voters. U.S. Representatives hardly start work before it is time for another election. But this two-year term was absolutely intentional by the founders to prevent entrenched public officials. A short campaign time period would save money and leave many officials with more time for the country's business. When combined with term limits, the campaign spending cap and time limits work together for a more efficient and sensible way to pick new representatives. Perhaps the role of the television ad would be minimized.

The professional lobbying system in the United States has become the third major contributor to abuse of the American political system. The right to redress grievances is locked up in the First Amendment, as described in the earlier discussion of corrupting influences. Professional lobbyists are the most successful bill writers and supporters in the private sector. Their activities are not necessarily bad. Registered lobbyists in Washington furnish Congressmen and Senators with research and background data on various subjects, and they actually provide a useful service for the representatives and their professional staff members. Many private citizens, organizations, and businesses employ professional lobbyists to help advance legislation that supports their causes.

The problem isn't the ability to lobby, but the perversion of the activity that has grown around it. This has become an extraordinarily lucrative business for lobbyists, and where large places of profit exist, greed and corruption are sure to be found in equally large doses. So, retired government officials become lobbyists with deep contacts, and soon, backs are scratched and palms are crossed. The great American practice of lobbying should be forever continued, but efforts to check the abusive practices are needed in order to prevent dilution of the wisest element of a free people, public opinion.

The first step to normalize specialized lobbyists would be to eliminate the progressive income tax system. This system, with its deductions, credits, and exclusions, enables the professional lobbyists to achieve power and privilege for their clients. If the nation's tax system is returned to a method solely for collecting revenue instead of controlling people and businesses, then the power of lobbyists may be reduced. Without opportunity for financial gain, many of these people might return to contributing to the country's productivity.

There are excessive gifts and unreasonable luxury trips that elected officials receive in a perversion of the lobbyist system. There should be strict controls on this activity with severe limits on gifts, or an elimination of gifts altogether. The tax laws of the country do not allow gifts between business associates of more than twenty-five dollars without triggering a tax event. A similar figure might be applied to Congressmen and Senators; that is, no trips, and no gifts more than twenty-five dollars. Anything more would be unlawful. In truth, though, should any official of the government be allowed to accept a gift from a lobbyist?

Another restriction could include a prohibition on former legislators and government officials working as lobbyists. When activities and relationships of this nature are permitted, it is simply an open door to corruption and distortion of the idea of a government for free people. The entire operation of professional lobbyists should be reevaluated and heavily regulated to prevent the continued corruption that has become part of the very operation of the American government.

TEMPER POLITICAL POLICIES – REVISE LEGISLATIVE METHODS

The legislative process in Congress today is a corruption of changes and alterations by the party unions to gain political advantage, not for responsible conduct of the nation's business. Parliamentary rules have been modified and perverted when necessary to force legislation into law. Similarly, bill riders and earmarks have been combined with hasty legislation to misrepresent rulemaking and pass laws in secrecy.

New and stricter legislative rules are needed to prevent the Congress from working around fundamental principles of parliamentary procedures.

Malfeasant, or deceitful, manipulation of rules are often described as a "long standing tradition of doing it this way." Explanations like this are an immediate alarm of treacherous behavior. Thomas Jefferson encouraged both legislative bodies of his era to strictly adhere to the base principles, because departing from primary rules sets up the opportunity for dangerous innovation. All Americans should recognize that any method used to skirt the rules of legislative procedure or Constitutional requirements are moves to take power and defeat the democratic process. Unless a rule is meant to promote openness in the legislative process to keep the American public informed, then it should be abolished.

Without question, one of the most abused actions that infuriates Americans is the use of earmarks and riders on legislative bills. Even though the use of these congressionally directed spending projects result in expenditures of about two percent ($75 billion) of the total budget, Americans despise them because it is an abusive and secretive practice. Their use is often recognized as unethical and deceitful, because there is little openness. Unfair rewards to a specific segment of the nation are usually restricted to the more powerful members of Congress, or as a bargaining bribe to secure a vote on a different issue. Earmarks are often passed without debate, which eliminates openness and accountability. Because Congress wants to avoid publicity of earmarks, they are hard to identify, and the efforts to keep them secret invites unethical and corrupt activity with lobbyists and contractors.

A recent passage of an Afghan War Bill is a typical example of this abusive practice. In order to secure votes to continue funding of this military conflict, there were many riders and amendments on unrelated issues attached to the bill to increase Congressional support. There were provisions for spending to avoid layoffs of government workers and teachers, to add Pell Grant money for education, and relief for the Haitian natural disaster. Another example is the rider on the infamous health care bill that included tax breaks for adoption credit. How can special benefits such as these, for a small segment of the country, be considered as providing for the general welfare of all people as set forth in the Constitution?

Naturally, the list of spending bills with unrelated appropriations is extraordinary. At campaign time many comments to discredit the voting record of an opponent are the result of earmarks. For instance, one candidate may claim the other did not support a war bill to take care of the troops in action. On the other hand, the opposition replies that the vote against the legislation was because of an abusive rider attached to the bill at the last minute. What could be more deceitful and confusing for voters? Who can judge the intensions and record of an individual when it is shrouded in secrecy and innuendo?

Abusive practices such earmark riders, and allowing approval of provisions such as "deemed as passed," should be eliminated from current legislative rules. Many different presidents have requested a control of the practice with authorization for line item veto power. For decades, the abusive power of the Congress has seen fit to deny this control, against the public opinion of the people. In the name of honest and reasonable management of the country's resources, the Congress should eliminate this practice altogether. There would be no need for line item veto, because there would be no secret provisions to favor a specific interest. And, it would eliminate the huge temptation for corruption. Let each action stand on its own merits, be presented openly to all Americans, and let each member of Congress vote accordingly.

Finally, there is the abusive practice of hasty rulemaking. This became most evident during the deliberations regarding the expansive new health care bill. The tremendous push to pass this comprehensive bill into law left many Americans in disbelief at the assault on the legislative process in order to make this a law. Now, more problems, and more flaws and holes are found in the huge bill. During the rush, the members of Congress and their staffs were not permitted adequate time to study and digest the provisions of the bill. Few, if any, took the time to determine whether its provisions were Constitutional, and it was beyond understanding when the country was encouraged to "pass it now and find out what is in it later." What prudent businessman or project manager would commit such a sophomoric error? But the herd mentality of party unions ignored all reasonable warnings and stepped off the cliff anyway.

Alexander Hamilton would never have settled for it. He warned that quick decisions are more often trouble than benefit, and he personally needed time to dig into a problem to understand it. This was the total purpose of the legislative process, in his view, where differences of opinion may sometimes slow a good plan, but more importantly promote deliberation and judicious consideration. There's nothing really new about these ideas. The obvious purpose for forcing the hasty passage of the health care plan was to advance a narrow political agenda without consideration for the original purpose of the republican Constitution, which is public opinion. The controlling party wanted it passed before the make up of Congress could change with the next election. The idea of public opinion was smashed at the hands of unreasonable zealots through the perversion of legislative methods.

Clearly, this needs to be stopped, and a method used by the rulemaking arm of administrative law could be applied to all areas of government. This is the use of a time limit for public comments on proposed legislation. Many agencies use the tool of Notice of Proposed Rulemaking. When rules or changes in board law are proposed, they are posted for public comment. A similar method should be applied to legislative actions according to size and scope. Voting on a very large bill, such as the health care bill, should be restricted until a reasonable period of time has been allotted for public review and comment. The members of Congress experienced this somewhat during town hall meetings, and many didn't like what they heard. Some actually began to avoid public contact, because the issue obviously had not been adequately researched or explained. Remarkably, a lot of the members of Congress tried to explain or defend the bill without the benefit of having examined it before discussing it at home. Horatio Bunce would have had a difficult time supporting such Congressional behavior. Nevertheless, it should be done in the open and in a reasonable period of time to allow a circumspective review of proposals and issues.

During a period for public review, the author of every bill should be openly identified to the public. In the cases of the health care bill and the economic stimulus bill of 2009, contractors, not Congressional staff or other members of government, created these bills. Of course, private citizens and organizations may draft and submit bills for consideration by the Congress, but the source should be open and obvious to all Americans. The Apollo Alliance drafted the stimulus bill, which included support for social programs and other earmarks, but it was also called an emergency provision and was hastily driven into law to save the nation's economy. If such a bill were presented to Americans with its source of authorship and a time limit for comment, then the opportunity for abuse could be reduced. A similar time period for public comment is needed for every board rule and administrative law created by all agencies and special advisors to the president. No rule should be a secret buried in a huge and incoherent regulation.

The common sense of the people should prevail. Legislative methods should be changed to eliminate secretive practices of all elements of the government, including the House, the Senate, the White House, and all government agencies. There should be time for consideration and study, and it should be open to all citizens for review and comment. Earmarks should forever be eliminated so that one day citizens of the future can look back in disbelief at the abusive practices that were used, and with gratitude to the honest representatives that changed it. Career politicians and their deceitful practices to promote their personal agendas must go, and with them, the equally oppressive and secretive legislative rules.

TEMPER POLITICAL POLICIES – RECONSIDER 17TH AMENDMENT

The Seventeenth Amendment probably tipped the balance of power between federal and state governments. The founders of the Constitution envisioned the purpose of the Senate as a protection of States' rights. The primary purpose of the Senate in reviewing bills from the House was meant to determine if the nation could afford a given program, and to evaluate its effect on individual rights and freedoms. The Senate was meant to check any tendency by the House toward excess problem solving, and to balance the majority by considering the entire needs of the country and its states. The protection of individual and states' rights were perhaps the central issue and sticking point for many members of the Constitutional Convention, and so the original provisions in the Third Section of the First Article of the Constitution for selecting Senators were specifically established to protect the rights of individual state governments. Even so, there were individual members of the initial Convention that believed Senators should be elected by popular vote, the way it is today. Later, the move to change to the election of Senators by popular vote was submitted by the House about five times but was defeated each time by the Senate. Eventually, though, a corrupt Senator from Illinois had basically purchased his seat by bribing his State Legislature. That affected public opinion, and the Seventeenth Amendment was ratified in 1913.

But should the Seventeenth Amendment be reversed? Many people believe the Seventeenth Amendment gives the country two houses for the people and dilutes the protection of States' rights as envisioned in the original version of the Constitution. The Tenth Amendment in the Bill of Rights guarantees all powers not delegated to the federal government nor prohibited to the federal government by the Constitution are left to the States or to the people. Here is where many citizens believe the Seventeenth Amendment steps on the guarantees of the Tenth Amendment and waters down the powers of the states; and, as a result, the constant encroachment in local affairs and its unceasing dictation of laws by the federal government.

Today, the federal government is involved in local schools, roads, housing, welfare, hospitals, banks, transportation, communication, energy, natural resources, air, land, waterways, and endlessly on. Is this the direct result of the Seventeenth Amendment, or of the wishes of the people? The question should be asked and the impact of this Constitutional change reviewed. If the people at large prefer local control again, and want the federal government to back out, then the provisions of the Seventeenth Amendment and its effect on States' rights should be reviewed.

It might be possible that a Constitutional Amendment to closely define federal government powers could similarly restore States' rights. By refining limits of commerce, general welfare, and federal powers, the repeal of the Seventeenth Amendment might be unnecessary. But its impact on balancing the power of the majority should be considered, too. The ideas of revising the First Article and Seventeenth Amendment should be considered together to decide the recommended form of change. The aim should be to settle the dispute on federal power and restore corresponding States rights.

RESTRICT SPECIALISTS

Several specialty groups were created by the Constitution and subsequently through federal laws. The creators of the Constitution recognized the light and dark side of human nature, and created many provisions within the Constitution to keep special groups in check to avoid development of dictatorial powers over the rights of common citizens. The Supreme Court was established by the Constitution to judge the Constitution itself on what it says. But through the years the nine individuals in this branch of government have trended toward acting as an extension of party passion for power and privilege.

Congressional rules have allowed the existence of unionized government employees for many years. The inherent conflict of interest in this arrangement advances the basic union ambition for power, privilege, and greed. It has resulted in too many federal workers at too high a pay rate with too many benefits in comparison with the average American worker. It is unfair to all Americans and adds to the bulky cost structure of the federal government.

Also established about one hundred years ago by Congress is the Federal Reserve Banking System. This private board of bankers has unsuccessfully tried to control the private economy and inflation at great harm to common people. It can be argued that its policies have caused more extreme fluctuations to the economy and distress to the everyday citizen than if the economy were left to operate according to market fundamentals of supply and demand, and their policies leave many businesses guessing at the impact of changing federal policies on their own investments and long-term plans.

Figure 10-3 can be used for reference in following the ideas for restricting specialists in their activities.

RESTRICT SPECIALISTS – SUPREME COURT

The Constitutional framers' original intent for the Supreme Court was to judge cases in law based upon the laws of the United States established by the Constitution. In order to protect judges from subservient influences of the other branches of government, such as the way English judges were controlled by their King at that time, it was decided that judges should be appointed for life. They could not be removed from office as long as their behavior remained satisfactory.

The root purpose and power of the Supreme Court is established in the Third and Sixth Articles of the Constitution. The second paragraph of Article Six establishes the Constitution as the supreme law of the land, and the third paragraph binds all officers of federal and state governments to its supremacy by their oath of office to support the Constitution. The specific power of the Supreme Court is set forth by Article Three, which authorizes the Supreme Court System, its inferior courts, and its areas of jurisdiction.

The founders viewed the Constitution as the instrument of the rule of the people that was founded in the marvelous concept of the common law jury. The power of the common law jury was described in the Lessons Learned discussion of the rule of people versus board rule. The original idea of the common law jury was that it would decide both fact and law. It was not required to accept the judge's interpretation of the law, but was free to decide for itself what the law required. Primarily, the jury was restricted to preventing the government from taking a person's life or property. Remember, the founders believed the jury system was the people's defense against being overpowered by judges and the government.

Restoring Self-Government by the People
Restrict Specialists

- Supreme Court – Reverse Court's independence from law of the people
  ✓ Identify specific qualifications for serving as justices
  ✓ Establish term limits for justices
  ✓ Provide veto power over rulings when ratified by three-fourths of States
- Government Unions
  ✓ Abolish unions for all public service employees
  ✓ Return federal workers to protection by the people's statutes
  ✓ Use private contractors in place of government workers
- Federal Reserve
  ✓ Compare Federal Reserve System versus Congressional control
    ▪ Abolish authority to manipulate money supply and economy
  ✓ Limit authority to supervising banking policies
    ▪ Abolish Federal Reserve and assign this responsibility to Congress

Restoring Self-Government – Restrict Specialists
Figure 10-3

The common law jury was more or less abolished in 1895 by the Supreme Court when it ruled that juries must accept strict judicial instructions on the meaning of law as determined by the judge. Even if the jury believed a law to be unjust, it was required to follow the judicial interpretation and to rule only on the facts of the case. Thus the power of the common law jury, and the fundamental power of the people for self-rule, was abridged by the Supreme Court to its form today. This subtle change in viewpoint of the common law jury, combined with life terms for justices, has gradually evolved into the situation today where the Supreme Court has used judicial interpretation to tell the people what the Constitution means, and judicial review to declare laws void and assume power over the other branches of government. In order to restore the government of the people, the Court must be returned to serving public opinion and the power of the people to establish their own laws.

The Constitution's creators did not lightly consider the appointment of justices to office for life, and there were differing views on its merits. John Adams, for example, believed justices should be individuals that were very experienced in the law and who had exemplary morals. He feared the corruption of justices if they were subject to removal from office at the whim of the Executive or Legislature, such as was often the example of the English system of their day. As a result, he believed justices should be subservient to none and appointed for life. The idea still makes sense, and this is the system inherited from the founders that remains in existence today.

But there was an alternative view. Thomas Jefferson did not think the Supreme Court should be set up to rule without checks and balances, and that no human could be trusted for life. Jefferson recognized the modern explanation of the existence of the law of statistical distribution in human nature, but it was called common sense wisdom and understanding of human nature in their time. He knew the character of all judges would be as honest as all individuals, but not more so. The population of justices would be made up of those that were extremely honest, those that were extremely dishonest, and those in the middle that could be persuaded by the dominant group. It's the same today in the high court where the struggle continues between accepting the law of the Constitution and making obscure interpretations of it. There are extremes at each end and the dominant individuals may influence the middle. Jefferson believed that once appointed without elective control the justices are free to exercise their passions without the restraint of the public. And so it is today.

When there is a vacancy today on the Supreme Court, the political maneuvering that occurs to slant the court in an intended direction perfectly illustrates the political nature of the Court. Instead of a jury of impartial judges to rule on the content of the Constitution, it has evolved into a political group with the same passions for party, power, and privilege as those joined in the quest for power and distinction in the other branches of government. When Franklin Roosevelt began the move toward supreme federal power and his ambitious programs for involvement in private lives, he tried to use the Court to support his agenda. When this failed, he tried to increase the size of the Court from nine justices to fifteen so he could appoint six more justices during his administration that would support his New Deal plans and slant the Court in his favor. Fortunately, this ambitious grab for dictatorial power was rejected by the Legislature.

The ideas of judicial interpretation and review started almost immediately from the beginning of the U.S. Government. Jefferson again criticized the developing interpretations when he wrote that judicial action should preserve the original meaning of the Constitution and not what may be squeezed out of its text or invented from the wording. Further, during his first term, the idea of judicial review was first used, and Jefferson believed it established judicial power over the other branches of government by declaring laws void. He thought judicial supremacy would replace Constitutional supremacy and effectively remove the powers of a self-governing society. He believed the ultimate power of free people was in the people themselves. If the elite believed the people were too unenlightened to exercise their own control, Jefferson thought the people could be informed through education.

Today, judicial interpretation and review has resulted in growing judicial activism. The justification for judicial activism is usually described as court decisions based upon public policy and modern doctrine. The danger of this idea lies in the opportunity for a small group of individuals to assume the power of the people to decide public opinion. It defeats the entire precept of a self-ruling public.

Perhaps similar restrictions on power that have been suggested for the legislative and executive branches of government are needed for the judicial branch as well. If the Constitution is to be adjusted to rebalance power for modern times and to correct past errors and abuses, then maybe another look at the function and current restrictions on the court system is needed, too. Term limits for justices, veto power by people over court decisions, and more specific criteria for justice eligibility to serve on the court should be considered.

Thomas Jefferson, in his criticism of lifetime appointments, suggested that justices should be appointed to serve for a set period of time. He proposed up to six-year terms with the opportunity for renewal by the President and Senate as is done for initial appointments. His idea was to reduce the Court's independence from the law of the people. Today, the Court may assume a political slant that continues for many years without being checked because of entrenched life long members. With term limits, the construction of the court would be more in tune with the direction of the people's laws as the membership is routinely changed. Accordingly, if the President, Congressmen, and Senators are to be subject to term limits, then so should the Supreme Court Justices. If their terms were set at six years, similar to Senators today, then a limit of two terms would result in a maximum of twelve years' service on the Supreme Bench.

Most Americans today accept the absolute power of the Court to decide matters of constitutionality. Remarkably, many of the early constitutional minds did not accept its absolute power. Remembering the ideas of self-government by public opinion through the concept of the common-law jury to decide both fact and law, it is easy to understand the position of many of the founding individuals that the Court should exist strictly as a balancing branch of the federal government to support the will of the people. Jefferson believed there should be a veto power for the Congress and States if the rulings of the Supreme Court were contrary to the will of the citizens. He suggested that Court decisions might be overturned by a vote of two-thirds of Congress, or three-fourths of the State Legislatures. The entire purpose of Jefferson's suggestion was based upon the principle of the common-law jury, or the people's law.

Finally, if the Constitution is to be revised to bring the power of the Supreme Court into balance with the other branches, then perhaps qualification requirements for justices should be added such as is done for Congressmen, Senators, and the President. The advice and consent of the Senate has become a political sham when the President submits a candidate to the Senate for consideration. The political maneuvering to block an appointment, discredit the candidate, or to hurry a candidate into office is somewhat repugnant to modern Americans. Naturally the idea of the process is to avoid abuses of the appointive power of the President and "stacking" the Court to support an Executive agenda. The system worked well when Franklin Roosevelt attempted to influence the Court by pushing for more appointments. Even so, there are still candidates and judges with experience limited to scholastic theory. By adding a paragraph for qualifications, the primary credentials for a candidate could be used to screen potential appointees, and the Senate could then focus on the individual's commitment to the Constitution and support of people's law.

By establishing term limits and specific qualifications for justices, and by providing the Congress and States the ability to overturn decisions that do not support the people, then the power of the Court will be returned to its function as a balancing branch of government. Such changes should further balance the power between government branches and reduce the opportunity for the Court to make laws and establish policy through judicial interpretation and review without the consent of the people of the land.

RESTRICT SPECIALISTS – GOVERNMENT UNIONS

In the business world the introduction of unions to the cost structure results in inherent inefficiencies and waste. Companies that must absorb the extra costs of bulky contracts, stewards, meetings, and dues find it difficult or impossible to compete with a business that enjoys freedom from the added overhead. Still, it is a fundamental right and freedom for individuals to join together in the common cause of bargaining with their employer if there is a majority of workers in favor of it, and it should be as fiercely protected by Americans as freedoms of the Bill of Rights.

The presence of unions in government jobs is a differing situation that breaches the rights of private citizens. It begins with a conflict of interest that exists when government employees can directly influence the management of their activities through contributions. The private American citizen pays the wages and benefits of government workers through the contribution of taxes. The government worker uses a portion of these wages to pay union dues. The union organization uses a portion of its dues to support the campaign of a particular candidate for political office. In return, the elected official supports the union workers with approval of pay increases, improved health subsidies, and generous retirement programs. All of the pay increases, health care payments, and retirement contributions are at the expense of the private citizen. What could be clearer? During contract negotiations, government unions are sitting on both sides of the bargaining table, causing a conflict of interest that should be abolished.

Today this situation has resulted with government workers earning a higher-than-average salary with extraordinary health care payments and retirement plans. They earn more than the average private citizen. They receive a higher payment of health care premiums than the average private citizen. They receive matching retirement plan contributions higher than the average private citizen, and they can retire earlier with cost-of-living adjustments to their pay that few private pensions offer. They receive more vacation and holidays than the average private citizen. Much of this is the direct result of the contribution of union dues to campaign funds, and the rest is from slack management by elected officials. Worse, the government officials that negotiate these contracts often receive the same benefits for themselves.

The primary aim of any union is security and protection. In the case of labor unions it is the never-ending push for higher pay and larger benefits. But every grant of security to one group results with insecurity for the rest of society, in this case the private sector. The excesses of the government reduce the opportunities for the rest of society. The main aim in contributing to the campaign of a potential employer, such as a congressman, simply feeds the aim of a union for personal gain, power, privilege, and greed. When political leaders, who are federal workers themselves, are in collaboration with labor, it is at the expense of the community. The poorest and the unemployed suffer. Middle Americans carry the load.

Government workers should never receive more pay or benefits than the national average for similar skills and responsibilities in the private sector. Routine wage and benefit surveys should be used to control and adjust their compensation packages. Unions commonly use security and protection as a justification for their existence. One hundred years ago the country didn't have the employment protection laws of today, so the union movement was necessary to expose this need, but today, the federal laws of the good people of the country assure labor protection. If government employment laws establish the compensation packages, then their protection is assured, and the nation is relieved from the threats of union strikes or other misconduct to get its way.

The alternative to abolishing unionization of government jobs would be to turn over the operation to private companies where possible. By using private enterprise to operate government activities, then unions could petition for certification with the private employer. But strikes by public service workers must be prohibited as a condition for employment. Where private operations are impractical or not possible, unions would be abolished. But the American people are entitled to the lowest cost and most efficient operation possible.

Surely, one of the most liberating adjustments by federal and state governments would be to eradicate permissible government unions. These jobs should be returned to conservative levels and the security of the private citizen considered above that of the government employee. If these individuals want high pay and extraordinary benefits, they should enter the competitive world.

RESTRICT SPECIALISTS – FEDERAL RESERVE

The Federal Reserve System in use today is another example of Congress avoiding its fiscal responsibilities as established by the Constitution. The current system was established in 1913 during the first of the three great government expansions in the last one hundred years. As a result of earlier financial panics, there were several different attempts to establish government regulation of the economy through a central banking system. One was formed in 1791 just after the Constitution was adopted, but Congress did not renew its charter during President Madison's term of office and its operation was discontinued. There were various other banking systems that were started and later discontinued in the 1800s. The country suffered several banking panics, but a major breakdown in 1907 caused huge stock market declines and frenzied runs on banks and trusts that resulted with firm calls for reform of the banking system. Following these cyclical crises a number of private bankers secretly met with Senator Nelson Aldrich in 1910 at the exclusive retreat on Jekyll Island, Georgia to draft provisions for a new central banking system. It was enacted in 1913 with the passage of the Federal Reserve Act. This system has been in effect, with more than a dozen Congressional modifications, ever since.

The Federal Reserve is a system of private banks that work with the federal government. The Federal Reserve Board of Governors is composed of seven members appointed to a term of fourteen years by the President and confirmed by the Senate. The primary purpose of the central banking system was to supervise banking in the United States and address banking panics. Today, its function has grown considerably to include managing the nation's money supply and financial markets, stabilizing inflation, and strengthening the U.S. economic position in the world. Its record is poor. The effect of manipulating the nation's money supply and trying to influence the financial markets has resulted in some of the most extreme fluctuations in the economy, extraordinary inflation, crushing recessions, and currently the U.S. position in the world economy continues to deteriorate to the point that its leadership is threatened.

The law of infinity of actions provides a common sense explanation for the Federal Reserve's failure to adequately manage the U.S. economy. Simply stated, it's too complex. There are too many variables and interactions in the national and world market to be fully understood and controlled. The country appoints a group of academic theoretical economists that try to apply finite and unproven theory to a limitless economy of interactivity. Economists use a static analysis to extrapolate solutions, while people do something else in the real world to adapt to the situation; it's constantly changing, opposing, and interacting. They would do well to remember the lessons left by the father of economics, the great philosopher during the Era of Enlightenment, Adam Smith, who wrote, no statesman or council should be trusted with authority to regulate private citizens in how to use their resources, and it could never be more dangerous than in the hands people who are presumptuous enough to believe themselves equipped to exercise it. Alexander Hamilton agreed that the wealth of nations depends upon an infinite variety of causes including situation, climate, nature of government, the genius of citizens, and many more that are too complex to be hardly conceivable. Even so, economists of today valiantly attempt to model and predict the economy and its actions. To be sure, they have learned to understand a great deal, but the problem remains far beyond the scope of total understanding. Yet, in the arrogance of modern academia, mathematical economists of today, such as the Federal Reserve Board, attempt to manipulate the economy in the belief that they understand the total results of their actions. It just doesn't work.

If the government were honest with itself it would admit that it has no business interfering with the economy, especially if it can admit that the world economy is too complex to adequately control. If the economy could be regulated satisfactorily, then there would never have been a Great Depression, never inflation near eighteen percent, never a Savings and Loan disaster, never a sub-prime mortgage balloon and collapse, never a crushing recession with accompanying huge unemployment, and never many other unsettling fluctuations. The very idea that government can prevent, control, or mitigate economic problems has long been proven false. In fact, its involvement likely has caused or intensified extreme economic problems.

The economy and markets should be left to themselves to operate according to natural actions and interactions. Government can't prevent it or even ease it, despite its overconfidence. This would mean the Federal Reserve authority to manipulate the money supply and adjust economic conditions should be abolished. The expansion of the money supply is but another of the government's Ponzi-like schemes that deteriorates the worth of goods and savings. Each time the Federal Reserve authorizes an increase in the money supply, referred to today as quantitative easing, the prices of stocks and securities are affected, usually upward. The people receive a sense of relief as the values of their 401(k) plans are improved or restored, while in reality, the buying power, or true value of their savings, is diminished. It's a diabolical shell game.

It is time to review the current Federal Reserve System to determine both its worth and effectiveness, just like any good business would do in periodically reevaluating all of its systems and programs. It is likely that the Federal Reserve should be strictly limited to balancing banking actions throughout the country, if not eliminated altogether. Whether such a system is needed or not is so complex that no one really knows, and the opinions on it are about as numerous as the parameters it tries to monitor and control. One thing is certain, it has not been successful in stabilizing the economy, and this is reason enough to reexamine it. It is past time for the Congress to accept its responsibility to adequately control this beast, and perhaps send it to the recycle bin.

NATIONAL CONCERNS

The country today is involved in a national discourse on spending, debt, and government's role in daily life. The concern of the common citizen can be summarized as a conversation about the balance between physical and human resources. At the time the Constitution was formed the primary idea of government was to provide defense and fair play, and with little provision to provide for unfortunate citizens as the business of government. The changes of the last one hundred years have left the country debt-ridden and locked in debate over items such as social insurance, welfare, immigration, and different energy sources. Again, by studying the wisdom of the early founders, and by applying good business principles of common sense and fiscal responsibility, there are other options besides the run-of-the-mill thoughts of career politicians pandering to their public.

Alternatives for dealing with national concerns are condensed in Figure 10-4. It outlines proposed controls for social insurance and welfare, and for immigration security. Renewed emphasis on physical resource priorities and bringing back American economic strength anchors the narrative.

Restoring Self-Government by the People
National Concerns

- Social Insurance and Welfare
  - ✓ Limit Social Security and Medicare to needs-based programs
  - ✓ Increase payroll payments for Social Security and Medicare
  - ✓ Social Security changes
    - Establish federal repayment plan on trust fund bond loans
    - Eliminate ability of Congress to "borrow" from the Trust Fund
    - Establish private Social Security accounts protected from federal borrowing
    - Eliminate eligibility of high-income candidates
    - Protect retirement age eligibility on needs basis
    - Consider long-term phase out of the program
  - ✓ General Health Care Revisions
    - Establish private portable-for-life health insurance plans
    - Allow all plans to be available in all states
    - Set up coverage degrees from comprehensive to catastrophic
  - ✓ General Welfare and Human Resources Plans
    - Constitutional Amendment to authorize it
    - Establish maximum spending limits as a percent of GDP or national budget
- Immigration
  - ✓ Enforce current immigration laws
- Physical Resources
  - ✓ Develop infrastructure to restore national competitiveness
  - ✓ Eliminate debt, reduce Human Resource spending, stay out of wars
  - ✓ Research
    - Increase support of the space program and its agency
    - Establish national research policy for all energy sources
  - ✓ Subsidies
    - Abolish all subsidies, tax incentives, deductions, and credits
  - ✓ Economy
    - Eliminate federal debt and reduce spending
    - Let free markets operate to restore American genius and industriousness

Restoring Self-Government – National Concerns
Figure 10-4

NATIONAL CONCERNS – SOCIAL INSURANCE AND WELFARE

The ideas of social insurance and welfare for American citizens was really never considered as the role of government by most of the individuals involved in the creation of the Constitution. Thomas Jefferson thought charity is not the business of government. He thought charitable spending by the government wasted the people's labor while pretending to take care of them. Decades later, Horatio Bunce, who today probably would be called a conservative Constitutionalist, (See Chapter 7) reminded Representative Crockett that the national treasury is, "not yours to give."

Nevertheless, social insurance and welfare programs have been born through creative, and somewhat deceitful, Constitutional interpretation. In 1913 the progressive income tax on citizens was implemented, legally and via Constitutional Amendment, and the clash of American classes was magnified. The sweeping reforms of 1935 brought Social Security to the country and the beginning of an unaffordable major debt monster that has been mismanaged by the governing class. Medicare and welfare programs were initiated in 1965 and beyond, and these programs have continued to grow beyond bounds at the hands of a growing governing class with little priority for supporting the Constitution, but with major priority for personal career gains. Today, the Constitutional interpretations to add human resource programs and add controls and regulations to daily lives are the major source of the split between Americans. Average Americans, who are able to work and contribute, generally want the government out of their lives, want to keep the bulk of their earnings, and expect the government to provide common benefits for all, such as defense and fair trade. Those who are unable to work, and those who have chosen not to work, want more support from the government, including food relief, housing help, free medical care, and income for spending on additional comforts of life comparable to those that the working class have obtained. They believe they deserve it. The governing class believes in the program that offers the most return, that is, the most votes to further their political lives of power and privilege.

This large split of factions in the country, compounded by the mismanagement by the governing class, has resulted in an oppressive debt, an economy floundering under the restrictions of both heavy debt and government interference, and extraordinary unemployment for those wishing to support themselves. The country is left with broken national pride.

Beginning with the first large social insurance program, that is, Social Security, there is little doubt that this enormous program must be modified to control its size within the limits of national income. First, the distinction between paid-in programs and not paid-in (welfare) programs must be identified and accounted for separately. A partial example of the differences in types of human resource programs is shown in Figure 9-14. The imperative idea is that the government must honor its promises to individuals who are part of paid-in programs. These folks have been required to pay an insurance premium to the government during their working lives and were promised there would be supplemental income and medical insurance during old age. Conversely, the not paid-in side of human resource spending involves those who cannot or will not work during a part or all of their lives. For these folks, the government pledges to care for them with no restrictions on the amount of the national income designated for them.

The Social Security program is threatened with extinction because the governing class has avoided its responsibility in favor of remaining in office. Honestly, if an elected individual tried to change it alone, the result would be loss of office and long forgotten by colleagues. By accepting trust fund accounting methods that work like a Ponzi scheme, politicians have for decades pushed it upon future generations. There are two ways to solve the problem: reform Social Security to new standards, or eliminate it entirely. Ethically, either of these actions must be phased in over many years in order to assure the government's promises to those who rely on the programs today and in the near future. In any case, if the actions are not started before the nation's debt has exceeded its ability to support the program, it may be necessary to end it suddenly and with great harm to innocent Americans who have been required to contribute to the program for their entire lives.

A logical step toward saving the program would be to change the trust fund accounting deception. Contributions should be separated into private accounts and protected from a Congress borrowing to supplement its spending habit. The idea of putting Social Security contributions into a common fund and then allowing the government to borrow it for other uses, with little or no intent to repay it, is the obvious source of the problem. Now, there aren't enough new investors in the Ponzi scheme to continue the plan. Individual accounts would operate like an annuity or similar benefit plan, and each person would be able to see what would be available to them; it would be their investment in their own future, not a payment of debt heaped upon them by preceding generations. Anyone, who has paid into the system should not receive a greater-than-average return on their investment; in other words, they should not be permitted to draw from the income of younger generations as it has been done for the last seventy years.

The next important step, if the program were run like a business, would be to establish a long-term plan to repay the debt to the Social Security system. It's negotiable. It may be necessary to consider the total owed on bonds and debts by the general treasury, and to settle upon an amount to be repaid. It should not be zero, but should be a number that in good faith the government can commit to honoring. Repaying this debt will probably increase debt pressure on the country, but the prudent action would be to cut other programs, including not paid-in spending, in order to honor the government's promises.

In reviewing numerous conflicting reports from the government and the governing class, it's difficult to really know the situation, but most reports suggest that individual accounts and repaying the debt to the program will not be enough to save Social Security. Future changes may benefit young Americans, but presumably immediate help is needed now. If it is to continue through the crisis and remain in some form for future Americans, more changes will be necessary. Here is where the Social Security program should be changed to a needs-based system, where it will be paid only to those individuals that need it. If needs-based rules are enacted immediately, then a sufficient amount of pressure on the system may be relieved. It will be somewhat of a broken promise to some Americans, but supposedly these will be the ones who don't need the payments at all. It becomes a perfect example of revocable statutory rights, and the unfairness and ineffectiveness of central planning.

Today, Social Security recipients already receive graduated payments based upon their working income. As pointed out earlier in the discussion of the national budget, replacement of working income by Social Security ranges from ninety-four percent for low-income workers to twenty-six percent for those who have paid in the maximum. The highest-income worker receives a higher dollar amount, but not a proportionally larger amount, than the lowest-income worker, because of the large difference in percentage of working income allotted to each individual.

A needs-based modification would simply phase out payments to individuals who don't need the Social Security income. Each case today should be reviewed according to current income from private pensions, investment and passive income, and other sources of supplementary income. For example, an individual today that receives eighty percent of their working income from pension payments would be subjected to a reduced Social Security payment. This would likely affect many of those fortunate enough to have worked for prosperous companies that maintained generous benefits. Total income for those at eligible Social Security ages would be compared to their average working income, and Social Security payments would be phased down and out for high-income individuals. Here is where the class warfare begins again. There are affluent individuals that already receive eighty to more than one hundred percent of their pre-retirement age incomes and add the Social Security payment, too. A lot of retired government employees fall into this category. These individuals should be eliminated from the Social Security payroll in the near term. It is an unquestionable default on a government promise, but it is unlikely to harm those who don't need it, and it may be enough to salvage the system in the near term of fifteen years or so, and beyond.

The default on promises made by the government regarding Social

Security is nothing new. Most government ideas suggested today for correcting the problem involve increasing the full-retirement age. Usually, in order to protect the promise to the elderly already receiving payments, it is suggested that an increased retirement age would be enacted upon folks younger than say fifty-five. Naturally, this was done in the 1980s, supposedly to save the system then. How fair is that? Based upon an arbitrary cut off date, some folks began receiving full retirement benefits at a younger age, while younger folks paid more and longer into the system, but had to wait longer for the same benefits. Did this really work? Evidently not, because thirty more years of malfeasance have left the program just where it was in the eighties. If it's enacted again, will the system find itself in dire straights again in thirty years? If the management methods are not changed, and the Ponzi scheme is not eliminated, then the likelihood is great that the problem will remain for future generations to deal with. In addition, increasing the retirement age most hurts the lowest-income worker, and those without generous pensions. Take government employees for example. These folks can retire with large, cost-of-living-adjusted pensions in their fifties, and at tax payer expense, and the tax payer is often the lowest-income worker. How right is it to penalize a low-income worker by requiring them to work longer to receive the benefits of their government social insurance while paying taxes to support a federal worker who has been receiving a cost-adjusted pension for ten or fifteen years earlier?

If the decision is made to increase the retirement age for Social Security recipients, then it should be accompanied by raising the retirement age requirement for federal workers. Workers, who have been forced to pay a larger part of their income for Social Security, and without benefit of a private pension plan, should not be forced to wait longer than the government workers they support. Government pensions plans should not be available any sooner than the Social Security rules. At the present time it is age sixty-two, and the benefit payout should be reduced at comparable rates. This stops the individual who retires at fifty-five, draws a government payment that is paid for by the working class, finds another job to build a larger nest egg, and then hops on board the Social Security train. In any event, increasing the retirement age is not the answer and is destined to fail again.

The Medicare program is an absolute parallel to the Social Security problem; it must be reformed or eliminated according to Constitutional choices. But if it is to continue, again, the problem should be separated into two parts: paid-in, and not paid-in recipients. The not paid-in side of the program has been named Medicaid. Medicaid and uninsured health care should be accounted for in the federal budget and controlled as a separate category.

Immediate actions for the Medicare program would include a change to a needs-based program similar to the suggestion for the Social Security plan.

Everyone has been forced to pay in to the plan, but not everyone has an equal need. Some are fortunate enough to be eligible for an employer plan that continues into retirement, or that can be used as a supplement to Social Security. It's not uncommon for government retirees to again receive the luxury of these programs. More private companies each year elect to terminate retiree participation in the group health insurance plan.

The original intent of Medicare was to provide health care insurance for "uninsurable" older individuals with pre-existing conditions. Of course, they were denied insurance as a direct result of government regulations on health care insurance. So, 1965 was the banner year for commencing this huge program. Today, it is already a somewhat needs-based plan. Each person that totally participates in the Medicare program is required to pay a portion of the medical insurance premium. The Social Security Administration evaluates the tax returns for participants, and as total income increases, so does the amount of the medical insurance premium. As a Medicare participant's income increases, per their tax return before last, the portion of the Medicare insurance premium may grow by several hundred dollars per month. So, it is likely that the individuals who have paid the most into the Medicare program throughout their lives will probably be required to augment the payments for those who have contributed the least.

Since the Medicare plan is already somewhat graduated, then it would seem to follow that those who need it least, or those who have alternative plans, would be phased out of the Medicare system. Those who don't need it won't receive it. Those who can easily afford alternatives won't receive it. But before folks can be removed from the Medicare rolls, there must be alternative forms of health insurance available to all citizens. This is where a sensible change in health care laws to allow equal competition is necessary before folks can be phased out of Medicare.

Healthcare insurance is one of the problems today for folks ready to retire. If individuals have had medical insurance with their employers and suffered a major medical event, such as cancer treatment, heart attack therapy, diabetes, and other disqualifying ailments, they are tagged with the infamous "preexisting condition" term. As long as these folks remain with their employer's group health plan, their insurance can be continued. At retirement, though, if the employer does not extend medical coverage for its retirees, then the individual must find an independent source of insurance. In 1965 this was virtually impossible, because insurance companies would not accept a person with a preexisting condition, such as a recent heart attack victim. Today, the situation is somewhat similar. Insurance companies will deny coverage, but some states offer an alternative. It is often referred to as the "high risk pool." An individual with a preexisting condition can apply for medical coverage through this method and cannot be denied due to a preexisting condition. Naturally, there's a catch. It is extraordinarily expensive. Although the individual must pay the entire premium without partial assistance from an employer, the actual cost of the insurance is much higher, because the applicant with a preexisting condition is considered a high risk. These medical premiums can quickly exceed $10,000 or $12,000 per year for a single person expecting to pay first expenses of $1,000 to $5,000 deductible. It is out of reach for the common citizen. This would be the situation for a retiree under age sixty-five.

Once the retiree reaches age sixty-five Medicare is available without restrictions for a preexisting condition and at a much more affordable price, because the government subsidizes the insurance premiums, so the premiums are a nominal percentage of the person's retirement income. This was the original intent of Medicare insurance.

Medicare does not offer total coverage; that is, it pays a percentage of expenses like the majority of employer sponsored health care plans. But, many retired folks don't feel financially secure enough to be able to pay the costs for a catastrophic event, so they elect to purchase supplementary health insurance. Some are fortunate to be able to use continuing coverage from an employer as the supplementary plan, and often this is less expensive. Others, that want a supplementary plan, must sift through more than a half-dozen different supplement options, and purchase one of these. Their additional cost easily can be in the $5,000 range.

What really, then, do Americans want from health care? Is health care a fundamental right? Many claim it is. Of course, what they are referring to is a vested right, not an unalienable right. Vested rights, such as health care, Medicare, and so forth, keep the government in the business of human resources.

Probably no American wants to see a fellow citizen denied health care. It just doesn't seem right. The answer may be locked simply in government regulations. The medical insurance industry is extremely regulated by administrative laws. It's clear that all programs are not available in all states. A typical example can be observed with available Medicare Advantage programs. One area of the country may have a dozen or more available insurance choices, while a few miles away, but across state borders, there may be three or so. How equitable is this to all Americans?

First, the health care laws need to be revised to accomplish three priorities: each person's health care plan should be portable for life, all programs and companies should be available in all states, and a variety of options for personal situations should be available. A health care plan that can transfer with individuals throughout their lives would allow them to maintain payments and coverage as long as they wish it, without the threat of termination in the event of developing a major illness. The insurance companies would be able to collect premiums for a lifetime to offset later expenses. This change would take employers, and government, out of the health care business. Employers that choose to do so might simply offer a payment of a certain amount for all employees to use on health care. So, the person that changes jobs frequently may keep the same insurance, and the portion of the premium paid by the employer may vary from zero to one hundred percent of the premium cost. This person would then be able to carry their insurance from the beginning of their working life through retirement.

At the same time, employers could get out of the health care insurance business if they elect to do so. Providing health care payments to employees would return to a competitive option. Those who choose to provide it would do so to attract top-notch workers. Employers should never be forced by government to be the source of health care insurance. It started out as a fringe benefit, then grew to be expected, and now the government believes it should be imposed upon businesses.

It's obvious that a portable plan could not work with the current restrictions on coverage within state boundaries. Is this equal trade in commerce? All plans should be available in all areas according to the business decisions of the insurance companies. Where there is an adequate market, free enterprise will fill the need. The clumsy and restrictive situation that varies by state today is the direct result of clumsy and restrictive regulation by government.

With portable policies and the lifting of state restrictions, the insurance companies should be free to offer varying degrees of coverage for their clients. Some individuals live hand to mouth and don't have any money in reserve. Frequently, these people want comprehensive medical plans that pay virtually all expenses. Others don't need to have every office visit paid, and may even want a high deductible program, so they are more interested in catastrophic coverage, such as a plan to pay the $200,000 bill on a heart attack. Everyone doesn't need a family plan, either. The young, single person, in good health and just starting a career, may simply want a policy for a major event such as a car accident.

In all likelihood, tailoring the health care laws to permit free enterprise across state lines, with portability for life, and with numerous degree-of-coverage options to suit different situations, would eliminate the need for government intrusion into the health care of private citizens. But what about the folks who simply can't afford health care? The cost of a policy would simply take too big a bite out of their paycheck, or they are unable to work, so they receive public assistance for food, housing, and other forms of income. For a lot of people the Medicaid program is used, but it is normally limited to children of parents below a poverty line, or disabled persons. Many more citizens do not qualify. If the government is to remain in the human resource business, then their help should come in the form of subsidized insurance premiums. This should be added to the long list of not paid-in human resources that the government operates today. Individuals who qualify would seek assistance at the same time they ask for food stamps, housing assistance, and such. The government would pay for part or all of their private health premiums according to their situation. A disabled individual, for instance, might remain in the program for life, with all the same privileges of portability, national scope, and variety of options. Today, the American people do not tell those receiving food assistance where they must shop. It seems a health insurance subsidy would help the same people make their own choices without direction of a bureaucracy.

Still, there is the issue of health care costs. It goes up every year. There's a lot of blame and finger pointing. Doctors and hospitals are accused of greed and inefficiency. The insurance companies are high on the target list for greed. But don't forget trial lawyers and the blame of lawsuits and malpractice insurance costs for physicians and hospitals. Many years ago it was simpler when people expected to pay for their medical expenses. The doctor came to the house, checked out the patient, and then sent a bill that the family paid out of pocket. Some families had a somewhat inexpensive insurance policy to cover expenses for major illnesses and hospitalization, and many did not. A lot of folks simply didn't like buying insurance.

Certainly it has changed today with the advances of technology in medication and the hospital. Physicians use expensive machines that can look deep into the body for diagnosis and treatment. Thousands of expensive wonder drugs have been developed to control the effects of illness. The unfortunate consequence is that the cost is too much for the average American budget, so insurance is needed if, and when, an illness or accident strikes. Tort reform has been suggested. It might help, but probably not much. Many industries have asked for limitations on lawsuit judgments in the past by claiming that the liability insurance costs made the costs of their products unaffordable. There is likely a degree of truth in the remark, but when tort reform has been enacted, the expected reduction in cost simply didn't materialize. The costs of the product continue to rise. To be sure, the health care industry, in association with the insurance companies, should support defined and ongoing cost reduction programs in order to offer a cost effective product. If tort reform is needed to add a degree of fairness to the situation, then by all means pass it.

Today, the country must deal with the provisions of a new health care plan developed by the governing class and its private contractors. Many of its key abuses are listed in Figures 8-5 and 8-7. This huge and intrusive legislation has stretched the boundaries of the Constitution and ignored true governing principles of public opinion. Many of the provisions, such as adoption credit and the requirement to report gold sales greater than $600, simply have nothing to do with offering equal provisions for American health care.

The government's move into the human resources business more or less started with the advent of Social Security, or at least this was the first substantial leap into the business of social insurance. It was enabled by the authorization to collect graduated taxes from individuals to support the program, and about 1965 the idea of welfare for unfortunate and deserving individuals was commenced. The passage of the legislation to launch ideals of The Great Society widened the great rift between factions of the country. There are those that believe it is a necessary part of a centralized democracy to assure equality for all citizens. The basic idea of a central democracy is the assumption that all people share the same needs, morals, and purpose in life. Elementary laws of nature do not agree with such assumptions. Those against a government becoming the administrator of a huge welfare plan believe such programs violate the most basic freedom of the individual to enjoy the results of their personal efforts and achievements without having it stripped from them without their consent.

Nevertheless, the use of Constitutional interpretation has left the country with a huge, expensive welfare system to fund and administer. Obviously many citizens today believe the government can be used to soothe the effects of natural disasters and to provide subsistence assistance to those who are unable to provide for themselves. The question is, though, what is a reasonable amount? Should the country sacrifice funding of physical resources, infrastructure, or defense? Should the country redistribute all of its money to the point that roads, bridges, airfields, communication, and defense are reduced to nothing so that a very few elite can support the majority of the country receiving public assistance? It sounds like a feudal government. Today, the government has elected to borrow money to give to the deserving few. Evidently the belief is that the country will continue to grow and prosper until the economy is large enough to repay the borrowed money. When is this expected to begin? A common sense look at the debt history in Figure 5-1 suggests no time soon; the $8.3 trillion debt in 2006 has exploded to more than $15 trillion in 2011, and the Congress is arguing over allowing it to grow larger.

If the Congress is expected to rationally run the U.S. Government like the good stewards of the treasury they were elected to be, then the welfare spending on not paid-in services and benefits must be limited to affordable levels. The expenses for paid-in and not paid-in programs are shown in Figure 9-14. Good stewards of the treasury should limit the percentage of the budget that can be spent on not paid-in benefits. If there isn't enough to go around, then the benefits must be reduced or revenue increased through taxes. Is it logical that when the country suffers during recession, millions are out of work, and the economy barely can be maintained, that the not paid-in benefits should remain at the same levels? Just like the government workers that are not suffering layoffs or pay reductions, those on the welfare rolls may continue to receive payments at pre-recession levels, while the everyday taxpayer may receive pay reductions or part-time layoffs, but is expected to carry the same share of the welfare load without relief.

The welfare programs should not be continued without a Constitutional Amendment to authorize their existence according to prevailing public opinion. If it's the people's will, then an amended Constitution will settle the fractious dispute. Firm budgetary limits must be established to abolish borrowing in order to fund welfare projects. Limits are needed to protect all Americans and their income, and to protect the security of the country. If it is the nation's will to provide welfare in a controlled manner, and if similar restraints are developed for the paid-in programs as previously discussed, then the nation can settle down to working together for the prosperity of its children, and in peaceful acceptance of the new Constitutional provisions that are passed openly and supported by the public opinion in majority.

NATIONAL CONCERNS – IMMIGRATION

Another human resource issue of national concern is the immigration policy of the United States. One of the Congressional enumerated powers established by the Constitution and listed in Figure 4-1 is to establish uniform rules of naturalization. It follows, then, that it is one of the first responsibilities of the President to enforce the laws established by Congress. The predicament of the country today with millions of illegal aliens in the United States is the direct result of decades of neglect by both the President and Congress to enforce these laws and to protect the country's borders. Protecting border-states was perhaps the primary driving factor in forming the first union of states.

There has always been a history of fear and hysteria concerning immigrants. In the country's early history during the presidency of John Adams, there was a fear of being overrun by fleeing French citizens and Caribbean refugees. There was also a fear of the "wild" Irish trying to escape the horrors of the Irish Rebellion. Later, there have been fears of too many Chinese, Japanese, and Germans. Today, it is Mexican citizens. The major difference, though, for many Americans, is that so many of the Mexican people have entered in an under handed and illegal way. The problem seems to have grown for decades until it has caused pressure on the average citizen and government spending as a whole. Again, the country is split over the solution, and career politicians use it for political advantage, rather than taking careful and rational actions to protect the interests of the country and to protect the border-states. If a candidate can appeal to the raw emotions of a group of people, such as Hispanics, in order to collect their votes and help ensure a continuing career, then the career politician is simply not deterred in driving a wedge between Americans.

As a result, many politicians believe the solution to the illegal alien problem can be found by waiving the country's naturalization laws to overlook illegal entry into the U.S. Generations of Presidents and the Congress have avoided enforcing existing law in order to avoid ruffling the feathers of the Hispanic group and losing their votes. The core action is to support the Constitution and the law of the land. Don't ignore the law, but openly change it if it is not satisfactory. George Washington left this insightful advice during his Presidency. Without the Constitution, a free people's mutual contract, then a self-governing people have nothing.

Clearly, there would not be a major illegal alien problem in the United States if the naturalization laws had been enforced in the first place. It would have been impossible for an illegal alien to provide adequate documentation to find employment. Without jobs, there would be no desire for people to secretly enter the country, because only those with proper documentation could find work. Similarly, without proper documentation, welfare benefits could be denied, and thus another reason to enter the country without papers would be eliminated. Unbelievably, though, some states support the idea of providing welfare benefits to illegal immigrants.

The solution to the problem lies in the law. If the laws of the country are properly enforced, illegal employment will be eliminated. The flow into the country probably will be reversed. Those planning to invade the country's borders will soon abandon their ideas when it is learned that it is nearly impossible to find work without documentation, and those that are currently in the U.S. illegally will soon want to return to their homeland, because there will be no work for them, either. A large majority of illegal aliens maintain allegiance to their homeland, not the United States, and so they will return to their original homes and families. It is there they should work to advance the cause of their own nation.

In today's world, however, there is a more insidious threat to the border-states and the country at large. It is the terrorist threat from hostile aliens. After the attacks on the country in 2001, and the continuing military actions by the U.S. in retaliation, these same enemies continue with schemes to enter the U.S. and kill its citizens. Here again is one of the primary reasons for developing a union of states; defense of the country and its borders. It is important for the country's leaders to assess the terrorist threat to enter the country through unprotected borders and to implement satisfactory surveillance and restraints. First, the border citizens deserve the protection as promised by the Union. Second, the country at large deserves protection as promised in the Constitution.

The neglect in enforcing naturalization laws and in protecting the nation's borders is a crucial element of Congressional and Presidential malfeasance. It has continued for decades until it has reached crisis proportions. By enforcing existing laws first, and then by implementing satisfactory protections at the border, order and security can be restored, with honest treatment for all citizens and legal resident aliens.

NATIONAL CONCERNS – PHYSICAL RESOURCES

The original purposes for establishing the Union of the States with a Constitution were for a united defense, coordination of central services, and to provide a united position in foreign relations. The central services included assuring fair trade and equal treatment of physical resources. The budget today, as shown in Figure 9-13, can be categorized into super-functions. These include defense, human resources, interest payments, administrative functions, and physical resources. The physical resources function is subdivided into energy, natural resources, commerce, transportation, and community development. Science, space, and technology are listed under other functions, but might be considered spending on the physical resources of the nation, also.

The country's physical resources are part of the foundation of its strength and stability. Three forms of economic real wealth have been reviewed: agriculture, mining, and manufacturing. Thomas Jefferson referred to four pillars of prosperity: agriculture, manufactures, commerce, and navigation. Jefferson believed this basis of prosperity must not be encumbered with too many regulations or oppressed by fiscal demands. His advice unhappily has been forgotten. Today, the nation's business and commerce are thoroughly crippled by mountains of regulations and taxes. United States companies are at a decided disadvantage when competing with other countries that enjoy operating under minimum restraints.

Government investment in physical resources and infrastructure is diluted, because a larger part of the budget is needed each year for human resource commitments. There is less money available for research and the infrastructure. Instead of the government investing in national projects that are too large and beyond the capability of private enterprise, it thins its commitments for keeping the country's infrastructure strong, in deference to huge human resource plans. Instead of attempting to control and regulate industry, the government should aid free commerce by helping build or repair efficient roads, bridges, airfields, communication systems, and other projects for the mutual benefit of all people. Perhaps nothing contributed to economic booms more than the development of the fabulous interstate highway system conceived in the fifties. This was an example of government participating in building a national infrastructure for national security and commerce. It's probable that even those who conceived it did not envision the full effect that it would have for the country's economy.

Competition and spending on physical resources are not incompatible with human services so long as they are balanced within the limits of affordability, and human resources are not permitted to make physical spending programs ineffective. It is the productivity of the American workers that has made America great. Allowing human resource programs to grow out of control, to the point that is necessary to borrow money to pay for them, restricts American productivity and weakens the economy. The huge debt is largely the result of overspending for human resources and the national defense. The cost of the long, drawn-out wars in the Middle East have cost far more than the country could afford for many years. The debt on these wars must be repaid as soon as practical. When war costs are combined with growing human resource spending, it has become impossible for the economy to grow enough to pay the country's expenses. Fiscal limits on human resource spending must be established, probably as a percentage of income, to free the genius and achievement of true contributors to the economy.

NATIONAL CONCERNS – PHYSICAL RESOURCES – RESEARCH

The federal government has a long history of involvement in research and development of resources and for national security. One of the most prominent is the Manhattan Project of the Second World War where government resources were utilized to develop an atomic weapon. Following this, for many years the government has been the primary provider of enriched uranium to fuel nuclear power plants, and the government invested research and development for alternative enrichment methods, such as the more efficient gas centrifuges. Perhaps the most dominate research and development activity for the last fifty years has been the space exploration programs of NASA.

The government continues to use the resources of its universities and private contractors to do research and development, but it has allowed much of the work to be distorted by subsidies. Many of today's development projects have become beasts of political maneuvering, both by the contractors and by career politicians. Each project should stand on its own merits and its practicality should be justified without hidden tax credits or false incentives to support it.

One of the great benefits of NASA's programs has been its willingness to freely share developed technologies for use in private industry. Many modern contributors to the quality of American life today are the direct result of NASA research. It includes communications, medical advancements, transportation, computers, and more. Entire industries with great jobs have been born from the effects of space exploration programs. In fact, the entire world has benefited from America's space exploration efforts. Unbelievably, though, America's governing class has chosen to ignore, or doesn't understand, the fabulous benefits of NASA activities. It has been decided to scale back the program. It is the unfortunate result of the need for cash to pay for a monstrous human resource commitment to not paid-in supplements and welfare. If allowed to continue, the payments to the nonworking citizenship will drag working folks into their ranks and smother the nation's economy and hopes.

Space exploration should be aggressively resumed. It shouldn't receive a disproportionate budget share, but it must be continued strongly. The best technology, the best jobs, and the best economic help will come from the cutting edge of efforts to explore the solar system. It fires the imagination and the pride of the American spirit. The net result will be a better quality of life for people at all levels. It fuels the opportunity for the disadvantaged to grow, instead of leaving them helplessly tied by the strings of public assistance.

Research programs similar to the NASA plan should be implemented in the search for new energy sources. But the government must provide its support without prejudice or interference. All sources of energy should be given opportunities to develop and be evaluated. Those that are economical and affordable will succeed on their own merits when the time is right. The main competitors today are petroleum, natural gas, coal, and nuclear energy sources. Sadly, the competition among these methods has been biased as a result of government interference. Restrictions on exploring new sources and using new methods stifle development of cost effective energy sources. Subsidies should be dropped, unreasonable restrictions removed, and each energy source must be allowed to offer itself at a real cost. The markets and American ingenuity will decide which is best.

Eventually, everyone knows, much of the inexpensive energy of the twentieth century will be exhausted. Either alternative sources will be found, or lives will change drastically, everywhere all over the Earth. The conversion may be disruptive and inconvenient, or it may occur naturally through the effects of market forces. Of course, many fear the continued use of fossil fuels harms the environment. As a result, another race is on to develop a form of clean, renewable energy. It is so important to the country's security, economic development, and apparent ecological preservation that the government could reasonably choose to help with research and development. Simultaneous programs to develop economic delivery of new energy resources are needed. But this should be done without the undue influence of tax credits and subsidies. All these do is distort and confuse the search for the best solution.

The green revolution that is developing in the twenty-first century includes a wide variety of new energy sources and ingenious ideas. It should be no surprise if the genius of the free American society is a primary developer of new and clean energy sources for the future. Entrepreneurs are exploring the use of plant matter, solar power, wind and wave power, geothermal energy from the depths of the earth, tidal forces, hydroelectric energy, and more. It can be an exciting time to live when the next type, or types, of energy have been developed into economical applications. It will mean the continuing prosperity of Americans and the rest of the world. The entire world will benefit from the next great discovery, but it will not come from the central planning of the U.S. government, or any other government.

The interference of the federal government by attempting to persuade the American people in a certain direction by manipulating their behavior with subsidies, favored loans, and tax credits will only delay the discovery of the best solutions and tie Americans to the wishes of the governing class. Like all similar subsidy and tax incentive programs before, the current government plans result with investments in favorite and preferred companies. The favorites receive a disproportionate advantage and grow richer to allow them to continue to contribute to their sponsors' political campaigns. It's conflict of interest, again. There are glaring examples. The wind farm program sponsored by the governing class includes special tax breaks for participating companies that often allow them to avoid paying any taxes. The situation with General Electric shows this effect. GE owns about half of the wind farms in the country today, and their tax credits from these developments have given them a huge advantage over competitors. The company avoids paying income tax and can funnel a portion of the tax savings into the campaign coffers of their government sponsors.

Many Americans are interested in electric cars. But is it time, yet? The cars are extremely expensive, and the useful life of the battery package for a totally electric powered car has been projected to be about seven years. The cost to replace the battery package may be about $6,000 or $7,000. But the government is offering a tax credit for some of the first individuals that buy an electric car. The idea is to help make up the large cost difference, and this in turn will help the manufacturer refine the product.

Even with a tax credit, though, the owner of an electric car may never break even. Figure 10-5 compares hypothetical electric and gas cars in three different case scenarios. The pay back period, or the time required to recover the extra cost of the more expensive electric car depends upon roughly four factors: the difference in purchase prices, the cost of gasoline, the number of miles the motorist expects to drive each year, and the equivalent miles per gallon for each vehicle. Two columns under each example case of Figure 10-5 show comparisons between electric and gas cars under different circumstances. The purchase prices for the cars were estimated at $40,000 for the electric vehicle, and $22,000 for an average sized gas machine. Two different gasoline prices were used: in Case 1 the gas price is estimated at $3.50 per gallon, and a more expensive gas estimate was used in the second case example. Annual mileage driven in each case is shown as 15,000 and 25,000 miles respectively in each case. Finally, the miles per gallon estimates used were twenty-four mpg for the gas car, and an equivalent rate of fifty mpg for the electric car.

Sharp consumers who do a little quick arithmetic quickly realize that the extra $18,000 they would have to pay for an electric car ($40,000 - $22,000) will never be recovered by their gas savings.

Savings and Payback for Electric Car

	Case 1		Case 2		Case 3 No Tax Credit	
Estimated Gasoline Price	$3.50 per gallon		$4.50 per gallon		$4.50 per gallon	
Miles Driven per year	15,000		25,000		25,000	
Type of Car	Electric	Gas	Electric	Gas	Electric	Gas
Estimated Cost						
Manufactured Cost ($)	40,000	22,000	40,000	22,000	26,400	22,000
Less Tax Credit ($)	7,500	-	7,500	-	-	-
Net Cost after Credit ($)	32,500	22,000	32,500	22,000	26,400	22,000
Electric Car Premium ($)	10,500		10,500		4,400	
Estimated Driving Cost						
Cost per Gallon	3.50	3.50	4.50	4.50	4.50	4.50
Miles per Gallon	50	24	50	24	50	24
Cost per Mile ($)	0.070	0.146	0.090	0.188	0.090	0.188
Miles per Year	15,000	15,000	25,000	25,000	15,000	15,000
Fuel Cost per Year ($)	1,050	2,188	2,250	4,688	1,350	2,813
Cost Savings per Year ($)	1,138		2,438		1,463	
Years to Save Premium	9.2		4.3		3.0	
Replacement Batteries						
Replacement Cost ($)	6,000		6,000		6,000	
Years to Payoff Batteries	5.3		2.5		4.1	
Years to Recover Total Cost						
Electric Car Premium ($)	10,500		10,500		4,400	
Replacement Batteries ($)	6,000		6,000		6,000	
Total Cost ($)	16,500		16,500		10,400	
Years to Recover Total Cost	14.5		6.8		7.1	

Savings and Payback for Electric Car
Figure 10-5

The government knew this, too, so they offered a $7,500 tax credit to entice early buyers to try out the new technology. Federal bureaucrats believed this would help auto manufacturers continue to refine their electric products. So, after the tax credit is deducted the consumer effectively pays about $10,500 more for the electric car, shown as a premium in the figure. Then, following the arithmetic in the first two cases, the driver would save about $1,138 per year if gas is cheaper and less miles are driven, and an owner that would have paid more for gasoline and covered more miles would save up to $2,438 each year.

The net result is that it could take a little more than four years for the more active driver to recover the $10,500 premium, but something like nine years to save the difference in the first case. Nine years is longer than the projected battery life of the electric car. If the cost of replacement batteries is figured into the example, the electric car could take over fourteen years to pay off the extra costs; and – new batteries would be due again!

The consumer has to be quick to get the tax credit, however, because it applies only to the first 100,000 units or so that are built. Even so, the governing class can't seem to write a comprehensive tax bill that isn't subject to abuse. The latest on electric cars is the golf cart fiasco. Certain golf cart designs meet the requirements for the tax credits. As a result, enterprising golf cart manufacturers noticed it and advertised that a new $6,400 golf cart could be obtained for free with tax credits.

So what would be a reasonable deal for an electric car? Case 3 of Figure 10-5 shows a possible scenario with no tax credit. If electric car costs can be developed to achieve a selling price of around $26,400 for a driver of 25,000 miles per year who is countering gas prices of $4.50 per gallon, then the electric car driver would make back the extra $4,400 cost in about three years; that's not too bad. Car companies must do more about the battery life, though. Even though the electric car owner in the third case would be saving money for the next four years, the specter of a new battery package still hangs over the owner like dark cloud.

Another problem right now is the flammability of lithium, the primary element of electric car batteries. Current batteries are susceptible to catching fire, so car companies encapsulate them in a safety case for protection. Unfortunately, there have been some battery fires anyway, so the problem isn't totally solved yet. American engineers will solve it, though.

It's obvious to common-sense Americans that the electric car technology is not quite ready, but apparently not to the elected officials who sponsor the special give-away. Instead of plowing money into false incentives such as tax credits, if the government would sponsor independent research for all Americans to use in competition, then suitable development might be achieved, and at a faster rate, too. Instead, the bureaucrats have already decided that this is the automotive fuel of the future, and they have tried to influence wealthy Americans to try it through a give-away program at the expense of modest income citizens.

If and when the technology is ready, then car sales will be brisk, electrical charging stations will be built, and the dependence on gasoline will be phased out. Enterprising individuals, companies, and the free market system will see to it in short order.

The new effort is to push Americans into using more expensive, but presumably more efficient, fluorescent light bulbs instead of the common incandescent bulb. This push by the governing class is not so much tax credits, but by board rule of administrative law. A penalty is proposed for those who refuse to make the change. Remarkably, the leading producer of fluorescent bulbs is General Electric, again.

The list of subsidies and tax credits for green energy is exhaustive. There are ethanol subsidies to lower the cost of ethanol in hopes that it will be used. The tax credit list includes solar panels, heat pumps, specialized heat pumps, water heaters, and furnaces. The idea of credits and subsidies to encourage citizens to pay more for equipment and energy sources that help the environment sounds noble. But it masks the harm it does to the country and the development of true and economical sources of energy. It plays to preferential favorites, hampers development, and leads the nation into blind canyons. If the people authorize the government to spend tax money to help in the search for new energy sources, then it should be limited to research. Programs and spending should be distributed equally and according to the prevailing probability of success for each type. But the American market should be the determining factor for the success or failure of each alternative energy source. No subsidies and no tax credits should be allowed to cloud the true cost and efficiency of any single source.

NATIONAL CONCERNS – PHYSICAL RESOURCES – SUBSIDIES

As unequal and abusive as are many of the green energy subsidies today, the country's record of subsidizing favored industries is long. One of the first manufactures to receive subsidies was the farm industry. Farmers have begged for help from the government almost since the Union's birth. Today, the agriculture subsidy list would fill a set of encyclopedias. Certain crops, such as milk and organic farms receive subsidies. One of the more remarkable situations involves the land banks. This preposterous program has left most Americans scratching their heads. Here, the government pays individual farmers to do nothing; that is, to leave their pastures idle in order to draw a generous subsidy check from the U.S. government. Who dreams up this stuff? For many years, the voting strength of the agricultural community was enough to persuade the career politician to hand out gifts like this to the voting public. Today, though, large agribusiness companies receive the majority of the subsidy money, so Americans aren't really giving a hand out to the family farm, but to giant corporations. Many wealthy individuals and celebrities, such as entertainers and sports stars, collect on the advantages as well. By designating a portion of their estates as organic farms, these wealthy non-farmers reap tax breaks in yet another example of the abuse of central planning programs. The true solution, of course, is no subsidy or tax break. Every product should stand against market forces on its merits. Naturally, the prices will rise when subsidies are removed, but the true price will be known, and the market will make a natural selection.

But the non-farming citizen can receive a subsidy, too; there are dozens of programs. One of the largest is the mortgage interest and real estate tax deduction for homeowners. It's another inequitable treatment of taxpayers. In reality today, most of these deductions go to folks who have very large mortgages with hefty real estate taxes. The low income homeowner with a small loan and modest taxes usually does not get the tax break, because their payments are too low to qualify for the deduction. Those who still can't afford a home receive nothing. But they pay real estate taxes, too, theirs is included with the rent, so the landlord takes the deduction. Those who don't receive a deduction contribute to those that do. It's difficult to see the fairness of it all.

The subsidy list goes deep. The depreciation dodge is a big one for all businesses. Assets that are resold may be depreciated over and again. Those who use this method for reducing the tax bill often wind up repaying part of it later, and it adds enormous complications to the accounting. Depletion is a similar tax reduction method used by businesses that deal in consumable products such as gas, oil, and timber. In addition, many workers receive a per diem allowance for meals while they are on travel and are able to deduct a standard amount from their taxable income. In 2010, it was possible to claim a standard meal allowance of $46 to $59 per day while on business travel, and the income deduction can range from fifty to eighty percent of the allowance. If the individual receives eighty percent of the maximum, this means the people pay $47.20 of the person's meal expenses each day.

Government flood coverage is another example of a subsidy to encourage people to live in dangerous areas, such as coastal flood plains. Each year the newscasts are filled with flood disasters and reports that the U.S. government is providing financial help to rebuild. The tragedy for the folks is terrible, but why must cautious citizens pay to rebuild these properties year upon year? Worse, many of these cases involve property owned by very wealthy Americans, such as Malibu or other exclusive shore property.

All subsidies should be stopped. The government has no authority to be in this business. The abuses are infamous. The waste is enormous, unreasonable, and deceitful. Some Americans, that know how to work the system, reap monumental benefits from the treasury while most never receive a single payment. Let the markets work openly, honestly, and without interference from a governing class working in its own self-interest.

NATIONAL CONCERNS – PHYSICAL RESOURCES – ECONOMY

What has happened to the American economy? Why has its growth slowed to a snail's pace? Where is the world leadership that Americans have come to expect from their homeland? Perhaps nothing perplexes and worries the mature American public more, especially those who experienced the grand era of U.S. inventiveness and economic leadership in the last century. Today U.S. economic leadership appears to be vanishing, or already gone.

There are many reasons for the complex problem of the country's sour economy and high unemployment so there can't be a single solution for the problem. Market forces, such as supply and demand, are primarily influenced by the activity and health of three parts of the American economy; these are individuals, corporations, and the government. The government and private individuals are hampered by burdensome debt. Healthy corporations are reluctant to invest until their confidence is restored in the demand side of market forces.

The long economic sleep is probably rooted in the unmanageable debt burdens of both individuals and the government. The loss of jobs associated with the poor economy is complicated by the migration of jobs to foreign countries. In turn, high debt and lost jobs caused fallen market demand that is likely to continue for several years.

Accumulation of huge debt has continued for decades. The amount of private individual debt has increased for more than thirty years until it burst and collapsed around 2007. This situation means consumers aren't as able or likely to spur economic growth.

Government debt is the direct result of poor management of the nation's business by the governing class. Combined with long and expensive wars, the long history and development of social spending on welfare and social insurance programs have built a debt obligation that may be insurmountable. The debt problem persists at all levels: federal, state, and local. If the trend isn't reversed soon, then the security of American freedom may be at stake, and its citizens vulnerable to the substitution of the Constitution with central planning by the governing class.

The huge debts coupled with the limitless migration of American jobs to other countries are major economic problems. Millions of jobs have been transferred to other countries in the last twenty-five years. Thousands of factories have been closed. Call centers, engineering, and accounting jobs have been sent to the Philippines, India, and China. Thousands of factories have been set up in Mexico and China, and yet the migration of millions of Mexicans to the U.S. continues.

The result of the mass transfer of American production has caused America to evolve from a nation of producers to a nation of consumers. Production of much of the three forms of real wealth, agriculture, mining, and manufacturing has been lost. Now, the nation has begun to consume without producing. The country's residual wealth is being consumed with unemployment and welfare programs as more Americans everyday are left without employment. A country founded on the ingenuity and industry of its people is left with a breaking, or broken, national spirit.

Heavy, burdensome debt and massive job migration cause falling market demand. According to the elementary economic concept, supply and demand will seek a balance. Some theorists believe the main constraint on economic growth is supply, and that technical and financial innovation will improve productivity and foster growth in the labor force. This has been true somewhat for much of the country's history. Henry Ford's assembly line ideas are an example of this principle that has advanced beyond imagination. The difference today is that new jobs are sent offshore as fast as they are developed. Americans have been told that only the most technical, advanced, and high-paying jobs will remain in the U.S., so there is no worry over the tremendous losses they have experienced. It just hasn't developed as envisioned.

The concept of relying on technical innovation really didn't consider the second side of the market idea of demand. If there is no demand, there is no need for more supply, and the market is dead. Demand today, is met by foreign producers. Healthy corporations have been criticized for "sitting on mountains of cash." Of course they are. With diminished market demand, smart business managers won't hire people to stand around, or buy more equipment to stand idle. Corporate investment will naturally resume when dictated by natural market forces. With no demand there are no jobs, and there is no recovery. This is the situation the country faces at present. It will return at some point, but it may remain years in the future. As long as the productivity related to innovation is shipped offshore, economic recovery will be slowed, and America's decline continued.

For the believers in government controls with its theoretical specialists, it is natural to turn to the government to fix the economy. They expect government actions to create jobs through more programs and financial manipulation of market forces. The truth is that the government can't make real jobs. Raising taxes or printing more money in order to put more people on a government payroll will never solve the productivity problem the country faces. This only adds to the debt, which is one of the main problems in the first place. When the nation reduced its production of real wealth, the ability of the working person to earn and grow was restricted or lost altogether. The jobs lost to other countries will not return until America can compete again. In the meantime, the country will remain in the doldrums as it adjusts to its new position in the world market.

The idea of financial innovation to develop the economy has turned out to be misleading and more damaging than helpful. The current extended time period, with monetary interest rates essentially at zero, has substantially reduced the power of the Federal Reserve to manipulate the economy. Fortunes have been made, but not by hardworking, productive workers, but by slick bankers and speculators. The money created isn't real wealth, but fantasy money that can go up in smoke – vanish – in a moment. The use of the government and its pseudo regulations to advance the business of financial innovation has left the country with unpaid mortgages and desperate citizens that were injured when the house of cards fell. There is no substitute for hard work, honest and straightforward accounting, and operating within the limits of the country's financial means.

Government intervention is not the solution, if for no other reason than the principle of infinity of actions; it is simply not possible for bureaucrats to predict the future or understand the total consequences of their actions. Each new government program results in unexpected market reactions. There are always clever people ready to take advantage of a new situation arising from deficient government programs. Subsidies and tax credits are excellent examples of backlash and abuse resulting from market interference. Central planning by the government results in huge swings from one problem to another. A glaring example of this resulted when the government decided it should be a vested right for all citizens to own their own home. The abuses and tragedies that have resulted from government's great experiment with the mortgage market are prominent subjects for economics textbooks. The specter of the massive health care bill of 2010, and the idea of the vested right of health care, will likely follow the pattern.

The real government solution is to eliminate the debt and establish a competitive tax system that allows Americans to compete again in the world. These actions are likely to restore lost jobs from foreign countries to American soil and stimulate market growth. Market growth means market demand and real, productive jobs that contribute to real wealth of the USA.

The U.S. government should stop its interference in the free market system and let its citizens live in freedom. This will be the only solution to lost jobs and a flagging economy. If the income tax system were eliminated, or at least the government drain on corporate earnings reduced, it is likely that the U.S. economy will return to a booming economy. Given half a chance to compete, the ingenuity and productivity of a free people will release a pent up economy and initiate one of the greatest booms of prosperity the country has ever seen.

But as long as the governing class, with its theoretical scholastic ideas, continues to restrain Americans, tax Americans, regulate Americans, and add Americans to the dole, the country will continue to languish for years to come. It is conceivable that America's strength may be lost to a new era. If the idea of central planning, vested rights, and a governing class continues to replace the Constitution of a free people, it may never return.

CHAPTER ELEVEN

OUR TURN

THE LAST ONE HUNDRED YEARS of federal malfeasance have brought the country to a fork in its course. It can continue the path of a centralized government with its failed programs and debt, a path made possible through Constitutional interpretation instead of Constitutional change. The alternative path is one to restore the freedom of self-government as envisioned and designed by the dedicated American founders. It means a renewed dedication to the Constitution, and the willingness to follow its provisions, but to change it openly and with the approval of the public opinion of society.

American countrymen today are alarmed at the tremendous split in viewpoints of the country and wonder what has happened to its character. Is the country too diverse? Has it become uncivil and ugly? Why can't the political parties work together in their representation of the people?

The answer may have been written more than two hundred fifty years ago from the rich mind of David Hume. He believed the answer to equalizing factions lay in decentralizing government. As American leaders today continue against all odds to try to solve everyone's problems at the federal level, the rift between U.S. citizens expands. As federal bureaucrats ignore the principles of the infinity of actions and available time in their efforts to retain power, they drive a wedge between their constituents. When the decision was made that the "general welfare" clause of the Constitution applies indefinitely to all facets of life, the fracture of the American grit began and continues to grow. Instead of leaving the business of religion, schools, health care, and every minute aspect of American life to individuals and their local governments, the federal government has tried to take everything to its own hand. When the control of American life is returned to the people, the chasm between them will begin to close, to heal, and the national spirit restored.

The return to the principles of self-government will soothe the people with a new contentment. They know they can't judge every particle of government business, but they know an educated public can properly support freedom. They know when they are free to manage their own affairs, in their own way, through their own skill and effort, then they can prosper and grow.

The alternative is the path called big government, bureaucracy, or centralized democracy. It means an ignorant society that is controlled by an elite few. It means control by a combination of theorists and slippery negotiators that will try to equalize everyone's lives and put all citizens in the same category. Push back by the citizenry occurs, because it's contrary to the freedom of the human spirit to be restrained, and so the split occurs, the country quarrels among itself, consideration for others and compromise are lost, and on the cycle continues for an unhappy nation. Is it your turn to read, think, and speak up?

YOUR TURN

Each individual must consider the situation of the country and decide whether to let it continue like it is or to return to the security of the Constitution. Shall the United States continue under the rule of people's law through its mutual contract? Shall the freedom of self-government be limited to providing for national defense, regulating fair commerce, and establishing equal and just laws for all?

Or, shall the people put their fate in the hands of a governing class of career politicians? Shall there be statutory rights from the government with unequal restraints on personal existence, and perhaps on unalienable natural rights? It's a personal choice with no right or wrong answer. Unfortunately, the centralized plan often harms those who refuse it. Which fork to take is the people's choice until the freedom to choose is lost.

For over fifty years the poetic call by President John Kennedy to "ask not what your country can do for you; ask what you can do for your country," has been repeated in books and papers, on radio, and television. Nearly every American has read or heard it. Perhaps today is the time for a new generation to answer this call by becoming more familiar with the workings of their government, and by taking a greater hand in keeping up with it. If the citizens of 1913 had been more like Horatio Bunce, then maybe the restraints on the federal government would have held firm.

Americans shouldn't elect politicians because they want a representative who knows what is best for them. Instead, they should choose someone to represent the aims and goals of public opinion in their towns, districts and states. Nearly all of the founders believed the government can never be trusted; it's the statistical distribution of human nature. They warned that an ambitious government will inevitably become severely authoritarian, and it is the job of free people to keep their unalienable right to self-govern by keeping the government within the boundaries of power conferred to it by the people in their mutual contract, the marvelous Constitution. After the Congress is seated, and has been co-opted into the culture of the central city, it will be your turn to keep elected officials more interested in the Constitution than their political careers. Then, following the example of citizen Bunce, and President Kennedy's challenge, it will be your turn to read, think, and keep up.

My Turn

It is the natural course of things, the law of entropy, for the Constitution of a free people to be slowly eroded into control by a large government. The last one hundred years have proved this point. Without the vigilance of the free people and their efforts to put effort into maintaining the principles of self-government, then self-government will naturally collapse and the founders' great experiment will be at an end.

Now is time to shake the empty promises of the governing class, eliminate failed programs, and restore Constitutional self-rule. It begins with the changes to preserve freedom that are outlined by Figure 10-1.

The time is past due to cast off the chains of the progressive income tax by reversing the Sixteenth Amendment so Americans can reclaim their individual freedom and breathe free again. This would eliminate all subsidies and dampen the abuses by lobbyists and the temptation for corruption of political officials. It will end the absurd notion that each individual should pay "their fair share" according to the judgment of the governing class, instead of an equal investment in the unique union of free people. It is time to end the unfair tax that robs individuals of the right to keep the fruit of their own hard work, and to give freely according their own wishes. The abolition of the progressive income tax will restore American's freedom to work, succeed, and choose their way of living according to nature's gifts.

Equally important is the requirement to protect the solvency and security of the country with balanced budget requirements. The country is bound to a debt of $16 trillion that exceeds its national output of less than $15 trillion. The budget of the United States should be limited to a fixed percentage of the Gross Domestic Product as established by legislation or Constitutional Amendment, preferably the latter. In coordination with this provision, each element of the budget should be similarly restricted to a percentage of the entire budget, and proper laws established to require the budget to be maintained within established limits. This would mean a welfare payment would be tied to the prosperity of the country. If a certain percentage of the country's output results in a $500 dollar payment in good times, but must be reduced to a $450 payment if the country is suffering, then that should be reasonable. All would suffer together. When workers and producers lose jobs, then welfare recipients should be pared, too, instead of riding the nation into oblivion.

In order to keep within budget limits, the business of the country must be operated like any nonprofit operation. If the GDP is down, then the size of government must be reduced or modified to meet the budget requirements. Clearly, today the government is too large for the size of a reasonable budget, so the federal operation should be resized according to a long-term plan for achieving the requisite adjustments, ten years or so.

In addition to changing the income tax system and including balanced budget requirements, it will be necessary to join together to specifically redefine government powers as established by the Constitution. It is needed both to eliminate the argument over the meaning of applicable sections of the nation's contract, and also to determine the purpose of government as desired by the public opinion of the current generation. It should be asked if the hybrid society that provides social spending for certain citizens should be continued. If so, then it should be put in the Constitution and controlled with Constitutional budget limits. It should not be hidden in an abusive tax code and the vague use of "general welfare" and "regulate commerce" statements. Let it be in the open, instead of being implemented by bureaus working around it. And leave it open for future generations. If they don't want a hybrid society, then they should have the right to change the Constitution according to the wishes and public opinion demands of their society. This was the vision of James Madison and the other founders.

Finally, it's time for free people to eliminate the governing class that has established itself in the federal government. The history of the last two hundred years is proof enough that the trust of the people should not be left in the hands of career politicians. Representatives of public opinion are needed, not a group of theorists that believe they should be the conscience of the people and choose the American lifestyle. It begins by returning the status of elected officials to being representatives and not federal employees. The powers of the executive branch must be restrained to prevent rule by bureaucratic laws. Following this, legislators must be removed from all federal employee programs, their pay reduced to a stipend for service, and the further restriction of term limits should be imposed in order to eliminate the class of career politicians from society.

These first steps are viewed as the most important to reclaiming individual freedom. After these changes the public can join with representatives, that are not career politicians, to tackle the legislation rules, curb the specialists, and address national concerns. With taxes returned to an equal system, the budget spending held in check by law, the powers of government clearly defined for the living generation, and the executive branch finished with lawmaking activities, the business of government for a self-governing people can be returned them.

TRANQUIL REVOLUTION

If the people choose to return to the early principles of the founders, a people's revolution will be needed to restore self-government. It should not be a revolution of confrontational demonstrations. These have been used with some success, but by and large they are destructive failures. The new people's revolution should be one of peaceful dispute, with no harm to others, like those described by Gandhi and Martin Luther King, Jr. It should be one of discussion to develop and identify public opinion with implementation through the vote. The government should remain the government of the voters, by the voters, and for the voters.

The change of the people's revolution should be accomplished peacefully within the provisions of the Constitution. To begin, the people must elect only officials to serve the good of the country, not those in search of a self-serving political career at the expense of the people. They must want change according to the will of the people and want to eliminate the governing class.

True public servants are needed to seek and prepare Constitutional Amendments that support public opinion. Real public opinion will be identified through the ratification process of Constitutional changes. If true representatives cannot be found to advance the people's revolution, then it will be necessary to seek a Constitutional Convention. This can come from the local level and established by the States. It's the special safety outlet that the founders of the Constitution left for the people. If the government assumes too much power and refuses to operate according to the will of the people and within the limits of the Constitution, then the people may exercise the rights established by Article Five of the Constitution to restore their authority.

These actions are necessary to restore the American dream. It's the dream of the freedom of choice in birth, life, and death. Our truest security is in one another. It is the freedom of the natural rights of our souls.

ABOUT THE AUTHOR

The author is from the Southwest United States. He has worked and lived at various times in all fifty states, and has had numerous international work assignments that include the hotbeds of industrial change in Mexico, China, and India.

His experiences in the book include more than forty-five years of engineering and business experience in fields ranging from nuclear applications to cryogenic process equipment, and from process cooling towers to automatic machine design. After his retirement from industry, he prepares income taxes for the unfortunate Americans who struggle with this creation of the federal government.

www.ingramcontent.com/pod-product-compliance
Lightning Source LLC
Chambersburg PA
CBHW030250290526
45785CB00001B/30